BRAND STORYTELLING

INTEGRATED MARKETING COMMUNICATIONS FOR THE DIGITAL MEDIA LANDSCAPE

Keith A. Quesenberry
Messiah University

Michael K. Coolsen
Shippensburg University

ROWMAN & LITTLEFIELD
Lanham • Boulder • New York • London

Acquisitions Editor: Natalie Mandziuk
Acquisitions Assistant: Yu Ozaki
Sales and Marketing Inquiries: textbooks@rowman.com

Credits and acknowledgments for material borrowed from other sources, and
reproduced with permission, appear on the appropriate pages within the text.

Published by Rowman & Littlefield
An imprint of The Rowman & Littlefield Publishing Group, Inc.
4501 Forbes Boulevard, Suite 200, Lanham, Maryland 20706
www.rowman.com

86-90 Paul Street, London EC2A 4NE

British Library Cataloguing in Publication Information available

Library of Congress Cataloging-in-Publication Data available
978-1-5381-7637-5 (cloth)
978-1-5381-7638-2 (paperback)
978-1-5381-7639-9 (electronic)

∞™ The paper used in this publication meets the minimum requirements of American National
Standard for Information Sciences—Permanence of Paper for Printed Library Materials,
ANSI/NISO Z39.48-1992.

Brief Contents

Detailed Contents

PART II: Foundations of IMC Storytelling

PART III: Stories for Different Media

Acknowledgments

I would like to thank Natalie Mandziuk at Rowman & Littlefield, for shepherding this book to publication, and Michael, who first helped me bridge the professional practice and academic research worlds. Of course, there is more to life than this. I also am a proud husband and father. Thank you to my family for their love and support. Without you, this book surely would not have been possible. And all of life takes faith, which comes from the one above (John 8:32). —Keith

I would like to thank Keith for his wonderful friendship, collaboration, and mentorship over the course of this long and fruitful storytelling adventure. I thank my wife and daughters for their substantial and unconditional support of my professional and academic pursuits—with them, my career is profoundly fulfilling. I'm also grateful to my father, who showed me that passion for learning and teaching can make a truly wonderful life. —Michael

About the Authors

Keith A. Quesenberry M.S. IMC is an associate professor of marketing, a researcher, and an author with Messiah University; he has taught graduate and undergraduate courses at Johns Hopkins University, Temple University, and West Virginia University. Quesenberry spent 17 years in the marketing and advertising field as an associate creative director and copywriter at ad agencies such as BBDO and Arnold Worldwide, creating strategies and campaigns for start-ups and Fortune 500 brands, including Delta Airlines, Exxon Mobil, PNC, Campbell's, and Hershey. Quesenberry is the author of *Social Media Strategy: Marketing, Public Relations and Advertising in the Consumer Revolution*, now in its third edition.

Dr. Michael Coolsen is a professor of marketing at Shippensburg University and an awarded professor, researcher, and consultant. A social scientist and expert in data analysis, he has spent his career researching consumer behavior. Before his doctorate in social psychology, he was a senior project director of marketing research at Arbor, Inc. (since merged into GfK Custom Research). His research has appeared and been published in *Psychology Today*, *Harvard Business Review*, *Advertising Age*, *PRWeek*, *Journal of Interactive Marketing*, *Journal of Current Issues & Research in Advertising*, *Journal of Marketing Theory and Practice*, and *International Journal of Integrated Marketing Communications*.

Introduction

Inspired by the latest research, professional practice, and ancient wisdom, this text draws from Aristotle and Shakespeare to neuroscience, plus the authors' own research and professional experience to reveal a formula for crafting powerful brand stories. A five-act story structure is explained and applied to various media from viral advertising videos, and content marketing to social media, print ads, and in-store experiences.

The reader is guided through a step-by-step process from brand to buyer, illustrated with templates and case studies demonstrating brand storytelling in action. The storytelling method is uniquely presented within a traditional campaign strategic process of marketing strategy, consumer insight, creative brief, to the media mix, creative execution, campaign pitch, and analytics for evaluation and optimization.

The authors bring a distinct perspective based on four decades of experience in both the marketing research and advertising creative fields working for start-ups to Fortune 500s combined with their academic research on what does and doesn't work in marketing.

This text presents a balance of research and theory with practical application and case studies within a classroom-friendly framework for undergraduate or graduate courses. It is also appropriate for marketing communications professionals seeking a guide to integrating storytelling into their brand communications.

A distinctive modern approach presents the strategic plan and campaign process from a digital- and social media–first perspective. Digital and social media perspectives are not just add-ons or afterthoughts. TV and radio include connected TV (CTV), streaming, and podcasts. Outdoor media include digital boards, mobile devices, and geotargetting. Public relations includes earned, shared, owned, and paid media. Digital is baked into every chapter for today's environment, in which digital ad spending has surpassed traditional media. New technologies in Web3, such as NFTs, cryptocurrency, and the metaverse, are also addressed.

Other chapters tackle important topics in executing integrated marketing communications (IMC) plans considering law, ethics, and analytics. Legal regulations for truth in advertising and Federal Trade Commission guidelines, such as influencer disclosures are explained. Professional ethics are presented from a real-life perspective with examples students and professionals may face in their careers. The last chapter covers analytics and advanced methods of conducting descriptive, predictive, and prescriptive research for IMC campaign planning and measurement.

Unique perspectives and key features include:

- The reader is taken on a journey from the ancient wisdom of Aristotle and Shakespeare to neuroscience and the authors' research to reveal a formula for brand stories.
- A five-act story framework is explained and applied to media from PR, viral advertising videos, and content marketing to social media, print and in-store experiences.
- A step-by-step process from brand to buyer is illustrated with templates and case studies demonstrating brand storytelling in action.
- A digital- and social media–first perspective is presented every chapter for IMC campaign planning in an environment where digital ad spending has surpassed traditional.
- Each chapter includes an introduction to discipline foundations through key figures; main content sections explaining concepts with examples, templates, and stats; a main case study; questions; exercises; and a list of key concepts for review.
- Key terms are bolded and defined throughout and featured in an alphabetic glossary with an index of key concepts, figures, tables, companies, and cases for easy reference.
- A separate section explains how the strategic process is different from a plan book and pitch to sell the recommendations to management or clients with a story approach.
- Legal and ethical considerations are described in the way that they may be experienced by professionals within a more complicated digital environment.
- Plan/campaign research for evaluation and optimization of IMC executions is included for descriptive, predictive, and prescriptive analytics.
- Instructor resources include chapter outlines, learning objectives, test banks, PowerPoint slides, forms, templates/worksheets, examples of assignments, and syllabi.

PART

I

Why Story Matters and the Story Formula

Frame of Reference

Storytelling Perspectives

PREVIEW

To begin our journey through brand storytelling in integrated marketing communications (IMC), we will start with a story about an innovator in the digital media landscape. Michelle Phan may have been known as the first social media influencer, but she knew that her strength was storytelling. Phan says, "Platforms—they come and go, but storytelling is forever."[1] From Phan's story, we explore how storytelling has been discussed in the media, the science behind storytelling, and how storytelling has been applied in various marketing communications professions. We end with our main case study about Microsoft's Chief Storyteller.

CHAPTER 1 LEARNING OBJECTIVES

1. Describe the origins of influencers and storytelling in digital media.
2. Analyze recent media attention paid to brand storytelling.
3. Understand the science behind storytelling's influence.
4. Apply storytelling to professional practice examples.

1.1 Michelle Phan: Storytelling Influencer

Michelle Phan, who garnered over a billion views as YouTube's biggest beauty star, knows the power of storytelling. When she took a break from social media in 2016, her 9 million subscribers were deeply saddened by the loss. One fan commented, "I really miss you! Feels like you were my best friend."[2] She was one of the original vloggers and the world's first influencer. Phan doesn't need case studies to explain how powerful story is; she is the original case study going from working in her mother's nail salon to the cover of *Forbes* magazine and helping to launch and run two successful companies.

Other people describe Phan as an entrepreneur and influencer, but if you ask her, she says she is a creator who works with different media, whether video or beauty products. A **creator** is someone who brings something new or original into being.[3] For over a decade, Phan's creations included GIFs on a Xanga blog, top 10 lists on Myspace, and videos on YouTube and Instagram. Michelle Phan's formula of personal storytelling combined with authentic makeup instruction was in stark contrast to traditional beauty advertising created by the big brands.[4]

In an *Allure* article, Phan recalls Lancôme spending thousands of dollars on tutorial videos that were getting only a couple of hundred views, yet a YouTube search of "Lancome makeup tutorial" would bring up Phan's videos. She was using the brand's makeup and getting 800,000 views per video. In one of the first influencer agreements, she began making monthly videos for the luxury skin care company.

Phan says the marketers at Lancôme "didn't understand why people weren't watching their videos." While other marketers and business owners were trying to figure out the power of story, Michelle went on to cofound subscription beauty company Ipsy, which today generates up to half a billion dollars in revenue each year. Then, she left Ipsy to acquire EM Cosmetics from her partnership with L'Oréal and is now focused on growing that company.[5]

The lesson here is that while Phan's success was built on mostly new digital platforms, those platforms changed over the years. Phan is "platform agnostic."[6] The common thread was her ability to tell stories that resonated with an audience. This helped her build her personal brand and then two company brands generating billions of dollars in revenue. Phan and her companies figured out how to tell compelling stories across an integrated mix of social, digital, and traditional media channels.

An example of the power of story is Phan's video "Why I Left." With over 14 million views, it tells her life story of following her dream to go to art school instead of medical school, how she found financial support through YouTube videos, the unhappiness of success, and her withdrawal from that life.[7]

After a yearlong journey of losing herself to find herself, she discovered that "You can't buy happiness, but you can create it." She ends the video by explaining the transformation she achieved going through her life story. "Back then I was just showing you how to look more beautiful. Now I want to show you how to feel more beautiful." The video ended announcing her revamped EM Cosmetics.[8] Today, in an ever-changing media landscape, marketers must learn to be platform agnostic while telling their brand product story.

Beauty influencers have told their stories on various platforms, such as YouTube, Instagram, and TikTok. Getty Images: Majpodile.

1.2 Storytelling in the News

A Google search of "storytelling in business" generates 157 million results. A Google search of "storytelling marketing" generates 356 million results. Over the past decade, news articles have pronounced storytelling as the future of marketing,[9] the new strategic imperative of business,[10] "an irresistibly powerful strategic business tool,"[11] and "one of the biggest buzz words in business."[12] Trade publication stories have described how "great storytelling can make your business stand out,"[13] that "it is a way to a stronger startup,"[14] how "storytelling can transform your business,"[15] and how you can "win more business through the art of storytelling."[16]

Storytelling News versus Storytelling Practice

CRM Magazine states that marketers need a story to tell and "brand storytelling has become an essential element of company success."[17] FastCompany.com did a three-part series on the science of storytelling,[18] and *Entrepreneur's* branding issue emphasized the power of storytelling. Author Anne Tugend explains that storytelling is "how savvy companies are satisfying the public's never-ending hunger for content."[19]

No matter where you turn in recent years, the business press is talking about the importance of storytelling. Businesspeople and marketers have been using strategic concepts such as the purchase funnel or AIDA (awareness, interest, desire, action) model since the 1920s and the four Ps (product, place, price, promotion) since the 1960s. Why does it seem like just recently they are waking up to the power of story?

It's easy for marketers and communications professionals from advertising and public relations (PR) firms to focus on what has worked in the past. In IMC strategies, the use of tried-and-true strategies, such as coupons, direct mail, and product demonstrations, abounds while story seems to be hit or miss. Yet case studies and research confirm that storytelling has been proven to be more effective.[20] For example, SoulCycle was started by two women who wanted a cardio routine that "made their hearts sing." From one studio, they've grown to 17 in New York and Los Angeles, telling the stories of their instructors and members through social media and their blog.[21]

Why the repeated reminders to professional marketers to use storytelling? Few marketers and communications professionals learned strategies from a story perspective. Even when they have a story of success, they seem to forget or fail to attribute the success to a story foundation. That's why so many news articles pronounce story as the future and keep calling for it. This is why storytelling articles, webinars, courses, and conferences keep popping up to educate about storytelling.

Many marketers and the communications professionals they hire simply aren't employing strategic storytelling on a regular and consistent basis. Again, it's easy to turn to old gimmicks. Yet somehow, we've missed one of the oldest strategies in the world. As we'll learn in chapter 2, Aristotle laid out the basic structure for storytelling in *Poetics* written over 2,300 years ago.

Story is needed more than ever. Products and services today often struggle to find differentiation. One bank's checking account has very similar features and benefits to the next bank's. Even if you have a truly unique product or service, that difference doesn't matter if no one knows about it. You must attract the attention of your audience. **Attention** is the process by which a consumer selects information to interpret and when they are aware of stimuli in an environment.[22] Without attention, marketing messages are useless. And story is one of the best ways to grab an audience's attention.

It used to be that marketers could buy attention with guaranteed reach and frequency in ads. Long gone are the days of mass audiences tuned into the big broadcast networks to watch hit TV shows such as *M*A*S*H*, *Seinfeld*, and *Friends*. Today, we consume media in a streaming multiverse where there's an overabundance of choice and a seemly infinite number of channels and shows for niche interests. In 2021 there were over 200 TV streaming services.[23] Even the biggest budgets find it hard to buy media interruption.

Shifts in Digital Media Shift Approaches to Storytelling

David Lubars, the former chief creative officer of BBDO North America, saw this environment coming in 2009. After judging that year's Cannes Lions Advertising Festival, he predicted that "The way the world is heading is voluntary engagement."[24] Appropriately, today the festival has been renamed the Cannes Lions International Festival of Creativity, acknowledging the increased importance of branded communication across disciplines. With digital media, a power shift occurred toward the consumer. In this age of voluntary engagement, the power of story is needed more than ever.

In 2022, the Cannes Titanium Grand Prix winner went to a campaign that told a powerful story to change the narrative about victims of violence. In Great Britain, Kiyan Prince was murdered by a student outside his school. Kiyan was a youth soccer (football) player with the talent to go pro. EA Sports partnered with the Kiyan Prince Foundation and introduced him as a player in EA Sports FIFA 21. They also told his story on digital billboards, advertising, Tops Trading Cards, and through earned media PR. Kiyan's father, Dr. Mark Prince, said, "I want my son to be remembered not for the tragedy of his death but for the triumph of his achievements."[25]

For the most part, mass audiences reachable by a couple of national network TV ads are a thing of the past. Getty Images: Majpodile.

Despite these changes in practice, many texts and curriculums still teach strategic frameworks that don't consider story. If it is discussed, it is often an add-on, footnote, or one of many techniques. Unless storytelling is built into the strategic process from the beginning, it can be easily forgotten until the next business trade article brings it back to the top of mind. But an 800-word article often isn't enough to change an entire approach to IMC strategy. Many are still struggling to get their story told and told well, even when they know it is important.

It is easy to forget or discount new realities or simply continue to turn to the old perspectives and strategic foundations that were built on mass media. Fred Bertino, former president and chief creative officer of Hill Holliday, captured the storytelling deficit well in an *Advertising Age* article describing account reviews. Bertino explains how 9 out of 10 prospective clients respond with the same answer when asked why they're looking for a new advertising agency: "Well, to tell you the truth, we think we've got a great story to tell and we're just not getting it out."[26]

Specialized agencies and consultants have emerged to help. One is the consultancy Narrative Builders. CEO Deb Lavoy says a good narrative can lead to a thousand stories that can be told to key stakeholders, including customers, employees, and investors.[27] Narrative Builders isn't alone. A Google search on storytelling agencies returns 14 million results. Yet why must storytelling require a specialized agency or be an add-on? If IMC is planned with storytelling in mind, the power of story will be built into every strategy and technique.

Another significant change to consider for the modern practice of IMC is how the COVID-19 pandemic changed customer behavior and the customer experience. A Facebook IQ study found that 81 percent of people have changed their shopping habits since the pandemic and 92 percent say they will continue that behavior long term.[28]

Many of these changes have to do with digital media. The CMO Survey reports digital marketing spending rose 15.8 percent from August 2020 to August 2021. Now, 58 percent of marketing budgets are spent on digital, and that is projected to grow another 14.7 percent. As can be seen in Figure 1.1, only 9 percent are in the early stages of digital

Figure 1.1. Company progress toward digital transformation.

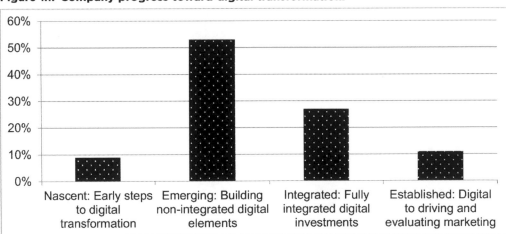

Source: Christine Moorman, "Managing and Measuring Marketing Spending for Growth and Returns," The CMO Survey, (August 2021), https://cmosurvey.org/wp-content/uploads/2021/08/The_CMO_Survey-Highlights_and_Insights_Report-August_2021.pdf.

transformation. Most marketers are already using digital elements and are well on their way to full digital integration.[29]

At the heart of these changes are new technologies and options that have changed how, where, and when people make purchases and purchase decisions.[30] The Facebook IQ study explains that "[Customers'] desire to have control in all aspects of their shopping journey is shifting the consumer–brand relationship."[31] Customers are taking the lead in the brand–customer relationship. This increased desire for control and personalization also applies to people's desire to control the content they want to consume.

Consumers increasingly want to dictate their own stories. IMC professionals should make room for an evolving brand story with many authors. Using celebrities to help tell a brand story is a tried-and-true method that is still relevant today. But now, this also includes influencers such as Michelle Phan and consumers themselves through user-generated content. Celebrity social media influencers are a big focus in marketing, but an **influencer** is anyone who has an impact on others' decisions.[32] You don't have to be a Kardashian to have influence. Influence opens the door for **user-generated content**, the content that comes from a brand's audience but is marketing the brand.[33] The trend is clear: story and digital need to be built into IMC plans from beginning to end.

An example of a company using influencers to help tell the brand story is Nike's YouTube Shorts videos. YouTube Shorts allows users to create short videos no longer than 60 seconds on their phones. It offers features similar to TikTok videos, and many post these videos with the hashtag "#shorts."[34]

One example is the shorts video "Pro skateboarder Ishod Wair finds balance in the midst of a hectic career. #shorts" In this Nike video, Ishod shares what it is like to be an athlete as you get older. He explains the conflict in his life story of deciding to keep skating and having fun while knowing that it is destroying his body faster. To keep skating, he needs to train harder and make changes in his life. The video ends with the question, "What are you working on?"[35]

An example of user-generated content helping to tell a brand story is Johns Hopkins University Hospital. Through its social media accounts, it doesn't simply share facts about complex health care services. It conveys its health care expertise through the stories of its patients. One YouTube video is titled "Convexity Meningioma: A Hollywood Stuntwoman's Story." The video communicates information about the expertise of Johns Hopkins' doctors and its state-of-the-art technology, but it is told through a personal story.

> Hollywood stunt woman Jill Brown received an incidental diagnosis of a benign convexity meningioma brain tumor after a stunt went awry. Watch as she recounts what led her to travel across the country to have her surgery performed at The Johns Hopkins Hospital in Baltimore.[36]

As a viewer, you get invested in her story, the complication of her life, and the conflict facing this diagnosis. You want to see the resolution and how her story turns out. In the end, the doctors are able to save her life and provide a happy resolution.

1.3 The Science Behind Storytelling

Storytelling has been researched for many years in many contexts. A review of studies reveals evidence of the effectiveness of stories and clues as to the best ways to apply story or narrative to marketing communications.

The Key to Attention Is Evoking Emotions through Story

A basic tenet in advertising is that if an ad hopes to generate a response it must first attract attention, yet just grabbing attention is not enough. Hooking an audience for sustained attention is needed for the audience to get involved in a message, remember it, and be motivated to act. Researchers have found that the best way to hook an audience is through their emotions and the best way to make them feel is through dramatic stories.[37]

With digital media, it is easier than ever to avoid advertising. A *New York Times* article described the problem well: "As advertisers bombard consumers across platforms like Facebook, television, and billboards, consumers are trying, and even paying, to get away."[38] The ability to hook and maintain an audience's attention has become more important than ever.

In one study, researchers found that the way to hook an audience is to evoke emotion through story. TV ads that had a narrative by telling a story drew more interest and positive feelings, making people feel less like they wanted to avoid the ad and more likely to stay interested.[39] People may hate ads, but they love a good story—even if it is an ad.

Story is one of the most effective ways to create an emotional response. Feelings matter in attitudes toward the ad but also in memory. The more you make someone feel (emotional intensity), the more they'll remember your ad appeal. How? It happens through brand stories that make people feel sympathy and empathy. Studies reveal sympathy is felt first.[40] **Sympathy** is a feeling of concern for someone else.[41] That feeling can then be turned into empathy. **Empathy** is the ability to understand and share the feelings of another person.[42] First, you may feel sorry for a character, but as the story progresses, you can feel their emotions.

Consumers get involved in the meanings of ads mostly through empathy.[43] When viewing or reading a story, you develop relationships with the characters. You begin to understand and share their feelings. Through the empathy developed in a story, an audience experiences the relevance of the products or services. They perceive similarities between aspects of their own identity with those portrayed by the characters in the ad. This identification can lead to actions the marketers want their target consumer to take.[44]

These emotional responses of sympathy and then empathy are seen as a powerful path to persuasion that affects the audience's attitude toward the ad and the brand and their memory of the message.[45] Social scientists have explained persuasion through narratives via transportation theory. **Transportation theory** is a mechanism to affect beliefs whereby an audience is drawn into the world of a narrative by becoming involved with the characters through conflict and an identifiable beginning, middle, and end story line.[46] Narrative transportation increases connections with ad characters, intensifies emotional involvement in the ad, and reduces counterarguments for the product.[47]

Best friends share empathy through stories, just like the best brands do.
Getty Images: JGI Jamie Grill.

The Key to Emotional Response Is Dramatic Story Structure

Some researchers approach story from different perspectives but have found similar evidence pointing toward a universal story structure that mimics classical drama. **Classical drama** is a chronologically organized plot that draws an audience into recognizing the feelings of the characters (sympathy) and sharing in them (empathy).[48]

The neuroscientist Paul J. Zak has studied how stories change people's attitudes, beliefs, and behaviors. Zak discovered that changes in the chemicals produced in the brain are related to story. These neurochemicals are cortisol, which is associated with attention, and oxytocin, which is associated with emotions. In experiments, blood draws to measure these chemicals were taken before and after participants heard a story. Character-driven stories caused the brain to produce more neurochemicals, leading to empathy. The amount released predicted which people would then donate money to the charity related to the story.[49]

In further studies, Zak developed ways to measure the level of neurochemicals in real time while people watched a story. To produce empathy that motivates action, the story must sustain attention, and that attention is best obtained by tension. **Tension** is an emotion of inner striving, unrest, or imbalance.[50] If the story creates tension, the audience is more likely to feel the characters' emotions and are then more likely to mimic their behaviors.[51] This only happens with a specific story structure formed through a dramatic arc.

Zak's first study measured response to a more complete story. A father tells the audience his two-year-old son Ben is dying of a brain tumor and that it is hard to be happy around him knowing that he will die in a couple of months. Yet through this struggle, he finds courage

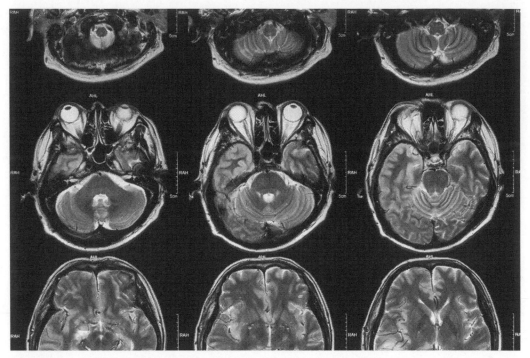

Emotional stories activate regions of the brain that make us feel empathy and sympathy that lead to immersion in a brand message. Getty Images: Stockdevil.

and vows to be happy around Ben. The story has a beginning, where the audience gets to know the characters, and a middle, where tension is created by the difficult decision the father must make, but the audience does not know what decision he will make. It has an end, where the father decides to be happy around his son, thus releasing the tension. Because this full story engaged more of the brain, it led to increased donations by participants to a childhood cancer charity versus participants who simply heard facts about childhood cancer.[52]

In another experiment, Zak showed participants only part of the same story—a video of Ben and his father at the zoo in which they are enjoying looking at the animals. Ben is bald, and his father calls him a "miracle boy." But the viewers don't learn anything more; they are not told the full story. This flat story structure didn't produce the rising and falling tension of the other. In this experiment, people lost interest halfway through. Levels of brain response waned, and not many donated to the charity. Without a full dramatic arc, empathy transportation did not occur.[53]

Jonathan Gottschall, author of *The Storytelling Animal: How Stories Make Us Human*, explains that without the information about the sick child, "you don't get emotional transportation, you don't get chemical changes in the brain, and you don't get the behavior change."[54] Zak calls the activation of these two networks in the brain (attention and emotion) creating immersion. **Immersion** is creating emotionally resonant experiences that lead to a higher likelihood of immediate action and easier recall later.[55]

Studies of TV ads and viral advertising videos by Quesenberry and Coolsen have produced similar results with dramatic stories leading to consumer action.[56] A study of viral ad videos coded them for a dramatic arc (based on a five-act scale). On average, videos that told a more complete story arc of four and five acts gained four times the shares of flatter zero- to three-act structures.[57]

Table 1.1. Viral Advertising Videos by Story Acts

Acts	Percentage of Sample	0–3 Acts vs. 4–5 Acts	Number of Shares
0 Acts	31		
1 Act	21		
2 Acts	10		
3 Acts	4	66% (0–3 Acts)	4–5 Act videos gained
4 Acts	9		four times the number
5 Acts	25	34% (4–5 Acts)	of shares compared to
			1–3 Act videos.

Source: Keith A. Quesenberry and Michael K. Coolsen, "Drama Goes Viral: Effects of Story Development on Shares and Views of Online Advertising Videos," *Journal of Interactive Marketing* 48 (2019, November): 1–16.

Despite this fourfold increase in just one-third of the videos told four- and five-act stories (see Table 1.1). In the study, over 50 percent of YouTube advertising videos had no story arc with zero acts or just one act. Half of video ads never reach a conflict in act three that produces the tension Zak and other researchers say is key to response.[58] We will learn more about this five-act dramatic structure in chapter 2.

In some ways, marketing communications professionals need to relearn the power of story. Before the trade articles and research, TV ads started as brand-sponsored dramas. Chuck Ross recalls these early days in *Television Week*. In the late 1940s and early 1950s, major advertisers such as Kraft sponsored weekly dramas. The *Kraft Television Theatre* on NBC was a show produced by their advertising agency. Most ads were through integrated marketing and product placement, leading to sales success.[59]

Eventually, sole sponsorship of programs with ad agencies producing the shows stopped. Then, we moved to the model we have today of multiple 30- to 60-second ad slots sold to multiple sponsors. With the proliferation of digital and social media, we have in some ways come full circle. More marketers are turning back to brand-sponsored content. Ross explains, "What was true back then is true today—that viewers pay attention to engaging programming."[60]

1.4 Storytelling in Professional Practice

With or without research, many marketing, advertising, and PR professionals have learned the power of story via decades of experience crafting IMC campaigns for their clients. There has been a joke in the advertising industry for years that most creatives on Madison Avenue would rather be writing screenplays for movies in Hollywood. Yet, the best communications professionals know they need to craft those stories in their ads.

Early Brand Storytelling in Advertising

In the 1980s and 1990s ad agency Hill, Holliday, Connors, Cosmopulos was known for its creativity and storytelling. In 1986, it won Advertising Age Agency of the Year and its campaign for John Hancock Life Insurance was recognized as one of the best of the decade. At first, it was misunderstood by the ad industry and was feared by the company's insurance agents because of its untraditional "soft-sell" approach.[61]

Yet the "Real Life, Real Answers" campaign hit home with the people who matter—the target audience. Each commercial told stories of real problems its target audience faced and ended with the message that John Hancock services could help. The campaign's powerful storytelling was eventually acknowledged by the industry winning the Grand Prix at the Cannes International Advertising Festival and a Clio for Best National Ad Campaign.[62]

Fred Bertino, former president and chief creative officer of Hill Holliday, knows the power of story. As quoted in *Advertising Age*:

> For us, telling the story of our client's brands in advertising and marketing campaigns is no different than telling a story in a great novel or feature film. We don't think of ourselves as being in the business of creating ads. We're in the business of telling powerful and compelling stories that connect with audiences on a deep emotional level.[63]

Telling brand stories worked well for the agency's clients and its own business. Under Bertino's leadership in telling brand stories, Hill Holliday grew from $300 million to $1.2 billion in revenue, becoming the 13th-largest agency in the United States.[64]

In the early 2000s, *Brandweek* highlighted various creatives turning to storytelling to create brand messages. Former Wieden+Kennedy creative director Jerry Cronin left the ad agency to work at BrightHouse creative consultancy. There, he began creating what the agency called advertainment. **Advertainment** is a form of entertainment created with the purpose of advertising something.[65] One project was a six-minute film called "The Scout," which aired in 90-second chapters on ESPN for Sears Craftsman tools. These branded ESPN shorts told the story of a baseball scout past his prime who discovers his next star—a 12-year-old boy who mows a baseball stadium with his Craftsman lawn mower.[66]

Other examples of advertainment from the 2000s include a one-minute short film created for fashion designer DKNY by Lord + Partners. "Road Stories" followed an actress driving cross-country to pursue her career. The docudrama was shown in DKNY stores and given out via DVDs, and print ads featured stills from the film. Ogilvy & Mather experimented with a series of webisodes for American Express starring Jerry Seinfeld and Superman. The five-minute shorts were hailed as branded entertainment and were directed by storytelling Hollywood movie director Barry Levinson.[67]

Industry professionals such as Byron Lewis seem to have known the power of story for most of their careers. Lewis first and foremost considers himself a storyteller. He is also an Advertising Hall of Fame member and founded UniWorld, the oldest African American owned and operated ad agency. Lewis credits his first job as a social worker as helping him understand everyday people's lives. When they became his audiences for ads, he turned to telling their stories for his clients. One of Lewis's first successes was a Quaker Oats–sponsored show called *Sound of the City*, which told the story of African Americans moving from the South to urban areas.[68]

Byron learned that stories can be told in many advertising forms. In an interview for *Advertising Age*, the 81-year-old pioneer said he is a big believer in digital advertising. "It is absolutely a remarkable way to build your brand, to build what they call 'buzz' and to be able to check and measure the effectiveness of your story . . . but that may be one of the problems with the digital space. You still have to have the story."[69]

As the digital space grew and social media became more prominent, many brands turned to old mascots for storytelling. In the 2010s, *Advertising Age* noticed revivals of brand characters such as Charlie the Tuna, Mr. Peanut, M&M's, and Captain Morgan. Brand mascots were revived because digital media made it easier to create story lines in new ways across various media. Previous cartoon brand characters were limited mostly to TV ads.[70]

Brand characters are not the only stories to tell. Luke Sullivan, award-winning copywriter, has written some of the most creative and effective campaigns for big brands. Sullivan explains, "What is advertising but telling compelling, memorable stories about brands?" For over 30 years, he has learned that narrative is key to improving ad creativity. He also has learned that to have a narrative, you need tension. He suggests studying a client's product category and looking for built-in conflicts—cultural tensions that can be turned into stories.[71]

Early Brand Storytelling in PR

PR professionals have long known the power of storytelling. A large part of PR is pitching stories to the media on behalf of clients for publicity. **Publicity** is the non-paid-for communication of information about a company, product, or service through media.[72] What marketer or brand manager doesn't want free media coverage when it is positive?

Edward Bernays, known as the father of public relations, knew the power of story. He famously used story to sell more bacon for his client Beech-Nut Packing. At the time, most Americans ate a light breakfast, but Bernays asked 5,000 doctors if a larger meal in the morning would be better for people's health. Of those surveyed, 4,500 agreed that more energy at the start of the day would be good. He let the experts tell the story in news articles, and that led to people eating bacon and eggs as a breakfast mainstay. Today, 70 percent of bacon is eaten at breakfast.[73]

Dan Edelman began his PR agency in the 1950s. It was one of the first to bring attention to products by getting its stories in newspapers and on television.[74] Edelman introduced the concept of telling stories through the media to sell products and build corporate brands. Edelman also developed the first media tour. Richard Edelman, Dan's son, has helped lead the agency to become the world's largest PR firm.[75] He also knows that PR today is much more than news

Publicity can tell positive or negative brand stories which can greatly impact the effectiveness of IMC strategies. Getty Images: Simonkr.

clippings. The practice has become more accountable for producing marketing results. At a PR Week conference, Edelman said, "We have to improve our ability to deliver tangible results, namely sales, not simply awareness or change of attitude among opinion formers."[76]

While PR professionals have been pitching stories for decades, we must be careful to distinguish a news story from a dramatic story. News articles and stories are often used interchangeably. Yet as OHO interactive points out, "the differences between the two are night and day." While news informs, stories inspire. News is about what people have done recently, but stories are about people and who they are.[77] This can be seen by comparing the structure of most news articles with a dramatic arc structure.

One of the most widely used forms by a journalist in mass media writing is the inverted pyramid. An **inverted pyramid structure** is a news story form that places the most important information in the lead paragraph, then details such as the background in the remaining paragraphs from most to least important.[78] This structure is good for delivering quick facts as people skim the news, but it is not good for hooking an audience and sustaining attention.

Dramatic stories follow a different structure where the background is provided first and emphasis is on characters and emotions. Dramatic stories follow a narrative arc to transport people into situations and move them along a journey to feel what the characters are feeling.[79] **Dramatic structure** is the structure of dramatic works, such as books, plays, and films, with a beginning, middle, and end that follows the journey of characters (see Figure 1.2).[80]

An example is a commercial for Kerrygold butter. A news story or press release about Kerrygold butter would start with the background and facts of the butter. It is all natural and made from grass-fed cow's milk to give it a rich and creamy taste. Instead, the Kerrygold butter TV commercial opens with parents waking up a son early in the morning. Then, using Kerrygold, they prepare a meal late at night. The son walks in, sees them at the table, and says, "You, you waited for me?" Mom hugs him and says, "Happy first day." The commercial ends with the announcer saying, "Nothing tastes like together. Kerrygold. Crafted with milk from grass-fed Irish cows."[81]

PR professionals have been searching for ways to tell more dramatic stories. One Public Relations Society of America conference offered PR training on storytelling.[82] Steve Clayton, chief storyteller at Microsoft, offered similar training at the Social Media Conference for PR, Marketing and Corporate Communications. At the conference, Clayton explained, "We are bombarded with information.... So, how do we promote our product/services and tie it back to the bottom line? It sounds obvious, but the real secret is this: Start with a great story."[83]

Figure 1.2. Inverted pyramid news structure versus dramatic story arc structure.

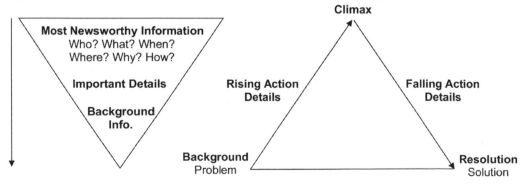

1.5 CASE

Microsoft's Chief Storyteller

As a company, Microsoft was not good at storytelling and not getting better. Instead of continuing to hire traditional communications professionals, Frank Shaw, corporate vice president of communications, saw an opportunity to try something different. Steve Clayton was a Microsoft systems engineer telling great Microsoft stories on his personal blog. Shaw created a new position, essentially turning what he did on his blog into a full-time job.[84]

With no formal training in journalism or PR, a test came early. An op-ed by an ex-Microsoft executive in *The New York Times* lambasted the company for having zero innovation. Clayton didn't know traditional crisis communications strategies, but he did know how to tell stories. Instead of issuing a standard press release, he sought out real people doing interesting work. In 30 interviews, real stories of innovation by Microsoft employees emerged.[85]

Early on, Clayton ran into roadblocks when his blog posts had to go through the traditional channels such as the legal and PR departments. The gatekeepers were treating blog posts like press releases. Eventually, he was given the freedom to publish stories outside of traditional structures. Now, he has a team of 35 people focused on storytelling in their own department.[86]

His team introduced Microsoft Stories to the website, revolutionizing the old Press Pass, which cranked out press releases. Instead of a standard press release about the features and benefits of Windows 11, Microsoft Stories features articles crafted by one of the department's storytellers. One of the articles tells the story of Charles Taylor and his journey from being a kid in a little North Carolina town interested in tech to college and becoming a product manager at Microsoft. The article goes on to seamlessly weave other team members' personal stories into a narrative about their inspiration for the key features of Windows 11.[87]

It's hard to argue that a company isn't innovative when you get to know people personally who are passionate about their product and how they innovated features to help improve their customers' lives. Today, instead of getting his blog posts edited by PR professionals, he is holding workshops at PR conferences teaching them how to be better storytellers.

Microsoft is not alone in hiring storytellers. Nike has had a chief storyteller since the 1990s. Many companies have added chief storytellers in recent years. IBM and GE have chief storytellers, and so do tech start-ups such as Wefunder and Trilingual.[88] What is a chief storyteller? A **chief storyteller** is an employee of an organization tasked with telling the brand's story to both internal and external audiences.[89] In many ways, Michelle Phan is her own chief storyteller. She created the stories first, then created two beauty industry businesses out of her storytelling.

This chapter has explored the seemingly new interest in storytelling for business and marketing communications in the news. Then, we dug into the research that supports the power of story and ended with examples of luminaries who learned the power of story through professional practice in advertising and PR. In the next chapter, we will put together these areas into a dramatic form that covers them all, giving us a template to follow in creating dramatic stories for IMC strategies.

QUESTIONS

1. Why does storytelling keep coming up as the key to business and marketing success yet so many examples exist of story not being used in practice?
2. Do you think all businesses need a chief storyteller, or should people in current positions simply begin telling brand stories?

EXERCISES

1. The storytelling research speaks for itself. Or does it? Storytelling research says that facts don't move people. How would you use storytelling to sell storytelling to marketing communications professionals? If you had one TED Talk to present the facts, how would you practice what you are preaching?
2. This chapter started with a beauty influencer and ended with a computer systems engineer. Both were amateur creators who turned their passions and storytelling into professional careers. Find two or three other examples of successful professionals in different industries where it is evident that their ability to tell stories was a key part of their success.

KEY CONCEPTS

Advertainment
Attention
Chief storyteller
Classical drama
Creator
Dramatic structure
Empathy

Influencer
Inverted pyramid structure
Publicity
Sympathy
Tension
Transportation theory
User-generated content

Plays to Pyramids

Aristotle, Shakespeare, and Freytag

PREVIEW

Our brand storytelling journey continues with some history. Like any good super hero movie there is an origin story. Storytelling has been around for thousands of years, and we'll leverage that ancient knowledge to tell brand stories today. We begin with Sir Ernest Shackleton's famous newspaper ad, "MEN WANTED for hazardous journey, small wages, bitter cold, long month of complete darkness, constant danger, safe return doubtful, honor and recognition in case of success."[1] From this early twentieth-century explorer, we'll travel to ancient Greece, the Renaissance, and modern Hollywood to unpack the origins of dramatic storytelling. The Apple case study provides an example of a long-running ad campaign told through five-act stories.

CHAPTER 2 LEARNING OBJECTIVES

1. Discover the history of drama in early ads and current entertainment.
2. Understand Aristotle's theory of drama.
3. Examine Freytag's Pyramid and Shakespearean play's story structure.
4. Compare Campbell's The Hero's Journey and Harmon's Story Circle.
5. Apply five-act dramatic structure to professional practice examples.

2.1 Sir Ernest Shackleton Ad

The quote above is an often-referenced advertisement written by Antarctic explorer Sir Ernest Shackleton. It was placed in the London newspaper *The Times* to recruit sailors for his Nimrod Expedition in the early 1900s. It's said the response was so great that he was overwhelmed with 5,000 applicants. This has been celebrated and studied as one of the best ads of all time praised for its brilliant copywriting. Great story, right? Well, it may not be true.

The Ad Is Dramatic and So Is the Story about the Ad

Since 2001, there has been a contest to win $100 and a case of Madeira for anyone who could provide a copy of the original source of this Men Wanted ad with the date and name of the newspaper it appeared in (see www.antarctic-circle.org/advert).[2] After 20 years, no one poring over archives, personal records, and historical artifacts has been able to track down the source. Many, including *Smithsonian* magazine, have now conceded that the ad is probably just a myth.[3]

The Shackleton ad has been cited in countless books and articles as one of the greatest ads, has been used in classes to teach writing, and has even appeared on T-shirts. If it is just a myth, is it now useless? Before quickly dismissing something as "just a myth," first, consider the real purpose and power of a myth. **Myth** is a traditional story of ostensibly historical events that serves to explain a practice, belief, or natural phenomenon.[4] With that perspective, the Men Wanted ad can still be useful as an illustration of good copywriting.

True or not, the Shackleton ad helps depict the practice and power of good writing built around an intriguing dramatic story. Even the story of the ad possibly being a myth draws an audience further in holds attention and adds drama.

What's drama? **Drama** is a state, situation, or series of events involving an interesting or intense conflict of forces.[5] The men going on the expedition would face conflict with the

The story of Sir Ernest Shackleton's Antarctic expedition and the ad written to recruit crew members is full of drama. Frank Hurley, "Shackleton's expedition to the Antarctic Sir Ernest Shackleton to the rescue," 1916. Library of Congress Prints and Photographs Division.

intense forces of nature. But the thought of someone creating a hoax around the ad draws interest. We want to know who and why. These situations or events of interest and conflict produce tension and evoke emotion. You know you are watching, hearing, or reading a drama when you feel it.

Drama Is One of the Most Popular Forms of Entertainment Today

Drama grabs our attention, holds our interest, and leaves us wanting more. This has been proven in many ways, even beyond what we already learned in Chapter 1. A report from the TV ratings service Nielsen reveals that dramas are the most popular primetime genre (44 percent of all viewership), followed by sports (22 percent) and reality shows (16 percent).[6] Yet any fan will attest to the fact that there is plenty of drama in sports and reality TV as well.

Watching LeBron James's Cleveland Cavaliers beat the odds and the Golden State Warriors or following the Chicago Cubs on their curse-breaking journey to a World Series title had plenty of conflicts of forces that make a great drama.[7] These stories drew the attention of more than just the local fans—it felt like the entire world was following them.

The top reality shows also draw us into the intense moments of *America's Got Talent* or *The Voice* and the personal conflicts of *The Bachelor* and *Survivor*. Have you noticed how reality show producers seem to cast for personal conflict and editors cut clips in a way to tease impending conflict, tension, and drama in upcoming episodes?

Sporting events and reality TV finales command some of the largest single-episode TV audiences. Not surprisingly, these top genres also earn the most advertising dollars. Yet marketers that create and buy the ads that are inserted into dramatic entertainment somehow forget to add that attention-grabbing drama to their brand communications.

Good dramas tend to unfold over time, telling parts of the story and leaving the audience wanting more. Top TV dramas, such as *The Big Bang Theory* and *Grey's Anatomy*, in the United States[8] or *Doctor Who* in the United Kingdom last 10 years or more.[9] The story of the Chicago Cubs' losing streak and the curse of the Billy Goat was especially intriguing because of their buildup over seven decades.[10] The reality show *Big Brother* has been on the air in the United States and the United Kingdom for over 16 years.[11] However, marketers often try to tell everything in every ad, social media post, and press release, packing in all the features and arguments to purchase the product or service.

The powerful aspects of a drama, such as mystery, tension, and intrigue, take time to build. Viewers of popular broadcast TV shows, such as *24* or *Lost*, or streaming shows, such as *Stranger Things*, or listeners of the podcast *Serial* know that feeling of ending one show and wanting more.

This desire to know the rest of the story is so strong it leads to binge-watching. **Binge-watching** is watching many or all episodes of a TV series in rapid succession.[12] With the right strategy, marketing communications professionals can harness this type of interest and dedication to their brand. To learn how, we'll first look to Aristotle, the first person to study dramatic composition.

2.2 Aristotle's Theory of Drama

Over 2,300 years ago, Aristotle wrote *Poetics*, the oldest surviving writing on dramatic theory. Aristotle analyzed elements of drama from relationships between characters and actions to the response of audiences. Most would not consider a book written in 335 BC as relevant to marketing and communications in the twenty-first century. The concept of **modern marketing**, moving goods from producer to consumer through advertising and sales, has only been around since the late 1800s. Marketing as a management discipline only emerged in the 1950s. In the last couple of decades, marketing practice changed dramatically with social media and digital marketing. How is an ancient Greek philosopher relevant to integrated marketing communications (IMC) today?

Aristotle Described the Structure of Drama

Much of Aristotle's *Poetics* is focused on drama, which we have described as attracting and holding attention. From brand websites and social media to traditional advertising and public relations, brand communication must attract and hold the attention of its audience. Without attention, messages are not received, and actions are not taken to meet marketing or communications objectives. If drama attracts and holds attention and can cause a response in the audience, then good brand communication should be dramatic, but what makes a good drama?

Regarding his writings, Aristotle considered the plot to be the most important element, something even more important than character and narration. One of the early researchers

Much of what we learn about story began in Greco-Roman amphitheaters where plays were first developed and refined. Getty Images: Diana Vioget.

of drama in advertising was Professor Barbra Sterns from Rutgers University. In describing Aristotelian plot, Stern used key terms such as conflict, complication, crisis, suspense, surprise, and solution. In a presentation at a conference, she summarized an Aristotelian view of plot:

> Many plots contain conflict, defined as an oppositional relationship between two characters or forces. A complication occurs when the conflict works itself out in one or more crises, often arousing suspense when there is uncertainty about what is going to happen. A solution is reached, frequently by means of a surprise ending.[13]

Besides the elements described above, a plot delivers meaning by arranging events into a unified chronological order. Aristotle described a plot as having a beginning, middle, and end with events that must relate—one event causes another.[14] The plot arouses emotion and delivers drama with opposing forces but also with a progression that explains what happened and why.

Aristotle said that in a good plot, each occurrence happens from a previous occurrence. A story is unified when you can't remove or reorder parts without changing the plot meaning. If something is removed or moved and the meaning remains intact, then it is superfluous. He further explained that the three parts of the plot are complication, turning point, and denouement. The turning point is a change of fortune where everything goes from good to bad or bad to good. The complication is what leads up to the turning point. The denouement, also called unraveling, is what follows the turning point.[15]

Aristotle Described Other Key Elements of Drama

It is useful to note that Aristotle's *Poetics* also introduced concepts such as mimesis (imitation of reality in art) and catharsis (a purging of strong emotion). Art and emotion are key aspects of telling a good story. He also argued that the best plots were complex where change arises from a reversal of the situation. What was expected doesn't happen, and the opposite occurs instead.[16] Finally, much of a story and plot are held together by the characters. The characters create the action, arouse the emotion, and must connect with the audience.

If your audience can't relate to the characters, they will not invest time in the story. Aristotle indicated that a character should have four traits for a good plot and story. First, characters must have qualities that will earn the respect of your audience. The characters' qualities must make sense based on their identity and must be believable, and the characters' traits must be consistent.[17]

A current example of this was a short-listed entry for the 2022 Cannes Lion Titanium.[18] Agency BBH New York created the campaign Black-Owned Friday for Google. It told the story of Black Friday, one of the busiest shopping days of the year, and refocused the story on a different set of characters—small Black-owned businesses represented with the hashtag #BlackOwnedFriday. The story spread as new businesses were highlighted every Friday and consumers shared their own, resulting in over half a billion PR impressions.[19]

Aristotle was naturally curious about all aspects of life and the world. As we will learn later, being curious about all things is a key to being creative and generating creative ideas. Through his curiosity, Aristotle systematically studied whatever subject he was interested in. He studied it and then attempted to make it understandable and meaningful through philosophical interpretation. This process developed into an early form of the scientific method. He formed a hypothesis and then tested it through experiments that could be repeated for the same results.[20] The scientific method is used to study stories and reveal many of the findings, insights, and theories explained in this book.

Aristotelian dramatics has practical marketing communications applications. Key elements to attracting attention and arousing a response in a marketing or communications target audience include opposing forces, conflict, complications, suspense, solution, and a cohesive progression of what and why. This is a good start. Yet Aristotle's *Poetics* only goes so far. For the next building block of brand storytelling, jump ahead 1,900 years and 2,200 years, respectively, to William Shakespeare's five-act plays and Gustav Freytag's Pyramid.

2.3 Shakespearean Plays and Freytag's Pyramid

Shakespeare is widely considered one of the greatest dramatists of all time. He wrote plays that captured the entire spectrum of conflict and emotion—key elements of Aristotelian drama. Known throughout the world, the works of William Shakespeare have been performed in countless cities and countries for more than 400 years.

Shakespearean Plays Follow a Popular Dramatic Form

BBC News Magazine reports that Shakespeare is more popular than ever. No writer past or present has as much work in daily circulation—not even J.K. Rowling or Bob Dylan can get close to influencing the lives of billions of people.[21] There are over 70 Shakespearean festivals held every year. One fan, Eric Minton, has kept track of Shakespearean productions on his website, documenting nearly 2,000 since 2011.[22] What can be learned from Shakespeare about creating dramatic brands and IMC strategies to drive interest and action?

Before discussing Shakespeare's historical dramas, comedies, tragedies, and tragic comedies, first, consider Shakespeare's business background. It is a little emphasized fact that William Shakespeare was first a successful business owner and entrepreneur before becoming famous for his plays. He started as a member and owner of a theatrical company for which he acted and later began to write plays part time.

A key business decision came in 1599 when Shakespeare and his business partners invested in their own theater, the Globe on the Thames River. Later, Shakespeare individually purchased leases of real estate near Stratford, which eventually doubled in value, earning him enough money to devote his full-time attention to writing. As a business owner, Shakespeare went from a family of modest means to being one of the wealthiest men in his town,[23] which is a good reminder that the purpose of brand storytelling drama is to build a business. Shakespearian art was not "art for art's sake"; it had an objective to generate revenue and profit.[24]

Shakespearean plays follow a five-part structure where part one explains the situation, presents the characters, and begins the action. Part II advances the action by introducing complications. Part III brings everything to a head, and the direction of the story changes. Part IV illustrates further developments that lead to the end of the story. Part V provides the final revelation and resolution.[25] Looking at this structure more closely provides an idea of the detailed planning that went into creating a dramatic Shakespearian story.

Shakespeare's *Romeo and Juliet* follows a five-act dramatic story structure the inspiration behind the method presented in this book. C. Birney, "Romeo and Juliet," Detroit Publishing Co., 1882. Library of Congress Prints and Photographs Division.

Romeo and Juliet follows this pattern (*spoiler alert*). Act 1 introduces the Verona, Italy, setting and the characters of Romeo and Juliet and establishes conflict with the feud between the Montagues and Capulets. In Act 2, complications arise as Romeo and Juliet fall in love but cannot see each other because of the feud. They decide on a secret wedding. In Act 3, tension peaks as Juliet's cousin, Tybalt, attacks the Montagues by killing Romeo's close friend, Mercutio. Romeo avenges his death by killing Tybalt, marries Juliet in private, and is then banished.

Act 4 advances the story as Juliet's parents arrange a marriage to another man named Paris. Juliet creates a plan with Friar to get out of the unwanted marriage by faking her death and sending Romeo a letter revealing she's not dead. Act 5 leads to the final revelation. We learn Romeo never received the letter. Discovering Juliet dead, he kills Paris and then kills himself. Juliet wakes up from a sleeping potion to find Romeo dead and kills herself. The families learn of the secret wedding and vow to end their feud.[26]

Consider how the segmented structure of *Romeo and Juliet* allows the plot to develop and create the maximum amount of drama. The story progresses yet has room to breathe and build the conflict, complications, suspense, and emotion. To learn more about the power and form of Shakespeare's five-part structure, look ahead a couple of hundred years to Gustav Freytag.

Freytag Developed a Pyramid Structure for Drama

Gustav Freytag was a successful German writer whose play *The Journalists* is considered one of the most popular German comedies. His novel *Debit and Credit* was also an international hit.[27] However, he is most known for his system of dramatic structure. *Freytag's theory* of five-act dramatic form was first published in *The Technique of the Drama* in 1863 and symbolized as **Freytag's Pyramid**, a sequence of five structural phases in drama (see Figure 2.1).[28] This advanced Aristotle's three-part classical narrative structure of a beginning, middle, and end to a more precise five-act structure utilized by Renaissance dramatists such as William Shakespeare.

Freytag proposed that a drama is divided into five units called acts and these acts combine to form the dramatic arc: exposition, complication, climax, reversal, and denouement. His book is said to be a model for the first Hollywood screenwriting manuals written in the early 1900s. To create drama in a play, for a brand and an IMC strategy, Freytag's Pyramid provides a process to build a story of interrelated events to evoke emotion and audience response.

In this model, **exposition** sets the stage by introducing character and setting, followed by a **complication**, which is an inciting moment that creates conflict-producing tension. A series of events build up to a **climax** where the story (plot) takes a turning point for better (a comedy) or for worse (a tragedy). The **reversal** is results of the climax as a series of events or falling action moves the plot toward a resolution. **Denouement** is when the conflict or complication is resolved and tension is released.

Freytag's study and analysis were based on five-act plays but have been applied to novels, demonstrating that dramatic structure is also a literary element.[29] His pyramid is seen as a powerful story tool for the most successful fiction,[30] has become an underlying element of classic Hollywood narratives,[31] and has been suggested as a solid structure for captivating and convincing public speech.[32] Each act in this model is further explained below:

Act 1 Exposition: Characters, time, setting, and past events are established. Conflict develops into tension between opposing forces or characters such as a protagonist and antagonist. This act ends with an inciting moment, setting the story in motion toward the rising action of complications.

Act 2 Complication: The story becomes more complex. Interests clash, and plans are made as action rises and tension mounts. The protagonist's efforts to reach their goal is complicated by additional conflicts and obstacles. Frustration builds as opposing forces and circumstances intensify.

Figure 2.1. Freytag's pyramid structure for dramatic story form.

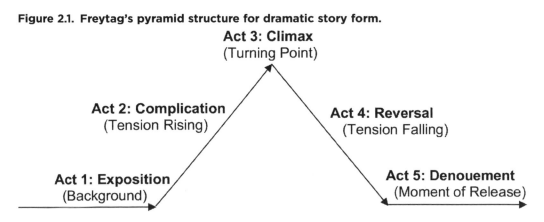

Act 3 Climax: The conflict reaches a high point. This turning point for the protagonist could lead to victory or defeat. A change happens for better or for worse. In a comedy, things have gone badly for the protagonist and now go well. In a tragedy, things go from good to bad for the protagonist.

Act 4 Reversal: Consequences of the climactic turning point play out. The falling action results from the reversal where the protagonist won or lost. Momentum slows as characters head toward a final resolution. In a comedy, it looks like all can be saved. In a tragedy, it looks like all may be lost.

Act 5 Denouement: The conflict is resolved to create normalcy for the characters and a sense of release of tension and anxiety. A comedy ends with the protagonist being better off. A tragedy ends with the protagonist being worse off.

You can see the value of dramatic five-act structure related to plays and movies or videos, but much of brand communication is written. Why apply dramatic theory to written story-telling instead of narrative or literary theory? There are unique differences between dramatic theory versus narrative theories.

Alterative Story Theories Fit within Five-Act Dramatic Form

The narrative theories of novels are rich in literary structures developed by many scholars.[33] Yet literature and narrative theories are developed for the analysis of the written word alone. Plays, films, TV ads, online/social media videos, events, and in-store brand experiences require the full elements of sight, sound, and motion. As David Bordwell in *Poetics of Cinema* says, "Literary texts conjure up worlds from mere words, but the film presents us with a rich array of images and sounds that immediately presents a dense realm."[34]

Dramatic theory is more useful to the marketer, communications, and IMC professional because it can apply to multimedia, whereas literary theory focuses on writing alone. If screenwriters are taught plot structure formulas to increase cinematic success built on the voluntary engagement of audiences seeking out the films, then the dramatic forms of plays and films should aptly apply to today's marketing environment where consumers increasingly and voluntarily choose to engage with brand communication.

Why five acts instead of just three? Some assume Aristotle proposed a three-act structure because he said a plot has a beginning, middle, and end. Yet Aristotle never referred to acts, and Greek dramas did not have acts. Later, Roman dramas did adapt to units or acts in drama. The leading Roman poet Horace proposed the number of acts should be five, not three. Horace's drama *Art* helped establish the five-act standard. The five-act form guided play-wrights and publishers for centuries in Europe, including Shakespeare.[35] Yet modern writers drifted back to the less nuanced three-act structure.

By the early twentieth century, most operas and plays started to favor three acts. Many scholars are unsure why, but this adopted norm in theater was then adopted in the film industry where a three-act structure was emphasized in screenwriting manuals starting in the 1970s.[36] Recently, some have proposed alternative act structures. American film theorist Kristin Thompson argues that films should be constructed in four parts,[37] and many call for a return to Shakespeare's five-act structure, arguing that the three-act structure is "egregiously simplified" and leaves "a gaping hole known as 'Act II' [that] is wholly crucial to your story's success."[38]

There are other alternative story theories. The largest are "story grammar" theories, which explain that stories are composed of elements such as setting, characters, location, time,

Table 2.1. Story Grammar Theory Elements as Related to Freytag's Five-Act Drama

Story Grammar	Setting, Explain Affairs, Establish Goal	Initiating Event, Enternal Response	Attempts at Goal	Outcome	Reaction to Outcome
	Act 1	Act 2	Act 3	Act 4	Act 5
Freytag's Five-Act Drama	Exposition (Background)	Complication (Tension Rising)	Climax (Turning Point)	Reversal (Tension Falling)	Denouement (Movement of Release)

theme, event, goal, plot, episode, attempt, outcome, and resolution.[39] **Story grammar** is a rule system describing parts of a well-formed story and the order in which they are presented. Many teachers use story grammar to promote reading and writing skills in children and to develop a "sense of story."[40]

Neil Cohn provides a useful way to think about these alternative forms by laying out the commonalities between the various theories. Cohn synthesizes the various story grammar theories of Gee and Kegl, Mandler and Johnson, Rumelhart, Stein and Nezworski, and Thorndyke into basic categories.[41] These categories can then be related to the five acts in Freytag's theory of drama (see Table 2.1). Story grammar theories can be seen as expanded explanations of the structure established in Freytag's five-act dramatic form.

Reading teachers help students identify the elements within a story using a story map. A **story map** is story grammar presented as an outline. Carl B. Smith suggests an outline for teaching students about the characteristics of literature through a story map of setting, plot, mood, and theme. Identifying these key elements of a story helps to show the path through a story.[42] Table 2.2 is Smith's outline for a story map that helps identify key elements of a story. The elements still need to be put into a structured order as seen in the last column. The questions help identify key elements that happen in the five acts, creating a dramatic arc.

Table 2.2. Outline for a Story Map Related to Freytag's Five-Act Drama

Setting	Where is the action?	Act 1
	When does it happen?	Act 1
	How would you describe the place?	Act 1
Plot	Who is involved?	Act 1
	What is the beginning of the situation?	Act 2
	How would you describe the conflict?	Act 3
	How is the major conflict worked out?	Act 4
Mood	What are your feelings during different events?	Acts 1–5
	How did verbal/visual cues create certain feelings?	Acts 1–5
Theme	What conclusions did you draw?	Act 5
	What set of values are emphasized?	Act 5

Adapted from Carl B. Smith, "Story Map: Setting, Plot, Mood, Theme (ERIC/RCS)," *Reading Teacher* 44, no. 2 (1990): 178–79.

2.4 Campbell's The Hero's Journey and Harmon's Story Circle

No discussion of story would be complete without mention of comparative mythology. **Comparative mythology** studies myths of various cultures and identifies common themes or underlying similarities.[43] Understanding myths is important to facilitate communication. If you understand the myths of a group of people, you can understand a model for their human behavior. Myths provide clues to universal story themes and universal characters to be used in universal story structure.

Campbell's The Hero's Journey Follows Dramatic Story Form

Joseph Campbell's works are the most popular examples of comparative mythology. Campbell was an American author and editor who studied the universal functions of myths in various cultures and common mythic figures in a wide range of literature. In 1949, he published *The Hero with a Thousand Faces*, defining a common plot of all hero myths. This monomyth or **The Hero's Journey** is a common heroic narrative where a protagonist sets out, has transformative adventures, and returns home.[44] George Lucas used Campbell's blueprint for the *Star Wars* movie script, and it is the underlying structure for other popular movies, such as *The Matrix* and *Lion King*.[45]

There have been many adaptations of The Hero's Journey. The longest versions contain over 17 stages, yet all have some form of the hero beginning in the ordinary or known world, being called to adventure to go into the unknown or extraordinary where a great ordeal happens. The

Campbell's hero's journey is a common mythical story across cultures that also follows a five-act drama story arc. Getty Images: AscentXmedia.

hero is changed and returns with special knowledge and reward. Along the journey, the hero meets mentors, helpers, and adversaries while facing trials and feeling both courage and doubt.

Harmon's Story Circle Is a Condensed Dramatic Form of The Hero's Journey

Dan Harmon, the executive producer of *Rick and Morty* and the creator of the NBC show *Community*, has developed a condensed eight-stage version of The Hero's Journey known as the Story Circle. The **Story Circle** is a simplified narrative arc adapted from The Hero's Journey.[46] In Harmon's version, a person in their ordinary world is challenged with a need. They accept and go out into the unknown searching for a resolution. They find it in a great challenge. They succeed, take a reward, and return home a changed person who changed things.[47] Dan Harmon explains the Story Circle structure as "(1) When you, (2) have a need, (3) you go somewhere, (4) search for it, (5) find it, (6) take it, (7) then return, (8) and change things."[48] An example of Harmon's Story Circle was a top Super Bowl ad in USA Today Ad Meter for 2022. The ad for Kia's all-electric EV6 features a lonely robotic dog for sale in a store window. The ad finished fourth out of 64 commercials based on consumer votes.[49]

Robo dog (1) needs companionship as he sees a happy real dog jumping on its owner (2). He needs to go somewhere to find that happiness (3). As Bonnie Tyler's song "Total Eclipse of the Heart" begins to play, Robo dog sees the owner of the Kia EV plugging it into a charging station. The car drives away, and Robo dog begins to chase it. Robo dog runs through the streets searching for the EV and man (4). After many obstacles and challenges, Robo dog finds the car parked (5) and jumps toward it as his battery runs out. Robo dog awakes to take his new owner as the man recharges him from the car (6). The man puts Robo dog in his car to return home (7). Robo dog is changed; he is happy as he rides with his head out the car window (8).[50]

These popular story frameworks also match the five-act dramatic form. As can be seen in Table 2.3, The Hero's Journey and the Story Circle can be broken down to Freytag's five-act structure but provide a further point of view that helps focus the story on the emotional growth of a hero protagonist.[51]

Table 2.3. Campbell's Hero's Journey and Harmon's Story Circle Related to Freytag's Five-Act Drama

	Known World		Extraordinary World		Known World
Campbell's The Hero's Journey	Call to Adventure, Refuse Call, Meet Mentor	Accepting Call, Crossing the Threshold	Tests, Helpers, Grand Trial	Reward, The Road Back Home	Restore Order, Take New Place in Old World
	Order		Chaos		Order
Dan Harmon's Story Circle	When you, Have a need	You go somewhere, Search for it	Find it	Take it, Then return	And change things
	Act 1	Act 2	Act 3	Act 4	Act 5
Freytag's Five-Act Drama	Exposition (Inciting Moment)	Complication (Rising Action)	Climax (Turning Point)	Reversal (Falling Action)	Denouement (Movement of Release)

The Hero's Journey and the Story Circle focus on a hero protagonist. Yet stories star different characters, and like people, brands can have different personalities. Brand archetype can also become a key to determining the story that needs to be told in IMC strategies, which we will explore in Chapter 3.

Shakespearean dramas are more popular than ever. Four hundred years later, Shakespeare still sells. This businessman-turned-playwright knew the formula for success. Hero's journeys in blockbuster films such as *Star Wars* and *The Matrix* also use drama to attract an audience. Both can be used to add drama to brands today. How do five acts apply to modern marketing communication? The next section and the end-of-chapter case will provide examples.

2.5 Five-Act Advertising Campaigns

The chapter started with the mythical story of Antarctic explorer Sir Ernest Shackleton's Men Wanted ad from the early 1900s. Now, consider real advertising campaigns that have been successful since the 2000s. These modern-day examples use the five-act dramatic form in IMC campaigns.

Five-Act Dramatic Form Ads Make the Best Ads of the Century

In 2015, *Advertising Age* updated its list of the 100 best advertising campaigns with the 15 best ad campaigns of the twenty-first century. It explained how in 15 years since the 1999 list, marketing communications "has experienced an incredible upheaval as digital media and interactivity changed the dynamics of how consumers see and pay attention to brand messages."[52]

Today, there is more pressure than ever to create engaging brand experiences. Let's look at some of the most popular campaigns from *Advertising Age*'s list with BMW films, Dove's Real Beauty, Red Bull's Stratos, and Apple's Get a Mac.

In 2001, the ad agency Fallon and marketing client BMW launched BMW films, which became one of the earliest examples of viral advertising and content marketing. The marketers and agency were bold in stepping away from traditional interruptive advertising to engagement on the internet through BMW film's website. These mini-movies told complete stories where the car and brand took center stage. They even hired A-list Hollywood directors and actors, and the expense paid off.

The films cost BMW $25 million but created a PR value of $26 million. The brand also experienced a dramatic sales increase of 12.5 percent in the year of the film series release and helped to create a new award at Cannes, winning the first Titanium Lion.[53] The Titanium category of the Cannes Lions awards was created to acknowledge campaigns that didn't fit into traditional media categories, such as radio, billboards, and TV ads.[54] In late 2016, the brand brought back BMW films with the YouTube release of "The Escape," featuring the original "The Hire" actor Clive Owen. Within months, the new film had reached 6 million views.[55]

Another campaign on *Advertising Age*'s list is Dove's Real Beauty. In 2006, Ogilvy & Mather worked with Dove to launch an innovative campaign that continues today. Dove's Campaign for Real Beauty features real women as characters in opposition to the beauty industry and its unrealistic portrayals of women. Tensions rise as advertisers' tricks are revealed, problems of low self-esteem are explained, and tension is released as Dove presents an alternative solution and a promise to make the situation better through education efforts.[56] These dramas sell more than an education initiative. In the first year of the campaign, Dove sales were $2.5 billion. Ten years later, they had risen to $4 billion.[57]

Red Bull's Stratos is another example of dramatic brand storytelling making the *Advertising Age* list. In 2012, Red Bull captivated the world with this dramatic story by sponsoring and documenting Austrian skydiver Felix Baumgartner's free fall from 24 miles above the earth. He broke five world records while the brand broke the rules of traditional marketing. Andrew Keller, CEO of Crispin Porter + Bogusky, described the event by saying, "Red Bull does such a brilliant job thinking of marketing as an action not as messaging."[58]

Red Bull's branded content event created real sports drama, and the world followed with earned media attention. Stratos was broadcast on nearly 80 TV stations in 50 countries. The live webcast was distributed through 280 digital partners, drawing 52 million views—the most-watched live stream in history. Red Bull Media House won a Sports Emmy for Outstanding New Approaches—Sports Event Coverage. The effort was credited with helping to increase sales of Red Bull by 7 percent immediately following the Stratos project.[59]

Five-Act Dramatic Ads Go Viral on Social Media

Another dramatic marketing effort was the popular "#LikeAGirl" campaign. In 2014, the Always brand and advertising agency Leo Burnett launched the #LikeAGirl advertising video on YouTube, and it went viral. As an already proven viral hit, they aired a shortened version as a 2015 Super Bowl ad that was watched more than 90 million times; was the number two viral video globally; and drove unprecedented, earned media coverage.[60] Was this documentary-style viral video a five-act story? This last ad will be considered in a story act table, which can be used as a template and worksheet when planning out brand stories (see Table 2.4).

Reported results of this viral video, traditional TV ad, and then viral advertising campaign include 96 percent positive sentiment for the campaign and brand and over 1,100 earned-media placements generating over 4.4 billion media impressions in just three months. The brand achieved a higher-than-average lift in brand preference with purchase intent increasing more than 50 percent among the target audience. Furthermore, the story changed the audience's beliefs. In a follow-up study, nearly 70 percent of women and 60 percent of men said, "The video changed my perception of the phrase 'like a girl.'"[61]

Table 2.4. Always "#LikeAGirl" Applied to Freytag's Story Framework

Story Act	Elements of Story Act Development
Act 1 Exposition Characters, setting, basic conflict are established, leading to tension. An inciting moment begins rising action of complications.	Characters are introduced as a director (off camera) and actors (on camera) trying out for an audition. Conflict develops into tension as the director asks them to run like a girl and to throw like a girl. Their reactions begin to make the viewer feel uncomfortable. The act ends with an inciting moment when the viewer realizes the negativity of their interpretations of the phrase in their acting.
Act 2 Complication Tension mounts as the main character's efforts to reach a goal meets conflicts and obstacles. Frustration builds as opposing forces intensify.	The story becomes more complex. Interests clash as action rises. Tension mounts as a question is posed on the screen: "When did doing something 'like a girl' become an insult?" The protagonists' goals to earn a spot in the commercial are complicated when they realize what they have been doing.
Act 3 Climax The conflict reaches a high turning point that could lead to victory or defeat for the main character, resulting in good or bad consequences.	The conflict reaches a high point. The director confronts one boy directly by asking, "So do you think you just insulted your sister?" The turning point of the climax is a realization of how wrong this popular saying has been.
Act 4 Reversal Events play out in falling actions from the reversal in the climax. Momentum slows as the characters head toward a final resolution.	The result of the conflict plays out as the same question is asked of young girls. The falling action happens as each young girl acts like a girl with strength and positive images. A fact is posted on the screen: "a girl's confidence plummets during puberty . . ."
Act 5 Denouement Conflict is resolved and tension is released, creating normalcy. Comedy ends with the main character better off and tragedy being worse off.	The phrase in Act 4 continues with ". . . but it doesn't have to." The question is posed a last time to a young girl: "What does it mean to you when I say run like a girl?" She responds, "It means run as fast as you can." Girls end better off in this story as a call to action is posted: "Let's make #LIKEAGIRL mean amazing things." Hopes are raised as the viewer is invited to "Rewrite the rules" and "Share what you do #LIKEAGIRL."

2.6 CASE

Apple's Get a Mac

Earlier in the chapter, we discussed that a good drama unfolds over time. Some TV and movie producers, directors, and editors are masters at telling parts of a story and leaving the audience wanting more. When ad agency TBWA created the Get a Mac campaign for Apple, it understood this concept. Launched in 2006, this campaign ran for four years and comprised 66 commercials that told the brand story of the Macintosh. It had main characters representing the hip Apple Macintosh and the nerdy competitor Microsoft Windows PC. It set up the idea of competitive forces so well that the campaign is commonly known as "Mac vs. PC."

A typical commercial started with the familiar characters introducing themselves: "Hello, I'm a Mac, and I'm a PC." PC is uptight in a drab tan suit. Mac is dressed casually and is easygoing (Act 1 Exposition). Next, a problem is introduced, such as PC sneezing like crazy in the direction of Mac. Tension rises as we worry about Mac getting sick (Act 2 Complication). PC warns him to stay away, but Mac pulls out a handkerchief (Act 3 Climax). The action turns as Mac says not to worry because he doesn't get viruses. Mac remains calm as he helps PC by wiping his nose (Act 4 Reversal). As Mac wipes PC's nose, PC crashes and falls to the ground (Act 5 Denouement). The spot ends with the resolution of a Macintosh product shot and the call to action "Get a Mac."[62]

This same plot form played out in many ways 66 different times as the brand engaged consumers with stories highlighting unique product benefits in entertaining stories. Did the story sell? Although other factors contributed, Apple's market share of personal computers went from roughly 2 percent in 2005, a year before the campaign started,[63] to over 8 percent market share by 2007, a year after the Get a Mac campaign launched.[64]

Like Shakespeare, Steve Jobs knew that good drama sells. Think of the typical Apple keynote and the closely coordinated dramatic buildup to Apple product launches. These efforts have the signs of Shakespearian drama and Aristotelian plot, including opposing relationships, suspense, uncertainty, a solution, and a surprise ending.[65]

This chapter has explored the origins of drama in Aristotle's *Poetics* in 335 BC and can be applied to brand communication such as Always' "#LikeAGirl" campaign in 2015. In later chapters, we will discuss how the basis of most of these successful brand stories emerged out of research into consumer insights. The next chapter will explain a strategy for uncovering consumer insights and setting a foundation for brand story.

QUESTIONS

1. Which of the alternative story frameworks do you feel are most helpful to understanding and creating brand stories: Aristotle's theory of drama, Shakespearian plays, Freytag's Pyramid, story grammar theories, The Hero's Journey, Story Circle, or story map?
2. Can you think of a successful advertising campaign example that didn't follow a story structure? If so, why do you think that it was an outlier?

EXERCISES

1. Look at the list of words describing Aristotelian drama: conflict, complication, crises, suspense, uncertainty, and surprise. At first glance, most marketers would think of this as a list of things to avoid being associated with a brand. But these are building blocks of drama, and drama attracts and holds our attention. Think of one way your brand (or your favorite brand) could leverage one or more of these characteristics and implement them in a marketing channel.
2. Brands are about relationships, and building relationships takes time. People wouldn't still be watching *Romeo and Juliet* today if they met and married in the first scene with no conflict. Take an audit of your (or your favorite brand's) current marketing. Is it trying to pack everything into each piece of communication, or is it letting the brand story unfold over time?

KEY CONCEPTS

Binge-watching

Climax

Comparative mythology

Complication

Denouement

Drama

Exposition

Freytag's Pyramid

Myth

Modern marketing

The Hero's Journey

Reversal

Story Circle

Story grammar

Story map

Dramatic Brands

From Form to Function

PREVIEW

Next on our brand storytelling journey, we consider the strategic foundation for story. A great story will not be effective without a solid marketing communications strategy. Often, that begins by asking why. Simon Sinek says, "People don't buy what you do; they buy why you do it. The goal is not to do business with everybody who needs what you have. The goal is to do business with people who believe what you believe."[1] The people who buy why you do it are the ones most likely to pay attention to and voluntarily engage with brand communication in digital media. From why, we explore the concepts of inside-out marketing, connecting brand story to buyer story and brand identity to buyer identity through social psychology. Our case study looks at Patagonia's strategic foundation of not wanting its consumers to consume.

CHAPTER 3 LEARNING OBJECTIVES

1. Examine the concept of the Golden Circle as it relates to storytelling.
2. Understand how inside-out marketing leads to better brand storytelling.
3. Consider the concepts of brand and buyer story and identity.
4. Apply these strategy forms to professional practice examples.

3.1 Sinek's Start with Why

Simon Sinek's TED Talk is titled "How Great Leaders Inspire Action," but the most popular phrase is "Start with why." This idea of why inspiration and the larger framework of the Golden Circle has driven the video to become the third most watched TED Talk on TED. com. It's been viewed over 55 million times and subtitled into 47 languages.[2]

Simon's inspiration comes from observation of the world's most influential people, such as Martin Luther King Jr., Steve Jobs, and the Wright Brothers. Sinek makes the case that these great leaders have little in common except that they all think, act, and communicate in a way opposite from almost everyone else.[3] The difference? They start with why they do what they do, then move on to the how and the what, which is opposite of most people, who start with what they make.

Strategic Thinking Starts at the Beginning, Not the End

This reordered thinking is called the **Golden Circle**, a model to explain how legendary leaders achieve what others just as smart, hardworking, and funded do not.[4] Leaders who inspire action and build successful companies don't start with what they are making or how they are making it. They start with why. Why is a purpose, cause, or deeply held belief. Why does not involve making money; making money is a result. People don't buy your product to make you money. Sinek says, "people won't truly buy into a product, service, movement, or idea until they understand the WHY behind it."[5] Steve Jobs was a leader who understood this.

On the 10th anniversary of Steve Jobs death, Apple CEO Tim Cook shared, "Steve believed that 'people with passion can change the world for the better.' That's the philosophy that inspired him to create Apple. And it lives in us today."[6] Notice that Cook didn't say Steve's vision was to build the world's most valuable brand or create the world's first smartphone.[7] Jobs wanted to "put a dent in the universe" by having faith in people, not technology.[8]

Apple inspires people to "Think Different," which is the advertising tagline that represents Job's vision. First, the focus is on why—to inspire people to think differently. Tim Cook's tweet tribute to Job's said, "People with passion can change the world for the better." That's the why. Next is how the company does it, the unique ways it makes things, the design that sets it apart. And finally, it lets people know what it makes, the specific products or services such as the smartphone. The result is helping to create the world's most valuable brand.

3.2 Inside-Out Marketing

Why is often harder to explain than what. Why requires stories. People can't know why you do what you do unless you tell them a story. Then, they'll want to know what you do and how you do it. Many marketers and communications professionals get this backward, communicating from the outside in. In other words, they start with what, then explain how, and may or may not get to why (see Table 3.1).

Table 3.1. Outside-In versus Inside-Out Marketing Strategy

1.	**What** (Product/Service)	1.	**Why** (Emotions/Motivations)
2.	**How** (Features/Benefits)	2.	**How** (Features/Benefits)
3.	**Why** (Emotions/Motivations)	3.	**What** (Products/Services)

Look for the Motivations behind the Brand

When creating an integrated marketing communications (IMC) strategy or campaign based on storytelling, don't start with the product and services, features and benefits, facts and figures. When we communicate from the inside out, we're talking directly to the part of the brain that controls behavior. Inspire and motivate through the emotions, then follow up with the how and the what, allowing people to rationalize their decision.

If you think about it, most decisions we make begin with an emotional why, such as "I love ice cream and I want some. It will taste soooooo good." We have already decided, and then we look for the how to rationalize our decision, such as "It's made with natural ingredients in a way that respects the environment and supports the causes I care about." Ben & Jerry's knows this. The company doesn't just list all its flavors or "euphoric concoctions" on its website. It also tells its story of how, which supports the brand why. The quote below is from Ben & Jerry's website:

> We love making ice cream—but using our business to make the world a better place gives our work its meaning. Guided by our Core Values, we seek in all we do, at every level of our business, to advance human rights and dignity, support social and economic justice for historically marginalized communities, and protect and restore the Earth's natural systems. In other words: we use ice cream to change the world.[9]

After deciding to buy ice cream, we also look for the what to rationalize our decision, such as "It has fewer calories, less sugar, and higher protein." Halo Top knows this. The brand doesn't simply communicate nutrition facts; it tells a story of its what supported by the why on its website.

> Why did we want to make light ice cream that tastes like ice cream? Well, it's pretty simple: we liked ice cream so much, we wanted to eat it more. So, we created delicious, creamy light ice cream that's 280–380 calories per pint, so we could do just that. Some might say we have an ice cream problem, but we see it as more of a solution.[10]

Despite the popularity of Sinek's TED Talk, putting why first is not a popular marketing strategy. Many times, you will have to research the history of the company, learn about the founders, and ask questions to get to the why. Sometimes, your marketing or business client may even fight you on it. It's human nature to want to rationalize product arguments—ignoring the fact that we don't make our own personal decisions this way. Often, we're not self-aware of why we do what we do.

Consider the success of the health care platform Noom. The artificial intelligence fitness tracking, nutrition, sleep, and stress management app is in the Inc. 5000 ranking of fastest-growing US private companies. Noom addresses the why of eating habits before providing the how and what to solve these habits.[11] As Saeju Jeong, the CEO and cofounder, explains:

> I was determined to find a fix for a system that had become too focused on sick care, instead of health care. Most everyone knows that they should eat healthier, exercise more, be less stressed, get better sleep, but most of us don't know how. Noom gives you the how—and the why that empowers you to take control of your health.[12]

When asked why we made a decision, we search for the facts, features, and benefits to rationalize it to others. But the facts are not what drew our interest and drove our decision in the first place. It's not surprising that marketers forget this. Marketers live and breathe their products and often believe people are just as interested as they are. If they just lead with the amazing features, people will buy. But marketing communications professionals need to remind them that this is not true.

Often, Differentiation Doesn't Come from Product Features

The problem of the tendency to lead with rational facts is compounded by the fact that many products and services today are not unique. Their points of parity far outnumber points of differentiation. **Points of parity** are the elements of a product that make it similar to products in a category. **Points of differentiation** are the attributes that make the brand distinctive from competitors'. Points of differentiation are the brand's competitive advantage. Often, a brand's product and service features are so similar that the only way to create differentiation is through the marketing and branding strategies themselves.[13]

Sometimes, the rational argument tendency will manifest itself as a preference for one type of rational argument. For example, some marketers may want to always lead with price promotion. **Price promotions** are when products are offered at a discounted price.[14] This can be great for short-term enticements, but you must be careful about leading with an irresistible price. Always making your brand story about price can lead to a price war where few in the market win. A **price war** is repeated cutting of prices below those of competitors.[15] A price war between airlines in the 1990s led to spiraling price reductions and record losses for everyone in the industry.[16]

It's not too often that your client has a truly unique product that is creating the product category or a unique segment. If so, build your story around that. Most of the time, you'll be working with smaller differences or creating the difference with the brand story. The why and telling a story can be the brand's point of differentiation.

How many times does a truly innovative product such as the iPhone come along to create smartphones? Today, the iPhone relies on incremental improvements to differentiate itself from strong competitors, such as Samsung. For example, the rational what message of a slightly improved camera, chip, and storage in the iPhone 13 was delivered by leading with the why message of how you can make a dent in the world as an aspiring director with "Hollywood in Your Pocket."[17]

Yet many don't start with why and don't remember the importance and power of the story. Despite all the trade articles and research, only a quarter of the brand advertising videos on YouTube tell a full story if any story at all.[18] Yet the research points to emotional appeals that drive interest and action. Inside-out marketing strategies drive results.

If you or your marketing client are worried that putting why first and not making your why about making money will hurt the company financially, consider the Apple example— now the world's most valuable brand. Also, consider two examples in the ice cream market that we just learned are telling stories of why.

Ben & Jerry's is the best-selling brand of ice cream in the United States, generating $863 million in revenue in 2020. That's over 22 percent higher than its closest two brand competitors Blue Bell and Haagen-Dazs (see Figure 3.1).[19] When Unilever bought Ben & Jerry's

Figure 3.1. Leading ice cream brands in the United States (sales in million US dollars).

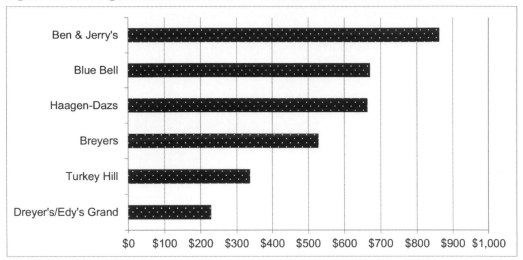

Source: Dairy Foods, "The leading ice cream brands of the United States in 2020, based on sales (in million U.S. dollars)." Chart. December 21, 2020. Statista. Accessed October 6, 2021. https://www.statista.com/statistics/190426/top-ice-cream-brands-in-the-united-states/.

from the founders, Ben Cohen and Jerry Greenfield, the company was strategic enough to keep the brand why and the brand story the same. It knew it was buying the why and how as much as the what.

Halo Top's story is slightly nuanced. After initial success, Halo Top's sales declined—33.5 percent in one year from 2018 to 2019.[20] According to a Mintel report:

> While Halo Top's value proposition is low calories, which would seem to resonate among a consumer base cognizant of health goals, diet positioning must be handled with care. . . .; 62 percent of frozen treat buyers agree that they would rather eat a small amount of indulgent, high calorie ice cream than an entire pint of low-calorie ice cream.[21]

The brand's what of eating an entire pint of low-calorie ice cream didn't match many of its targets' true desires, but Halo Top has found a sweeter story to tell with a new what—ice cream pops. Halo Top Pops are seen as permissible indulgence because they are portion sized and more associated with health and being guilt free. The target audience is more receptive to a low-calorie story for pops versus pints. While Halo Top ice cream sales declined 7.9 percent in 2021, new Halo Top Pops sales increased 110 percent.[22]

Successful Brands and Sales People Often Have a Noble Purpose

Story and the Golden Circle aren't just powerful in the business-to-consumer market; they also drive success in the business-to-business (B2B) market. Companies and salespeople who put what and money first don't perform as well as their peers who tell a why story. In Lisa Earle McLeod's research, she found that salespeople who sell with a noble purpose, outsell salespeople focused on sales targets and quotas.

Your brand story can help products stand out in competitive categories such as ice cream leading to consumer decisions in the frozen food isle. Getty Images: Anderson Ross.

A **noble purpose** is being in service of something bigger than yourself and adding value for your customers. The why you are selling is to help customers. Salespeople who focus on their customers' lives sell more than those focused on the sales numbers. Other research has found companies that put improving people's lives at the center of what they do grow three times the rate of competitors.[23]

McLeod explains, "Purpose creates competitive differentiation and emotional engagement."[24] If you're thinking that there are similarities between McLeod's and Sinek's message, you're right. McLeod says that financial targets don't motivate and shouldn't be the center of a business narrative. Financial results are an outcome, not a driver for sales performance.[25] As Sinek says, making a sale is not why. Making a sale is a result of starting with why, or as McLeod puts it, your noble purpose.

Lisa Earle McLeod has her own why, how, and what story to tell in her bio that explains her noble purpose and results in sales of her consulting services to B2B clients.

I'm a former Procter & Gamble sales trainer who realized early on that I have a knack for decoding human behavior. When I was 15 years old working at Donut King in Arlington, VA, I sold over 700 donuts in a single shift. When the owner, a first-generation immigrant, looked into the cash register that night, his jaw dropped. A huge grin spread over his entire face. He grabbed me and hugged me. In that moment I knew, helping people make money is a noble endeavor.[26]

3.3 Brand and Buyer Story

Having the right story where brand why, how, and what match consumer why, how, and what is important. If they don't match, you won't achieve desired results. That's why Hummer buyers wouldn't switch to a Prius even if they were concerned about the environment. The SUV buyers' why didn't have the right how and what. That is, until GM reintroduced the Hummer as an all-electric SUV.

Psychology Plays an Important Role in Telling the Right Brand Story

Psychologist and chairman of the market research firm Archetype Discoveries, Clotaire Rapaille, says people buy SUVs so they can feel dominant. He calls this the code for SUV or the unconscious association with the product. Through this mental highway, people make decisions.[27] No matter how bad the Hummer was for the environment, the typical Hummer driver had no interest in an environmentally friendly Prius. It was off code. The Prius brand story didn't match their personal story. Even now that the Hummer EV is environmentally friendly, the all-electric message takes a back seat on the website where "off-road dominance" is emphasized.[28]

Unconscious codes for products apply to other markets. It can help explain how Halo Top experienced a dip in sales. From Mintel consumer market research, we could surmise that the code for a pint of ice cream is a guilty pleasure. Another trend in the ice cream market is increased portion and calorie control options in pop cycles. Thus, the code for pop cycles would be a slightly different position of a guilt-free treat. Ben & Jerry's message is on code with "euphoric concoctions" for pints. That story matches the story or code many are looking

Most SUVs are sold with the story of "off-road dominance" not "environmentally friendly."
Getty Images: Chris Clor.

for in pints of ice cream. Halo Top ice cream was off code with low-calorie pints. Now Halo Top is getting results with its on-code story "light ice cream that tastes like ice cream" in pops.

No matter what product, service, or brand you're working on, ask yourself if the story matches the code or story the consumer wants in the product. The brand's why must match the consumer's why. Steve Jobs used computers to change the world by attracting customers who wanted to change the world. Ben & Jerry's uses ice cream to change environmental and societal impact by attracting customers who want to indulge their sweet tooth while not spoiling the planet or society. Halo Top uses pops to change our world by attracting customers who want to enjoy ice cream without guilt. Top salespeople use a noble cause to change their client's world by attracting business customers who want genuine solutions that help them, not their salesperson's commission check.

More likely than not, your client, whether a start-up, midsized regional business, or Fortune 500, will come to you with an outside-in marketing plan (see Table 3.1). You will be tempted to simply take what it sells and begin your IMC strategy or campaign. But as we just learned, your IMC plan will not be effective if you are telling the wrong why, how, and what story or telling part of the story—simply what you are selling. First, you'll need to flip the marketing plan to discover the why and possibly the how.

Think of this flip as creating an inside-out marketing plan. Your client will be quick to tell you exactly what the company makes, all the features and benefits, the facts and figures. Your client may even tell you the great ways of how the company makes products and services. Getting to the why usually takes more work.

In Chapter 1, we learned that the power of story comes from emotions. Jak's research connected oxytocin release with more charity donations. The what fact of children having cancer was not enough. The why of the charity is expressed through the story of an individual father's struggle in being sad his child is dying but trying to smile to make his boy's last days happy. This character-driven story went beyond what (childhood cancer charity) and how (cancer research), to express why (help dads to not have to live this difficult story).[29]

Why is the heart of story. It drives the plot, characters, and emotions of sympathy and empathy.[30] How do you get to why of your marketing client's brand? Ask questions or conduct research to discover the following:

1. Why does the company exist? (Simply to make money is not acceptable.)
2. What does the company stand for?
3. Is there a greater problem it is trying to solve?
4. Is it trying to spread a bigger message?
5. Does it support a specific cause or community?
6. Is it dedicated to being the absolute best?
7. Does it have a mission or vision statement?
8. What is the founder's story or reason for starting the business?

You may also need to flip the marketing plan to a more customer-centric mindset. **Customer centric** means understanding who your most valuable customers are and delivering the most value to them. Notice how this is different from the adage "the customer is always right." Peter Fader, creator of the customer-centricity concept, argues that there are wrong customers and that companies need to focus on the right customers for strategic advantage.

Not every customer is right for a Ben & Jerry's pint, Halo Top Pop, Hummer, or a Prius. Why waste time and money trying to speak to everyone? Part of telling the right story is identifying the right customer.[31] For any IMC plan to be efficient and effective, you need to start with a narrow, well-focused target audience. Then, you will have a much better chance of matching brand story to consumer story.

Archetypes Can Help Define Brand Personality

Another tool that can help ensure you begin with a strategic foundation for your IMC plan and creating brand stories is archetypes. For example, a brand with the archetype "outlaw" such as Harley Davidson will attract "outlaw" customers who want to identify with that image and the "soul-satisfying rumble" of the powerful American engine.[32] A brand with a "creator" archetype such as Vespa Scooters attracts customers who identify with creator narratives and a scooter "celebrating the sunny spirit" and European heritage.[33] Understanding personality archetypes can help match brand code and story to the right customer as well as help to identify what type of characters to place in IMC stories to draw consumer attention.

Carl Jung, a Swiss psychologist and psychiatrist, developed the concept of archetypes. Jung believed people have instinctive patterns or universal characteristics that are expressed in certain behaviors and images.[34] In literary devices, an **archetype** is a character in a story created based on a set of qualities identifiable to readers or audiences. The most common archetype is the **hero**, or the protagonist, of a narrative who displays characteristics of courage, perseverance, and sacrifice.[35]

In Chapter 2, we discussed The Hero's Journey. Yet stories include different characters, and like people, brands can have different personalities that should match their customers' and

Vespa has a different "creator" European heritage archetype than Harley Davidson's more "outlaw" American heritage image. Getty Images: Dimensions.

Table 3.2. Jung's Universal Personality Archetypes

Creator (Innovation)	**Magician** (Power)
Sage (Knowledge)	**Jester** (Pleasure)
Innocent (Safety)	**Every person** (Belonging)
Explorer (Freedom)	**Lover** (Intimacy)
Outlaw (Liberation)	**Caregiver** (Service)
Hero (Mastery)	**Ruler** (Control)

Source: Conor Neill, "Understanding Personality: The 12 Jungian Archetypes," Conorneill.com, April 21, 2018, https://conorneill.com/2018/04/21/understanding-personality-the-12-jungian-archetypes/.

potential customers' in the target audience. Archetypes can be shortcuts to tension, establishing conflict quickly through contrasting characters to elicit audience attention and action.[36] They signal to your audience that your brand is talking to them and is worthy of attention. Archetypes can help an audience relate to characters quickly, thus avoiding detailed descriptions and expanded expositions.[37] Jung identified 12 universal mythic character archetypes, which we can apply to both people and brands (see Table 3.2).[38]

Margaret Mark and Carol S. Pearson wrote a seminal book on this topic called *The Hero and the Outlaw: Building Extraordinary Brands Through the Power of Archetypes.* Mark and Pearson use Jung's 12 archetypes to classify brands, consumer markets, and consumers. They argue that companies should identify brand meaning or archetype and then use it as the basis for establishing relationships with customers. The brand archetype becomes the filter through which all brand visual and verbal messages pass through.[39]

Some scholars have found that consumers don't just select brands that match their personality; they seek brands that match their ideal selves. The difference is that your actual self includes both the good and bad aspects of your self-concept. Your ideal self includes the aspects to which you aspire.[40]

This explains how Nike and their ad agency Wieden+Kennedy creates ads that target top performance athletes, yet they're not the only ones who relate to Nike ads and purchase Nike products. Breaking the two-hour marathon barrier is not something most runners get close to attempting. Yet Nike's quest to help elite runner Eliud Kipchoge break this record was chronicled in the 2017 IMC campaign *Breaking2*, which promoted Nike Vaporfly running shoes. Eliud missed the record by 26 seconds, but by 2019, he was able to break the barrier in another attempt, proving "that if you are relentless in pursuing a goal, anything is possible."[41]

A very small percentage of runners could get close to breaking long distance–running records (their actual self). Yet many runners aspire to run as fast as Eliud runs (their ideal selves). These people include back-of-the-pack runners just trying to break four- or five-hour marathons or trying to get a personal record in their next 5K. Enough nonelite runners view their ideal selves as fast that Vaporfly shoe sales drove Nike's marketing share in the running market category to a record high by 2019.[42]

Products affirm a consumer's ideal self. Researchers have found products aligned with the consumer's ideal self are evaluated more favorably and bring about more positive changes in the consumer's emotions and personality. These affirmation feelings go above and beyond the product's utilitarian value. Nike's Vaporfly technology can make you run faster, but the feeling of being an elite runner is much greater than any actual physical improvement.[43]

Products can help sculpt a consumer's ideal self just as a relationship partner can help you achieve your aspirations and goals. With increased consumer participation in two-way communications through social media, this idea of brand relationships is stronger than ever.

3.4 Brand and Buyer Identity

"Who am I? Who do I want my future self to be?" Everyone seeks to answer these timeless questions.[44] Today, consumers turn to brands to help them define their ideal selves. Therefore, it is important to match brand and buyer identity in the stories you tell. Beyond traditional brand identify guidelines, which include design elements such as fonts and colors, we must also consider brand character qualities, beliefs, and personality.

Brands Can Build Community around Their Products and Services

Identity is the experiences, relationships, and values that create one's sense of self.[45] Identity is expressed through beliefs, qualities, personality, looks, and expressions that make a person or group. A brand acting as a person to form relationships with its customers needs a social identity. Your brand's identity should match your ideal customer's ideal identity. There should be enough connections to form an attraction like in a real personal relationship.

Psychologists describe personal identity as the things that make a person unique, while sociologists describe **social identity** as the collection of group memberships that help define the individual. Brands that become communities can become one of the memberships that help define their target audience of ideal buyers. A **brand community** is a group of people with social relations structured around being admirers of a brand.[46]

Think about how many people today place brand stickers on their laptops, water bottles, or cars. Why do they put these stickers on the things they own? Because it helps personalize them. Each brand represents a piece of their ideal self. Why do they wear T-shirts and hats with brand logos? Is it because they want people to know that they have a cooler with extra-thick walls, pressure-injected polyurethane foam insulation, and rotomolded construction? Or is it because that brand logo is a social cue to others that their life is "Built for the Wild" like their cooler? People wearing YETI brand apparel and posting pictures of their outdoor adventures to the hashtag #BuiltForTheWild symbolize a lifestyle and membership to a group described in YETI's story on its website:

> In 2006, we founded YETI Coolers with a simple mission: build the cooler we'd use every day if it existed. One that was built for the serious outdoor enthusiast rather than for the mass-discount retailers. One that could take the abuse we knew we'd put it through out in the field and on the water. One that simply wouldn't break. We decided early on that product innovation would come from necessity and firsthand experience—not from market research and data analysis. Today, YETI products perform when it matters most—whether that be an excursion into the remote Alaskan wilderness, chasing redfish on the Gulf coast, or just getting together with friends in the backyard.[47]

Products such as coolers can tell the story of a lifestyle that the product's features enable leading to brand communities. Getty Images: Thomas Barwich.

When there is an understanding of brand and buyer social identity, a bond can be formed through a consistent visual and verbal story told in IMC consumer touchpoints. Psychologists believe stories are fundamental to social interaction, so this brand/buyer story sharing and interaction will form bonds.[48] Micro-connections through the narratives in IMC establish a group social identity built around brand community.

Every time YETI posts a picture on Instagram of its products in the wild, it is sharing a glimpse of a story of a particular outdoor adventure. When it reshares customers' own photos of their outdoor adventures with their YETI products, it is building that brand story with them. When interacting and co-developing stories with your buyers, the group social identity can build strong brand loyalty. Perhaps this could even grow to become "loyalty beyond reason," as Kevin Roberts, CEO of communications agency Saatchi & Saatchi, calls brands that are *Lovemarks*. Roberts explains that "when a deep emotional connection is cultivated, anything, anywhere can win loyalty that protects against preference attacks from competitors touting new features, deals, and design." **Lovemarks** are brands that recognize that the heart rules the head in decision-making.[49]

Brands Contribute to a Consumer's Identity

To be intentional about these brand stories and communities, a strategic tool can be helpful. A brand buyer identity template or worksheet (see Figure 3.2) helps to plan and guide the

Figure 3.2. Brand/buyer social Identity template and worksheet.

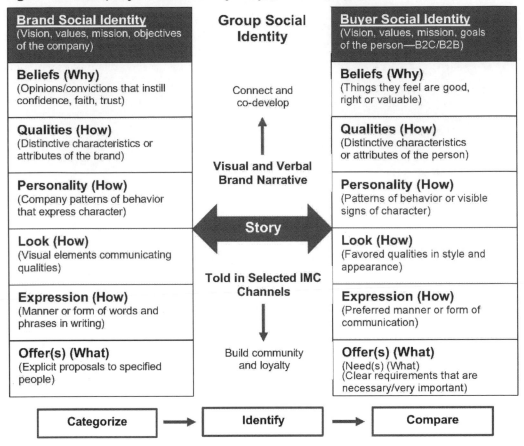

visual and verbal brand narrative told through various IMC media channels. This brand/buyer identity model follows a three-step process explained in social identity theory (illustrated at the bottom of the template/worksheet).

Social identity is a person's sense of who they are based on their group memberships. The groups people belong to are an important source of pride and self-esteem, giving them a feeling of belonging. To increase self-image, people are motivated to enhance the status of the group. To do this, they categorize groups, identify with one, and then compare and favor that group over others in the same category.[50] This can happen in many ways, including abilities (artistic vs. scientific), design preference (contemporary vs. country), team loyalty (Eagles vs. Cowboys), and brands (Apple vs. Microsoft).

A brand's social identity should be informed by the organization's vision, mission, and objectives to make up the social identity of the brand. Following Simon Sinek's model, these are its why. A brand's why also informs brand beliefs. What are the opinions or convictions of the organization that instill confidence, faith, and trust in employees, investors, and customers? These are brand beliefs.[51]

Next in Sinek's model is how. The organization's how helps inform brand qualities. What are the distinctive characteristics or attributes of the brand? These make up a brand's qualities.[52] What pattern of behavior would best convey the character of the brand? This is brand personality.[53] Are there important brand visual elements, such as colors, logos, fonts, and image style? These are visual components that make up a brand's look.[54] How would you describe brand voice or form of words and phrases in written communication? This is brand expression.[55]

Finally, consider the what from Sinek's model. Capture main offerings as explicit proposals to specified people. These are brand offers. What are the specific products and services offered? What are their main features and benefits?[56] What a brand offers is where many marketers and communications professionals begin and end, but that doesn't lead to audience-engaging brand stories.

The buyer's social identity is similar yet from a slightly different perspective. This is informed by the target audience's personal vision, values, mission, and objectives in a business-to-consumer context or informed by the target business's vision, values, mission, and objectives in a B2B context. Describe the things they feel are good, right, or valuable (beliefs); the distinctive characteristics and attributes of the person (qualities); signs of their character or patterns of behavior (personality); favored qualities in style and appearance (look); and preferred manner or form of communication (expression). Capture the clear requirements that are necessary or very important to this buyer (needs).[57]

Often, needs come out of complications, obstacles, or pain points that cause tension, which we can see in the YETI founders' brand story. They were frustrated by the quality and performance of coolers that didn't live up to their outdoor lifestyle. Building your brand narrative around these and positioning your products and services as a solution to release that tension can be very powerful.[58] As we learned in Chapter 2, tension is a building block of story in Act 2 of Freytag's Story Framework.

Does the client's brand social identity match the buyer's social identity? If these are significantly off in key areas, you may have to adjust the social elements of the brand, or perhaps you need to realign your target audience to buyers who have more elements in common with the brand. If the client's brand social identity does not match the buyer's social identity, then as Clotaire Rapaille of Archetype Discoveries may say, your brand is "off code." The visual and verbal stories told through the IMC strategy should help the target audience move through the three-step socialization process to story making with the brand.

The brand narrative will lead potential consumers into categorizing the brand personality and offering and identifying as belonging to the brand community. As members of that social group, they will compare the brand favorably over competitors'. Having a brand social identity can help guide IMC content creation and buyer social media engagements, setting a standard of authentic brand communication. Perhaps one day, the brand logo will become a "lovemark" that they proudly display on their laptop, water bottle, car, hat, or T-shirt.[59]

A Brand That Sells Its App through Key Beliefs, Not Key Features

Going back to Noom's inside-out marketing strategy, its brand story of solving the problem of "a system that had become so focused on sick care, instead of health care," created a convergence of complementary and interdependent brand and buyer social identities between the company and its consumers. Both are now part of a group identity that "takes control of their health."

As such, once the customer succeeds in Noom's program, the brand's story is passed onto the customer's own story of overcoming the tension and adversity of failed attempts at getting healthy. Noom's website testimonials highlight the passing of this story torch: "I've learned a lot about the psychology of food and the mental blocks we all have as we go through change. I sleep a lot better, am far more mentally alert, and feel more confident."[60] This powerful and shared narrative may help to explain the company's growth of 140 percent in three years.[61]

Inherent in Noom's brand story is the broader approach to improving the health of the entire population. The brand's vision or why is to change people's bad habits to encourage weight loss via a broader healthy lifestyle and prevent weight-related diseases, such as diabetes and high blood pressure.

The company's unique story and value proposition effectively drive home a point of differentiation for it in a weight-loss category that typically highlights the what of its diet plans, such as restricting calories, counting steps, and stepping on the scale every day. Noom's mission doesn't emphasize mundane and often "off-code" messages. Consider what we learned earlier in this chapter with Halo Top's initial low-calorie positioning failure.

Noom takes a more empathetic approach to what the traditional, nonemotional fitness tracking apps can offer, moving from points of parity to points of differentiation. As Saeju Jeong states, "Empathy is not a thing you can generate out of A.I. technology." In Chapter 1, we learned how empathy plays a key role in the effectiveness of storytelling on consumer behavior. It took Noom a few years to come to this conclusion, but it has paid off well for the brand.[62]

Throughout the first three chapters, we have talked a lot about markets being made up of consumers looking to buy products and services. From that market, we target a segment or group of consumers or buyers with our IMC strategies. The **consumer** is the ultimate user of products, services, or ideas. This could be Michelle Phan's EM Cosmetics targeting moms to buy makeup for themselves. However, a consumer can also refer to the decision-maker who buys a product or service but is not the ultimate user.[63] For example, Cheerios targets parents to purchase cereal for their children. Yet not all desired actions are to buy and consume a product or service.

At other times, the target consumer of an IMC message is a decision-maker in a business that buys on behalf of others. They may not be the ultimate consumer of the product or service. A member of the buying center at a baby stroller manufacturer may buy components, such as wheels, from suppliers that are assembled into the final jogging stroller to be sold to parents. A human resources director may be the target audience for a health insurance provider, such as Blue Cross. They make the decisions on what benefits to offer at their company. Employees use the service, such as maternity care for those about to become a parent.

3.5 CASE

Patagonia's Consumers Don't Always Consume

Marketers don't always want consumers to consume. Patagonia famously ran an ad with the headline "Don't Buy This Jacket." Patagonia sells clothing, but its overall mission is, "We're in business to save our home planet. We aim to use the resources we have—our voice, our business, and our community—to do something about our climate crisis" (https://www.patagonia.com/activism/). Patagonia balances selling new clothes with its overall mission to protect the environment that its target audience enjoys.

Patagonia Wornwear encourages consumers to consume less by trading in old Patagonia clothes to be resold. This helps to reduce the company's carbon, waste, and water footprint (https://wornwear.patagonia.com). The company tells this brand story in a variety of formats, from traditional ads featuring products to Twitter pleas for climate action. On YouTube, Patagonia features documentaries that tell how Salvar Una Cuenca is running to save a watershed and that show employees demonstrating how to repair a zipper to extend the life of its jackets (https://www.youtube.com/c/patagonia).

Sometimes, marketers want consumers to consume more or consume something different. An example is Campbell's sharing recipes featuring its soups as the main ingredient to increase the frequency of purchases of its canned soup. Campbell's tells stories of busy adults showing how to make quick and easy meals for their families. The brand's stories are told when and where its target audience is looking, with posts such as "Get hammy with your Easter leftovers" on Pinterest (https://www.pinterest.com/jjcauthen/campbells-kitchen-recipes/).

Gatorade doesn't want people to consume more sports drinks during workouts but wants athletes drinking Powerade to switch. Gatorade tells stories where characters are training for games or races, which positions the brand as performance hydration for serious athletes.[64] Yet it doesn't just tell stories of pro athletes in TV commercials. Gatorade knows when and where its target is telling their stories. They created a free app called "Highlights" to help teen athletes capture and share videos of their best sports moments. The brand makes them the star of the story while boosting user-generated brand content.[65]

Marketers may also want target audiences to take action through less consumption or nonconsumption. A nonprofit or government agency often wants audiences to consume less, such as with a public health campaign or natural resource conservation effort. The Truth anti-tobacco campaign has used stories for decades with the goal of eliminating teen smoking. Now, it is telling truth stories to reduce teen vaping and opioid use. In the 1990s, it used **public service announcements (PSAs)**, or promotional messages carried by the media at no cost as a public service.[66] PSA TV ads reached their audience on popular teen shows. Today, The Truth campaign tells its stories on social media, such as Instagram and YouTube, and on The Truth website (https://www.thetruth.com).

In this chapter, we began with Simon Sinek's simple observation that why motivates successful leaders, organizations, and customers. This inside-out way of thinking about marketing is essential to storytelling to connect the brand's story to the buyer's story. We also considered how buyers seek brands and brand communities that match their ideal selves. Finally, we learned that not all marketers will have the objective of enticing consumers to consume more. In the next chapter, we will set the stage for a story-focused IMC plan by understanding the marketing mix, IMC touchpoints, and media mix.

QUESTIONS

1. Why do so many marketers and the IMC campaigns they create focus only on what they make instead of why they make it and why the customer truly buys it?
2. What companies do you feel have strong brand communities, and what are some key elements that have enabled those communities to grow?

EXERCISES

1. In this chapter, we looked at several examples of companies, such as YETI and Noom, where their why or mission is told through stories in their IMC messages. Does a company's mission always match its IMC message? Visit the websites of several brands, and read their mission/vision statements. Their statements can usually be found under an "About Us" or "Our Story" tab. Then, look at some of their latest ads and social media posts. Does the message emphasized in the company's IMC communication match its mission, or why?
2. Do you know why you buy what you buy? Look at the brand on your shirt, hat, and shoes and the logos on your laptop, water bottle, or car. What why of the brand story matches your why or story of your ideal self? Are there any products or services that you buy for utilitarian function only? Or do they all have some why story that is calling you to join the brand community? Fill out the brand/buyer social identity template and worksheet for your brand and target audience or for yourself and one of your favorite brands.

KEY CONCEPTS

Archetype
Brand community
Consumer
Customer centric
Golden Circle
Hero
Identity
Lovemarks

Noble purpose
Points of differentiation
Points of parity
Price promotion
Price war
Public service announcements (PSAs)
Social identity

PART

II

Foundations of
IMC Storytelling

Set the Stage

Marketing, IMC, and Media

PREVIEW

As we journey into Part II of this book, we'll learn about the origins of brand storytelling within the foundations of integrated marketing communications (IMC). This includes a look at innovators in the field, an understanding of the Four Ps marketing mix, IMC touchpoints, and the media mix. We'll begin with marketing discipline innovator Philip Kotler. Kotler understood that IMC is more than the integration of disciplines or media, saying, "Integrated marketing communications are a way to examine the entire marketing process from the point of view of the receiver."[1] From the Four Ps, we look at the origins of IMC in the 1990s, the consumer touchpoints of IMC today, and how to reach consumers through those touchpoints via a media plan.

CHAPTER 4 LEARNING OBJECTIVES

1. Discover the origins of the Four Ps and IMC.
2. Understand the changing marketing mix.
3. Identify the key consumer touchpoints in IMC.
4. Evaluate various media mix options in IMC.

4.1 Kotler's Four Ps and Schultz's IMC

Philip Kotler is a marketing author, consultant, and emeritus professor of marketing at Northwestern's School of Management. He is also known as the father of modern marketing and credited with popularizing the concept of the marketing mix, or the Four Ps—the essence of marketing strategy.[2] Have you heard of the Four Ps? Understanding these Ps of the marketing mix helps you create a successful IMC strategy.

The Marketing Mix Sets the Foundation for IMC Strategy

The **marketing mix** is the combination of controllable marketing variables a firm uses to achieve sales objectives in the target market.[3] The variables of the Four Ps are product, price, promotion, and place (or distribution). The **target market** is a specific portion of the total population most likely to purchase a particular company's products or services.[4] A **market** is a collection of people who wish to buy a specific product, known as an industry or business sector.[5] An example of a market is everyone who wants to travel by airline. All the companies that provide this type of travel compete in the airline industry. Markets also tend to be country specific, meaning that companies create different marketing mix strategies based on the country in which they are marketing.

Have you heard the phrase "birds of a feather flock together"? Marketers look for flocks of people to position their products toward compared to their competitors. To select a target market, they segment the broad market into groups of people with common characteristics via bases of segmentation. Bases include demographic, psychographic, behavioral, and geographic segments, each with multiple variables (see Table 4.1). Secondary consumer research via market research companies, such as Mintel; company primary surveys; and focus groups reveals clusters of customers with similar needs and preferences. Multiple relevant bases and variables, such as age, income, lifestyle, benefits sought, and region, form the market segments.

Each combination of bases and variables is often given a profile description, such as business travelers, family leisure travelers, low-fare seekers, or elite luxury travelers.[6] Marketers then decide which market segments are most likely to purchase their offering compared to their competitors. The marketing mix of product, price, place, and promotion is tailored to that customer segment's preferences through positioning. **Positioning** is the way consumers view competitive brands or products in a market.[7]

In the marketing mix, marketers must have a product. A **product** is a bundle of features, functions, benefits, and uses capable of exchange. It can be both tangible and intangible, such as an airline ticket, which is a tangible thing, and the rest of the trip, which is an intangible thing, or it can be a service, such as beverages, snacks, in-flight internet and movies, change

Table 4.1. Bases and Variables of Consumer Segmentation

Geographic	Demographic	Psychographic	Behavioral
Region, climate, growth rate, population density	Age, gender, ethnicity, income, education, occupation, family	Values, beliefs, attitudes, lifestyle	Usage rate, brand loyalty, benefits sought

policies, and frequent flyer rewards.[8] Businesses also need to decide what to charge. **Price** is the amount a customer must pay to acquire a product.[9] The price can be one time, a monthly subscription, or another form of payment option.

In addition, marketers and business owners decide how to get the product to the target market. **Place (distribution)** refers to carrying the products to consumers and the extent of market coverage.[10] A product could be available nationally or just in one region or in store and not online. Airlines can be regional, national, or international and only fly out of specific hubs. Finally, you need to let people know about the product and entice them to purchase it. **Promotion** is marketing communications or the promotional messages and media used to communicate to a target market.[11] Today, this happens through IMC.

Typically, a marketer or business owner determines the marketing mix in a marketing plan. Then, as a marketing communications firm or professional, they hire you to create an IMC plan to promote the product to the target market at the price and place they have determined. Where the marketing mix ends, IMC takes over (see Figure 4.1).

IMC Takes Over Once the Marketing Mix Is Set

IMC has its roots with another Northwestern professor, Don E. Schultz. He is known as the father of IMC. He was a former advertising professional turned professor at the Medill School of Journalism, Media, and Integrated Marketing Communications. In the early 1990s, he worked with the American Association of Advertising Agencies to study a new practice of IMC being used by advertising professionals. Out of that research came the concept of IMC and the first published text on IMC.[12]

The practice of IMC calls for the integration of what were previously seen as separate methods or disciplines: advertising, sales promotion, direct marketing, and public relations. Today we must also add the integration of the new emerging disciplines and methods of digital marketing and social media marketing, personal sales, and alternative media (see

Figure 4.1. Four Ps marketing mix and IMC mix.

Figure 4.1). IMC also calls for a focus on consumer-centric communication to meet the needs and desires of the customer. **Integrated marketing communications** align and coordinate all marketing communications from the consumer's perspective to present a cohesive whole that persuades them to purchase.[13]

In Chapter 3, we discussed the importance of inside-out marketing in the context of starting with why before how and what a company sells. If you don't know the why, you can't tell an effective story. Another important component of a successful IMC strategy is understanding the marketing mix from an outside-in perspective—the consumer's perspective. As we collect the key components of the marketing mix strategy, we will seek to present them from an outside-in context from the consumer's point of view. The goal is to develop an inside-out marketing mix combined with an outside-in IMC strategy to connect brand social identity to buyer social identity.

4.2 Understanding the Marketing Mix

Telling the right story to the right people requires understanding the main components of a company's marketing mix. A first step in creating an effective IMC plan is to collect information about key components of the marketing plan from your client. When first working with a client, ask the following questions to ensure you understand the context within which your IMC story will be told. If your client doesn't know some of these, fill in the blanks with your own research.

Vision/Mission: Why does the company exist? To make money is not motivating for employees or customers. What does the company behind the product/service stand for and where is it headed? Think: solving a greater problem; spreading a bigger message; supporting a cause, community, or the environment; or being the absolute best at something specific.

History/Backstory: How did the company start? People buy for rational and emotional reasons that can come from an origin story. Discover the company's human side of founders starting in a garage, making a childhood dream come true, an event that put a cause on their heart, or something they needed but couldn't get. Did they struggle and overcome adversity? Even big companies benefit from showcasing their humble roots.

Marketing Objectives: What numbers must be met? Define a couple of main objectives the IMC plan must help meet, such as sales, market share, leads, awareness, volunteers, or donations. Ensure that the objectives meet SMART guidelines. **SMART** is specific (quantified such as X% or $X), measurable (data you can access), achievable (not too high), relevant (support vision/mission and address problem/opportunity), timely (due date such as X months or by 20XX year). The marketing objective is usually tied to an annual goal that must be met within the yearly marketing budget that justifies the marketing spend with a return on investment.

Products/Services: What is the IMC plan selling specifically? What are the product and service offerings, lines, and versions? Capture specific features but also try to describe the consumer benefit. From the consumer's perspective, how do the company's offerings compare to those of its main competitors?

Industry Overview: What market category/industry does the product compete in? Is the overall category growing or declining? What trends are important? Are there gaps in offerings?

What do consumers care about most? What are the consumer's pain points? Describe the main threats and opportunities in the industry and for your client's success specifically.

Target Market: What group is most likely to have the need for your client's specific product offering? Define with relevant demographic (gender, age, income, education), psychographic (attitudes, values, lifestyle), behavioral (products used, brand loyalty, usage), and geographic (region, climate, population) bases (see Table 4.1). Is there more than one significant segment? With geographic bases, consider place. A product with national distribution needs promotion in all regions, but a local business can focus on local media markets and digital geotargeting.

Key Competitors: Who are the company's main competitors? Identify top competitors by market share/sales in the same industry and/or by replacement products/services outside the category. Who is the company trying to catch, and what company is trying to catch it? What does the company do differently than its main competitors? For nonprofits, consider organizations that serve similar needs.

Place Strategy: What are the ways the consumer can purchase and experience the product or service? A single distribution channel or multiple channels? The company's own physical or online store or through channel partners such as retailers or brokers in physical or online stores? Are there geographic boundaries? Is distribution exclusive (one or a few outlets), selective (select outlets in specific locations), or intensive (in as many outlets as possible) in market coverage?

Price Strategy: How do the customers pay for the product or service? Do they pay all at once or per month? Is there a free sample or trial? What forms of payment are taken? How do the prices compare to those of the company's main competitors? Is the pricing premium (high price set to reinforce prestige image), value (set to customers' perceived value), or economy (low price set to sell higher volume)?

Positioning Statement: Summarize all the information into a positioning statement written to the target market. Follow a template, such as "For [ideal market segment], the product is [concise description], which is ideal for [describe best use/application of product] and better than [identify primary competitor] because of [cite differentiation and other evidence to back up a claim of superiority]."[14]

Budget/Time: What money will be spent to meet marketing objectives within a specified time frame? If the client needs help, marketing budgets can be determined by the following methods: all you can afford (what's left over), percentage of sales (percentage of projected/past sales, consider industry standards), match the competition (spend what main competitors spend), or objective/task (calculate what it will take to meet objectives). Time frames tend to correlate with the yearly marketing budget based on a calendar year. Time frames can vary for movie releases, elections, events, or fundraising campaigns that have a specific end date.[15]

For a visual template of this process and to organize responses/answers, see Figure 4.2 marketing strategy template worksheet. You will notice in the template worksheet the addition of boxes between industry overview, target market, key competitors, place strategy, price strategy, and positioning statement. These boxes are designed to translate or present client answers into an IMC consumer perspective for each category.

From an industry overview, determine the consumer's unmet needs that this company can satisfy. From the target market, determine the group of people who need this the most. By learning about key competitors, describe why that group should pick this company over

Figure 4.2. Marketing strategy template worksheet.

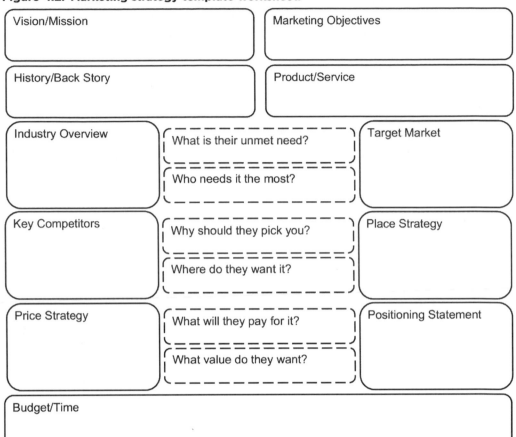

the others. In understanding the product's distribution, explain where and how the customer likes to buy. From pricing strategies, explain the customer's view on how and what they're willing to pay. Considering the positioning statement, summarize the value the customer will feel they are receiving.

Before moving on, an important distinction should be made. As the IMC agency, your job is not to make marketing mix recommendations outside of promotion. You are merely collecting this information. However, in the process of asking these questions and collecting research you may discover some places where you feel the client may benefit from a new product, place, or price strategy. Clients will welcome suggestions, but your focus and the expectation is that you will help them meet the main marketing objectives with the current marketing mix of products, pricing, and places the products are sold. As the IMC expert, it is your job to meet the objectives through promotion strategies and tactics.

An example of the increased importance of understanding the broader marketing mix and marketing objectives in IMC is the shift in performance measures occurring within the discipline of public relations. During the PR Week Annual Conference in 2016 Richard Edelman, president and CEO of the PR firm Edelman, said:

The swim lanes between PR agencies and sister firms in digital, advertising, and media buying will be blurred. We have to improve our ability to deliver tangible results, namely sales, not simply awareness or change of attitude among opinion formers. This is our time, but only if we reposition our business as communications marketing, with equality of the disciplines. We must be able to appeal to the CCO and CMO.[16]

4.3 Identifying IMC Touchpoints

Once you understand your client's marketing mix, determine the right places to tell the IMC story. You want to select the best consumer touchpoints to reach the client's target market. The target market, or whom the client wants to sell to, becomes your target audience, or the group you want to reach with your IMC plan.

A **target audience** is the specific group of consumers most likely to want a product or service and the group who should see marketing communications. Yet a target audience isn't always the entire target market. Sometimes, a specific campaign or promotion will be aimed at a subset of the target market.[17]

It is also important to note that defining a specific and often narrow target market or target audience doesn't mean they are the only ones who will want to buy a company's products or services. As with the Gatorade case discussed later in this chapter, targeting high school and endurance athletes doesn't mean they are the only ones who will purchase Gatorade. Consider a middle-aged jogger who just runs a couple of miles a week to stay in shape. They don't relate to the story of a marathoner but think, "If Gatorade is good enough for a marathoner, it is good for my three-mile run."

In a business-to-business (B2B) context, marketers consider target markets and target audiences through various buying roles that one or more people perform in a buying decision. The **initiator** is the person who first thinks of buying a product or service. A **decider** is the person who ultimately determines whether, what, where, and how to buy. The **buyer** is the person who handles the actual purchase. The **user** is the person or persons who use the product or service. Finally, a **gatekeeper** is the person who controls access to the decision-makers and influencers.[18] In a B2B context, a smaller company may have just one or two people who serve all these roles. A larger company may have people in all these roles as part of a buying center. Brand stories may vary based on buying roles.

B2B target audiences are segmented with different variables called firmographics based on company size, industry, geographic market, and business needs. **Firmographics** are data used to segment companies into meaningful categories for B2B marketing.[19] B2B target audiences can be segmented into job titles or members of professional organizations. Some also determine B2B target audiences via technographics. **Technographics** are data used to segment companies based on the technology they use such as hardware, software, tools and applications.

Marketing clients typically dictate the target market and audience defined by bases and variables of segmentation as seen in Tables 4.1 and 4.2. Yet as a marketing communications professional, you should not assume that the provided target is always the right target. Sometimes, businesspeople are good at their business but are not the best marketers. Even top marketers at Fortune 500s can get it wrong. If you don't start with the right target audience, your IMC strategy will not be successful and will not meet the marketing objectives the client is hiring you to achieve.

Table 4.2. Bases and Variables of Business Segmentation

Geographic	Demographic	Behavioral
Region, climate, growth rate, population density	Experience, income, industry, occupation, company size/sales, previous or new relationship	Usage planned or special purchase, bidding, contract, invoices, business needs

Also, remember that clients are often hiring you because current marketing efforts are not working. There is a problem that needs to be solved. Sometimes, it's a wrong message, content, media, SEO, or social media problem. But it can also be a wrong target audience problem. How do you know you have the right target audience? Consider these common misconceptions.

Don't assume your target is your social media followers. A client for the social media agency BSquared defined its target audience as 18- to 24-year-olds. It had the most social media followers from this age group. Yet BSquared looked at additional social listening data beyond the brand pages and digital advertising data. It found that the next two older age groups accounted for 90 percent of sales compared to just 10 percent of sales from the younger group.[20]

Don't assume everyone that could use the product is your target. We will learn in this chapter's case that when Gatorade shifted to a mass-market target of hydration for everyone 18 to 49 years old, sales declined 10 percent. The brand's core audience of competitive athletes got the message—Gatorade was not for them. The aspiring athletes got the message as well. Only when they focused back on niche audiences with increased targeted digital ads did sales return.[21]

Don't assume the people who use the product are your target. For years, Proctor & Gamble's Old Spice experienced declining sales. Consumer research revealed women purchase 60 percent of men's body washes. For the first time, the men's brand created an IMC campaign targeted at women. Within a year, sales grew 125 percent, surpassing competitors to become the number one brand in the category.[22]

Don't assume your target audience is current customers. When sales level off or decline, marketers may need to reach a new group of people who are not current users. The market for two-door coupes has been declining for years. The Ford Mustang Mach-E all-electric SUV is designed to reach a new audience. Targeting current Mustang drivers would not be effective because the car was designed to gain EV market share from Tesla. In the first year of sales, 70 percent of Mach-E buyers were new to the Ford brand.[23]

Don't assume there is only one target audience. There may be multiple target audiences that influence a purchase decision. Colleges know that parents influence high school students' college choice. Therefore, enrollment strategies often include a primary target audience of high school students with a secondary target audience of parents of high school–age children. Messages and media must be targeted to both because they view different media and may value different benefits of the college. Different variations of the brand story may have to be told.[24]

Don't assume the target is consumers of the product. Other key stakeholders can be selected for corporate communication and PR to manage the company's reputation with employees,

Sometimes, women can be a purchase decision-maker for men's products leading to a different target audience for an IMC plan. Getty Images: Cavan Images.

investors, suppliers, regulators, and the media. When the Crockpot brand faced a PR crisis, other target audiences became important. An episode of the popular show *This Is Us* featured a story where the main character was killed off in a fire caused by a faulty Crockpot. On social media, outraged fans threw away their slow cookers. The brand's PR agency, Edelman, responded quickly with a message to multiple stakeholders assuring the public that Crockpots were safe. Instead of sales dropping, sales increased from increased exposure.[25]

After understanding the target audience, you need to plan your media. This includes paid traditional, digital, and social media advertising; earned media opportunities through PR; and brand-created communications with digital and social media content marketing. A good model to organize the media mix is the PESO (paid, earned, shared, owned media) model created by Gini Dietrich at PR agency Spin Sucks (see Figure 4.3).[26] In the PESO model, Dietrich categorizes media based on the new realities of digital media and integration of disciplines practicing across media types.

Paid media is anything where the brand pays for its message to appear in front of any audience. This includes TV ads, billboards, social media ads, sponsored content, and email marketing to purchased lists. **Earned media** refers to getting media to talk about the brand in newspaper and trade articles, on broadcast news and podcasts, or in blogs, without payment. **Shared media** are nonpaid forms of social media where the brand talks about itself, consumers talk about the brand, and they both talk directly through social networks, reviews,

Figure 4.3. The PESO media model.

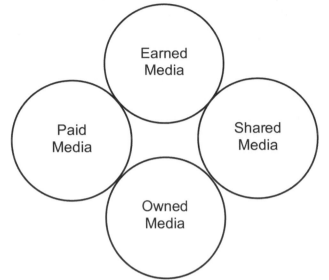

Source: Modified (with permission) from Gini Dietrich, "Why Communicators Must (Finally) Embrace the PESO Model," Spinsucks.com, (January 4, 2022), https://spinsucks.com/communication/pr-pros-must-embrace-the -peso-model/ © Spin Sucks. To learn more about the PESO Model and see the full PESO Model Diagram, visit: https:// spinsucks.com/communication/peso-model-breakdown/.

forums, and consumer blogs. **Owned media** is content created by the brand on platforms it owns and controls, such as websites, corporate blogs, videos, webinars, brand podcasts, and email to lists of brand subscribers.[27]

4.4 Planning the Media Mix

Once you have confirmed your target audience and understand the various forms of media, you need to plan what consumer touchpoints will be used to tell the brand story. From the IMC consumer perspective, answer how the target audience will experience this message.

Advertising: Do paid messages in traditional media, such as TV, print, radio, outdoor, transit, and newspaper, fit the target audience's media use and the brand's budget?

Public Relations: Can you make the message newsworthy? What earned media will reach the target audience via news stories, newscasts, podcasts, events, and conferences?

Digital Marketing: How will the target audience find the message online? Start with a user-centered website optimized for search, then consider search ads; content marketing; email; online ads; and video, affiliate, and mobile marketing.

Social Media: Where is the target audience active on social media? Look at social networks, blogs/forums, messaging apps, ratings/reviews, and podcasts. Consider geotargeting, crowdsourcing, influencer marketing, social care, user-generated content, and social ads.

Direct Response: Will the target audience want to purchase through direct calls to action in mail, catalogs, email, social media, website, texts (SMS), TV (infomercials), radio, newspaper, and social selling? Collect or purchase databases of email and/or physical addresses.

Sales Promotion: What special offers could get the target audience to buy, try, or rebuy? Consider discounts, samples, gifts/premiums, coupons, vouchers, competitions, sweepstakes, joint promotions, or special financing.

Personal Sales: High involvement products/services or B2B sales require a salesperson for prospecting, customization, demonstration/trial, and after-sale service to maintain lasting relationships and generate referrals. Salespeople need to be integrated into IMC strategy.

Database Marketing: Database marketing, also known as customer relationship management (CRM), uses databases/software to build long-term relationships with customers for retention, extension, and acquisition with special communication, services/offers, and rewards often through loyalty programs. CRM also enables the personalization of messages to individual buyers or segments of your larger target audience.

When various forms of the marketing communications mix come together, ensure they are integrated into both verbal and visual messages and are consistent through brand storytelling. For a visual template of this process, see Figure 4.4 IMC strategy template worksheet.

Notice that some components carry over from the marketing strategy template worksheet with communication objectives added. **Marketing objectives** focus on a direct return on the firm's marketing investment, such as reaching a specific level of sales, revenue, or

Figure 4.4. IMC strategy template worksheet.

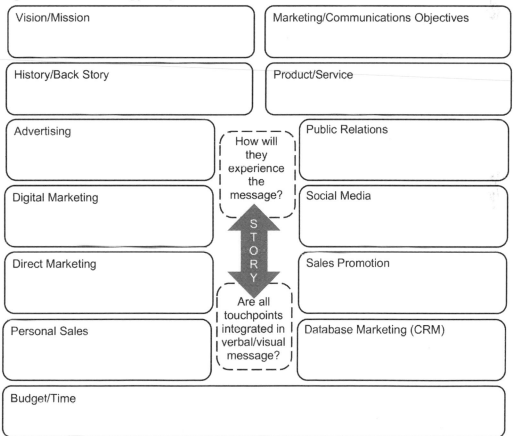

market share. **Communications objectives** focus on effective communication, such as a specific level of advertising recall or brand or product awareness or a measurable change in attitudes, brand image, or reputation. Companies may also determine a measure such as retention of existing customers is important and set a retention rate or percentage as an objective.

IMC plans begin with a revenue-based marketing objective but may also have communications objectives. For nonprofits, the marketing objective may be expressed as reaching a specific level of donations, volunteers, or event attendance. Marketing and communications objectives should not be IMC touchpoint specific. "Increase sales 20 percent in the next year" is a marketing objective. "Increase consumer engagement by opening a product Instagram page in the next year" is not a marketing objective; it is a strategy and tactic recommendation. "Increase Instagram followers 20 percent in the next year" is not a marketing objective; it is a metric measuring the communications success of this strategy and tactic.

Measuring specific strategies and tactics will come later in the strategic process by identifying key performance indicators (KPIs) and metrics in a measurement plan. In this phase of IMC plan development, simply capture the overall marketing sales or communications awareness objective to be achieved from all IMC consumer touchpoints. Specific strategy and tactic recommendations come in the next phase of the strategic process.

Once you have determined key consumer touchpoints, paid advertising media needs to be planned for the most efficient and effective spending of the budget. **Media planning** determines the types of advertising media used, the amount of budget allocated to each (media mix), and the specific time schedule for each media vehicle.[28] A McKinsey Global Media Report (see Table 4.3) reveals the shift from traditional advertising to digital media spending. Digital media spending surpassed traditional for the first time in 2019. The

Table 4.3. Advertiser Media Spending by Media Type (Media Mix)

Media Type	2019 Percentage of Mix	2020 Percentage of Mix	2021 Percentage of Mix
TV	30	30	29
Radio	6	5	5
Print	6	4	3
Out of home	4	2	3
Traditional media	**46**	**41**	**40**
Search	25	27	28
Nonvideo social	12	13	14
Video social	5	5	5
Nonvideo display	7	7	7
Video display	4	5	5
Other digital	1	1	1
Digital media	**54**	**59**	**60**

Source: "Five questions to answer before you finalize your media plan," Mc Kinsey.com, November 18, 2020, https://www.mckinsey.com/capabilities/growth -marketing-and-sales/our-insights/five-questions-to-answer-before-you-finalize -your-media-plan.

What media mix will reach your target audience in an increasingly crowed traditional and digital media landscape? Getty Images: Zsolt Hlinka.

COVID-19 pandemic further increased this shift. By 2021, 60 percent of advertising budgets were spent on digital media.[29]

In addition to determining the media mix and schedule, media plans set objectives to expose a percentage of the target audience to the brand product message a number of times. This occurs through reach, or the breadth of an ad's spread across a group of people, and frequency, or the number of times they see it. The idea is that marketers must reach a minimum number of a target audience a minimum number of times to see results. Yet if a person sees a message too many times, you may be wasting money on someone who has already acted or who will never act.

An example of a media objective for Gatorade would be "Reach 70 percent of male and female high school athletes age 15–19 a minimum of three times a month in the next year."[30] In the United States, this would be 21 million people. To reach 70 percent three times a month requires 540 million impressions. That sounds like a lot, but consider that Gatorade's previous target of men 18–49 was 65 million people. To reach 70 percent three times a month requires 2.3 billion impressions.[31] Based on this chapter's Gatorade case, the brand was paying to reach a group of people who were spending less, and the company was spending more to do it!

The Media Mix Is Evaluated through Several Measures

The impressions or exposures of the brand story to the specified target audience are planned, measured, and bought via multiple metrics. **Reach** is the number or percentage of people or households of a defined population exposed to a particular advertising media vehicle or media schedule during a specific time.[32] **Frequency** is the average number of exposures received by a portion of a defined population that was reached.[33] **Impressions** are each time an ad is shown; they are often calculated as Reach (#) x Frequency (#).[34] A media plan with high reach and low frequency may get lost in a crowded media environment, and a plan with low reach but high frequency could overexpose some and miss others.[35]

Impressions are measured differently in traditional and digital media. In traditional media, **advertising impressions** are an estimate of the audience for a media insertion (one ad) or campaign.[36] They can be based on average or previous viewership for a TV program, listenership for a radio station or subscribers, and newsstand sales for a printed magazine or newspaper. **Internet impressions** are a single display of online content to a user's web-enabled device. They are a direct measurement of exposure of a specific ad in a single digital media appearance.[37] Other measures of media follow.

Gross rating point (GRP) measures the size of an audience reached by a specific traditional media vehicle or schedule during a specific time.[38] Purchasing an ad on a TV show with a 2.0 rating means you reach 2 percent of people in a group, such as adults 18–49 or women 25–54.[39] GRP (%) = Reach (%) × Average frequency (#).[40] The top-rated TV series in 2021 was *Sunday Night Football* with a 4.8 rating, reaching 26 percent of adults 18–49, or 6.2 million people. *The Bachelorette* was number 10, with a 1.9 rating, reaching 10 percent of adults 18–49, or 2.3 million.[41] Purchasing a 30-second TV ad on *The Bachelorette* costs $170,278, while a 30-second TV ad on *Sunday Night Football* costs $789,718.[42]

Different cost models are available with specific forms of internet advertising. **Cost per impression (CPI)** is an internet advertising metric that defines cost according to the number of impressions.[43] **Cost per click (CPC)** is an internet advertising metric that is the amount spent to get an advertisement clicked.[44] CPC is the cost structure for Google Search ads sometimes called PPC or pay per click ads. **Cost per acquisition (CPA)** is the total cost of acquiring a customer based on dividing the dollar amount spent.[45]

All these forms of measurements can make media planning difficult when considering media options. Media planners often use **cost per mille (CPM)**, which is the cost to reach 1,000 people or households to compare the cost effectiveness of two or more alternative media vehicles.[46] Table 4.4 compares the average CPM for forms of traditional and digital media.[47]

Looking at average CPMs may lead you to recommend running only Google Display ads because they're the cheapest, yet remember what a banner ad is and its limitations of a small space on a web page many may not see. There's a term called **banner blindness**, which refers to the tendency of internet users to ignore banner ads.[48] They don't compare to the

Table 4.4. Average CPM per Media Type

Traditional Advertising Costs		Online Advertising Costs	
Platform	**Average CPM**	**Platform**	**Average CPM**
Radio	$10–$20	Google Display Ads	$3.12
Newspaper	$10–$45	Twitter Ads	$6.46
Billboard	$13–$22	LinkedIn Ads	$6.59
Network TV	$20–$30	Facebook Ads	$8.60
Super Bowl Ads	$36	Instagram Ads	$8.96
Magazine	$140–$1,300	YouTube Ads	$9.68
Direct Mail	$500–$1,000	Google Search Ads	$38.40

Source: "Online Advertising Costs in 2021," TopDraw.com, March 26, 2021, https://www.topdraw .com/insights/is-online-advertising-expensive/.

storytelling power and impact of the sight, sound, and motion of a TV ad on the big screen, yet when looking at CPM, buying all TV ads isn't efficient either.

The cost of a Super Bowl ad seems outrageous at $4 million, but with an audience of 111 million people, the CPM is $36. Super Bowl ads also tend to generate pre- and postgame earned media attention. However, if your media budget for the year is only $4 million, you don't want to spend it all on one ad—your frequency would be one. Each media vehicle has its pros and cons and is good for different strategic reasons. Multiple factors besides CPM need to be considered when planning media.

One exception to the mass audience focus of linear TV ads is **connected TV (CTV) advertising**, which combines the technical capabilities of digital advertising with the user experience of television. As more people cut the cable cord and switch to streaming TV services through smart TVs and streaming devices, TV ads become more targetable, customizable, interactive, and cost efficient.

CTV ads use first- and third-party data to target more specific audiences with custom messages based on demographic, geographic, psychographic (interests), and behavioral bases. For example, website visitors and CRM data could create a remarketing TV campaign such as social media remarketing. You could run CTV ads targeted only to people who had previously visited your website. CTV can also drive direct internet actions and use KPI metrics such as CPA. Connected TV ad spending is expected to double in 2023.[49] P&G says 70 percent of households are now reachable via streaming TV and has shifted spending from network age–gender linear TV deals to CTV buys that match custom audiences.[50]

The Media Mix Can Be Made More Efficient in Several Ways

One way media planners gain efficiencies is to stretch media budgets through flighting and pulsing (see Figure 4.5). Instead of running ads continuously during the plan year, **flighting** alternates between running an advertising schedule and stopping ads. This saves on media costs, considering consumers will remember past ads before they need to be run again. Products with seasonal sales use flighting to run ads during peak sales periods. A related strategy is **pulsing**, which combines continuous advertising with intermittent planned spikes in ad runs.[51]

Again, considering this chapter's Gatorade case, we can calculate the value of a narrow target audience. Based on the media objective for a target of men 18–49, it would cost $66

Figure 4.5. Flighting or pulsing media schedules can make media buys more efficient.

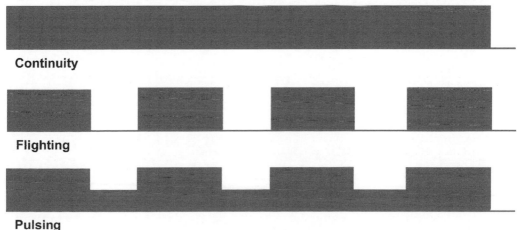

Continuity

Flighting

Pulsing

million to reach 70 percent of the target audience three times a month on broadcast TV and $21.2 million on YouTube. In contrast, to reach 70 percent of male and female teens 15–19 three times a month would only cost $16.2 million on broadcast TV and $5.2 million on YouTube. Reaching a broad audience with paid ads would be much more expensive. Do the diligent work up front to ensure your marketing client has a narrow target audience of the most profitable customer so the client can have the most efficient media buy.

Once media research is complete, put together a media plan to determine the media mix and allocate the media budget. Table 4.5 is a paid media planning template worksheet separated by media type (TV, radio, print, search, social, display) and media vehicle (publication/platform). Dates should consider continuous, flighting, or pulsing media schedules. Once total spend is calculated, determine the percentage of the total budget by media type and traditional versus digital.

Your media type percentages in the media planning template can be compared to the national averages in Table 4.3 earlier in this chapter to see how your budget compares to national benchmarks. To put together a detailed media plan and media buy, media professionals use software tools that collect consumer and media data into one system, such as SRDS (next.srds.com), MRI-Simmons (mrisimmons.com), Nielsen & Scarborough (nielson.com), and ComScore (comScore.com).

Table 4.5. Paid Media Planning Template Worksheet

Media Objective			Total/Monthly Media Budget		
Type	**Dates**	**Name Publication**	**Description**	**CPM**	**Spend**
Television (Total: Ave. CPM, Total/Percent Spend)				$	$ %
				$	$
				$	
				$	$
Radio (Total: Ave. CPM, Total/Percent Spend)				$	$ %
				$	$
				$	$
Print (Total: Ave. CPM, Total/Percent Spend)				$	$ %
				$	$
				$	$
Traditional Media (Total: Ave. CPM, Total/Percent Spend)				$	$ %
Search (Total: Ave. CPM, Total/Percent Spend)				$	$ %
				$	$ %
				$	$ %
Social (Total: Ave. CPM, Total/Percent Spend)				$	$ %
				$	$ %
				$	$ %
Display (Total: Ave. CPM, Total/Percent Spend)				$	$ %
				$	$ %
				$	$ %
Digital Media (Total: Ave. CPM, Total/Percent Spend)				$	$ %

4.5 CASE

Gatorade Isn't Hydration for Everyone

Gatorade learned the importance of a narrow target market after shifting to a broad target of men 18 to 49 years old that positioned Gatorade as hydration for everyone. In 2007, the brand created campaign ads featuring both athletes and nonathletes. Targeting a larger group and positioning your product as a solution for more people should lead to increased sales, right? That's not what happened. Instead of increasing sales, going after the broader mass market led to a sales decline of 10 percent while competitor Powerade grew 13 percent.[52] Why did this happen?

Brand marketer Sarah Robb O'Hagan began to analyze the company's customer data and research. She discovered that high school athletes made up 15 percent of Gatorade's customers and marathoners made up another 7 percent. Yet this 22 percent generated 46 percent of all sales revenue. When Gatorade started telling a different story of Gatorade is hydration for everyone, the core athlete audience got the message that Gatorade was no longer for them.

The brand social identity no longer matched the main buyer's social identity (see Figure 3.2). Instead, the serious athlete identified more with the group social identity of Powerade through the brand story it was telling. Robb O'Hagan realized this and recommended returning to a narrow target market and positioning strategy. Gatorade went back to telling a story that Gatorade is hydration for serious athletes. In the core segments, Gatorade's best customers responded, and sales returned. Revenue increased 9 percent in 2011 alone.[53]

Today, Gatorade's targeting can get even more specific with digital marketing. The company also knows that targeting a smaller niche market increases sales to the broader audience. In 2015, the brand launched a new strategy targeting "the 'competitive athlete' who exercises 4-6 times a week, wins on the field, and attributes a large part of their identity to playing sports." While this customer segment is only 14 percent of the US population and less than half of Gatorade sales, it influences tens of millions who aspire to be competitive athletes.[54]

In Chapter 3, we learned about consumer preference for social identity through ideal selves versus actual selves. The broader market wants to drink Gatorade not because it's hydration for everyone but because it's hydration for the serious athlete they desire to become.

Morgan Flatley, chief marketing officer of Gatorade and Propel, says the brand learns about this core audience by spending time on the field with them. The marketing team observes real problems that Gatorade products can help solve. To tell the right story to the right people, you have to know what it is like to be someone in the target market. You don't have to be a serious athlete, but you have to research, know, and understand them to have a customer-centric IMC perspective.

Gatorade also helps its core athlete target market by creating digital content that adds value through information, education, and entertainment. A team monitors social media conversations to ensure that content is resonating with this audience. As technology improves, personalization to individual customers will grow. Gatorade plans on creating more customized training programs, content, stories, and experiences.[55]

This chapter has explored the key concepts of the marketing plan, integration of IMC touchpoints, and media plan as a foundation for marketing objective success. We learned the importance of selecting the right media mix and having a narrowly focused target market and audience for more effective IMC plans and more efficient media buys. Chapter 5 will focus on creativity. How do you find inspiration for the right combination of verbal and visual message stories to be told in the selected consumer touchpoints and media mix?

QUESTIONS

1. With the increased power of the consumer through social and digital media, do you think the Four Ps framework is still relevant today?
2. Are there any broad markets left today, or must all brands have a narrow target market?

EXERCISES

1. Pick a national brand, and look up its annual report, visit its website, and view some of its ads and social media. Determine which market or industry it is in, and find an industry market report or other secondary research on consumers, trends, and competitors in the market. From this information, fill in the key categories in Figure 4.2 of the marketing strategy template worksheet. Summarize in a positioning statement: "For [ideal market segment], the product is [concise description], which is ideal for [describe best use/application of product] and better than [identify primary competitor] because of [cite differentiation and other evidence to back up a claim of superiority]." Without an understanding of the current situation, you will not be able to tell the right story to the right people in the IMC plan.
2. Based on the average CPMs for various traditional and digital advertising media (see Table 4.4), calculate the costs of reaching a broad versus a narrow target audience for Gatorade. Start with Gatorade's 2019 advertising budget of $134 million, and set media objectives, considering reach and frequency, for a narrow and broad target audience.[56] Calculate total impressions based on US Census population data (see Table 4.6). Allocate a media mix considering industry media type averages (see Table 4.4), calculating total costs per media and staying within the total advertising budget.

Table 4.6. Resident Population of the United States by Sex and Age (in Millions)

Age in Years	Male	Female	Total
Under 5	9.86	9.44	19.30
5 to 9	10.35	9.89	20.24
10 to 14	10.59	10.16	20.75
15 to 19	10.69	10.27	20.96
20 to 24	11.03	10.56	21.59
25 to 29	11.88	11.36	23.24
30 to 34	11.57	11.27	22.84
35 to 39	10.94	10.89	21.83
40 to 44	10.11	10.2	20.31
45 to 49	9.87	10.1	19.97
50 to 54	10.5	10.34	20.84
55 to 59	10.51	11.09	21.60
60 to 64	9.98	10.82	20.80
65 to 69	8.39	9.48	17.87
70 to 74	6.79	7.88	14.67
75 to 79	4.47	5.51	9.98
80 to 84	2.75	3.72	6.47
85 and over	2.41	4.24	6.65

Source: US Census Bureau, "Resident Population of the United States by Sex and Age as of July 1, 2020 (in Millions)." Statista, accessed October 31, 2021, https://www.statista.com/statistics/241488/population-of-the-us-by-sex-and-age/.

KEY CONCEPTS

Advertising impressions
Banner blindness
Buyer
Communications objectives
Connected TV (CTV) advertising
Cost per acquisition (CPA)
Cost per click (CPC)
Cost per impression (CPI)
Cost per mille (CPA)
Decider
Earned media
Firmographics Technographics
Flighting
Frequency
Gatekeeper
Gross rating point (GRP)
Impressions
Initiator

Internet impressions
Integrated marketing communications
Market
Marketing mix
Marketing objectives
Media planning
Owned media
Paid media
Place (distribution)
Positioning
Product
Promotion
Pulsing
Target audience
Target market
Reach
Shared media
SMART

Point of View

Consumer Insight and Creative Brief

PREVIEW

Next on our journey through brand storytelling in integrated marketing communications (IMC), we will learn the value of consumer insight to inspire the right stories with creative ideas. We begin with Advertising Hall of Fame creative Carol Williams. To develop strategic consumer insights, Williams says, "I have to remove the 'I' from how I see the world."[1] Then we'll apply a three Rs approach to being an influencer brand, learn how to uncover insights through consumer research, summarize strategy in a creative brief, and develop creative ideas. Our case study is an IMC campaign creative idea that increased Snickers market share.

CHAPTER 5 LEARNING OBJECTIVES

1. Discover the importance of point of view and the three Rs.
2. Understand how to uncover consumer insights.
3. Know how to complete a creative brief.
4. Learn a process to develop creative ideas.

5.1 Williams's Point of View and the Three Rs of Influence

Carol Williams is the second African American woman and the first with a creative agency background to be inducted into the Advertising Hall of Fame. Her creative insights were behind famous campaigns for Secret, Pillsbury, KFC, and Disney, which were not only creative but also delivered marketing sales results.[2]

Seeing through the Eyes of Others

Even though Carol Williams is very successful, her entry into the advertising business in the late 1960s was challenging. Her struggle helped inform her approach. In an interview, Carol describes the path to developing strategic advertising insights and great creative concepts. She recounts, "I was a black woman from the Southside of Chicago in a white man's world. As a matter of survival, I had to see differently. I became adept at seeing through others' eyes."[3]

The ability to see from others' points of view is key to her thriving career and to developing an effective creative strategy in an IMC plan. Carol urges us to use research, data, and insights to see through the eyes of the consumer to uncover the moments that matter and to search for insights to see, understand, and feel life's moments, rituals, and products from your audience's perspective.

When working on Secret deodorant, Williams explains, "[W]omen were perceived as soft, delicate creatures that didn't sweat."[4] Her famous line for Secret, "Strong enough for a man but made for a woman," embraced contradictions and traditional beliefs about the roles of men and women in society. She helped reframe the Secret brand to embrace the reality of a woman "working hard while celebrating her femininity."[5] This combination of cultural contradiction, or tension; brand message; and audience perspective resonated with the brand's target audience.

In Chapter 1, we learned the importance of tension in telling a story. Creative director Luke Sullivan suggested looking for conflicts or cultural tensions in the product category for brand stories.[6] This is what Williams did with Secret deodorant. Today, Carol runs her own agency, Carol H. Williams Advertising, and it is the longest-running independent multicultural marketing firm in the United States. There, the agency continues to search for insights by asking, "Whose eyes are you looking through when you view the world?"[7]

Target Brand Stories through a Three Rs Framework

A framework for seeing through others' eyes is to take a three Rs (relevance, reach, and resonance) approach. The three Rs concept has arisen around the idea of influence in the social media age.[8] Experts recommend relevance, reach, and resonance as criteria for selecting social media influencers for brands. In IMC from a story perspective, it is useful to consider the three Rs as a target for brand stories in which brands take a storyteller approach to become an influencer to build relationships around brand communities.[9]

Relevance is sharing stories relevant to your business and industry—what is pertinent to the market.[10] This is the cost of entry or having your story recognized as on the right subject. Fitness brands such as Peloton, NordicTrack, and Bowflex create verbal and visual messages and brand stories about working out and fitness. They don't create stories about financial planning, vacations, or electric vehicles.

No company has the resources to reach everyone in a market, and broad messages tend to fail. Markets are segmented, a target is selected, and the product is positioned to them. **Reach** is the number or percentage of people or households of a defined population exposed to a particular advertising media vehicle or media schedule during a specific time.[11] Reach is getting the brand story to the target audience. Peloton places brand messages (paid, earned, shared, owned) in media frequently read and viewed by its target audience.

Not everyone who receives the message responds or responds equally. A brand's best customers tend to be the most loyal fans and vocal advocates. When they become brand advocates reaching others in the market, this is called resonance. When a message resonates with someone, they want to share it as a signal of their identity to a group.

Focusing brand stories on this core target of your audience adds momentum to the message. **Resonance** is engagement generated through the prolonging of a message by reflection and amplification.[12] When the brand's social identity matches the buyer's social identity through brand story content, it has resonance, and the target audience reflects on it through engagement and amplifies it through sharing. These three factors combine into a graphic of concentric circles, like a target for IMC brand stories (see Figure 5.1).

The outside circle ensures the message is relevant to the market, the middle circle gets the message to the target segment, and the bull's-eye is the sweet spot where the most engaged customers take action and talk about the brand. Through its fans, the brand will resound. **Resound** is fans' echoing messages to widely celebrate a brand.[13] The **bull's-eye** is the center of a target, which is the precise point to achieve the desired results.[14]

Hitting the bull's-eye or sweet spot connects with a core group that responds, which turns your target into a speaker spreading the product brand story. Michelle Phan, from Chapter 1, is a good example of this principle. She was an influencer with relevance, reach, and resonance in the beauty market and then turned that into two successful companies with the three Rs.

Figure 5.1. Aim the verbal visual IMC story for relevance, reach, and resonance.

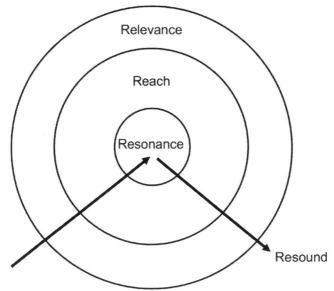

Peloton is another example. The company doesn't just sell stationary bikes; that is only the price of entry or relevance to the market. Its target segment or reach is people who struggle to work out on their own. A consumer insight in the home fitness market is a desire to work out, to the point of purchasing a stationary bike, only to lose motivation and have the equipment go unused. Peloton's resonance comes in addressing this tension by offering more than a bike and telling a different story.

With the equipment, Peloton sells membership to an online fitness club offering live online classes. Its story is not only one of equipment and sheer willpower but also of instructors and a community of like-minded enthusiasts who help motivate each other. Like Carol Williams and Secret deodorant, Peloton reframed the story to address the cultural contradiction and tension.

Peloton tells this story from the customer's perspective on its website: "Tap into motivation whenever you want." This emotional appeal is backed by the rational justification for purchase: "70 percent of members work out more than they did before joining."[15] A piece of equipment alone doesn't come with accountability and personal relationships. Peloton's story helped create the connected fitness market category, which led to 1.67 million monthly subscribers with an annual retention rate of 92 percent.[16]

5.2 Uncovering Insights

Engaging product messages and brand stories come from genuine human truths. Whether it's about the way women truly sweat or about what truly motivates people to work out at home, uncovering insights about your target audience is an important building block to a successful IMC plan. Airbnb provides another example.

In explaining a new IMC campaign for Airbnb, cofounder and CEO Brian Chesky said, "The number one reason people choose to travel with Airbnb is they want to live like a local. They don't want to be tourists stuck in long lines, fighting with the crowds to see the same thing as everyone else. Our hosts . . . welcome travelers from around the world into their communities." This insight was integral to the campaign message and big idea, "Why vacation somewhere when you can live there?"[17]

Without it, the Airbnb IMC campaign may have been relevant in the hotel market and reached a travel target audience but may have not resonated with a core segment to produce marketing results. In a crowded market, Airbnb reframed the travel story, differentiating its offering and addressing the contradiction and tension of wanting to tour a destination but not getting caught in tourist traps. Within a year of the campaign, Airbnb users in the United States and Europe rose by 17 percent.[18]

How to Get Actionable Consumer Insights

How do you get insights that lead to an effective IMC plan? You must be part scientist and part artist following a creative process. First, insights are gathered to develop creative work. **Creative work** is the visual and verbal combination that informs and persuades an audience about a product.[19] Creative work is part of advertising, public relations, marketing, and IMC campaigns. A **campaign** is a set of coordinated activities based on a common theme to promote a product through different media.[20] A campaign can also be called a strategy or plan.

Airbnb's consumer insight is that people want to live like a local when they travel staying in neighborhoods not tourist traps. Getty Images: James O'Neil.

As we can see with Secret, Peloton, and Airbnb, creative work and campaigns are based on consumer insights. There are hundreds of insights you could uncover about a target audience, but what you want are actionable insights. An **actionable insight** is a true understanding of people in the target audience and situations related to the product that can be used to meet marketing objectives.[21] Airbnb's insights become actionable through the platform, which connects travelers to locals and enables them to rent hosts' homes.

Actionable insights are collected in a creative strategy document with other information to help ensure the creative work is on strategy, increasing the chances that it will be effective. A document that captures these insights is a strategic document called a creative brief.

However, having an actionable insight and creative brief alone won't lead to creative work in a campaign. That insight needs to be combined with a big idea to produce the creative work. A **big idea** is a driving, unifying force behind brand marketing efforts.[22] Airbnb's big idea is "Why vacation somewhere when you can live there?" Big ideas can lead to campaigns if they have legs. **Having legs** means a campaign theme can be created for many different media, for a long period of time.[23] Big ideas connect the brand's stories to customers.[24] Airbnb does this through multiple visual and verbal expressions of the big idea in TV ads, digital media, and social media.

To produce creative work, follow a series of strategic steps called the creative process. Begin by collecting information about the target audience. Narrow down consumer insights into ones that are actionable in the IMC plan through creative work. Collect relevant information into a strategic document called the creative brief. Then create work with similar themes to form possible campaigns. The best are considered big ideas that have legs.

1. Consumer research
2. Consumer insights
3. Actionable insights
4. Creative brief
5. Creative work in a campaign
   (*A big idea that has legs*)

How do you find consumer insights? There are four steps to focus on consumer research: state your questions, dig through secondary research, conduct primary research, and interpret the data. When do you know that you have found a good insight? Cenk Bulbul, director of YouTube Ads, and Netta Gross, Google video marketing contributor, suggests looking for tension, "an issue or desire that your products haven't fulfilled for your target audience—yet."

Also, consider the activities, events, time of day, year, and life stage in which your target audience uses the product and emotions that might stir them.[25] As we have learned from multiple research studies and successful professionals, tension and emotions are powerful parts of a story.

The digital marketing firm Linkfluence explains the difference between mere research data and consumer insight. Linkfluence recommends that a good consumer insight be new, unexpected, and relevant.[26] See Table 5.1 for the four steps of consumer research and characteristics of actionable insights.

Table 5.1. How to Find Consumer Insights

Steps to Find Consumer Insights	Characteristics of a Consumer Insight
State your questions	New—It's not something previously widely known.
Dig through secondary research	Unexpected—It's something you didn't know about.
Conduct primary research	Relevant—It matches marketing objectives and the target.
Interpret the data	Actionable—It leads to clear next steps for ideas.

Before conducting any research, start by asking key questions that could provide insights for the creative brief to inspire a big idea. The following are questions to ask that can uncover insights that may inspire a big idea:

- What do people think about the brand leader versus your client's brand?
- What are current trends in the industry?
- What are people looking for in the product?
- What are things that prevent them from buying?
- What are their top concerns, problems, or pain points?
- Whose story isn't being told?
- What obstacles are in their way causing tension?[27]
- What job does the product serve?

Next, dig into secondary research and consider primary research. **Secondary research** discovers information previously collected for other purposes that is publicly available. **Primary research** is new research conducted to answer specific questions.[28] Always start with secondary research to discover what information is already available. You'll learn what questions need to be answered with new primary research.

Secondary Sources of Consumer Research

There are many sources for secondary and primary research (see Table 5.2). Mintel gathers consumer, trend, market, and competitor data in industry reports. MarketLine profiles major companies, industries, and geographies. The US Census Bureau not only provides demographics of geographic areas in the United States but also conducts hundreds of surveys each year. Statista is a portal with more than 60,000 topics of data from more than 10,000 sources.

Nielsen Scarborough provides trends, shopping patterns, media behaviors, lifestyle, and demographic information on US consumers. SRDS is a media planning platform that additionally offers Claritas 360 demographic and consumer behavior research. MRI-Simmons is also a media planning tool that also provides US consumer demographic, psychographic, attitudinal, and behavioral data on product categories and brands.

A source often forgotten is academic research, which can be found through Google Scholar or public and university library databases, such as EbscoHost. A smoking-cessation campaign for the Pennsylvania Department of Health was inspired by an academic journal study linked quitting smoking with the feeling people have in bad romantic relationships. The campaign told the story of a woman in an unhealthy relationship trying to break up with a boyfriend dressed as a cigarette. Finding the tension of knowing what is best but still struggling to do it tapped into emotions in the target audience that led to action. The campaign increased calls to a smoking quit line and more pledges to stop smoking.[29]

Primary Sources of Consumer Research

There are many primary sources of research. **Focus groups** involve a small group of 6 to 10 people who participate in a discussion led by a moderator. Focus groups are a form of

Table 5.2. Sources of Consumer Research

Secondary Consumer Research	Primary Consumer Research
Mintel (reports.minel.com)	Surveys
MarketLine (marketline.com)	Focus groups
US Census Bureau (census.gov/data)	Experiments
Statista (statista.com)	Observational
Nielson Scarborough (nielson.com/Scarborough)	Industry trade reports
MRI-Simmons (mrisimmons.com)	Website and web search data
Claritas 360/SRDS (claritas360.claritas.com)	Customer relationship management and databases
Academic research (ebsco.com)	Social media listening

qualitative research that collects exploratory data that are not initially quantified to further understand a problem. **Surveys** collect participant responses on facts, opinions, and attitudes through questionnaires with statistically representative samples of the larger population.[30] Surveys are a form of **quantitative research** that collects statistically large samples of empirical data, often to support findings from qualitative research.[31]

Think of quantitative research as something that can easily be converted into numbers, such as the percentage of people who answered specific given response options to a survey question. Qualitative research provides more details and nuance, such as direct quotes or answers to questions researchers didn't think of as a survey response.

Another type of consumer research is simply observing people. **Observation** is a form of qualitative research that collects data using multiple senses to examine people in natural settings and situations.[32] An example of observation data that led to a consumer insight is the California Milk Processor Board. After years of declining sales, the marketing client hired the ad agency Goodby, Silverstein & Partners.

The milk brand's previous ads conveyed the messaging of "Milk Does a Body Good." The ads worked as far as communicating that milk was good for you. In surveys, 93 percent recalled the message that milk was good for them. The problem was that message didn't lead to more milk sales—it led to less.[33] This is why IMC plans should begin with marketing objectives such as sales and market share. Exceeding a communications objective doesn't guarantee marketing success.

To help solve this marketing problem, the agency's consumer research included observing how people respond to running out of milk by placing video cameras in the refrigerators in the office break room after removing the milk. It revealed genuine exasperation of having food that goes well with milk but having no milk. The agency also had a group of consumers go without milk for a week and document their feelings in a journal. These observations of woe and despair provided inspiration for the creative work.[34]

The research led to an actionable insight called "milk deprivation." Creative work consisted of stories of consumers' emotional reactions to not having milk in different situations and the big idea "Got milk?" After one year, the new campaign increased sales by 6.8 percent after the previous year's sales decline of 1.7 percent.[35]

Other forms of primary research include **experiments**, which are observations performed to answer a question or solve a problem.[36] Today marketers can perform experiments with neuromarketing. **Neuromarketing** maps participants' brains using magnetic resonance imaging to record conscious and subconscious responses to brands, products, and advertising.[37]

When Frito-Lay switched its target audience from children to adults over childhood obesity concerns, it hired NeuroFocus to measure how adults feel about Cheetos. Results revealed that adults' brains responded strongly to Cheetos turning their fingers orange with cheese dust. This actionable insight, "a sense of giddy subversion enjoyed over the messiness of the product," inspired the big idea, "Bend the rules with mischievous fun." The Orange Underground campaign led to an 11.3 percent sales increase, which was nearly double the IMC campaign marketing objective of 6.4 percent.[38]

When researching for insights, strive to use a variety of methods because you may discover that one is not accurate. With the Cheetos campaign, focus groups contradicted neuromarketing findings. Before releasing the Orange Underground campaign, NeuroFocus tested an ad in the campaign with a woman pranking someone in a laundry mat by throwing orange

Cheetos into her dryer with white clothes. People in the focus groups said that they didn't like the ad, yet viewing the ad with their brain waves measured by an EEG (electroencephalogram) revealed they secretly found it to be funny.[39] This reveals a limitation of focus groups; people often don't know what they like or why.

Another consideration for consumer research insights is trade associations. Most industries have a **trade association** or a trade group founded by businesses in a specific industry to promote their common interests.[40] Some groups conduct research on behalf of their members. One group is the National Association of Convenience Stores (NACS). Some examples of insights from NACS Research found on the association's website include "Frozen Treats Sales Heat Up," "Mars Wrigley Sees 3 Snacking Trends Post-Pandemic," and "How C-Stores Can Adapt to Evolving Shopping Behaviors."[41]

Finding Consumer Insights through Digital Media

A final area to consider is digital sources, such as brand websites, Google web search data, customer databases, and social media. Social media includes social networks such as Facebook but also forums, blogs, and online reviews.[42] This research occurs through **social media listening**, which collects data from brand social mentions and broader relevant conversations to improve strategy. Social media offers real-time insights, large data sets, and a way to test and add context to other data. Some people refer to social media as the world's largest focus group.[43]

Linkfluence suggests using a good social media listening and analytics software tool and collecting brand mentions across social media to analyze for audience, sentiment, topics, and platforms.[44] See Table 5.3 for this social media consumer insight research process.

Social Partners says social data helps identify insights by combining facts from other research with observations found in social media listening. Look for disconnects in the data, such as conflicting attitudes held by the same group of people. Then use social media listening to confirm and discover why.[45] That gives you the tension on which to build a story to hook attention, produce empathy, and motivate action.

Heinz Ketchup leveraged the insight of conflicting attitudes about whether tomatoes are a fruit or vegetable into a successful IMC campaign. The disconnect or tension was confirmed through social media listening. That tension was leveraged in a story told through the big idea #tomatodebate released on National Tomato Day. The brand story intersected

Table 5.3. How to Conduct Research with Social Media Listening Analytics Software

Collect a large sample of brand mentions across social media, then analyze for:	
Audience	Learn age, gender, language, location of people talking about the brand.
Sentiment	See how social media users feel about the brand, product, and competitors.
Topics	Learn the themes, keywords, and concepts most associated with the business.
Platforms	Learn where they are talking about the brand and how the talk differs on each social media platform.

Source: Modified from Joei Chan, "How to Find Consumer Insights on Social Media: The Expert Guide," Linkfluencer. com, https://www.linkfluence.com/blog/consumer-insights-social-media-guide.

with an existing consumer story to take advantage of trending topics told through TV, digital, and social media.[46]

As marketers increasingly draw on the same sources for data, such as Mintel, Scarborough, Simmons, and Claritas, social media observations become a valuable way of differentiating an approach. Gareth Price head of insight at The Social Partners says, "Following the same data trails can easily lead to a homogeneity that fails to address the need to make communications memorable and distinctive from the market category in which a brand competes." Social media presents the opportunity to identify better and unique insights.[47]

5.3 Write the Creative Brief

From your research into the consumer, you should be looking for human truths, contradictions, and tensions. From these insights, certain perceptions and feelings about the brand or product probably need to change to get consumers to act and help solve your client's marketing problem and meet the client's marketing objective. These insights drive your creative message. Consumer insights plus information about the marketing, IMC, and media strategies are collected and summarized into a creative strategy document called a creative brief.

Creative Briefs Are Brief but Important

A **creative brief** is a strategic document used to develop creative content for IMC plans and campaigns. Creative brief formats vary but typically state the problem/opportunity, marketing objectives, target audience, current and future thinking, feeling, actions, main message, support points, style and tone, and requirements. It is useful to think of these as questions (see Figure 5.2 creative brief template worksheet). Creative briefs should be one page or two at most. They summarize the most relevant and required information for the creative team to develop the big idea, creative work, and IMC campaign.

Why are we communicating? briefly sums up the main reason the marketing client came to you and what the client wants to accomplish with the new IMC plan. This section includes specifics and quantifies factors such as sales declines for problems, sales increases for objectives, and reasons why this occurred such as a new competitor entering the market or a changing consumer trend.

Whom are we talking to? defines the primary target audience and any secondary target audience with specifics that quantify factors such as age and income range. Also, include a brief profile or concise biographical sketch of a typical person in the target audience. A profile could be a "middle-aged professional who is looking for ways to stay in shape amid career and family demands." These two sections come from information collected from the client in the marketing strategy (Figure 4.2 template worksheet) and IMC strategy (Figure 4.4 template worksheet). The next sections come from consumer research.

What do they currently think-feel-do? summarizes what a typical noncustomer thinks and feels about the brand and product that leads them not to buy. Write this as if it is the thoughts in the person's head, such as "I need to stay in shape but don't have time to go to the gym and don't have the motivation to work out on my own at home."

Figure 5.2. Creative brief template worksheet.

Brand: _____ Product: _____

Why are we communicating?
(Describe problem/opportunity, reason for the ad, campaign, plan,
and define the SMART marketing objectives that it must meet)

Whom are we talking to?
(Define demographic, psychographic, behavioral, geographic bases
and a profile description of a typical target audience member)

What do they currently think-feel-do?
(Explain current product positioning in relation to competitors
and what target currently thinks, feels, and does in category)

What would we like them to think-feel-do?
(Explain new product positioning in relation to competitors
And what we want the target to think, feel, and do in category)

What is the single most persuasive idea?
(In one sentence, the strategic message to move them from
one think-feel-do to the other to meet marketing objectives)

Why should they believe it?
(Bulleted list of specific support facts, product features
that validate the key consumer promise/persuasive idea)

What is the personality, style, and tone?
(Execution approach reflecting brand personality
considering style of look and tone of the message)

What are the specific requirements?
(List of media mix, TV, outdoor, social media platforms, etc.
measurable call to action and required elements/lines, etc.)

What do you want them to think-feel-do? should summarize what you want them to think and feel that would motivate them to take action to meet the client's marketing objective, such as "With Peloton I can bring the gym, instructor, and class into my home to give me the time and motivation I need."

What's the single most persuasive idea? is a single sentence that will move the target audience from what they currently think-feel-do to what you want them to think-feel-do. This is the strategic message that you need to communicate. It is not the final creative big idea, a creative headline, or a tagline. Those come later in the creative process. An example could be "Peloton brings the motivation and community of a gym to the convenience of your home." Delivering that single message, even in a clever headline or in an engaging story is not enough. You must back the message or claim with facts as support for it to be trusted.

Why should they believe it? is a bulleted list of the main product features, stats, and benefits that will make the audience believe your promise and move to the "do." We may make decisions with our emotions, but we rationalize them with facts.

What is the personality style and tone? helps to ensure that the creative work feels like it is from the same brand integrating individual ads. Describe personality traits, such as funny versus serious, formal versus casual, respectful versus irreverent, and enthusiastic versus matter of fact for the verbal message, and design elements of the visual message.

What are the specific requirements? lists the media mix so the creative team knows what specific forms of the message and story are needed, such as 30-second TV ads, 6-second You-Tube bumper ads, Instagram promoted posts, in-store signage, and PR live events. Also, list specific calls to action that drive the audience to where they can buy or learn more, such as websites, store locations, and phone numbers to call or text. Ideally, these are measurable with custom landing pages and coupon codes or form completions and downloads.

The creative brief directs the development of the creative work and the big idea that creates the IMC campaign or plan. It should be signed off by the marketing client agreeing to the focused direction for the creative strategy before the creative team begins brainstorming creative ideas. After the marketing client agrees to the creative brief, it is given to the creative team to begin work. When ideas are developed, they are compared to the creative brief to determine if they are on strategy. An ad or campaign may be creative, but if it doesn't fit the creative brief, it is not marketing.

The Creative Strategy, Brief, and Concepts Involve Different People

Who writes the briefs and develops the work? Creative briefs are often written by **account planners**, who are strategists who bring the consumer's perspective into the process of developing marketing communications. While others worry about sales, clients, media, and creativity, an account planner's job is to seek consumer truth and insight through research.[48]

If a firm doesn't have an account planner, the account executive handles research and creative briefs. **Account executives** serve as the main contact with marketing clients in a marketing communication firm. They coordinate the capabilities of the firm to satisfy the needs of the client and can also serve as the main research and strategic advisors.[49]

The creative team works from the creative brief to develop the creative work. A copywriter and art director make up a traditional creative team that conceptualizes or "concepts" the big idea and individual ads. **Copywriters** are writers of advertising or publicity copy,[50] and **art directors** are designers who coordinate ad type, photos, and illustrations.[51] You may have an expanded creative team that includes public relations and digital specialists. **Public relations executives** develop strategies for nonpaid forms of brand communication.[52] **Digital marketing specialists** develop online media, such as websites, online ads, and paid search.[53] **Social media strategists** plan brand social media connecting it to marketing objectives, advertising, and public relations built around the creative idea.[54]

Additional Consumer Research Tools

A tool that's helpful in organizing research for creative briefs is a **perceptual map**, which is a marketing research technique that plots consumers' views about a brand or product on horizontal and vertical axes of different attributes (see Figure 5.3).[55] Attributes are consumer perceptions ranked from low to high along a Likert scale. They are used to visualize the competitive landscape and understand how a client could create a unique position in the customers' minds by repositioning it into a quadrant where competitors are not located. This is what Snickers did, as we'll learn in the case at the end of this chapter.

Figure 5.3. Rational and emotional attribute perceptual maps.

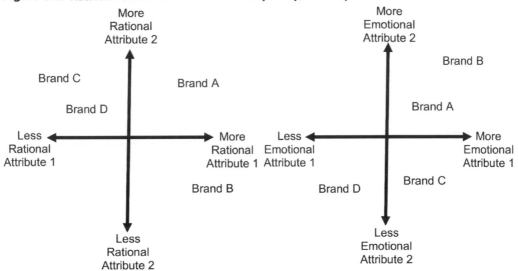

Jim Joseph of integrated communications agency BCW suggests creating two perceptual maps, one based on functional product attributes and one on emotional attributes. Theories and research indicate that consumers make decisions based on both rational and emotional reasons.[56]

The **elaboration likelihood model** is a theory where persuasion happens through a rational central route and an emotional peripheral route. The central route involves thoughtful consideration, with more time elaborating on the message and rational arguments. The peripheral route is not analyzed cognitively, with less elaborating, because more focus is on feelings evoked by the message and imagery.[57] While some products lend themselves to more elaboration and a rational message or less elaboration and an emotional message, it is best to include both routes or approaches in a brand story.

A research study analyzed 400 case studies of successful ad campaigns comparing large profit gains to the type of message or content—rational, emotional, or combined. Emotional-only ads performed twice as well as rational-only ads. Combined emotional and rational ads performed a third better than rational-only ads (see Figure 5.4). The caveat to these findings is that emotional-only campaigns tended to come from established products with high brand awareness such as Coca-Cola. Most consumers already knew the product and its benefits.[58]

For most campaigns, emotional and rational approaches should be used, especially in promoting newer products or lesser-known brands. Budweiser can use an emotional-only ad

Figure 5.4. Percent of campaign reporting large profit gains versus content approach.

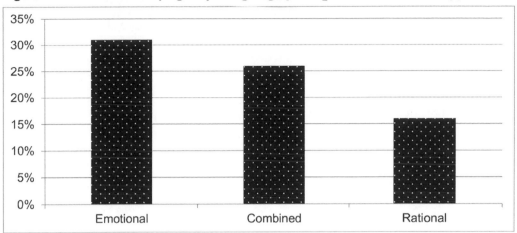

Source: Roger Dooley, "Emotional Ad Work Best" NeuroscienceMarketing.com, accessed November 3, 2021, https://www.neurosciencemarketing.com/blog/articles/emotional-ads-work-best.htm.

about Clydesdale horses on the Super Bowl because of the high brand association with beer after decades of ad spending. If consumers cannot already associate the brand with the product category and its main features and benefits, then a combined approach is best.[59]

PepsiCo can also focus on emotion-only ad messages in the Super Bowl, often featuring top entertainment stars such as Michael Jackson and Britney Spears promoting the "Pepsi Generation" and "The Joy of Pepsi."[60] But when PepsiCo introduced a new sparkling water brand Bubly, the company took a rational and emotional approach with the message "No calories. No sweeteners. All smiles." Smiles were brought to Super Bowl viewers and through integrated paid, earned, shared, and owned media with spokesman Michael Bublé, creating debate over whether it was pronounced "buh blee" or "boo-bley." The combined message and integration worked with 57 percent growth in the sparkling water category in six months, nearly tripling Bubly's market share, while competitor La Croix saw a 16 percent drop in earnings.[61]

5.4 Develop the Creative Idea

Now that you have the creative brief, the creative team begins coming up with ideas for the big idea and creative work. But where do ideas come from, and how do you get them? James Webb Young was an Advertising Hall of Fame copywriter who was very good at coming up with advertising ideas. He famously wrote an ad for women's deodorant that increased sales by 112 percent.[62]

Where Do Creative Ideas Come From?

Because of Young's creative marketing success, people kept asking him where his ideas came from. He didn't know, but he was curious enough to find out. Through self-reflection, he uncovered a five-step process for creating ideas and published them in the 1940 book *A Technique for Producing Ideas*. Aspects of this same process have been described by other creative people in vastly different fields, from fine artists and authors to researchers and engineers.[63]

Young begins by defining an **idea** as nothing more or less than a new combination of old elements. The production of ideas is about seeing relationships in bringing old elements into new combinations. Not every old element fits together with another. The creative person becomes adept at searching for relationships between facts to produce ideas. Being intentional about the steps improves the quantity and quality of creative ideas.[64]

Follow these steps for the creative process to produce your next idea:

1. *Gather Raw Material:* Collect specific information about the product and target audience. Always be collecting general knowledge about the world.
2. *Play Matchmaker:* Take different bits of raw information and view from all angles. Try all together, looking for a new relationship. Ask "why not?"
3. *Forget About It:* Make no direct effort to work on the problem. Play a game, run, see a film. Put it out of your conscious mind so your unconscious mind can get to work.
4. *Birth of the Idea:* If you follow the other stages, suddenly an unexpected idea will pop into your mind from your subconscious. It can happen anywhere and anytime.
5. *Optimize the Idea:* Compare your subconscious "Eureka" ideas to the creative brief. Get feedback from others. Refine ideas into practical usefulness to fit the creative brief.[65]

The process is simple but hard to follow. As adults, we lose touch with our creative mindset. A lifetime of school and work experiences set up barriers to seeing new relationships. If you are only taught to look for the right answer based on past solutions, how will you ever see new possibilities of solutions yet to be conceived? Think like a kid again.

Innovation author Paul Stone explains that to a kid every problem can be solved. We grow up learning what cannot be done through rules, teachers, and bosses who tell you no. Yet when we tell our children no, they say, "Why not?"[66] For example, an adult will tell you that babies can't roller skate, but a kid or creative person will say why not?

Why Can't Babies Roller Skate?

This is what the creative team asked when working on a Super Bowl TV ad for Evian. Evian's "Roller Babies" held the Guinness World Record for the most viral video of all time. In the famous Super Bowl Ad and YouTube video, an announcer and type on the screen opens saying, "Let's observe the effect of Evian on your body." The ad cuts to a close-up of a cassette tape in a boom box labeled "Rapper's Delight." A finger pushes play, and the camera pulls back to reveal a baby in a onesie wearing roller skates. Then a series of different babies are dancing and doing roller skating tricks in a park to the rap song. More type appears saying, "Naturally pure and mineral-based water supports your body's youth." The spot ends on the Evian logo and tagline "Live Young."[67]

Following Young's technique, we can imagine how the creative team concepted this popular Super Bowl ad and viral video. (1) They gathered specific knowledge about Evian

Generate creative ideas by following a process and working in teams to brainstorm potential big ideas for your brand stories. Getty Images: Robb Reece.

water, the target generation, how drinking water keeps you young, and general knowledge from music to trends and news. (2) They worked hard trying to fit different elements together. (3) They got tired and stopped working. Perhaps they went to a park and saw people rolling skating. (4) It didn't look like they were working, but their subconscious minds were. (5) Then, the idea popped into their head of roller skating babies.

It was written down with other ideas, and a creative idea was born and refined to deliver a product benefit through a nostalgic story. The older audience would relate to the old days of roller skating. It was checked against the creative brief to ensure it was on strategy. Instead of older people skating, the babies represented feeling young by staying healthy by drinking water. Putting babies in adult situations under the tagline and hashtag #LiveYoung became an unexpected big idea story with legs sparking a 10-year campaign for Evian.[68]

Creativity is about unlearning what is not possible and exploring possibilities from every angle. It is about asking the "naïve" questions only kids ask. The consumer insight helps you see the world as your audience. Young's technique helps you see the world as your younger and more creative childlike self. Also consider AI as a jump start for ideas not an end. Chatbot ChatGPT will answer questions and write an ad from data from the Internet. DALL-E 2 will draw anything. But they lack human nuance, insight, and refinement, can be wrong, biased and pose copyright issues.

5.5 CASE

Snickers' You're Not You When You're Hungry

Have you ever noticed that you're not yourself when you are hungry? The strategy and creative team working on the Snickers advertising account did, leading to a 10-year campaign that is at the top of what Cannes Lions and WARC (World Advertising Research Center) calls the "Creative Effectiveness Ladder" (see Table 5.4). The **creative effectiveness ladder** is a hierarchy of the main types of effects that creative marketing produces, from least to most commercially effective.[69]

The marketing problem the team faced was that growth for Snickers from 2007 to 2009 lagged other chocolate brands, meaning it was losing market share.[70] Snickers' marketing director realized that the company didn't need brand awareness. Most people were already familiar with the 80-year-old brand. What it needed was to get people talking about the brand so that it was top of mind for impulse buys. It needed a campaign that would spark word-of-mouth advocacy.

The solution came with consumer research and an actionable insight based on the traditional young male target audience. James Miller, global head of strategy for Mars at ad agency BBDO, described the findings: "Qualitative research identified an interesting insight: that there is a universal code of conduct by which men abide to stay part of the male pack. This was globally consistent among men, but also something that everyone could recognize or identify with."[71] Their social identity.

The insight became actionable in the creative brief's main message and support points as Snickers is "packed with peanuts" and "really satisfies" as a more substantial snack for when you're hungry but can't eat a meal. The creative team turned it into a big idea distilling the insight into the campaign line "You're not you when you're hungry." The big idea had legs in varied stories of guys becoming cranky, lethargic, or just silly, creating tension between them and the group. These symptoms of hunger are cured with a Snickers, the product hero that gets you back to yourself and accepted into the group again. With stories they connected brand social identity to target social identity.

Table 5.4. The Creative Effectiveness Ladder

6 – Enduring Icon	Creativity drives brand sales growth consistently with the same strategy or creative work over a long time (3+ years).
5 – Commercial Triumph	Creativity increases sales and market share beyond a single quarter or campaign period.
4 – Brand Builder	Creativity improves brand measures of awareness, consideration, preference, or purchase intent.
3 – Sales Spike	Creativity creates a short-term growth in brand sales, market share, or profitability.
2 – Behavior Breakthrough	Creativity changes consumer behavior relevant to the success of the brand.
1 – Influential Idea	Creativity maximizes engagement and sharing to overachieve in campaign metrics and media efficiency.

Source: James Hurman and Peter Field, "The Effectiveness Code," Cannes Lions and WARC, 2020, https://www.warc.com/content/paywall/article/the-effectiveness-code/en-GB/133006.

Figure 5.5. Snickers sales growth from phase one to phase three of the campaign.

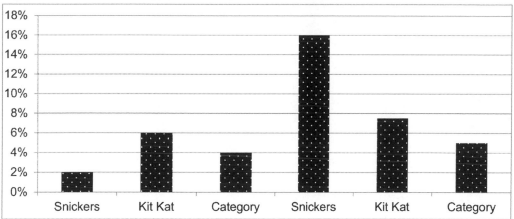

Source: James Miller, "Case Study: How fame made Snickers' 'You're not you when you're hungry' campaign a success," CampaignLive.com (October 26, 2016), https://www.campaignlive.com/article/case-study-fame-made-snickers-youre-not-when-youre-hungry-campaign-success/1413554.

The result was resonance and word-of-mouth advocacy to add new customers and remind current customers to purchase more frequently. Snickers repositioned the product in the market from a candy bar treat for dessert to a meal replacement when you're hungry and cranky. These hit both rational and emotional attributes on perceptual maps for the category.[72]

BBDO and Mars knew it was a hit launching the campaign in a Super Bowl ad with Betty White, when it topped USA Today's Super Bowl Ad poll. It became part of popular culture in political satire, memes, and tweets, generating three months of media coverage, 400 million media impressions, and a media value 11 times the company's investment. By year two, the campaign had exceeded marketing objectives with sales growth over its main competitor and the category (see Figure 5.5).[73]

The Snickers big idea had legs. It has been expressed in multiple media through many stories over a long period of time. It works with various messages for different communications objectives. David Tiltman, WARC vice president of content, says, "It's worked both as a brand-building message in mass-reach media and as a way to reinvigorate short-term sales campaigns."[74]

This chapter gave us foundations for IMC plan creativity applied to marketing problems. We learned the importance of point of view, the three Rs framework, and how to research consumers to uncover insights. From this, we formed a creative brief and learned how to develop ideas that are creative and on strategy for effectiveness. We learned where ideas come from and a process to create them. Snickers provided a model campaign that reached the top of the creative effectiveness ladder. In the next chapter, we'll look at how to tell strategic stories in each medium beginning with TV, radio, and online video.

QUESTIONS

1. Considering what we learned from Carol Williams, how well do you think you are able to see the world through other people's eyes?
2. Considering the elaboration likelihood model, do you think consumers make purchase decisions based mainly on emotional, rational, or a combination of appeals?

EXERCISES

1. A valuable form of consumer research is observation. Do some for a business you like, work for, or are using for your IMC plan. Follow these best practices. First, identify your objective. What are you trying to learn that you haven't uncovered in other research? Second, establish your recording method. Note taking is the most common. Third, develop specific questions to be answered looking for those insights in the observation. Fourth, observe and take notes. Visit the space, and be as unobtrusive as possible. Fifth, analyze behaviors and inferences. Connect what you observed to why it happened.[75]
2. James Webb Young's five-step method is a great overall process to follow to produce ideas. But on a smaller scale, there are many creativity exercises, activities, or brainstorming techniques that can help you to think in more creative ways and come up with more original ideas. Some examples include "Yes And," "Forced Connection," and "Alternative Uses." Find these and others, then try them out. Which ones do you find to be the most helpful?

KEY CONCEPTS

Account executives
Account planners
Actionable insight
Art directors
Behavior breakthrough
Big idea
Brand builder
Bull's-eye
Campaign
Commercial
Copywriters
Creative effectiveness ladder
Creative work
Digital marketing specialists
Elaboration likelihood model
Enduring icon
Experiments
Focus groups
Having legs

Idea
Influential idea
Neuromarketing
Observation
Perceptual map
Primary research
Public relations executives
Qualitative research
Quantitative research
Reach
Relevance
Resonance
Resound
Sales spike
Secondary research
Social media listening
Social media strategists
Surveys
Trade association

PART

III

Stories for
Different Media

Sound and Motion

TV Ads, Online Video, and Radio

PREVIEW

In our journey through brand storytelling, we begin a new part of the book as we consider how best to tell stories in different integrated marketing communications media and consumer touchpoints. We'll first begin with the history of advertising's creative revolution, which moved from rational arguments to emotional appeals. Yet as we put story into practice, consider what ad creative revolutionary Bill Bernbach said, "Nobody counts the number of ads you run; they just remember the impression you make."[1] Powerful brand storytelling can deliver exponential results.. We'll learn to do this through storytelling in TV ads and online digital video plus traditional radio ads and digital streaming audio ads. Our case study explores Motel 6's three-decades-long storytelling radio campaign, which has won creative awards and kept the brand at the top in market share.

CHAPTER 6 LEARNING OBJECTIVES

1. Discover the evolution of advertising approaches through different eras.
2. Understand how to create TV ads through story.
3. Know how to develop paid and earned online video with story.
4. Learn to develop traditional radio and streaming audio ads leveraging story.

6.1 Reeves's Unique Selling Proposition
and Bernbach's Creative Revolution

In Chapter 4, we learned that impressions are calculated as reach times frequency of ad placements. The media planner buys the required minimum impressions expected to reach the marketing client's objectives. Advertising leader Bill Bernbach was a firm believer in the exponential power of creativity. Bernbach believed a truly creative ad could add 10 times (1^{10}) the power to an impression, saying, "Properly practiced creativity can make one ad do the work of ten."[2]

A contemporary of Bernbach, Rosser Reeves believed the opposite. He was a creative executive at Ted Bates advertising agency and an early pioneer of advertising on TV, whom some call the "godfather of television advertising." Reeves believed in the power of impression alone and that advertising was for slogan repetition, not entertainment.[3] To Reeves, the power of advertising was simple impressions of a client's unique selling message. Repeat that simple message enough times, and people will buy.

Rosser Reeves's Unique Selling Proposition

Reeves's thinking formed the concept of USP, which he first introduced in 1930. A **unique selling proposition (USP)** is a benefit that prospects want that is unique from what competitors offer. In the early days of advertising, this approach was successful. However, this strategy and style of advertising began to wane as more products entered markets with similar features. Today, it is often hard to find a truly unique benefit of one product over another. It is often up to the creativity of the message to create brand and product distinction.[4]

USPs were developed with the help of George Gallup, who first introduced the practice of market research in 1935. Gallup polls gathered information about consumers to better advertise to them.[5] Another leader in advertising, David Ogilvy, worked for Gallup, learning firsthand the power of consumer research. He later credited much of his success in advertising, including founding the agency Ogilvy & Mather, to his experience working at Gallup.[6] Gallup is still surveying people today (news.gallup.com) and can be another valuable source for consumer insights.

One of Reeves's most successful USPs was "It melts in your mouth, not in your hands." At the time, M&Ms were unique in that they were the first candy-coated chocolate.[7] Reeves also wrote "Fast, fast, incredible fast pain relief" for Anacin aspirin. The noisy and repetitive Anacin TV ads were grating and annoying, winning a most obnoxious TV commercial contest. One person noted, "It seems they are trying deliberately to give the viewer a headache so he'll buy Anacin." Reeves admitted that the Anacin ads "were the most hated commercials in the history of advertising."[8] Yet he was still against creativity, warning that "it is the most dangerous word in all of advertising."[9]

Bill Bernbach's Creative Revolution

In contrast to Reeves's rational, straightforward message approach, Bill Bernbach believed in concept-based advertising where the creative idea was a crucial part of an ad and a single idea should be the focus of a campaign. In 1947, Bernbach wrote a letter to his board of directors at Grey Advertising saying he wanted to prove "good taste, good art and good writing can be good selling."[10] The letter didn't change Grey's approach, so he left and started the agency Doyle Dane Bernbach (DDB). Few would argue today that he hadn't proved his point. *Advertising Age* lists him as advertising's most influential person of the twentieth century.[11]

Known as the "Father of Creative Advertising," Bernbach was an early proponent of diversity. He hired some of the industry's first employees from diverse ethnic backgrounds and the first women to head up creative roles. He was also open to diverse creative approaches. Instead of USP and slogan repetition to ad nauseum, DDB favored unique stories promoting the brand with a strategic message while keeping consumer interest. With product parity, Bernbach saw creativity as the last advantage marketers could employ over their competitors.[12]

Building his ad agency during the same time, David Ogilvy was a big proponent of research. Ogilvy & Mather used research into what types of creative produced the best sales results. But Ogilvy also agreed that creativity played an important role saying, "you can't bore someone into buying your product."[13] He insisted it was better not to advertise than to run poorly designed and written ads.[14]

A powerful creative idea can meet and exceed expectations even for a company with a small advertising media budget, such as DDB's client Volkswagen in the 1950s. Not only was VW's budget small, but its marketing problem was big. DDB was challenged with selling a small ugly German car to the American public. At the time, big American cars were in style, and the perception of Germany wasn't positive with World War II still fresh in people's minds.[15]

VW tasked DDB to advertise the Beetle with just $600,000, a tiny marketing budget compared to Chevy's and Ford's yearly marketing budgets in the 1950s of $30 million and $25 million. Before creating any ads, DDB conducted observational research by taking the agency team to Germany to visit the Beetle factory. Bernbach was impressed with the pride the workers took in such a basic, no-frills "honest" car. While a budget car, the focus on quality, performance, and reliability was exceptional. The Beetle respected the customer's investment.[16]

The creative team took that approach with its advertising. Instead of talking down to the consumer, the ads treated them with respect. Ads made intelligent ploys emphasizing both the negatives of the Beetle being small and ugly and the positives of its performance and economy. This honest pitch was delivered through humor, irony, wit, and emotion.[17]

The Beetle campaign tapped into a cultural tension of pressure to consume for recovery after the Great Depression and World War II. This led to a never-ending pursuit of newer and better to "keep up with the Joneses." The VW ads gave people permission to be pragmatic, changing the perception of the Beetle as a small, ugly car to a bold, smart car.

One ad featured the 1951 through 1961 Beetles showing how their appearance hadn't changed, relieving pressure to have the latest model. One ad tapped into the public's great pride in the space program saying, "It's ugly, but it gets you there," showing a picture of NASA's Lunar Module and a VW logo.[18] The campaign was so successful that by 1971, the Volkswagen Beetle had become the world's best-selling car, surpassing the previous record holder Ford's Model T.[19] In the late 1990s VW brought back the new Beetle. Ad agency Arnold picked up DDB's legacy of intelligent sales pitches. One recalling how the old Beetles were underpowered said, "0–60? Yes."

DDB's creativity changed the perception of the VW Beetle as a small, ugly car to a bold, smart car and the best selling car model in history. Getty Images: Dorian Puztay.

Table 6.1. Periods in the Evolution of Advertising

Research and Repetition Era	Creative Revolution Era	Digital Disruption Era	Ultimate Revelation Era
1935–1950	1950–2000	2000–2015	2015–20??
Emphasis on research, unique selling proposition, and relentless repetition of rational product sales points.	Emphasis on honesty, respect of consumer intelligence, and creative craft of emotional brand storytelling.	Emphasis on technology tools, and analysis of vast digital data often to the detriment of creativity and craft.	Emphasis on a balance of technology tools to collect and analyze data combined with craft, creativity, and brand storytelling.

Source: Modified from Keith Reinhard, "Advertising Today," Stan Talks, YouTube.com, March 29, 2018, https://youtu .be/WIgXU2Z7700.

Periods in the Evolution of Advertising

If the advertising creative revolution began in the 1960s, are we still in it? Copywriter, art director, and creative director Keith Reinhard rose through the ranks to become chairman of DDB Worldwide for 16 years. In an interview, Reinhard described what he believes are the phases of advertising (see Table 6.1).

The **research and repetition era** (1935–1950), before the Bernbach-led creative revolution, was dominated by Gallup's market research, Rosser Reeves's USP, and media repetition. This era didn't value story. Next, Reinhard describes the **creative revolution era** (1950–2000) as adding humor, irony, wit, and emotion to ads that respected the intelligence of the consumer. Bernbach and others learned the importance of craft and the power of story over mindless repetition of sales points. After the creative revolution, new technology ushered in a digital age.[20]

The **digital disruption era** (2000–2015) brought digital data tools that made new connections between people and brands. Enormous amounts of data helped agencies better understand and locate prospects for their marketing clients. Yet some emphasized technology too much, forgetting important lessons learned in the previous age about human creativity.

We're now entering an age of the **ultimate revelation era** (2015–present) that takes what was learned in the creative revolution about emotional storytelling and combines it with the technology and data of the digital disruption. Reinhard says there's a difference between "creating a buzz and creating a brand," "a one-off stunt and a compelling brand story that endures," "an algorithm and a true insight into human nature," and "a click and a true connection." Most importantly, the new age will emphasize that there is a difference between "big data and big ideas."[21] Today, brands need authentic and compelling stories told consistently across all consumer touchpoints informed and optimized by digital data insights.

6.2 Brand Stories in TV Ads

No media makes an impression like the sight, sound, and motion of television ads and online video. Mark Dominiak in *Television Week* described the power of storytelling in TV ads: "They engage us on many levels—with the spoken word, with conjured visual imagery, with body language, and with raw emotion."[22]

Connecting Product to Consumer's Life through Story

No matter the media or consumer touchpoint, when developing creative executions, start with the creative brief. Remind yourself of the campaign purpose, the target audience, and the attitude change needed for the audience to act. Research finds that narrative communication (story) elicits attitude change when recipients become transported into a narrative.[23]

A way to transport them is to tell stories the target audience can relate to or recognize from situations in their own lives. Yet you cannot lose the product in the story either. To achieve brand product attitude change, you must link the product to the story. As the audience seeks to understand story meaning (comprehension), the brand product message will be carried (transported through the narrative) into an attitude change (see Table 6.2).[24]

Begin by brainstorming key situations or moments in your target audience's life based on consumer insights found in research. Then, consider ways to link that story to the product. How? Researchers Mattias and Reisinger suggest six ways:

- Make the characters in the story use the product.
- Have the product be a solution to a problem.
- Make the product essential to the story (couldn't be replaced).
- Make the product influence the behavior of the characters.
- Have the product provide story meaning, such as in a metaphor.
- Have the product drive the story, causing events or enabling characters.[25]

Consider the creative brief example from Chapter 5 for Peloton. Our target audience was a "middle-age professional mother or father who is looking for ways to stay in shape amid career and family demands." The attitude change needed was from "I need to stay in shape but don't have time to go to the gym and don't have the motivation to work out on my own" to "With Peloton, I can bring the gym, instructor, and class into my home to give me the time and motivation I need."

Think about a situation where a parent walks by a regular stationary bike unused and covered in coats on their way out the door each morning. It's a montage showing the passage of time, and every scene adds more stuff on top of the bike. Finally, they look at it tired and dejected, giving up all hope of using it, and put it in storage in the garage.

Table 6.2. Ensure Product–Story Link in Narrative Ads

1. Product	Brand product situation.
2. Link	Target audience life situation.
3. Story	Situation relevant to the product and target audience.
4. Comprehension	Audience understands story meaning.
5. Narrative Transportation	Product message carried through story.
6. Brand/Product Attitude	Attitude changes about brand and product.

Source: Matthias Glaser and Heribert Reisinger, "Don't Lose Your Product in Story Translation: How Product–Story Link in Narrative Advertisements Increases Persuasion," *Journal of Advertising* (2021, September): 1–18, Figure 1.

In the next scene, the doorbell rings, they open the door, and a Peloton instructor and class walk into the house with a Peloton bike. The instructor and class members jam into the small study, each taking turns encouraging the now-motivated parent to work hard and not give up. The scene fades to them on the Peloton bike, energized, with the instructor talking and graphics of others in the class on the screen. A voice-over announcer says, "Peloton isn't a home gym; it's a community that brings the gym to your home."

This ad tells the story of the lack of motivation people experience in purchasing home gym equipment—something learned in consumer research. As the audience processes the story meaning, "it's hard to work out on your own; it's easier with a community" the product is linked to the story as a solution. The story meaning—to get motivation through community—is transported through the narrative to attitude change, delivering the creative brief's main message, "Peloton brings the motivation and community of a gym to the convenience of your home." Once you create the basic TV ad concept, use the story act template worksheet (Table 2.4) from Chapter 2 to plan a complete five-act story (see Table 6.3).

Table 6.3. Five-Act Story Example for Peloton

Story Act	Elements of Story Act Development
Act 1 Exposition Characters, setting, basic conflict are established leading to tension. An inciting moment begins rising action of complications.	The setting and characters are introduced. Middle-aged mom or dad rushing out the door every morning. The tension forms as the unmotivated parent keeps walking past an obviously unused stationary bike.
Act 2 Complication Tension mounts as the main character's efforts to reach a goal meets conflicts and obstacles. Frustration builds as opposing forces intensify.	Tension mounts as time passes and every day the unused stationary bike simply becomes a place for the family to pile up their clothes, backpacks, and other unused items.
Act 3 Climax Conflict reaches a high turning point that could lead to victory or defeat for the main character, resulting in good or bad consequences.	Finally, they confront the situation. Seemingly giving up, they put the bike away in the garage. Yet one morning mom or dad opens the door to reveal a Peloton instructor, class, and bike coming to the house.
Act 4 Reversal Events play out in falling actions from the reversal in the climax. Momentum slows as the characters head toward a final resolution.	The result is the parent using the Peloton bike as the instructor and class members are in the home study encouraging and motivating them and they succeed.
Act 5 Denouement Conflict is resolved and tension is released creating normalcy. The main character is either better off or worse off.	The tension is released as the instructor and class members go away from the room, but we realize the gym has come to the busy parent virtually with Peloton solving the problem. They're better off than when the story started.

In planning out the five acts, the main character is the target audience facing a struggle based on the cultural tension of the expectation of self-motivation for exercise when most don't have it. Our main character (the target audience) makes it through improving their life in the end. If you go back to Chapter 2, Table 2.3, you will recognize elements of Campbell's The Hero's Journey and Dan Harmon's Story Circle in this example of a Peloton TV ad.

Craft the TV Ad or Video through a Script and Storyboard

Once you have the ad concept and five acts, put the TV idea into script and storyboard format. Internal and external audiences, such as creative directors, account managers, and marketing clients, need to understand the TV ad and ensure it is on strategy by comparing it to the creative brief. If approved, a production company and director also need a script and storyboard to film and edit. Create the script and storyboard following standard formats using common film production terms to describe camera shots and movements, audio devices, and editing techniques (see Table 6.4).

Table 6.4. Common Film Production Terms

Camera Shots
Long shot shows a subject in surrounding environment sometimes from a crane or drone.
Medium shot features a subject from the waist up to show surroundings.
Two shot includes two subjects in a frame often in dialogue.
Close-up tightly frames a face, making their emotional reaction the focus.
High-/low-angle shot looks down on a subject for a sense of superiority or up for inferiority.
Camera Movements
Pan is the camera moving horizontally left or right from a fixed location.
Tilt is the camera moving vertically up or down from a fixed location.
Tracking shot moves the camera sideways, forward, or backward on a dolly.
Dolly zoom moves the camera on a track closer to magnify a subject.
Zoom shot uses the camera lens to move closer magnifying the subject.
Audio Devices
Music is used to set a mood and evoke emotion to aid in telling a story.
Sound effect (SFX) is a specific sound added to a movement or scene.
Dialogue is a conversation between two or more characters.
Announcer (ANNCR) is seen and heard on camera delivering a brand, product message.
Voice-over (VO) is heard off camera narrating or delivering a brand, product message.
Editing Techniques
Fade-in is a dissolve edit from a blank screen to a picture.
Fade-out is a dissolve edit from a picture to a blank screen.
Cross fade is an edit that gradually fades one scene out and another gradually fades in.
Jump cut is an edit that cuts between two sequential scenes where the subjects move.
Superimpose (SUPER) places one image, graphic, or text over another.

Source: "Film Terms Glossary: Guide to 95 Film Terms," Masterclass.com, June 24, 2021, https://www.masterclass.com/articles/film-terms-guide#a-glossary-of-95-film-terms.

Every camera shot, movement, audio, and edit should emphasize the concept and message, advance the plot, and evoke the emotion of the story. Most ads and videos start with a long shot, called an establishing shot, to quickly convey a recognizable setting and characters. Close-ups are used for emotional reactions. Pans and tilts mimic head movements from the point of view of a person in the scene. Music genres, styles, or specific songs and lyrics elicit emotion and set a mood. Postproduction edits enhance the story and message.

These terms and descriptions are placed in a standard TV script and storyboard. A **television or video script** is a written blueprint or outline of a TV or video ad including both video and audio descriptions.[26] A standard TV/video script has two columns (see Figure 6.1). Video descriptions are in all caps in the left column, describing scenes, camera shots, movements, and superimposed graphics or type. In the right column, audio descriptions indicate music, sound effects, voice-over, announcer, or character dialogue. Ensure video descriptions align on the same row as audio to be heard at the same time.

Figure 6.1. Television and video script template worksheet.

Brand: _____ Product: _____

Time: _____ Title: _____

VIDEO	AUDIO
(DESCRIBE WHAT HAPPENS VISUALLY INCLUDING CHARACTERS, BACKGROUND, MOTION, AND TRANSITIONS.)	VO: *(What an announcer says, over the action and not in the scene.)*
	SFX: *(Describe the sounds)*
(MAKE SURE WHAT HAPPENS ON THIS SIDE MATCHES UP WITH THE SOUND HAPPENING ON THE AUDIO SIDE OF THE SCRIPT)	BETTY: *(What a specific character says.)*
	MUSIC: *(Describe music or specific track)*
SUPER: *(Words that appear on screen.)*	

Write scripts within the allotted time. Under "What are the specific requirements?" in the creative brief, ad types are listed, including print and digital size plus TV, video, and radio length. Typical TV ads are 30 seconds but can also be 60 and 15 seconds. A standard practice when launching a campaign is to use a 60- or 30-second commercial to introduce the concept and do a cut-down 15-second version to reinforce the idea, stretching the media budget to extend reach and frequency. This said, research indicates 30 seconds is an ideal length because it is long enough to make an emotional and intellectual connection but not too long to lose audience interest.[27]

Another approach for 15-second ads is to create unique concepts best told in short forms. TV ads that run at the beginning and end of a commercial break or are run in different dayparts are called **15-second bookends**.[28] You may start a story in one 15-second ad and then finish it in another 15-second ad at the end of a commercial break. For dayparts, a restaurant may use a 15-second story for breakfast in the morning and a 15-second story for dinner to run in the evening.

Once the script is complete, read it aloud, checking for natural sounding copy and dialogue. Time the script, accounting for pauses in dialogue, action, sound effects, music, and movement. If you go over time, the TV channel will not sell you a 37-second commercial slot.

After writing the television script, you want to create a storyboard. No matter how detailed your video descriptions, it is often difficult to envision visuals for scenes. A **storyboard** is a visual blueprint or outline of a TV script or video showing a series of images.[29] Draw out important scenes to help communicate the visual portion of the TV idea, finetuning the important visual aspects of the commercial (see Figure 6.2).

Figure 6.2. Television and video storyboard template worksheet.

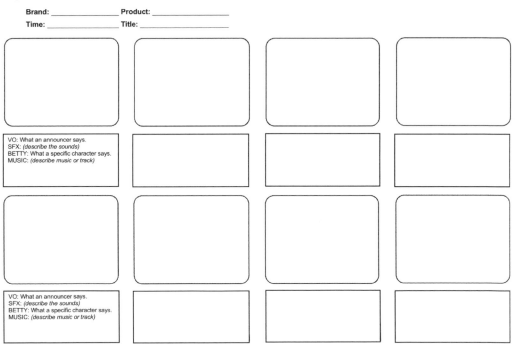

Consider the Peloton TV ad. In working on the storyboard, you may realize the script description may be expressed in a better way. Perhaps the script described the turning point with a close-up of the main character's face to show emotion. In sketching the storyboard, you could realize that a medium shot would be better to show the buried unused stationary bike in the same scene as the cause of the emotional reaction.

Often, art directors make simple line drawings for storyboards. That is enough to convey the idea. For an especially important campaign or pitch, agencies may hire professional illustrators to draw more detailed color illustrations, or the art director will take time to find stock photography to represent each of the scenes.

6.3 Brand Stories in Online Video

We have learned the foundations of concepting stories for the sight, sound, and motion of TV and video. We have learned key terms and standard formats for scripts and storyboards used in the presentation and production of TV and video ads. When it comes to online video, there are additional practices and standards unique to the main types used in IMC plans.

The following are various types of online video ads:

- Viral advertising videos
- CTV advertising (streaming TV ads)
- YouTube advertising videos

Both nonpaid and paid online videos are used for marketing communications, including viral advertising videos and YouTube advertising. Traditional TV ads are also now being placed on CTV/OTT. CTV is internet-connected TV, and OTT is video content streamed via the internet instead of accessed via traditional cable or satellite TV. With this new distribution model comes unique, targeting, interactive, and measurement capabilities that let the audiences interact with TV ads and advertisers in ways that they have never done before.

Viral Advertising Videos

First, consider the nonpaid form of internet advertising videos. **Viral advertising videos** are branded videos produced for the internet that facilitate and encourage people to pass along a marketing message.[30] Despite the name, no one can promise a viral video will "go viral." You can't guarantee viral views or a massive video hit like Old Spice's "The Man Your Man Could Smell Like," ALS "Ice Bucket Challenge," or Always "#LikeAGirl."[31] Yet there are best practices that can be followed to increase the chances of the viral spread of an advertising message without paying for reach through media ad placement.

As we learned in Chapter 2, storytelling in a full five-act structure produces increased views and shares in viral advertising videos. Quesenberry and Coolsen's research looked at a large sample of viral advertising videos from randomly selected brands in different industries over a year. Videos that told a more developed or complete story had significantly higher shares and views based on coding videos for the five-acts in Freytag's Pyramid: introduction, rising action, climax, falling action, and resolve.[32]

Having all five parts creates a dramatic arc or plot of a fully developed story—a formula for being interesting. But don't confuse brand storytelling with telling stories about the brand. Other research has found that the most engaging stories include branding but not overt sales messages. Plots in viral advertising videos should be built around characters and situations relatable to the target audience.[33]

While there is no guarantee that a video will "go viral," five-act stories about your target audience's life are a good start. As we learned in Chapter 1, a five-act story with tension transports the viewer into feeling sympathy and empathy for the ad's characters, which then elicits emotional resonance and immersion from the audience. Additional insights for concepting and planning a viral ad video come from studying memes.

Google's Engagement Project conducted research into **memes**, which are ideas expressed as visuals, words, and/or videos that spread on the internet from person to person. To study memes and how they spread, Google partnered with cultural anthropologists, psychologists, and creators of digital content to determine what motivates creating, curating, and connecting across the web.[34]

What they found is that people are attracted to the fascinating familiar—everyday moments framed in a different way or juxtaposed for a new perspective. The fascinating familiar elevates regular life moments by tapping into imagination and discovery. On the internet, unrelated images and clips can come together in a childlike way. Seeing babies dance or cats surf connects random components in our brains to form synapses that produce creative joy. Passing on the meme or story is about sharing the emotional response. The sharing of the video becomes a gift or moment of pleasure to someone else.[35]

We can learn insights into viral ads by studying memes which tell us to create the "fascinatingly familiar." Getty Images: Maskot.

Sometimes, TV ads can become a meme and a gift of pleasure to share. An example was Geico's "Scoop! There It Is" TV ad, featuring hip-hop duo Tag Team's 1993 hit "Whoomp!" The ad was named Adweek's 2021 ad of the year. Not only was it ad of the year, but it reignited DC "The Brain Supreme" Glenn (Cecil Glenn) and Steve "Rollin" Gibson's careers. It also became the biggest Geico commercial ever, which is notable for a brand with a long history of popular ads, including Cavemen and Humpday.[36] The popularity of the TV commercial shared on social media made it the most-seen ad in America and even turned into a real limited-edition ice cream flavor.[37]

Derek Thomas in *Hit Makers: How to Succeed in an Age of Distraction* explains hits in a similar way, saying that hit makers are architects of familiar surprises. People are curious to discover new things but don't like anything too new or unrecognizable. The right combination places the viewer in a situation between the anxiety of something new and the satisfaction of understanding it. When the viewer sees the relationship, they create meaning and get a rewarding feeling of "aha." Thomas says, "Great storytellers excel in creating tension followed by a cathartic release—aha"—a feeling they want to pass on by sharing with others.[38]

Facebook has also conducted research into memes. It found that adding the words "please post this" or "copy and paste" makes a meme twice as likely to be shared. Phrases that are easy to agree or identify with, such as "if you love your" or "share if you agree," also drive content sharing. When videos are promoted, include a call to action encouraging sharing.[39] Marketers often jump-start sharing with paid media to promote the initial discovery of viral ads. Also, consider timing the release of videos around a relevant time of year or trending topics to help drive discovery and sharing.[40]

Connected TV Ads Enhance Targeting, Interactivity, and Measurement

To guarantee reach and frequency, most marketers turn to paid forms of digital video advertising, such as CTV ads and YouTube ads. A unique characteristic of CTV ads is that they are highly targetable. Linear TV ads target the demographics of viewers watching channels or TV programs, and CTV ads offer enhanced targeting. When developing creative concepts, consider variations in the story, product, and characters based on primary and secondary target audiences.

Behavioral targeting is possible based on online browsing to target interests and lifestyles. CTV ads can also retarget via CRM databases targeting people who have visited brand websites, signed up for emails, purchased recently, or have not purchased in a while.[41]

Creating CTV ad variations is more expensive than customizing and personalizing a digital display, email, or mobile ad. Yet if you plan variations ahead of time, there can be cost efficiencies in filming and editing all versions in one production. Consider leaving space for customization by having on-camera talent record multiple script options and have announcers record variations on the voice-over, such as different highlighted benefits or calls to action.[42]

CTV ads also offer interactive capabilities enabling creative opportunities for engagement. Dynamic overlays can add photo and video galleries so the audience can view product options and feature descriptions. Overlays could show a product in customizable environments, such as furniture in different rooms and décors.[43]

Dynamic overlays can also include interactive store locators, live social feeds, games, coupons, sweepstakes entry, and e-commerce. You could produce several versions of a story and allow the audience to pick which one they want to view. A CTV ad for an SUV could begin with asking the viewer if they want to view an off-road or city ad. Then, it could show a gallery of features and options, help the viewer locate a local dealer, and generate a lead for a salesperson with a request for a quote or test drive.[44]

Unlike traditional TV ads, CTV ads are also more measurable. Because digital ads are trackable and offer direct actions, such as clicking through to a website, A/B testing can determine which versions of creative are most effective. Because of these attractive capabilities, 90 percent of advertisers and agencies planned to increase their CTV ad budgets in 2021.[45]

A sign that CTV ads are growing is streaming services, such as Netflix, which have traditionally been subscription only, announcing new ad-supported tiers. Netflix's "Basic with Ads" allows users to subscribe to Netflix for only $6.99 per month with 15- and 30-second ads appearing before and during shows and movies with preroll ads for new release originals. This is similar to Paramount+'s and Peacock's ad-supported basic tiers. Disney+ also plans an ad-supported offering.[46]

YouTube Ads Reach Large Groups of Consumers

The last category of online video is YouTube ads. YouTube is the second-most-visited website behind Google and the second-most-used social platform behind Facebook. YouTube has more than 2 billion logged-in monthly users, 74 percent of adults in the United States watch YouTube, and 94 percent of over-the-top (OTT) viewers watch YouTube on their TVs.[47] It's no wonder YouTube has become a significant channel for video advertising.

YouTube ads come in multiple formats, including skippable in-stream ads, nonskippable in-stream ads (bumper ads), video-discovery ads (in-display ads), and nonvideo ads (overlays and banners). Skippable in-stream video ads play during a video either pre- or mid-roll, meaning they appear at the beginning or middle of a video. Viewers can skip them after five seconds. They can be any length from 12 seconds to three minutes or more, and advertisers only pay when viewers watch past 30 seconds or click on the ad.[48]

Because 76 percent of people report they automatically skip ads, many marketers choose nonskippable in-stream video ads. These are 15 seconds long, run pre- or mid-roll, and are cost per impression. Bumper ads, the last video option, are especially popular for their reach and awareness capabilities. **YouTube bumper ads** are six-second nonskippable ads that run on YouTube videos pre-, mid-, and postroll. They serve as "bumpers," appearing in the beginning, middle, or end of a video, similar to TV ad "bookends."

Theodor Arhio, global director of creative and content at TBWA, says that bumper ads require unique concepts. Unlike TV ads there is no time for a backstory or to set up the scene.[49]

The following are the best practices for YouTube bumper ads:

- *Rule of one:* Focus on one feeling, one joke, one feature, or one question.
- *Establish the ad:* Drop a viewer right into the action, capturing attention immediately.
- *Time it out:* Spend four seconds on a feeling then two seconds on branding and call to action.
- *Build a flock:* Create individual bumpers in a series that also deliver a larger story.[50]

Global creatives at Google's Unskippable Lab, Ben Jones and Matt Lindley, suggest not thinking of a YouTube bumper ad as a cutdown of a traditional 30-second TV ad. Instead, think of it as a "bump up" of a print ad idea. They also address the myth that bumpers can't tell a story. No one makes a media buy for just one. Bumpers are typically bought as a series of three, four, or five. Concept bumper ads to work separately but also work as a group to convey a story.[51]

As an example, consider how the Peloton TV ad example in Table 6.3 could be broken down into a series of six-second bumper ads to tell the story.

The following is an example of a six-second YouTube bumper ad story for Peloton:

- *First six-second bumper:* Middle-aged parent rushing out the door to work glancing at an unused stationary bike with piles of backpacks, clothes, and boxes on top of it.
- *Second six-second bumper:* The parent putting the non–internet–connected stationary bike away in the garage
- *Third six-second bumper:* The parent excitedly opens the front door to a big Peloton logo box; cut to them happily working out with the virtual class and instructor on the screen.

6.4 Brand Stories in Radio

Our final category of ads in this chapter is radio. Radio ads include traditional terrestrial radio ads run on local stations and ads run on internet streaming services, such as Spotify, Pandora, Amazon Music, Apple Music, and iHeart Radio. In 2021, terrestrial radio accounted for two-thirds of radio advertising spending in the United States, while one-third went to digital audio services. Of the digital audio platforms, Spotify is the largest with 83.1 million US listeners, followed by 54.2 million for Pandora.[52] Not surprisingly, 75 percent of radio listening occurs in the car, and 88 percent of adults over 18 are weekly radio listeners.[53]

Radio Is Less Expensive but Still Effective

When considering radio following the sight, sounds, and motion of TV and video, it's easy to focus on the limitations. You only have audio to work with, and we've learned the importance of the visual and verbal brand message. Yet, limitations can open creative possibilities. Audio only doesn't mean you can't paint a visual picture. With TV and video, you can only create visuals that can be recorded in reality. Creating grand visuals in exotic locations with casts of thousands is not possible with most brand budgets. Radio can be used to tell stories via the imagination with descriptions, music, and sound effects.

In a classic demonstration of the creative power of radio, Stan Freberg recorded "Stretching the Imagination." In it, he creates "theater of the mind" using sound effects to drop whipped cream and a huge cherry into Lake Michigan, which has been drained and refilled with hot chocolate, to the sound of 25,000 cheering extras. Unlike TV, radio can stretch the imagination and budget.[54] While the average cost to produce a national 30-second TV ad is $350,000,[55] radio production costs are only around $2,000.[56]

In creating an ad for terrestrial radio or streaming radio, consider a similar process we discussed for TV ads. Begin by brainstorming situations in your target audience's life inspired by consumer insights. Then link the story to the product via one of the six ways suggested earlier in the chapter. This time, the concept must be told only via audio, representing both limitations and possibilities.

Image brainstorming a radio ad for Peloton where the target audience parent is asked by various family members where to place things: "Where should I put my coat?" "Where should I put this package?" "Where should I put my backpack?" Mom or dad answers repeatedly, "Just put it on the stationary bike." Finally, one child replies, "I can't find the stationary bike." An announcer says, "Has your stationary bike become too stationary?" Then with sound effects, we hear the mom or dad working out with a motivational talk by a Peloton instructor in a virtual class.

Radio Scripts Describe Sound to Paint a Picture in the Mind

Once you have the concept and story, put the idea into script format to present to internal and external audiences. A standard radio script is similar to a TV script format except that it only has the audio side (see Figure 6.3). Also, use standard radio production terms and descriptions as described in the audio devices section of Table 6.4. Like TV, look to "What are the specific requirements?" in the creative brief for length. Radio can be bought in 60-, 30-, and 15-second units. However, 60 seconds is the standard because it elicits a higher recall than 30-second radio ads.[57]

All audio descriptions need to be described with music, sound effects, announcer, and character dialogue. Music genres, styles, or specific songs and lyrics should be described and used to evoke emotion or set the mood. Character voices create dialogue and interaction between people in audio scenes. Announcers can deliver story transitions, brand and product messages, benefits, promotions, and calls to action. Don't forget to describe the announcer's and characters' voice style and tone. Radio relies heavily on sound effects to paint a picture. Describe in detail what they should sound like and when they should occur.

Read the script aloud to check for natural-sounding announcer copy and character dialogue. Time the script, accounting for all pauses in dialogue, sound effects, and music. As with TV, a radio station will not run a 67-second radio ad if you go over.

What sound effects would "paint a picture" of a beach vacation in radio for an ad promoting flights to Florida in the winter?

Figure 6.3. Radio script template worksheet.

Brand: _____ Product: _____

Time: _____ Title: _____

ANNR: | *(What an announcer says)*

SFX: | *(Describe the sounds)*

MUSIC: | *(Describe music or specific track)*

BETTY: | *(What a specific character says)*

Another consideration is that terrestrial radio stations have a local connection to specific metropolitan regions. If appropriate, take advantage of local knowledge, sayings, and references to customize messages to the community. The ice cream brand Turkey Hill made special flavors for professional baseball and football teams, such as the Philadelphia Phillies and Philadelphia Eagles, New York Yankees, and New York Jets plus the Buffalo Bills and the Pittsburgh Steelers. These regional flavors were only sold in these metro markets, and the brand created different radio commercials to run different radio ads in each city. Running Jets ads in Buffalo would not produce good results for the brand! Radio is also good for local businesses that have regional physical locations such as retail stores, restaurants, law firms, home improvement contractors, and insurance agents.

6.5 CASE

Motel 6 Leaves the Light on for You

Radio can be a powerful support medium or lead medium for the right brand. For over 30 years, Motel 6's success has been driven by its radio ads. What's unique is that the company has done it with a single announcer and music while still delivering engaging and relevant target audience and brand product stories. An example of a big idea with legs, Motel 6 has produced the longest-running radio ad campaign in history and has become a leader in the economy hotel market segment.[58]

In 1986, David Fowler, then creative director at The Richards Group, heard comedian Tom Bodett on NPR's *All Things Considered* and knew he was the perfect voice. Bodett, at the first recording session, ad-libbed the brand tagline "I'm Tom Bodett for Motel 6, and we'll leave the light on for you." The stories told before that tagline vary over the years to stay relevant but always deliver the main message that Motel 6 isn't a cheap motel. It is a smart decision for the budget-conscious traveler target audience.

An example of relevant stories in the campaign is a Motel 6 ad that ran on radio coverage of Super Bowl XLVII. In it, Bodett poked fun at smartphone auto-correct, delivering the famous line "We'll heave the bright on farm you. Close enough."[59] Unaided awareness of Motel 6 ads is 77 percent higher than the next-highest motel. Tammy Greenberg of the Association of National Advertisers says there are six key ingredients to the Motel 6 radio strategy:

1. Bodett's voice brings humorous commentary to a commoditized category with original music as a sonic brand identifier.
2. Fresh thinking combines relevant messaging to changing pop culture that evolves the promotion of the brand.
3. Whimsical, folksy, and funny, writing stays on message and sustains an iconic reassuring tagline for the brand's target audience.
4. Radio is perfect for a "dashboard brand" that drivers hear on the road, delivering the right audience at the right time.[60]

This chapter began with how advertising has evolved over the decades through the eyes of some of the industry's visionary leaders. Then, we explored processes and practices for brainstorming, presenting, and producing ideas for linear TV, CTV, viral video, YouTube video, terrestrial radio, and digital radio ads, emphasizing the unique role that a five-act dramatic story can elicit in viewers and listeners. When developing concepts, be sure to reference the creative brief to ensure each ad and medium is on strategy and consistent in its messaging and expression of the big idea for your IMC plan. In the next chapter, we will look at how digital and story can transform the traditional media of print and out-of-home.

QUESTIONS

1. How has the influence of TV ads shifted over time? In your life, what medium that combines sight, sound, and motion has the most influence over your purchase decisions?
2. A challenge in marketing communications is that most of the time, you are not the target audience. How has your personal experience clouded your views of what people in other demographics do in terms of digital and traditional media use? Find some research data that shows the difference.

EXERCISES

1. Go back to Table 6.1, Periods in the Evolution of Advertising. Do you agree with Keith Reinhard's descriptions? What evidence do you see of the ultimate revelation? Find a campaign you believe is still stuck in the digital disruption. What elements of the creative revolution is it missing? Find a campaign that is an example of the ultimate revolution. What key elements has it drawn from the creative revolution and digital disruption?
2. For practice, brainstorm some additional ideas either for the Peloton example presented in the text, your favorite brand, or for a brand you are working on for a project. Begin with consumer insights and a big idea. Then, concept ways to tell that story in a 30-second linear TV ad, 30-second interactive CTV ad, 6-second YouTube bumper ads, and a 60-second radio ad. Consider the creative brief. Does what you created tell the story consistently following standards for each medium while delivering the right message to the right people on strategy?

KEY CONCEPTS

Announcer (ANNCR)

Close-up

Creative revolution era

Cross fade

Dialogue

Digital disruption era

Dolly zoom

Fade-in

Fade-out

15-Second bookends

High-/low-angle

Jump cut

Long shot

Medium shot

Memes

Music

Pan

Research and repetition era

Sound effect (SFX)

Storyboard

Superimpose (SUPER)

Tilt

Tracking shot

TV/video script

Two shot

Ultimate revelation era

Unique selling proposition (USP)

Viral advertising videos

Voice-over (VO)

YouTube bumper ads

Zoom shot

The New Page

Magazine, Newspaper, and Out-of-Home Advertising

PREVIEW

Our brand storytelling journey continues by peering into the past and future of the more traditional advertising media, which continue to have unique strengths in integrated marketing communications (IMC) plans. We'll begin with lessons from innovators in the field of art direction and copywriting. Mary Wells Lawrence also provides lessons on creativity saying, "You can't just be you. You have to read books on subjects you know nothing about. You have to travel to places you never thought of traveling. You have to meet every kind of person and endlessly stretch what you know."[1] Drawing from these broad experiences and big ideas, we'll learn to tell stories in magazine, newspaper, and out-of-home ads which today each have their own forms of digital media components. Our case study tells the story of a billboard concept that helped to launch the IMC campaign and success of Chick-fil-A.

CHAPTER 7 LEARNING OBJECTIVES

1. Discover key practices in copywriting and art direction.
2. Know how to construct creative visual and verbal storytelling messages.

3. Understand how to craft magazine and newspaper ads with stories.
4. Learn to create out-of-home placements with a storytelling approach.

7.1 Lawrence's Copywriting and Krone's Art Direction

In Chapter 5, we first learned of the different positions and roles involved in planning and creating IMC strategies and campaigns. Copywriters and art directors are the main parts of a creative team that work together to concept big campaign ideas and create individual ads in those campaigns. When looking at print advertising, the skills and crafts of these positions become more apparent. To begin our look at creating print advertising, we will highlight two influential advertising creatives known for their individual craft in copywriting and art direction.

How Mary Wells Lawrence Innovated Copywriting

Mary Wells Lawrence is an American Advertising Hall of Fame copywriter who started her career at DDB working with Bill Bernbach but went on to be the owner of the creative agency Wells Rich Greene. She was the first woman president of an advertising agency and the first woman CEO of a company on the New York Stock Exchange.[2]

Her quote in the chapter introduction is a good reminder of what we have learned thus far. An effective IMC plan and campaign is more than creativity. All marketing communication must be rooted in a sound strategy based on research, the consumer's point of view, and relatable brand/consumer stories to tell. Wells Lawrence didn't write a line of copy until she first understood the product, the competition, and the mind of the target consumer, and she made sure she had plenty of raw material to draw from to generate creative ideas. Remember the key ingredients of the creative process we learned in Chapter 5?

This chapter focuses on the next forms of marketing communications in an IMC plan as components of the media mix. We will discover best practices and techniques for the specific media of magazine, newspaper, and out-of-home advertising. Yet a single, well-written, and well-designed print ad is only as good as the consumer insights, creative brief, and big

Mary Wells Laurence says that a copywriter must be a detective and a psychiatrist before being an artist. Getty Images: Fiordaliso.

campaign idea that came before it. As Wells Lawrence says, "When copywriting, be a detective and a psychiatrist before allowing yourself to be an artist."[3]

Before entering the advertising business, Wells Lawrence had a background in theater—something she brought to her advertising philosophy of selling dreams. She looked beyond a product's features and found new and exciting reasons for customers to buy. She knew how to tell a story about the products in a dramatic way. Selling dreams and entertaining ads was innovative at the time, introduced mainly by Wells Lawrence.[4]

Because of her innovative creative approaches and focus on product and consumer research, her advertising didn't just influence a company's advertising; it often influenced the product itself. That is what happened with her campaign for Alka-Seltzer at ad agency Jack Tinker & Partners. Most drug ads at that time focused on the pain the drugs would ease, resulting in ads that evoked unpleasant feelings. Remember Rosser Reeves and his most obnoxious TV commercial for Anacin aspirin in Chapter 6?

Wells Lawrence and her creative team flipped that traditional approach, deciding instead to entertain the audience. Yet before being "artists," they first became "detectives" and had the lab test the drug in Alka-Seltzer for claims and tried it themselves. They discovered it worked better when taking two at a time. As a result, Alka-Seltzer released a two-tablet pack, and Wells Lawrence wrote her now famous line "Plop, plop, fizz, fizz, oh what a relief it is." The ads themselves used self-deprecating humor—a first in drug ads. As a result, campaign sales doubled.[5]

In another example of breaking the traditional advertising rules, Wells Lawrence, now running her own agency Wells Rich Greene, published side-by-side print ads directly comparing her client's car, the American Motors Javelin, with the main competitor's Ford Mustang. This type of direct comparison was not something traditional automobile ads did at that time. This untraditional story approach led to a revival of the American Motors brand for several of its car models.[6]

Helmet Krone Revolutionized Art Direction

Another innovator during the creative revolution of the 1960s was The One Club Creative Hall of Fame and Art Directors Club Hall of Fame member Helmet Krone. While Mary Wells Lawrence was known for her copywriting, the verbal message, Krone was an art director who was a master of the visual message. Krone also worked with Bill Bernbach at DDB and was integral to the Volkswagen Beetle ads discussed in the previous chapter.

As an art director, Krone was known for his ability to take something familiar and change it enough to make it new. This approach was inspired by a challenge posed to him by Bill Bernbach. To break through advertising clutter, Bernbach encouraged Krone to design a new page for every brand in the same page size as the average magazine ad. This became known as the **theory of new page**, which states that you should create a completely new-looking page, in the same shape, using the same old elements, with every campaign.[7]

Krone strived to make his ads look like something other than an ad, especially a typical ad in the brand's industry, whether the ad was in the automotive, medicine, or electronics market. He also knew the power of branding. His graphic design was unique for every brand, and he stuck with those elements within "the page" to help define a brand's personality in its own advertising package. Yet these unique packages on the same page were not shockingly different.[8]

Krone's innovative design was typically based on a traditional layout, such as "two-thirds image above, centered headline, three columns of body copy below." But he knew there was power in taking the ordinary and making a subtle change. He once described this saying,

Art directors must create new designs within the same page with every campaign by starting with a blank page to create a "new page." Mordolff, "Blank page of magazine," Creative #157437187. Getty Images, http://www.gettyimages.com /detail/157437187.

"There's a German word for it, *Umgekehrt*—turned around slightly." Making a slight turn within the same page can attract attention.[9] This is something Google learned in its research on memes within the digital page. Attraction comes from the fascinating familiar—the ordinary framed in a slightly different way for a new perspective.[10]

As a masterful art director focused on the art of design, Helmet Krone also knew the main purpose of advertising. A purpose of creativity is to drive real business marketing results. In a DDB video interview called "God Is in the Details," Krone described this ultimate purpose: "I like to say that the Avis sales curve after six months of our advertising is the most beautiful piece of graphics that I have ever done in my life."[11]

In some ways, today's new page challenge is even more challenging because popular digital ad spaces, such as display ads, are smaller. One of the best display (or banner) ads of 2022 provides a good example.

Adobe sold its design software with a new page banner ad that simply tells the story of a picture you take and then what you can do with it with software such as Photoshop. On the left of a square banner ad is a picture of an outdoor scene that looks OK. On the right, divided by an Adobe brand color red slash, is the same photo in a much more attractive and brilliant form. The headline over the two images on either side of the red slash says, "Take It. Make It." The last visual element is the red Adobe logo in the top right corner.[12]

7.2 Brand Stories in Print

Is "the page" still relevant today with the rise of digital media? After years of decline, combined print and digital magazine audiences grew from 210 million in 2012 to 222 million in 2020. In 2020, nearly 60 new print magazines were launched, and 88 percent of US adults and 90 percent of adults under age 25 say they've read a magazine in the past six months. Intriguingly, 64 percent of 18- to 34-year-olds agree that "even in the digital age they love the touch and feel of a printed magazine."[13] Magazines and the other forms of printed media discussed in this chapter remain important parts of an IMC plan.

In-Print Ads Tell Stories about Your Audience

Research indicates paper-based reading is better at stimulating emotions and desires and has a higher comprehension and recall than digital reading. Print can also lead to digital action. When people notice a print ad, 68 percent take further action, such as visiting the brand website or social media sites.[14] How do you make someone notice your print ad?

The key to audience attention in any media—TV, radio, video, and print—is a story. In an *Advertising Age* article, "Consumers Ignore Ads That Aren't Telling Their Stories," Tom Neveril draws insights from his consumer research experience as an account planner at DDB Worldwide and his Storybrand Consulting. He emphasizes the importance of listening to customers to get their real stories, which can turn into engaging ads.[15]

Neveril came to understand this while researching surfers for a beverage client. When talking with them, he realized that they would ignore advertising for any product if it didn't tap into their stories. This was not because they don't want to know about a new beverage but because if it was only about the product, they wouldn't read it. The most read, watched, liked, and memorable ads are stories about the audience.[16]

For example, an ad in a surfer magazine with a big product photo of Long Board Energy and the headline "Fuel Up With 160MG of Caffeine, B-Vitamins, Guarana, and Taurine" would probably be ignored. Imagine a different ad inspired by real stories from surfers with an image of a tired surfer on the shore looking longingly at a nice set of waves. The headline and subhead say, "Whether You Stay in the Pocket or Get Barreled" and "Long Board Energy Gets You Back Out for the Next Set." At the bottom is a picture of the energy drink and body copy that weaves product features into a story about the surfer getting the energy to get back out into the waves.

In Chapter 5, we discussed Goodby, Silverstein & Partners' campaign for the California Milk Processor Board. One of the keys to the success of that campaign was listening to the stories of woe and despair recorded in the diaries of consumers who went without milk for a week. Some of those thoughts directly inspired individual ads in the campaign.[17] Those real movements from your target audience's lives can turn into engaging headlines and visuals for your client's print ads.

Telling a Tide to Go TV Story in Print

Tom Neveril provides another example with a Tide to Go ad that engaged a mostly male Super Bowl audience. We can take this example and see how it tells a five-act dramatic story. Instead of explaining the features of the stain-removal product, the ad "Talking Stain" told the story of an older man interviewing a younger man with a coffee stain on his white dress shirt (Act 1 Exposition and Act 2 Complication). The nervous interviewee talks up his organizational skills, but the stain outshouts him and distracts the interviewer (Act 3 Climax). The product is superimposed over the image with "Silence the stain, instantly" (Act 4 Reversal). The product erases and silences the stain, ending with a call to action to visit Talkingstain. com (Act 5 Denouement).[18]

On the website landing page, the story continued. The audience was invited to tell their own Tide to Go story with a chance for their talking stain ad to air on prime time TV. Some of the users submitted stories, which included "First Date," "Cop Pulling Over a Motorist," and "Man Taking to a Girl in a Bar."[19] These stories are relatable to the audience but also convey the product features of easy stain removal in a small package that's ready for any moment.

Super Bowl ads are known for their elaborate movie-like productions. How would a "Talking Stain" print ad tell this story? First, brainstorm a list of important moments a stain could ruin, such as a job interview, a first date, or asking a father permission to marry his daughter. The last situation is a big moment that stimulates emotions. A lot is riding on it! How could you tell this story in print around the big idea for the Tide to Go IMC campaign?

Imagine a photo of a young man dressed to impress sitting at a table with an older gray-haired man. The younger man is visibly nervous talking to the older man. Instead of looking directly back, his gaze is focused on a stain on the young man's shirt. A headline by the young man's mouth reads "I promise to take care of your daughter. Do I have your blessing?" Another is down by the stain and reads, "This guy can't take care of his shirt! How will he take care of her?" The subhead "Silence the Stain" is at the bottom with a product picture and body copy explaining the product features. Do you see how this combination of visuals and words tells a complete story in a print ad?

The Tide to Go campaign told relatable stain story moments such as this one, not just product features. Getty Images: Chip Somons.

Research has found that ads with images showing stories the target audience is familiar with attracted their attention and were easier to understand. When the images and words told the same familiar narratives, they experienced what the researchers call imagery fluency. Not only does this attract attention, but consumers experiencing imagery fluency are also likely to attribute that feeling to liking the ad. That feeling of liking the ad is then transferred to the evaluation of the product.[20]

7.3 Brand Stories in Magazines

Magazines are good at reaching target audiences via niche interests. Would your target audience be more likely to read *AARP, Seventeen,* or *American Baby*? Would they enjoy *Golf Digest, Runner's World,* or *Field & Stream*? Do they read *Country Living, Cosmopolitan,* or *Backpacker*? How about *National Grocer, Amusement Business,* or *Medical Product Manufacturing News*? Whatever your target audience, business-to-consumer or business-to-business, there is likely a magazine that piques their interest. Magazine readership also goes beyond subscribers. Each copy is passed along to an average of six readers per copy.[21]

Writing to the Verbal Components of Magazine Ads

Once you find a story about your audience and make it relevant to the product, there are key concepts, components, and practices to best tell that story in print. First, you must understand the key elements of most print ads: headline, main visual, subhead, product shot, body copy, call to action, logo, and tagline. The **headline** is the part of an ad designed to attract the reader's attention.[22] The headline works with the **main visual**, which is the photograph, illustration, or graphic in an ad used to gain audience interest.

Your headline and main visual should work together. Neither one should tell the complete story on its own. The reader should get part of the story from the visual and the rest in the headline or part of the story from the headline and the rest in the visual. This makes the ad more intriguing and engaging.

Former creative director Jim Aitchinson recommends a "bent" headline with a "straight" picture or a "straight" headline with a "bent" picture. Aitchinson explains:

> If the idea in the ad is being carried by the headline, it means the headline will contain a twist, a trick, a turn, a shock factor, it will be "bent." Therefore, the accompanying visual must play a subservient or "straight" role. If the idea in the ad is being carried by some creative twist in the picture, the picture will be "bent." Therefore, the headline must be absolutely "straight."[23]

A Tide to Go print ad with a headline "Gets stains out on the go" with a main visual of the product erasing a stain isn't very attention getting. The image is "straight," the visual is "straight," and each one completes the story on its own. Compare that to the engaging story told in our Tide to Go print ad example. The "straight" picture of a young man asking a father permission to marry his daughter tells part of the story. The stain shouting, "This guy can't take care of his shirt! How will he take care of her?" is the "bent" headline.

Another element of print ads is subheads. A **subhead** conveys specific details about the product while guiding the reader's attention to the body copy.[24] The "Silence the Stain" subheading in the Tide to Go print ad helps the audience understand how the product relates to the story and invites them to learn more in the body copy. **Body copy** is the main text of an ad, which provides more detailed information, such as product features.[25]

Print ads often have a photo of the package. A **pack shot (or product shot)** is a close-up photo or video showing a product and its package.[26] Pack shots can further convey main product features visually. A Tide to Go product shot would visually show how the size of the package makes it easily carried so you're prepared to erase a stain at any moment. A product shot also provides a visual cue to recognize it on a store shelf at the point of purchase.

Product shots in print, TV, and digital ads convey product benefits and provide visual cues for purchase. Getty Images: ATU Images.

An important part of print ads today is a **call to action (CTA)**, which is the next step a marketer wants the audience to take and how.[27] With more emphasis on the measurement of return on investment, most print ads must include a CTA. CTAs should tell the reader what to do and where to do it, such as "Visit Talkingstain.com to create your own Silence the Stain story, and your ad could air on prime time TV." This wasn't the generic Tide.com homepage. It was a custom website created specifically for the IMC campaign that made it more measurable.

The final components of a print ad are the logo and tagline. Logos and taglines provide consistency in IMC campaigns and help aid ad recall. A **logo** is a graphic design element used as a consistent symbol for a company, organization, or brand.[28] A **tagline (or slogan)** summarizes the main idea of a marketing campaign in a few memorable words.[29] If a brand runs the same tagline for a long time, it could become a catchphrase, such as Nike's "Just Do It." A **catchphrase** is a phrase often repeated and connected to a particular organization or business.[30]

Copywriters and art directors work in unison to create print ads. They come up with the main concepts and stories together. Then, the copywriter focuses on verbal components, and the art director focuses on visual components. A way to represent the verbal components of a print ad is a copy sheet (see Figure 7.1). The print ad copy template worksheet is like the TV and radio script template worksheets but focuses only on static image descriptions and words (not motion or sound).

For body copy, consider the personality, style, and tone of the brand found in the "What is the personality style and tone?" section of the creative brief. Is the brand funny versus serious, formal versus casual, respectful versus irreverent, or enthusiastic versus matter of fact? Write copy as a person with the brand personality talking to another person. Advertising copy should be conversational and not formal. Basic grammar and punctuation apply, yet more naturally sounding conversational copy is better than following all the grammar rules.

When Apple launched its tagline "Think Different," English teachers complained that it wasn't grammatically correct, saying it should be "Think Differently." Yet the grammatically correct version doesn't sound conversational.[31]

The standard format for body copy consists of an introduction, detailed paragraphs, and a conclusion. The lead-in paragraph connects the headline/subhead to the rest of the copy, piquing reader interest. The interior paragraphs stress the main features and benefits, detailing support facts from the creative brief. But don't simply list them. Craft product features seamlessly into an engaging story focused on the audience's point of view. The last paragraph pulls the ad together and invites the reader to action.

A classic example of standard copy format is the 1960s "Lemon" ad for the VW Beetle from DDB written by copywriter Julian Koenig and art directed by Helmet Krone. The visual for the ad is a close-up picture of the VW Beetle on a white background. After looking at the "straight" visual, the reader sees the "bent" headline "Lemon," followed by the body copy:

This Volkswagen missed the boat.

The chrome strip on the glove compartment is blemished and must be replaced. Chances are you wouldn't have noticed it; Inspector Kurt Kroner did. There are 3,389 men at our Wolfsburg factory with only one job: to inspect Volkswagens at each stage of production. (3,000 Volkswagens are produced daily; there are more inspectors than cars.)

Every shock absorber is tested (spot checking won't do), every windshield is scanned. VWs have been rejected for surface scratches barely visible to the eye.

Final inspection is really something! VW inspectors run each car off the line onto the Funktionsprüfstand (car test stand), tote up 189 check points, gun ahead to the automatic brake stand, and say "no" to one VW out of fifty.

This preoccupation with detail means the VW lasts longer and requires less maintenance, by and large, than other cars. (It also means a used VW depreciates less than any other car.)

We pluck the lemons; you get the plums.[32]

The first paragraph of this VW Beetle ad bridges the headline to the body copy, offering some explanation but not telling the whole story to invite further reading. The interior paragraphs take car features and weave them into the overall story. The conclusion paragraph is the call to action. The VW logo lets the readers know where to buy their plum. The Beetle print ad "Lemon" also demonstrates the five-act story form. This print ad of seven paragraphs and 165 words contains all five story acts, as can be seen in Table 7.1.

Creating the Visual Components of Magazine Ads

While the copywriter crafts the words, the art director crafts the ad layout. A **layout** indicates where the component parts of an ad such as image, headline, subhead, body copy, and logo are to be placed.[33] Layouts are planned through roughs to get ads ready to present to internal audiences, such as the creative director and account executives and then the external marketing client. A **rough (or thumbnail)** is a preliminary sketch of an ad layout.[34]

Art directors use thumbnails to brainstorm various options for ad design. A thumbnail is a small version of a rough layout, about the size of a thumbnail, so options can be drawn quickly. This is helpful when searching for the new page. The challenge is taking the same old elements within the same shape and creating something new in every campaign.[35]

Thumbnails are narrowed down to the most promising designs, which are then drawn in more detailed roughs closer to the actual ad size. The average full-page print ad in magazines is roughly 8 inches by 10 inches. Often, just the main headline, subhead, visual, and tagline are written and drawn to convey print ad ideas. In rough layouts, the body copy is typically represented with wavy lines. The actual print copy is presented on the copy sheet (Figure 7.1). See Figure 7.2 for an example of thumbnails and a rough layout for a print ad.

Once the concept, copy, and rough layouts are approved, art directors begin designing layouts to get the ready to run. This begins with more design on the computer using typography and photography considering additional design concepts and practices such as typography. **Typography** is using type and its principles to arrange text in a visually appealing way that best conveys a message.[36]

Typefaces should be selected that emphasize the message and brand voice. Serif type, such as Times New Roman, Garamond, and Goudy, is more traditional, whereas sans serif type, such as Helvetica, Gill Sans, and Arial, is more modern. Script typefaces are formal, whereas cursive looks personal. Novelty fonts convey specific concepts mimicking comic, computer, or scary type. Sometimes, brands will have designated or even customized typefaces you'll be required to use.

Figure 7.1. Print copy template worksheet.

Brand: _____ **Product:** _____

Title: _____

VISUAL: (Describe the image and look for the ad)

HEADLINE: *(Attracts attention)*

SUBHEAD: *(Details and lead into body copy)*

COPY: (Body copy story, sell and call to action)

LOGO: (Company or product logo)

TAGLINE: (Campaign line)

MANDATORIES: (Legal copy, copyright, address, social media icons, etc.)

Table 7.1. VW Lemon Ad Applied to Freytag's Story Framework

Story Act	Elements of Story Act Development
Act 1 Exposition Characters, setting, basic conflict are established leading to tension. An inciting moment begins rising action of complications.	Time and place and the main character hero or protagonist is set as a single car image, not on a road. Next, the headline "Lemon" is read. This is the inciting moment. The term lemon refers to new cars that have substantial defects. What was thought to be a car company boasting about their car is put into question, causing conflict and rising action.
Act 2 Complication Tension mounts as the main character's efforts to reach a goal meets conflicts with obstacles. Frustration builds as opposing forces intensify.	The story becomes more complex and advances as the reader discovers that this Volkswagen missed the boat. A chrome strip had a blemish that must be repaired. Obstacles frustrate the protagonist's (the Beetle's) goal to reach the United States and the road.
Act 3 Climax Conflict reaches a high turning point that could lead to victory or defeat for the main character, resulting in good or bad consequences.	The conflict reaches a high point. The antagonist is revealed with the introduction of inspector Kurt Kroner, who noticed the blemish and stopped this car from leaving the factory. This is the turning point for the car that led to a change for the worse—being held back from boarding the boat.
Act 4 Reversal Events play out in falling actions from the reversal in the climax. Momentum slows as the characters head toward a final resolution.	The falling action happens as it is revealed that there are 3,389 inspectors, checking 3,000 VWs a day. The details of the inspections reveal how tough it is for a VW to get through these tests. The conflict between the protagonist and antagonist unravels as we see the obstacles this Beetle faced only to get the final no, which kept it from leaving the factory.
Act 5 Denouement Conflict is resolved and tension is released, creating normalcy. Comedy ends with the main character better off and tragedy being worse off.	The final act is when the conflict is resolved, creating new normalcy for the characters and a sense of release of tension and anxiety. It is explained that the inspector's preoccupation with detail means the cars that make it through last longer, require less maintenance, and depreciate less. Even though this is a tragedy for this Beetle, it means that the consumer is the ultimate winner because the inspectors pluck the lemons.

Figure 7.2. Example thumbnails and rough layouts for ads help art directors plan out the best visual way to tell the brand story.

Getty Images: Martiana Vaculikova.

In a layout limit typefaces to one or two because too many can look cluttered and confusing. Stick to type choices in a campaign for consistency. Left-aligned type is easiest to read and is best for body copy. Center-aligned type is hard to read in paragraphs but is good for calling attention to headlines and subheads.

Computers don't always adjust the space between letters, words, and lines well and must be finessed with kerning and line spacing. **Kerning** is the space between letters and words.[37] **Line spacing** is the space between lines of type. If letters or lines are too far apart, it is hard to tell if they are part of the same word or paragraph. If they are too close, they become hard to read.[38]

In designing the layout, consider contrast to distinguish between elements, and ensure the type over colors or images is legible. Avoid too many colors or bad color combinations

Figure 7.3. The rule of thirds grid helps turn amateur designers and photographers into professionals.

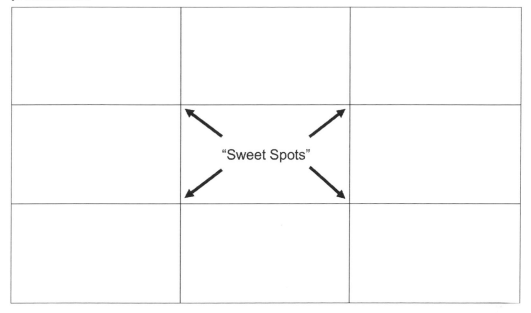

that may distract from the message and the brand's image.[39] Also, take into consideration the brand's design standards, including logos and brand colors.

Good design guides the viewer's eye across the page, letting them know what elements to look at and in what order. That is why headlines tend to be the biggest type in the top left or center of the page and logos and taglines are smaller at the bottom right. Create a visual hierarchy using size, placement, contrast, and white space to guide the reader to important elements.[40] **White space (negative space)** is the area found between design elements that enables them to stand out. However, white space does not have to be white. It can be any color, texture, pattern, or image that enhances communication and creates a hierarchy of elements.[41]

Good images and layouts also tend to follow the **rule of thirds**, which is a principle that divides an image or layout into thirds horizontally and vertically to place elements in an appealing, balanced way (see Figure 7.3). Most people place the subject of an image or layout in the center. However, placing the subject in one of the intersecting points, or "sweet spots," creates a more dynamic, natural, and interesting image or layout.[42]

7.4 Brand Stories in Newspapers and Out-of-Home Advertising

Next, we will focus on telling local stories through newspapers and out-of-home advertising. These types of media are unique in that they are very specific to local communities whether through a news publication with a regional circulation focused on community news or physical advertising placement seen only in that region. It is probably no surprise that many of the newspaper and out-of-home ads you see tend to be for local businesses, events, or national businesses with local store locations.

The Unique Strengths of Newspaper Ads

As we saw with magazines, print circulations of newspapers have declined significantly in the past couple of decades. Subscribers have been on a decline since the 2000s with website audience traffic increasing. In 2020, the estimated US daily newspaper circulation print and digital combined was 24.3 million for weekdays and 25.8 million for Sundays. While print circulations declined 19 percent for daily and 14 percent for Sunday during the COVID-19 pandemic, newspaper digital circulations increased 27 percent for weekdays and 26 percent for Sunday. Unique visitors to newspaper websites were up 14 percent.[43]

Like magazines, more than just subscribers see each edition. Newspaper subscribers will pass along the paper to an average of two other people. Many readers turn to newspapers intentionally to view ads because they often feature special sales, promotions, and coupons. In fact, 65 percent of adults say newspaper ads are influential in making purchase decisions.[44]

Despite the shift to digital and social media consumption, newspapers remain a strategic option in the media mix for IMC plans. Besides a few national newspapers such as the *New York Times*, the *Washington Post*, the *Wall Street Journal*, and *USA Today*, most focus on local communities. Newspapers with local newsrooms are the main source for community news. Many have gone beyond the printed page to deliver the local news through an integrated mix of print, website, and mobile. No matter the format, 90 percent of readers say their community newspaper keeps them informed.[45]

Newspapers are especially useful for the promotion of products and services with a local focus. This can be a local or regional business or a national company with local offices, stores, sales representatives, or events. Newspapers are good at reaching target audiences by location

Magazines target interests, while newspapers target local communities to serve a unique strategic role in an IMC plan. Getty Images: Hyeoncheol Gim.

and for fostering a sense of local community. Often, a newspaper media buy includes a combination of ads in the newspaper's print, website, and mobile forms for greater reach.

As an example, *The Philadelphia Inquirer* reports that its average weekly reach across the greater Philadelphia region is 1.8 million—higher than the 1.5 million reach for the local ABC TV affiliate. Its two print newspapers, *The Inquirer* and *Daily News*, reach 1.9 million monthly readers, and its digital newspaper, Philly.com, reaches 1.8 million monthly readers on desktop and 5.1 million on mobile.[46] This is an attractive medium for local businesses such as Chickie's and Pete's, Geno's Steaks, and ACME supermarkets. It's also a great medium for national chains such as Macy's to advertise sales at its local locations.

Newspaper ads tend to be good for local promotions, events, coupons, and sales, especially around holidays. Many people purchase the Sunday paper for the coupon inserts. They may also purchase a paper to look for sales during holiday weekends and Black Friday. **Coupons** are printed certificates offering price reductions for specific products for a specific period.[47] The main form of sales and coupon placements in newspapers is **free standing inserts (FSIs)**, which are loose papers, which contain ads or coupons, often in color, added separately to a newspaper.

Roughly 90 percent of coupons are distributed through FSIs, mostly through Sunday newspapers.[48] Because of its focus on local sales, newspaper advertising is also known as retail advertising. **Retail advertising** is local stores or merchants advertising national brands using sale ads in local media to entice customers to visit stores.[49]

Newspapers are also a good medium to place **cooperative advertising (co-op advertising)**, which is when national manufacturers partially pay for local ads placed by retail stores that feature their product.[50] Examples of co-op ads include a brand such as Under Armour partially paying for a Dick's Sporting Goods FSI to be the featured brand in the circular. An ice cream brand may pay to supplement newspaper costs for a local grocery store to feature its ice cream in a weekly sales ad.

Other forms of co-op ads include authorized resellers of certain services such as Verizon Mobile or local car dealers. Sometimes, a national brand such as Ford will create newspaper ad templates that dealers can customize with their local information to run in the newspaper. Other co-op ads may be more national partnerships such as McDonald's ads advertising Coca-Cola products or Dell Computer ads with "Intel Inside" promoting Intel computer chips.

There are special considerations for newspaper ad design. Despite the availability of color, most newspaper ads are black and white. Color ads don't reproduce well and are considerably more expensive. Unlike the fairly consistent size of full-page magazine ads, newspaper ads come in more varied sizes, ranging from very big 10 inch by 21 inch full-page ads to a small space 3.25 inch by 4 inch 1⁄16th-page ads. The quality of newsprint is not as high as glossy magazines. Ink tends to bleed, making images less crisp and smaller, thinner typefaces can disappear. Art directors should use larger, thicker, and bolder typefaces.

Avoiding clutter is good for any print ad, but in newspapers, it is especially important. Most ads will be placed on the large page with articles and other ads around it. Too much clutter will force the reader's eyes away. A nice, simple layout with a focused image, message, and call to action that uses white or negative space will stand out. Also, don't forget that many print readers have smartphones. Send them to a mobile app, a custom landing page, and brand social media with a call to action and URL or QR code to add an engaging digital component.

The Big Presence of Out-of-Home Ads

Another form of advertising that is especially effective for local targeting is out of home. **Out-of-home (OOH) advertising** is any advertising media found outside of the home but not inside a store.[51] Out-of-home ads appear outside in a community. Like radio and newspaper, they are often used for local businesses, national brands with local stores, and advertising local events. Most out-of-home ads are big and hard to ignore. You can't skip them, and people commuting to work will see them many times for high frequency. The most common forms of OOH ads include the following:

- Billboards (digital or traditional)
- Subway, train, and bus exterior posters and wraps
- Subway, train, and bus interior signage
- Street "furniture," such as park benches, bus stops, and kiosks
- Wall murals
- Moving billboards[52]

OOH ads attract attention but also drive action. Research indicates that 46 percent of adults searched online for a brand or product they first saw in an OOH ad. Consumers are also 48 percent more likely to click on a mobile ad after seeing the brand in OOH first.[53] Some of the best OOH ads are the ones people want to share. A creative billboard or bus shelter poster can cause people to take pictures to share with friends and others via social media.

A clever billboard or transit ad can "go viral." One in four people in the United States has posted a picture of themselves with an out-of-home ad to their social media.[54] The streaming music company Spotify created a sharable outdoor campaign when it customized billboards for specific zip codes and neighborhoods based on actual listener data. One in a Brooklyn neighborhood said, "Sorry, Not Sorry Williamsburg. Bieber's hit trended highest in this zip cod."[55]

Before creating an OOH ad, research the competition and location of placements. The best will not only be different from the competition in message and look but can also play off competitor boards. A high-profile unique placement could take a competitor's message nearby and create a playful, engaging moment for the target audience. Imagine a billboard for a local restaurant that says, "Best Wings in Town." A competitor's restaurant could place an OOH ad on the next or nearby billboard with the message "They haven't tried our wings."

Messages and images related to physical surroundings grab attention and are often more memorable.[56] Consider a billboard for headache medicine Anacin above the Lincoln Tunnel in New York City—one of the most congested commuter highways in the country. Then, when you come out of the tunnel but are still stuck in traffic, a billboard for a condominium in Hoboken, New Jersey, saying "If you lived here, you'd be home" is very effective.

Because OOH is locally focused, try to create messages that tell a unique story tied to the community. A Nike billboard in Atlanta could add a local spin with "Just Do It, Y'all." In Pittsburgh, it could be "Just Do It, Yinz." In Minneapolis, you might use "Just Do It, Dooncha Know." And in Southern California, it might say "Like, Just Do It."

Along highways, billboards are also good at providing directions. Restaurants and hotels will run a billboard a couple of miles away and tell motorists to take the next exit for a good night's sleep or a comforting meal.

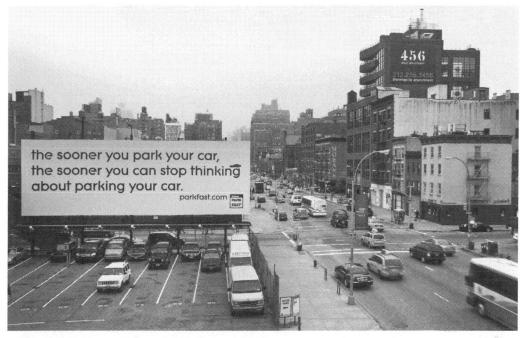

Billboards grab attention via placement and messages to local audiences that can make a big impact. Getty Images: Atlantide Phototravel.

Design for billboards is unique in that the placements are large, but the design must be simple with larger type because placements could have people driving past them at 65 miles per hour. The verbal and visual message must be clear and uncluttered. Promote one thing and focus on a single call to action. Be sure headlines, logos, and calls to actions, such as URLs, phone numbers, hashtags, or addresses, are easy to remember and large enough to see.

Keep OOH designs simple with fewer elements and make them legible. Avoid clutter and complex design elements. Avoid script typefaces for large, bold typefaces. Aim for high contrast when using images and colors.[57] Research indicates that ads with two message elements are 21 percent more likely to be noticed than ads with five message elements.[58]

When viewing a rough layout for a billboard, don't look at it close up like you would a magazine ad. Hang it on a wall on the other side of the room to represent how it will most likely be seen. A best practice is to limit messages to seven words or less. The exception is airports, train stations, subways, and bus stops where people are waiting or riding and have an opportunity to read more.[59] Either way, make it interesting. Most people carry smartphones with them everywhere they go, and 46 percent look up information after seeing something that interests them on an OOH ad.[60]

Sizes for OOH vary even more than those for newspapers. Standard highway billboards, whether digital or printed vinyl, are roughly 14 feet by 48 feet. Smaller billboard posters along smaller roadways are typically 12 feet by 24 feet. Junior posters often appear in downtown areas of cities and are 5 feet by 11 feet. Bus shelters are 69 inches by 46 inches. King-size bus posters are 30 inches by 143 inches. Besides standard posters on the sides and back or front of buses, bus wraps can make a big impact when the entire bus is wrapped in the ad.[61]

7.5 CASE

Chick-fil-A's Cows

Billboards don't have to be flat and can be creative with different shapes and three-dimensional options. When the fast-food restaurant chain Chick-fil-A was a much smaller regional food chain with a tighter marketing budget, it focused its advertising spending on billboards near local restaurant locations. To make the billboards stand out, its ad agency The Richards Group (TRG) developed a concept simple enough for a billboard but conceptual enough to tell an engaging story.

First, the agency did its research. Most fast-food restaurant billboards have a big picture of their food and a nicely designed typeface headline and logo. Being that most fast-food restaurants build their menu around hamburgers, the big food picture is typically a burger. With that in mind, imagine seeing something completely different.

You are driving down the road and notice a simple white billboard. There is no picture of a burger but some hand-painted–looking type, still dripping ink, which misspells "EAT MOR CHICKIN." By the time you read this, you notice real-sized, three-dimensional cows standing up there with one on the back of the other just finishing painting the "N" with a brush. Then in bright red, you see the Chick-fil-A logo, which has an illustrated chicken head as part of the "C."

In just three words, an image, and a logo, you just got a complete five-act story. You may still be processing it while you're driving down the road, but that is even better for full immersion in the brand story. You were still thinking about the brand long after you passed the billboard. In your head, you have to piece the story together to close the gaps. The billboard was a piece of a complete story, and the fun is in figuring out how and why the cows are up there.

Act 1 exposition introduces cows on a billboard as cows and not burgers. They've grazed below burger fast-food restaurant billboards long enough. They're taking action into their own hands, or hooves, causing tension and the inciting moment. Act 2 Complication and Act 3 Climax happen with the cows high off the ground with one balancing on the other. Will they fall and fail? Or will they succeed? Act 4 Reversal is seeing that they just completed the message and have overcome the obstacles. Act 5 Denouement is seeing the Chick-fil-A logo as the solution, releasing the tension for the cows. All is fine for our hero cows if you go to Chick-fil-A.

This billboard is a complete story, but also consider how the billboard first attracted your attention because it is fascinating and familiar. You have seen plenty of billboards in your life and have also probably seen plenty of cows. But the cows are usually in the field below the billboards and not up on them. The visual was "bent," and the line was a "straight" call to action. The ad agency proofreader probably tried to correct the spelling of the headline on the copy sheet, but the copywriter knew the misspelling was purposeful to the concept. How many cows did you have in your English classes in school?

Chick-fil-A first introduced the Cow campaign in 1995 as a three-dimensional billboard concept. What began as an economical and strategic media choice soon became "spokecritters" for the brand. In addition to clever roadside billboards, the "Eat Mor Chikin" cows are the focal point of Chick-fil-A's in-store point-of-purchase materials, promotions, radio and TV advertising, clothing, and merchandise sales.[62]

These billboards leverage a unique selling point and tell an entertaining story—the heroic story of renegade cows taking over billboards to encourage motorists to visit Chick-fil-A instead of burger-oriented fast-food restaurants.[63] When The Richards Group introduced the Chick-fil-A cows billboard campaign and the "Eat Mor Chikin" tagline in 1995, it helped to more than double Chick-fil-A's same-store sales. The continuation of the campaign for more than 20 years helped turn the regional chicken restaurant into one of the largest US restaurant chains with more than $6 billion in sales and over 2,000 locations in 43 states.[64] That is an IMC campaign concept delivering real business marketing results with a sales cure art director Helmet Krone would admire and exponential return on creativity Bill Bernbach would applaud.

This chapter has explored how to continue IMC campaign storytelling in the advertising media of magazine, newspaper, and out-of-home ads. These print media can be powerful storytellers. Take what we've learned about consumer insight and storytelling and combine that with best practices for crafting the verbal and visual messages in each unique print medium. In addition, we learned how many of these traditional media are taking digital media forms and driving measurable digital actions. Remember that IMC campaigns leverage multiple media to tell a more complete story. In the next chapter of our brand storytelling journey, we'll explore more media vehicles and marketing disciplines to tell brand stories in direct, digital, and experiential marketing.

QUESTIONS

1. Mary Wells Lawrence encourages us to "read books on subjects you know nothing about ... travel to places you never thought of traveling ... meet every kind of person ... endlessly stretch what you know."[65] With today's social media thought bubbles or echo chambers, how well do you think you are doing in gathering diverse perspectives for general raw material in the first step creative process that we learned in chapter 5?
2. Have you written off traditional media, such as magazines and newspapers? Are they making a comeback in their traditional print forms? Find the latest data. How have magazines and newspapers evolved to be relevant in new digital ways beyond traditional print?

EXERCISES

1. This chapter focused on the partnership between research, strategy, verbal, and visual creativity. Which of these do you feel that you are best suited for? Depending on your role in a business or organization, you may be called to do all, some, or just one. Either way, it is best to learn how to do each job and understand what makes good research, good insights, good writing, and good design whether you are the one doing it or not. Further explore key roles in marketing communications, such as marketing managers, market researchers, account planners, account executives, copywriters, and art directors. Read job descriptions, responsibilities, and qualifications, then match your skills and interests to one or two you want to pursue.

2. This chapter featured many examples in an 80-year-old time span from VW "Lemon" in 1960 to today's Chick-fil-A "Eat Mor Chikin." What are the common elements of all the examples of ads mentioned in this chapter throughout the decades? Even with the advancements in technology, there are basic elements that make IMC campaigns and the individual ads in those campaigns creative and effective. How would you sum up the keys to success across the decades?

KEY CONCEPTS

Body copy

Call to action (CTA)

Catchphrase

Cooperative advertising (co-op advertising)

Coupons

Free-standing inserts (FSIs)

Headline

Kerning

Layout

Line spacing

Logo

Main visual

Out-of-home (OOH) advertising

Pack shot (or product shot)

Retail advertising

Rough (or thumbnail)

Rule of thirds

Subhead

Tagline (or slogan)

Theory of new page

Typography

White space (negative space)

Connecting with the Audience

Direct, Digital, and Experiential Marketing

PREVIEW

Our journey in brand storytelling moves on with the origins of direct consumer marketing in the 1960s to the origins of customer relationship marketing in the 2010s. Social media expert Jay Baer connects story to social and digital marketing saying, "If your stories are all about your products and services, that's not storytelling. It's a brochure. Give yourself permission to make the story bigger."[1] In this chapter, we'll learn various forms and practices of direct marketing, the newer practice of digital marketing, and the latest practice of experiential marketing. We'll also look at the future of Web3 with NFTs, cryptocurrency, and the metaverse. Our case study describes a Taco Bell campaign that leveraged direct, digital, and experiential marketing through the power of story.

CHAPTER 8 LEARNING OBJECTIVES

1. Discover the origins of direct marketing and its current digital forms.
2. Know how to create effective direct marketing with stories.
3. Understand how to utilize digital marketing with a story approach.
4. Learn to leverage experiential marketing through storytelling.

8.1 Wunderman's Direct Marketing and Baer's Youtility

We have touched on the main forms of traditional advertising media of TV, radio, print, and out of home. In this chapter, we will discuss the practice of direct marketing that relied on traditional media but quickly embraced new technologies. We will also look at the newer practice of digital marketing and explore experiential marketing. To begin, we will look at two influential figures in the development of direct and digital.

Lester Wunderman Developed Direct Marketing in the Last Century

Lester Wunderman is an American Advertising Federation Hall of Fame marketer known as the father of direct marketing. He founded his direct marketing agency Wunderman, Ricotta & Kline in 1958 out of a hotel room. By the time he stepped down as chairman, Wunderman Cato Johnson had 65 offices in 39 countries with annual billings of $1.8 billion.[2]

Wunderman utilized techniques that sent personalized ads to preselected people for products and services they might want versus the broad approach of advertising to a general audience in mass media. Long before internet sales and interactive communication, Wunderman understood the power of data, communications, and personalization.[3]

Wunderman's direct marketing agency was an innovator in the use of databases to identify likely customers and to reach them at home with mailings, promotional letters, phone calls, and newspaper and magazine inserts. He first developed direct techniques still used today such as toll-free telephone numbers, postage-paid subscription cards, buy-one-get-one-free offers, and loyalty rewards programs. Each technique produced dramatic sales results for the agency's clients compared to the general advertising techniques of the era.[4]

Wunderman's tactics changed with technology, but the essence of his strategy remained the same. Know a product's consumers and reach them at the right place with the right message at the right time. He insisted that businesses collect detailed information on their audiences and target ads specifically to them.[5] This philosophy led to the modern practice of **customer relationship management (CRM)**, which combines database computer technology with customer service and marketing communications to provide meaningful one-on-one communications with customers.[6]

In 2010, Wunderman predicted, "We're in the death-knell of one-way conversations and the birth of the dialog system of marketing. The secret of the future is to listen to the customer, not to talk to him."[7] Today, his agency, Wunderman Thompson, continues to create targeted, personalized, and meaningful direct marketing through CRM, apps, and experiential marketing.[8]

A recent example of Wunderman Thompson's targeted ads was a campaign for Hellmann's mayonnaise that told the story of food waste. The average American family of four wastes $1,600 of food every year. The agency and its client discovered that most people waste food because they don't see the possibilities of the food they have in their refrigerator. They used experiential digital billboards combined with social media direct messages to target America's worst city for food waste—New York.[9]

Across the city, images of fridges appeared in digital out-of-home ads filled with the most wasted ingredients. For a bigger experience, a massive fridge was placed in Times Square. All ads delivered the headline "There's more in your fridge than you think" with the hashtag tagline "#MoreTasteNotWaste." Each ad also included a note in the fridge with the ingredients that said "Congrats for seeing more in the fridge. DM 'Seeing more' to @hellmannsmayonnaise on Instagram for a chance to win $1,600." For the first time, the agency bragged that no one responded to one of its ads. Of over 4 million people who saw the ads, zero found the message about winning $1,600 proving the point about overlooked food waste.[10]

Jay Baer Created the Concept of Youtility for This Century

Jay Baer is an author and speaker who heads the content marketing and social media strategy consulting firm Convince & Convert. One of the core concepts he has built his businesses and consulting upon is Youtility, which was first introduced in his book of the same name.

In Chapter 3, we learned that marketing should be customer centric, focusing on understanding your most valuable customers and delivering the most value to them. Youtility is about delivering value to attract your most valuable customers. Baer explains, "the difference between helping and selling is just two letters. Focus on help, not hype."[11] Trying to make your products more exciting is **hype**, which is extravagant or intensive publicity or promotion.[12] **Help** is making it easier for someone to do something by giving them something they need.[13]

Hype is hard because you're competing against everything else being hyped online, from movies to memes to TikTok videos to trending news. Help is easier. Customers have problems and are seeking solutions. To gain their attention, provide help by offering **Youtility**—marketing that is so useful that people would pay for it.[14]

There is another outcome of offering content that people would pay for but not charging them for it. Every day, people are bombarded with thousands of messages trying to sell them something. Finding something valuable for free is completely unexpected. Unexpected value evokes emotion. Evoking emotion increases the desire to share.

Research has found content that evokes emotions is more likely to be shared.[15] Stories that evoke happiness create more comments and stories that inspire more sharing. And the most viral content, which spreads quickly on the internet, tends to be surprising.[16] Delivering more than they expect for nothing is surprising—this creates joy and happiness at being helped and a story worth sharing, which generates word-of-mouth marketing.

People don't respond to rational arguments alone. Content that evokes happiness is more likely to be shared. Getty Images: LWA/Dann Tardif.

8.2 Brand Stories with Direct Marketing

We've already gotten a taste of direct marketing from Lester Wunderman's story and how his agency's practice of direct marketing evolved with the changes in technology and media from the 1950s to when he stepped down in the 1990s. How has the disciplined advanced? First, let's start with some definitions. **Direct marketing**, also known as direct response advertising, is using one or more forms of media, such as mail, email, and phone, to solicit a direct response from a customer making a purchase.[17]

Direct marketers use media to sell to customers utilizing databases to identify potential and existing customers and to customize messages and offers to those very customers. **Database marketing** is using computer databases to design, create, and manage customer data lists for locating, selecting, targeting, servicing, and establishing relationships with customers to enhance long-term value.[18] The main forms of direct marketing media today include the following:

- Direct mail
- Email marketing
- Telemarketing
- Infomercial
- Magazine
- Online ads

Despite being called "junk mail," direct mail is still one of the most popular forms of direct marketing. Average response rates for internal direct mail lists are 9 percent and for external lists, nearly 5 percent, while average email response rates are under 2 percent.[19] Consumer trust in direct mail is higher (76 percent) than in other forms of marketing, including search ads (61 percent), social media ads (43 percent), and banner ads (39 percent).[20]

Direct Marketing Begins with Lists

Determining your direct mail list is an important first step. It is key to efficiency and effectiveness and determines the visual and verbal messages. Lester Wunderman emphasized telling the right story to the right people at the right time. You need all three to be effective. For example, a replacement window company may create a direct mail message that drafty old windows cause high heating and cooling bills. This is the right message. But if its mail list includes people living in new housing developments and apartments, then it will send the message to the wrong people at the wrong time.

There are three main types of direct marketing lists for use with mail or email. **Internal database lists** are lists of a company's qualified leads and current customers, also known as CRM lists. These are people who have inquired about a company's products, responded to other offers, received a free trial, are a frequent customer, or are a loyalty club member. People on these lists tend to have higher response rates because the company knows the most about them and they know about the company. Internal lists are free.[21] An example would be auto dealers sending messages to customers whose state inspections are about to expire.

Response lists are lists of people who have responded to another company's offers, belong to certain organizations, or have indicated special interests through subscriptions to

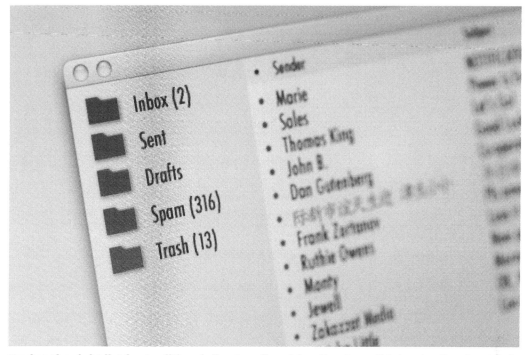

Having the right list for traditional direct mail and for direct email is key to direct marketing response. Getty Images: Epoxydude.

publications. Examples could be members of AARP (American Association of Retired Persons), subscribers to the *Wall Street Journal*, or customers of other companies such as Hilton Hotels.[22] These lists are the most expensive to purchase but can be rented to reduce the cost. On average, external lists can cost anywhere from .05 cents to .20 cents per name.[23]

Hilton Hotels would not sell its customer list to a competitor, such as another hotel chain, but may sell to travel-related businesses that its customers may find valuable, such as car rental companies, airlines, or luggage brands. The National Military Family Association may sell a list of its members to USAA (United Services Automobile Association), which is a company that offers insurance and financial services to US military members and their families.

Compiled lists are lists of people built from proprietary and publicly available data. They are less expensive than response lists and typically focus on targeting geographic areas or demographic characteristics. These lists are put together by companies obtained from telephone directories and government data, such as deed and property data, court records, and voter registration, and then combined with private data sources, such as credit card and survey companies.[24]

An example of a company that sells compiled lists is Experian. The company compiles consumer lists based on age, income, gender, marital status, homeownership, home value, and life stage or lifestyle. It also has specialty lists, such as high-income households, health enthusiasts, sports enthusiasts, and pet owners.[25]

Once you have your mailing or email list, you need to write and design the direct marketing content. Next, we will cover some of the key components and best practices for the main forms of direct marketing.

Direct Marketing Needs Compelling Offers

Most direct response advertising has an offer that can make a big difference in response. For example, all three of the following offers were tested in a campaign. Which one do you think produced the best results?

1. Half price!
2. Buy one, get one free.
3. 50 percent off![26]

The second option had a 40 percent higher response.[27] Despite these results, this does not mean all direct marketing offers should be buy one, get one free. The offer needs to be appropriate for the audience and product. Buy one, get one free for a tax filing service may not perform as well because you file your taxes only once a year. A marketer selling a high-ticket item such as a car probably cannot offer a 50 percent discount. But car marketers do offer special low-interest financing or specific dollar rebates.

Marketers must also be careful not to lower the perceived value of the product, service, or brand. Free attracts a lot of attention, but a huge response from people simply chasing free offers will not help build brand-loyal customers.[28]

These various types of offers are known as **sales promotions**, which are direct inducements that provide extra value or incentive for the product to create an immediate sale.[29] Sales incentives are used to lift sales temporarily, drive store or website traffic, clear out inventory, or generate a new product trial.[30] See Table 8.1 for common sales promotion offers used in direct marketing.

Table 8.1. Common Sales Promotion Offers Used in Direct Marketing

Product discounts typically offer a percentage off the price or reduce the price to a specific dollar amount for a limited time.	**Lifestyle discounts** provide discounts to certain types of customers, such as senior citizens, teachers, military, or full-time students.	**Holiday promotions** try to capture sales at times when consumers tend to spend more, such as Christmas, Halloween, or Valentine's Day.
Coupons are physically distributed printable pieces of paper or offer codes used to receive discounts.	**Flash sales** create a sense of urgency because they usually run for only one day or several hours.	**Bundles** encourage customers to try more of a company's products by selling them together for a discount.
BOGO is a buy one, get one offer to purchase one item at regular price and receive another free or at a discount.	**Giveaways** entice people to enter for a chance to win something, such as a gift or a trip.	**Free samples** are products offered in a small size or for a limited time and are often used to get people to try new products.
Loyalty programs invite customers to sign up to receive reward points for repeat purchases.	**Free shipping** can boost online sales for a certain time or for orders over a certain amount year-round.	**Free gift with purchase** entices customers to purchase more for a gift such as spending over $50 for a free bag.

Source: "Types of Sales Promotions (with Examples)," Indeed, April 1, 2021, https://www.indeed.com/career-advice/career-development/types-of-promotions.

How to Tell Stories in Direct Marketing

As we have learned throughout the book that the key to telling stories in any medium is understanding your audience and your brand and telling a complete story in five acts. How can you do this in a typical direct mail piece?

Let's say the marketing client wants to drive trial of a new product with a 30 percent off deal this weekend. A headline that simply says "30% Off This Weekend Only!" and a picture of the product communicate the offer but don't tell a story. Instead, consider Table 8.2, which uses common elements of a direct mail piece to convey the offer in a more engaging and emotionally memorable five-act story.

This story could also be told in a direct email to a list of men who have purchased Valentine's Day gifts in the past. This list could be purchased by the Napa Valley Wine client from a response or compiled list.

The Act 1 message would be the subject line of the email. The Act 2 headline would be in the email **preview pane**, which is the window in an email program where you can read part of an email without opening it.[31] The Act 3 headline, Act 4 call to action, and Act 5 P.S. could be sequential subheadings in the body of the email. When creating a direct marketing email, include the following essential elements.

1. *Sender Information:* Be strategic about the email address to make it look personal and credible, such as Jane@company.com.
2. *Subject Line:* Let the reader know what the email is about and entice them to open it.
3. *Preview:* Ensure the first lines of copy in the preview pane explain but also tease the content inside to further entice opening.
4. *Header:* The header is usually a visual representation of the brand logo and may include an image or call to action.
5. *Personalized Greeting:* Emails are digital letters, so make it personal with a customized salutation, such as "Dear John" versus "Dear customer," or no salutation at all.
6. *Body:* The main content uses short paragraphs, subheadings, images, and emphasis through bolding, color, and bullet points. A call to action links to a landing page.
7. *Footer:* The consistent information at the bottom includes company name, physical addresses, contact email for credibility, and unsubscribe link required by law.[32]

In all forms of direct marketing send customers to custom landing pages, not website homepages. This measures the effectiveness of different promotions and messages and is more effective in keeping customers on task for a response. A **landing page** is the web page a user is sent to after clicking on any link or call to action and should match closely with the previous message.[33]

8.3 Brand Stories with Digital Marketing

Digital marketing is the promotion of products and services to reach customers via digital media on computers and mobile devices.[34] Three related concepts include content marketing, native advertising, and sponsored content. **Content marketing**, also known as inbound

Table 8.2. A Sales Promotion Offer in a Five-Act Story Direct Mail

Story Act	Elements of Story Act Development
Act 1 Exposition Characters, setting, basic conflict are established leading to tension. An inciting moment begins rising action of complications.	**Outside Envelope: "Don't Disappoint Her This Valentine's Day."** This identifies the characters and setting and establishes the basic conflict while identifying the target audience.
Act 2 Complication Tension mounts as the main character's efforts to reach a goal meets conflicts with obstacles. Frustration builds as opposing forces intensify.	**Letter Headline: "Why give her overpriced flowers or chocolate that lasts just a day or two?"** This further explains the complication and increases tension highlighting obstacles to making her happy.
Act 3 Climax Conflict reaches a high turning point that could lead to victory or defeat for the main character resulting in good or bad consequences.	**Letter Subheading: "Show her your love lasts the entire year with a Napa Valley wine subscription."** This is the turning point as the potential solution to what to get this Valentine's Day.
Act 4 Reversal Events play out in falling actions from the reversal in the climax. Momentum slows as the characters head toward a final resolution.	**Call to Action: "Get a holiday 30% discount!"** After the solution is offered, the conflict of not knowing what to get her for Valentine's Day is pushed further toward resolution in a direct call to action special offer incentive.
Act 5 Denouement Conflict is resolved and tension is released creating normalcy. Comedy ends with the main character being better off and tragedy being worse off.	**P.S.: "Respond before January 31st to receive your first wine shipment by Valentine's Day with a free box of Ghirardelli chocolates!"** The P.S. removes any remaining doubt offering a box of chocolates with a sense of urgency to act now. Responding releases the tension as the conflict of the holiday is resolved.

marketing, is the publishing and distribution of text, video, or audio materials to consumers online.[35] Content marketing can include **native advertising**, which is the blending of marketing materials into a news media to provide valuable content but also a marketing message.[36] Related to this is **Sponsored content**, which is a popular form of native advertising where a brand writes an article and pays for it to appear on another website.

A survey of chief marketing officers reveals where they are investing their budgets to improve performance of digital marketing (see Figure 8.1). You can see that the company website is the most important. The second largest investment is digital media/search, which serves the purpose of driving traffic to the website.

Figure 8.1. Types of investments made to improve performance of digital marketing.

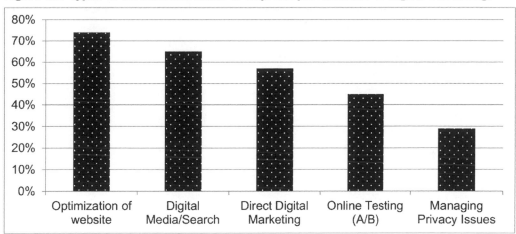

Source: Christine Moorman, CMO Survey. "Types of investments made to improve the performance of digital marketing according to CMOs in the United States in 2020." Chart. February 24, 2021. Statista. Accessed January 15, 2022. https://www-statista-com.ezproxy.messiah.edu/statistics/1223658/investments-digital-marketing-usa/.

Website Writing and Design Are Unique

For many businesses, the company website is the heart of its digital marketing. Good website writing and design understands target audience goals or their purpose for coming to the website. Good websites also communicate consistently in words and design. As we discussed for print ads, good design is important to create a visual hierarchy using size, placement, contrast, and white/negative space to guide the viewer to important elements.

Websites should follow brand guidelines with proper use of logos, fonts, and brand colors. Brand spokespeople or mascots and main images from brand advertising should be included for consistency. The tone and style of writing should be consistent with the brand personality or image. These should also support the creative concept verbal and visual message.

Easy navigation is important for websites. Fewer options, plain language, and using conventions such as "Home," "Contact," "About," and "Shop" make websites simpler to use. Establishing credibility is essential. Create trust with professional design, a prominent physical address, a phone number, an informative and personal about page, privacy policy, guarantee, and customer testimonials.

Calls to action are important and tend to perform better when they are designed as buttons. When creating forms to collect information, be sure to collect only the bare information needed. It is tempting to want to collect as much information as possible to build databases and lists, but too many requirements will reduce response.

When writing and designing a website, it is important to consider search marketing. **Search engine optimization (SEO)** is a process of improving website rankings on search engine results pages. SEO focuses on optimizing the website to appear higher in organic (vs. paid) search results. Typically, a digital marketing or SEO expert will perform keyword research and provide a list of keywords to be used for website pages. A **keyword** is a word or a combination of words, known as a key phrase, that people use in search queries.[37]

The keyword list is provided to the copywriter, who must use the keywords or key phrases regularly in the copy while still writing enjoyable copy that tells a story. The writer must be careful not to use too many keywords or use keywords unrelated to the content. Search engines can detect unrelated words or keyword stuffing and penalize the website's ranking.[38]

Best practices include using the keywords or phrases in page titles, headlines, subheads, and calls to action, plus highlighting or bolding them. Good copy design practices, such as bulleted lists, short paragraphs, and using images or graphics to break up information, also improve search results.

Search engines can't see images or graphs. Therefore, keywords must be placed in captions and alt text. **Alt text** is the alternative text used in HTML code to describe an image on a web page so it can be "seen" by a search engine. Keywords should also be written into meta-data descriptions. **Meta data** is information entered about a web page to provide context and information to search engines.[39]

Online Advertising Comes in Different Forms

Besides good website design, writing, and SEO, there are many forms of advertising used to drive traffic to websites. **Paid search advertising**, sometimes called pay per click (PPC), refers to paying for a website to appear on search results. These search result listings are designated with the word "AD" next to them. The advertiser doesn't pay for them to appear in results listings but must pay when a person clicks on the link.[40]

Search advertising is often called PPC, for pay-per-click advertising. PPC advertisers bid on keywords for their website to appear in results for relevant searches. More popular keywords require higher bids and higher costs per click. Because Google has over 83 percent of desktop search traffic, most PPC ads are placed through Google Advertising, followed by Bing Ads (Microsoft) and Yahoo Advertising (Verizon).[41] Google search ads have strict guidelines in the way that they must be written, with two-part headlines that are a maximum of 30 characters, a single description line that is a maximum of 80 characters, a display URL, and a type of ad extension.[42]

An important distinction to consider is that keywords for SEO often target noncustomers with nonbranded keywords. For example, a hotel may create content on its website optimized to "Seattle Waterfront Attractions" to capture the search of people considering a trip to Seattle. In its search ads, it may run a campaign for "luxury waterfront Seattle hotel" or "The W Seattle Waterfront," which would capture people further in the buyer's journey who have decided on the trip and are looking for a hotel or are previous customers looking specifically for the hotel brand name "W" in that location.[43]

Another popular form of online ads is **display advertising**, which is a graphic image, animation, or video displayed on a website, mobile app, or social network for advertising purposes.[44] Display ads are also called banner ads and can appear on desktop and mobile websites, in mobile apps, and on social media networks. Display ads are mostly bought through **display advertising networks**, which serve as an intermediary between advertisers and publishers. These networks hold an inventory of ads and then serve them to a network of publishers based on demographic, topic, interest, and remarketing lists.[45]

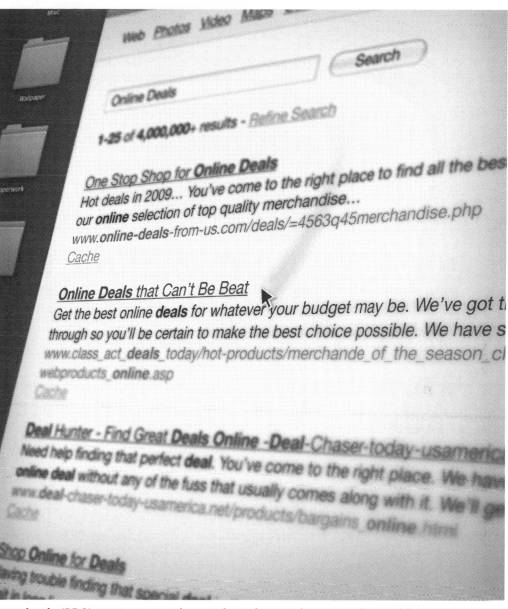

Search ads (PPC) pay to appear in search engine results pages along with unpaid organic results (SEO). Getty Images: SpiffyJ.

Top display advertising networks include Google AdSense, Facebook Audience Network, mMedia, Apple Advertising, Yahoo! Network, and Taboola.[46] Advertisers can also purchase display ads directly through high-profile publishers, such as *Sports Illustrated*, the *Wall Street Journal*, or The Weather Channel's website or app. Banner ads are the most common display ad but can take other forms, such as rich media, interstitial ads, and video. Table 8.3 describes common forms of display ads and key measurements marketers use to judge effectiveness.

Table 8.3. Key Forms and Measurements of Display Advertising

Types of Display Ads	Measurements of Display Ads
Banner ads are hyperlinked, image-based ads in the shape of a banner (horizontal rectangle) that appear at the top, middle, or bottom of websites or mobile apps, also sold as squares or vertical rectangles.	**Reach** is the number or percentage of people of a defined population exposed to a particular advertising media vehicle or media schedule during a specific time.
Rich media ads look like traditional banner ads but add interactive elements beyond static images, such as video, audio, and clickable elements, to make them engaging.	**Impressions** are each time an ad is shown and are often calculated as reach multiplied by frequency.
Interstitial ads take up an entire screen and appear as a separate web page before the user is directed to the page they want to visit.	**Clickthrough rate (CTR)** is a percentage of people shown an ad who click on it; often calculated as clicks divided by impressions.
Video ads are like TV ads placed in banner ads on websites and on social networks. Usually, they are played with the sound off with an option to turn the sound on.	**Conversion rate** is a percentage of people who visited a website and took action, such as buying a product, downloading an app, or subscribing to an email newsletter.

Sources: Chiradeep BasuMallick, "What Is Display Advertising? Definition, Targeting Process, Management, Network Types, and Examples," ToolBox.com, March 16, 2021, https://www.toolbox.com/marketing/programmatic-advertising /articles/what-is-display-advertising/; "Reach," Marketing-Dictionary.org, accessed October 25, 2021, https://marketing-dic tionary.org/r/reach/; and Rob Stokes, *eMarketing—The Essential Guide to Marketing in a Digital World* (Quirk (Pty) Ltd., 2021.

Telling Stories in Display Ads

Remember Jay Baer's quote at the beginning of the chapter? "If your stories are all about your products and services, that's not storytelling. It's a brochure."[47] How do you tell a story that is not a brochure in a small banner ad? A common method of creating banner ads is to use a series of static images that change over a time period. Each image can be used to tell a brand and customer story. These are created through an **animated GIF**, or a single file that contains a number of images or frames presented in a specific order.[48]

Consider the example in Figure 8.2 based on the Napa Valley Wine Valentine's Day promotion given earlier. Act 1 and Act 2 are combined in the first banner frame. The headline establishes the conflict while identifying the main characters. The banner ad would run close to Valentine's Day, and an image of heart-shaped chocolates gives further context. Act 3, the climax, is told in the second banner frame. This headline is the turning point, offering a solution to what to get for Valentine's Day.

Act 4 is the reversal in the third banner frame offer. Choosing this gift ensures the story goes well for the protagonist because he can save money and be the hero. Act 5 takes place on the landing page. The conflict of what to get for Valentine's Day is resolved, and tension is released because you get the wine subscription and the box of chocolates.

Figure 8.2. An animated GIF banner ad conveyed as a five-act story.

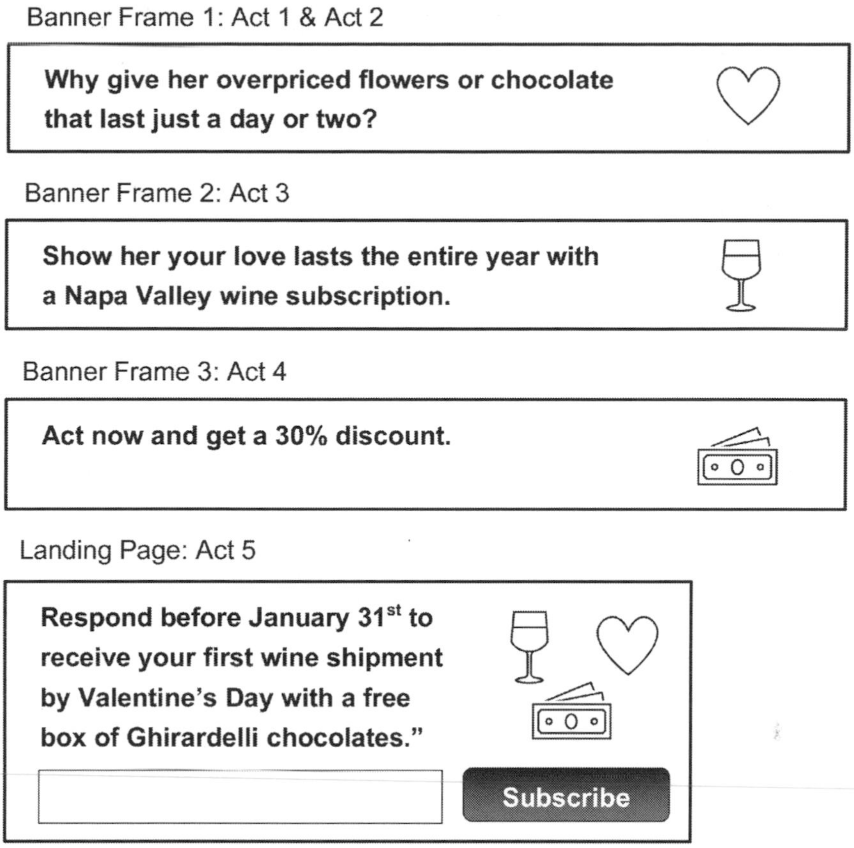

Banner Frame 1: Act 1 & Act 2

> **Why give her overpriced flowers or chocolate that last just a day or two?**

Banner Frame 2: Act 3

> **Show her your love lasts the entire year with a Napa Valley wine subscription.**

Banner Frame 3: Act 4

> **Act now and get a 30% discount.**

Landing Page: Act 5

> **Respond before January 31st to receive your first wine shipment by Valentine's Day with a free box of Ghirardelli chocolates."**
>
> **Subscribe**

Audience Segmentation Is Key to Response

A way to make digital marketing more personalized and thus more effective is through audience segmentation. **Audience segmentation** is dividing a target market into subsets based on demographics, needs, priorities, common interests, and other criteria to better understand and communicate to a target audience.[49] It can increase response rates and lower acquisition costs with more specific messages that resonate with customers' wants and needs. More personal messages also help brands stand out from the competition.

As an example, consider an amusement park promoting ticket sales. Its core target market is adults ages 25–45 with children living at home. This is the group most likely to plan and purchase tickets for immediate and extended family trips to the park. The park could build overall awareness through traditional TV, radio, print, and billboard ads with a general message and broad appeal showing kids, adults, grandparents, and teens having fun at the park.

With an IMC campaign, the digital and social media components present an opportunity to customize messages, imagery, and offers considering possible differences in wants and needs within the group. The amusement park could look to target an audience's stage of life and location differently. People in different stages of life may want different experiences at the park, including the following:

- Adults with young children (ages 25–34)
- Adults with preteens/tweens (ages 35–45)
- High school/college students (ages 13–24)
- Grandparents (age 55+)

People who live different distances away from the park may plan different types of trips:

- Multivisit locals (within 40 miles)
- Day trippers (40 to 100 miles)
- Overnighters (over 100 miles)

From these segments consider differences in content. How could messages, imagery, and offers vary for each segment's needs? Parents with young children probably respond to content focused on smaller rides. Parents with elementary and middle school kids look for more exciting attractions. High school and college students go with friends and look to ride the biggest roller coasters. Grandparents want to see grandchildren on rides, sit, rest, and enjoy shows and restaurants.

With the geographic segments, offers could get more focused. People within 40 miles would be most interested in season passes whether talking to families, teens, or grandparents. People 40 to 100 miles away are most likely interested in day trips. Those over 100 miles away may be interested in park and hotel packages.

Now, you can create a content segmentation grid by linking various segments together to determine how many content variations may be needed. See Table 8.4 for the 12 market segments (4 × 3 = 12) and content variations identified for the amusement park.

Going through this process, you will most likely end up with many possibilities, but not every segment will produce significant improvements. If the segment doesn't increase conversions, stop using it and try something else. The amusement park may discover that conversion for targeting multiday trips to high school/college students over 100 miles away is too low.[50] Some segments may not increase results, but overall, audience segmentation works. A brand loyalty study found that 75 percent of emails opened most frequently contain segmentation.[51]

Table 8.4. Target Audience Segments for a Regional Amusement Park

	Multivisit locals (within 40 miles)	Day trippers (40 to 100 miles)	Overnighters (over 100 miles)
Adults with younger children (25–34 years old)	Message 1 Image 1 Offer 1	Message 2 Image 1 Offer 2	Message 3 Image 1 Offer 3
Adults with preteens/tweens (35–45 years old)	Message 4 Image 2 Offer 1	Message 5 Image 2 Offer 2	Message 6 Image 2 Offer 3
High school/college students (13–24 years old)	Message 7 Image 3 Offer 1	Message 8 Image 3 Offer 2	Message 9 Image 3 Offer 3
Grandparents (55+ years old)	Message 10 Image 4 Offer 4	Message 11 Image 4 Offer 8	Message 12 Image 4 Offer 12

Different groups go to amusement parks for different reasons, which requires different messages delivered to segmented audiences. Getty Images: Zia Soleil.

The Future of Digital Marketing with Web3

There has been much hype in marketing about Web3 and related terms, such as NFTs, blockchain, and crypto. What does Web3 have to do with IMC and brand storytelling? First, let's begin with some definitions. **Web3** is simply a term describing a decentralized version of the World Wide Web built on blockchain technology and cryptocurrencies, which make the internet more assessable, secure, and private.[52]

Blockchain is technology that enables Web3. **Blockchain** is a distributed database shared among nodes of a computer network that maintains a secure decentralized record of transactions. Blockchain is most commonly used as a secure ledger for transactions.[53]

Blockchain also enables cryptocurrencies to exist. **Cryptocurrency** is a virtual currency secured by cryptography based on blockchain technology that makes it nearly impossible to counterfeit or double spend. Cryptocurrencies, such as Bitcoin, are purchased from crypto exchanges and are popular for trading and investment. While some marketers have added crypto for payment, Bitcoin is hardly used for retail transactions.[54] Marketers are mainly using Web3 in other ways such as NFTs. **Non-fungible tokens (NFTs)** are cryptographic assets based on a blockchain with unique identification codes that distinguish them from others. NFTs can represent physical assets, such as artwork or real estate, or they can be used to represent digital artwork. They connect artists directly with audiences, thus simplifying transactions and creating new markets.[55]

How does Web3 impact marketing communications? One impact of Web3 is that it gives users more ownership of how their data and information are used online. This means marketers will have less access to collecting and leveraging data from consumers. IMC professionals will need to be more transparent about how they collect and use consumer data. You'll need more creative strategies to reach target audiences and provide incentives to collect data from them.

As Web3 takes hold, there may be a shift from large social media platforms earning profits from content creators to content creators owning and controlling their content and profits. This means brands may need to shift from purchasing ads on platforms such as YouTube, Facebook, and Spotify to increasing relationships with content creators themselves.[56]

Another consideration is that cryptocurrency and NFTs offer new forms of incentivization for brands, their customers, and their audience. Imagine a brand creating its own NFTs and rewarding people who spend time on their website and apps or for responding to surveys and submitting new product or service ideas.[57] Web3 opens up creative possibilities beyond traditional rewards programs. Gamification rises to new levels when rewards can come in brand tokens based on crypto. As we head into a cookie-less future, this may be the new way to collect consumer digital data.

What is a cookie and why is it phasing out? A **cookie** is a small amount of data generated by a website and saved by your web browser to remember information about you.[58] Cookies are a good thing in that consumers don't have to reenter information when visiting websites and they can receive more customized communications and offers. Yet growing concern over internet privacy and the emergence of Web3 is leading to a phaseout of third-party cookies. Google has announced a phaseout of its third-party cookie in late 2023.

Marketers will have to increase first-party data by enhancing data collection and management. This includes communicating with customers in a transparent way and making the case for the value and personalization they will receive for sharing their data.[59] The cloud-based CRM platform Salesforce has has created NFT Cloud to enable Salesforce's customers to mint NFTs using their CRM and offer them as rewards or sell them on their existing commerce website.[60] An example is Chipotle offering rewards for the first 30,000 fans who visited their metaverse restaurant in Roblox. They were given vouchers for burritos at real-life Chipotle restaurants.[61]

Another option is to turn to new emerging identity solutions such as Unified ID and IdRamp, which allow advertisers to reach people who have opted in to tracking. Yet marketers will need to make the case to users why they should opt in. What value will they receive in exchange? Even then, there may be a sizable portion of the population who will simply decide that they don't want to be tracked on the internet anymore. Thus, marketers also need to prepare strategies to reach people without tracking them.[62]

It is important to remember that tracking someone online is a fairly new development and that marketing communications were effective before this level of targeting. Melinda Han Williams, chief data scientist at Distillery says, "The good news is you don't need to know who someone is to know whether they'd be receptive to your message. Today's artificial intelligence (AI) enables marketers to choose best impressions rather than the best users." We don't need to know everything about a user to target customers effectively. We've been using content-based targeting in ad media buying for decades with success.[63]

Examples of brands leveraging Web3 are Nike, the NBA, and Starbucks. Nike purchased RTFKT Studios in 2021 and began making NFT sneakers. Its first collection, called Dunk

Genesis Cryptokicks, sold 600 pairs in six minutes for a total of $3.1 million. Once brand fans own them, they can customize them using skin vials, which are created by different designers to add special effects and patterns.[64] The NBA created virtual trading card NFTs featuring brief highlight reels of top players. The cards are bought and sold online, building NBA brand community around collecting and trading cards of fans' favorite teams and players.[65]

Starbucks Odyssey which combines Starbucks' rewards loyalty program with an NFT platform. Instead of customers earning "stars" for perks, such as free drinks, customers earn NFT "stamps" by engaging in "journeys," such as interactive games, or taking on challenges to deepen their knowledge of Starbucks and coffee. By collecting the stamps, members gain points unlocking exclusive benefits such as a virtual espresso martini-making class, access to unique merchandise and artist collaborations, or invites to special events at Starbucks Reserve Roasteries.[66] Each of these journeys offers a unique opportunity to tell the brand's story.

8.4 Brand Stories with Experiential Marketing

Our final category of IMC storytelling in this chapter is experiential marketing, which utilizes multiple forms of marketing communications. **Experiential marketing** is a marketing approach that directly engages consumers and invites them to participate in a branded experience.[67] Experiential marketing includes broader events and more individual experiences. A brand customer experience can be a product demonstration, sponsorship, sampling, extra or personal care, or grassroots event. The right brand experience can stimulate an emotional connection and reinforce the essence of the brand.

A popular marketing experience is **sponsorship**, which is a fee paid for a property or an event in return for associated marketable resources.[68] Sponsorships can help create a brand experience with a sports, entertainment, or nonprofit event. A key is making sure it is a good fit. Years ago, Reebok decided to turn around a sales decline by marketing specifically to cross-fit athletes. Therefore, it makes sense that they were the title sponsor of the annual Cross-Fit Games for 10 years.[69] This came with event naming, signage, posters, and banners surrounding the competition. The brand social identity matched the target audience social identity.

Most football stadium sponsor names are not football or even sports brands. The sponsorship fit comes from the location. They tend to be companies with offices or headquarters in those stadium cities, such as Lincoln Financial Field in Philadelphia, Heinz Field in Pittsburgh, Wrigley Field in Chicago, and Levi's Stadium near San Francisco.[70] The Boston Marathon has a mix of sports brand sponsors, such as Adidas and Gatorade, along with local business sponsors, such as John Hancock and Sam Adams.[71]

What happens when the sponsor's brand story doesn't fit? When the Pittsburgh Steelers announced it would be changing the name of its stadium, the hometown newspaper, the *Pittsburgh Post-Gazette*, reported a fan backlash saying, "Steelers fans hate it." In 2022, Heinz Field was renamed Acrisure Stadium after selling the naming rights to a Michigan-based insurance company.[72]

Adam Bittner reported, "For 21 years, Pittsburgh's football stadium was named after one of the most visible food brands in the world. One that had deep local roots. Now, it's named after an insurance company many people have never heard of." One fan explained the mismatch saying that many major corporations are based in the Pittsburgh area and would have made much more sense, such as Alcoa, Dick's Sporting Goods, PPG, UPMC, and US Steel.[73] Longtime franchise quarterback Ben Roethlisberger commented on Twitter with the fan-started hashtag #ForeverHeinz, saying, "Home will always be Heinz Field!"[74]

Not only were Steelers fans upset; days after the announcement, they started a petition to remove the name.[75] Why such a backlash? Pittsburgh fans and their loyalty and support for the Steelers are deeply rooted in the history of the city itself. Pittsburgh may be a big city, but it is more a blue-collar town rooted in the industry and companies that built it. For many years, the three major sports stadiums were named after national and international businesses built in Pittsburgh; Heinz Field (Steelers), PNC Park (Pirates), and PPG Paints Arena (Penguins). The old Heinz factory is up the river from the stadium. PNC and PPG headquarters are across the river in downtown Pittsburgh.

In Chapter 3 we learned that when there is an understanding of brand and buyer social identity, a bond can be formed through a consistent visual and verbal story told in IMC channels (see Figure 3.2). Every time YETI posts a picture on Instagram of its products in the wild, it is sharing a glimpse of a story of a particular outdoor adventure. When Pittsburgh was suffering in the 1970s with the decline of the steel industry, citizens were uplifted by the Steelers dynasty in their run of Super Bowl wins. Much of the Steelers fan identity is about local pride and history. When the team sells the name of the stadium to a company from Michigan that is less than 20 years old, there is a mismatch. If If#YETI began posting pictures of stockbrokers in suits on Wall Street using YETI mugs, there may be a similar reaction with its brand fans.

Use In-Store Marketing to Continue the Brand Story

Experiential marketing can also be created through in-store brand experiences. These are expressed at the point of purchase through signage and branding in the company's own store or through signage purchased from retailers with in-store advertising and point-of-purchase displays. **In-store advertising** includes any advertising messages inside a store that sells a product. **Point of purchase** is a special in-store exhibit placed where the product is sold.[76] Forms of in-store marketing include the following:

- Shopping cart panels
- Above-aisle/end-aisle signs
- Window posters
- Floor graphics
- Digital screens
- End cap displays
- In-store sampling
- In-store events[77]

An example of in-store advertising that helps create a brand experience and tell the brand story is Starbucks' end caps. An **end cap** is a branded point-of-purchase display at the end of a shopping aisle in a store.[78] When Starbucks began selling its ground coffee and pre-brewed drinks in grocery stores, the products needed more than just packaging to tell the brand's story. Much of Starbucks' experience comes from the design of its stores.

In-store marketing firm Catman Global helped revitalize coffee aisle sales for the grocery store chain Safeway with an experiential marketing end cap. The key insight was that shoppers view coffee as a warm and emotional beverage occasion. Yet the coffee aisle at the grocery store lacked any café or at-home experience. Research told them that a more premium end cap would help tell that story with the emotional cues needed to stimulate purchase.[79]

The solution was placing Starbucks' products in a premium end cap featuring dark, natural wood grain, branded black and green colors, large Starbucks logos, and seasonal coffee features in a brand font poster. It brought a slice of the Starbucks café and story into the grocery store experience. The result was a sales increase of 18 percent for Starbucks and an increase in all coffee sales by 10 percent for Safeway.[80]

In-store marketing tells the brand story at the point of purchase and should reinforce other IMC touchpoints for experiential marketing. Getty Images: Prasert Krainukul.

Telling Stories Across In-Person Elements

When it comes to in-store storytelling, go beyond a single poster. Think about how to help bring the larger consumer and brand story to the overall physical brand experience. Each piece of communication should reinforce the larger story. Not all experiential marketing will happen in retail stores. An example is airlines, where their customer experiences occur at the airport and on their airplanes.

Southwest Airlines uses its terminals and planes to tell the larger brand story. The Southwest story is that airline travel doesn't have to be a hassle and it doesn't have to be uptight. The low price doesn't mean unpleasant—it can be casual and fun. This love of the customer is the heart of the brand's customer experience.

Signs in the Southwest terminal deliver important information in the casual brand font, bright happy colors, and funny brand voice. The digital sign showing a flight has arrived says, "Let us tidy up, and then we'll get you on your way." The sign letting passengers know that group A is boarding says, "Group A, now boarding. Aww yeah." A sign that shows boarding time is still 30 minutes away says, "Ahhh. There's still time for coffee."[81]

On the plane, flight attendants wear brightly colored casual polo shirts instead of formal, uniforms. When they deliver scripted safety information, they add a little humor. When introducing the plane's emergency exits, one flight attendant said, "There may be 50 ways to leave your lover, but there are only 4 ways out of this airplane." Another explained the safety features saying, "In the event of a sudden loss of cabin pressure, oxygen masks will descend from the ceiling. Stop screaming, grab the mask, and pull it over your face."[82]

As a final example, researchers studied a local European grocery store in a midwestern US town and found dramatic brand story told through the in-store experience. To tell the brand and customer story of what it might be like to be a French consumer shopping in France, several experiential in-store elements were used.[83]

The setting was established with chalkboard, window, and door signs outside describing everyday European products with foreign spellings and using foreign words. Inside the store, French music played, and there were cultural artifacts, posters, and other merchandising from foreign places. All store employees had multicultural experiences acquired through foreign travel, stays abroad, and knowledge of foreign languages.[84]

The brand story created through these elements matched the story of the customer's self-image of upwardly mobile middle class seeking encounters with other cultures. The customers and salespeople interacted by sharing stories about cultural experiences, describing how customers could use the products and how they tasted. All these in-store elements contributed to the experience of its being a genuine European grocery store in the midwestern town.[85]

8.5 CASE

Taco Bell Hotel

An example of a brand going all out to deliver experiential marketing is Taco Bell. Its marketing team, public relations firm Edelman, and lifestyle marketing agency UEG created a five-day total emersion in the brand. Image loving a fast-food restaurant so much that you would pay hundreds of dollars to fly to and stay in a hotel themed around the restaurant and its food. Many people did, and many more wanted to but couldn't. How did Taco Bell come up with such an unexpected marketing idea?

Jennifer Arnoldt, senior director of retail engagement + experience at Taco Bell, says that doing the unexpected is in the company's DNA and that first started with founder Glen Bell. Arnoldt explains, "Everyone else was making burgers and he decided to open up a taco stand. People didn't even know how to eat a taco or say taco. By doing the unexpected, and really having creativity at our core, Taco Bell is about disrupting convention."[86]

With this in mind, creating an entire resort hotel around the fast-food restaurant makes complete sense as a unique experience for your hardcore superfans. The Bell: Taco Bell Hotel and Resort was a five-day hotel takeover in Palm Springs, where paying attendees were completely immersed into the Taco Bell brand story.

The Bell Hotel and Resort experience kicked off months before the actual event with targeted seeding strategies and a focused public relations effort. One early email to brand fans and journalists teased The Bell's concept by asking recipients if they would like to be alerted when the rooms could be booked. More than 80,000 responded. Then a few weeks before rooms could be reserved, Taco Bell launched a website with teaser content and renderings of the soon-to-be-open brand destination. Rooms started at $169 per night and up to $299 per night for pool-view suites. When reservations went live, they sold out in under two minutes.[87]

How did they decide what to brand Taco Bell? Arnoldt said, "We looked at all of the hotel tropes, and asked 'How can we do it with the Taco Bell wink?'"[88] The Bell included branded bedrooms with Taco Bell art on the walls, branded pillows, towels, coffee mugs, and robes. The pool featured sauce packet floaties, a hair and nail salon offering styles inspired by the brand logo, and a gift shop selling exclusive Taco Bell merchandise. Branded activities were offered from yoga to live concerts.[89]

Of course, Taco Bell food was given freely, including poolside snacks each afternoon signaled by the iconic Taco Bell gong. Regular Taco Bell food was supplemented with special dishes from the brand's test kitchen, such as Taco Bell's spin on the club sandwich. The concept really leveraged the experiential travel trend of its target audience. With Instagrammable moments all over the resort, the brand experience traveled around the world beyond the in person attendees.[90]

In the end, 400 fans and 61 journalists traveled from 21 states to experience The Bell. With zero paid media, this experiential marketing effort generated 6 billion earned media impressions and 5,000 media stories. The Bell five-day experience drove more than 1.2 billion social impressions and over 40,000 social mentions while increasing sales by 7 percent.[91]

This chapter has explored how to continue IMC campaign storytelling in the tried-and-true area of direct marketing, newer forms of digital marketing, in an emerging new emphasis on experiential marketing. No matter the age of the practice or what combination of digital medium or physical location, story is an important driving force. In the next chapter, we'll continue our storytelling journey by considering how public relations has evolved with digital media and how storytelling plays an important role in earned media, social media, and influencer marketing.

QUESTIONS

1. Many people today spend much of their online time on mobile. Do you think all design should be mobile first, or is there still a place for desktop design as well?
2. Can you think of an experiential marketing event that you attended? What made it a success, and what could have been improved?

EXERCISES

1. Analyze your last direct response experience considering best practices learned in this chapter. What was the last direct marketing that you responded to? In what medium did it appear? Was it an email, direct mail piece, or something else? What caught your attention and why? How important was the offer and what was it? Was there a landing page, and what difference did that make? Do you know how and why you got on "the list"?
2. The Taco Bell Resort and Hotel experiential marketing is an excellent example of Youtility. The marketing was so good that people literally did pay for it. Think of another example of Youtility—a company creating marketing that you would pay for but weren't charged for. Is it direct marketing, digital marketing, experiential marketing, or another form of IMC that we have discussed? What are the key elements or insights that make it a success?

KEY CONCEPTS

Alt text

Animated GIF

Audience segmentation

Banner ad

Blockchain

BOGO

Bundles

Clickthrough rate (CTR)

Compiled lists

Content marketing

Conversion rate

Cookie

Coupons

Cryptocurrency

Customer relationship management (CRM)

Database marketing

Digital marketing

Direct marketing

Display advertising

Display advertising networks

End cap
Experiential marketing
Flash sales
Free gift with purchase
Free samples
Free shipping
Giveaways
Help
Holiday promotions
Hype
Impression
In-store advertising
Internal database lists
Interstitial ad
Keyword
Landing page
Lifestyle discounts

Loyalty programs
Metadata
Native advertising
Non-fungible tokens (NFTs)
Preview pane
Paid search (pay-per-click [PPC]) advertising
Point of purchase (POP)
Product discounts
Reach
Response lists
Rich media ad
Sales promotion
Search engine optimization (SEO)
Sponsorship
Youtility
Video ad
Web3

New Model for Newsworthy

Public Relations, Social Media, and Influencer Marketing

CHAPTER 9 LEARNING OBJECTIVES

1. Discover the origins of public relations and how the practice is evolving.
2. Learn to create effective public relations with brand stories.
3. Understand how to utilize social media marketing through storytelling.
4. Know how to leverage influencer marketing with a story approach.

9.1 Bernays's Public Relations and Dietrich's Spin Sucks

Our brand storytelling journey continues exploring the final consumer touchpoints in integrated marketing communications (IMC) plans—public relations, social media, and influencer marketing. First, we'll look at an influential figure in the origins of public relations (PR) and one driving changes in the field. Edward Bernays is often credited with helping to develop the professional practice of PR in the 1920s and was also known as "the father of spin." In 2014, Gini Dietrich published the book *Spin Sucks*, with a new approach to PR. Dietrich says, "Lie or spin the truth, and you will be found out. People will take you to task."[1]

A driving force of "being found out" is social media. We'll learn how brand social media communities, including influencer marketing, are important components of an IMC strategy. Our case study looks at how PR crisis communications and social media listening can turn into marketing with the right plan in place.

Edward Bernays and the Origins of Public Relations

Edward Bernays, known as the father of public relations, first helped the Committee on Public Information (CPI) persuade Americans to support World War I. Bernays was intrigued by his uncle Sigmund Freud's idea of hidden forces that drive behavior. He opened up a PR office in New York City with his soon-to-be wife, Doris Fleishman, to test some of these methods.[2] Edward and Doris called themselves "counsels on public relations." One technique they used was to devise events to generate news that would produce demand for clients' products. This indirect method was unique compared to the straightforward sales messages of advertising at the time.[3]

Bernays also helped to develop the PR technique of employing a third party as the messenger for client interests.[4] This included the now common practice of forming interest groups to advocate for something and the use of opinion leaders to change attitudes.[5] Bernays, along with others, used these indirect methods to develop the discipline of public relations.

An early example was Bernays's client, Venida Hairnet Company. Instead of directly advertising the product, the company publicized the dangers of workers wearing long, loose hair in factories and restaurants. As a result, many states passed laws requiring factory workers and food-service employees to wear hairnets, which indirectly increased Venida's sales.[6]

In another example, Bernays persuaded feminist protesters to march in the New York Easter Parade smoking cigarettes and calling them "torches of freedom." Women smoking cigarettes in public became a symbol of freedom, and the publicity helped to increase sales for his tobacco client. When Bernays later learned of the connection between cigarettes and cancer, he regretted those efforts and instead worked on efforts to ban tobacco advertising from radio and TV.[7]

In the article "The Original Spin Doctor," Bernays addressed criticism of his techniques: "If I tell you to pick out a certain tie and you think that's bad advice, you'll call it manipulation, but if I use reason, persuasion, authority, and tradition to show you why it's a good idea to wear that tie, you'll thank me for showing you facts."[8]

A recent modern version of PR reason, persuasion, and authority is PR agency Edelman's Facebook Messenger chatbot for LEGO. In consumer research for its client, Edelman discovered that 84 percent of people research gifts online and over 25 percent say it is stressful because they are overloaded with choices during the holidays. To help overloaded consumers pick the right gift, Edelman created the LEGO chatbot, named Ralph.[9]

Chatbot Ralph had a tone of voice based on the LEGO movie characters and used warm, inviting language; playful GIFs, and emojis to make shopping feel carefree, fun, and informed. The AI's advice was based on questions about price, age, personality, and interests; it gave custom recommendations with real-time localized stock updates from the store, LEGO.com, and offered a free shipping code. Ralph resulted in a reach of 2.69 million, 1.2 million post engagements, an engagement rate of 45 percent and an 8.4 times higher conversion rate than other ad formats.[10]

Gini Dietrich's "Spin Sucks" Approach to Public Relations

If Edward Bernays began the PR profession as a "spin doctor," then Gini Dietrich could be seen as leading an "anti-spin" movement. She has advocated for the advancement of PR practices on Spinsucks.com, a top-five PR blog, and in the book *Spin Sucks*.[11]

Dietrich's journey to *Spin Sucks* began with dissatisfaction in traditional PR practice. In 2010, Dietrich announced the PR firm that she had cofounded, Arment Dietrich, was no longer a PR agency. Instead, it was going to be an IMC firm.[12]

Dietrich developed the Spinsucks.com blog to point out outmoded PR practices. In the *Spin Sucks* book, she explains how many PR books tell you how to "spin" your message but that people are sick of spin. Companies must restore trust through open, honest, and authentic communication to earn the trust of customers and other key stakeholders.[13] Dietrick's new rules for effective, ethical communication include the following:

- Share stories more powerfully without sex or "truth-stretching."
- Tell the truth using techniques of storytellers.
- Create fresh, honest content compelling to humans and search.
- Engage successfully online and celebrate brand ambassadors.
- Transform online critics into fans.
- Converge paid, owned, earned, and shared media.[14]

The Public Relations Society of America links the negative aspects of spin to propaganda. An early term in PR, **propaganda** is messages designed to shape perceptions or motivate actions that an organization wants. Later in the twentieth century, the term took on negative connotations associating it with lies, deceit, and misinformation.[15]

An anti-spin approach to PR is needed as consumer trust slips. The latest Edelman Trust barometer consumer survey finds that 46 percent of people view media as divisive forcing disinformation for commercial gain. Yet the same survey reveals that 58 percent say they'll buy or advocate for a brand based on brand beliefs and values.[16] If a brand can get that story out, its beliefs and values, it will be trusted.

Dietrich suggests that marketers tell this truth by reading great fiction to know how to tell their brands' stories. In chapter 2 we discussed various narrative structures and saw how they align with the five-act dramatic framework presented throughout this book. This included story grammar theories (see Table 2.1) and story maps (see Table 2.2). In *Spin Sucks*, Dietrich explains that to tell the truth, you need a company story and that you can learn how to tell compelling stories by reading successful fiction writers to learn the structure they use in their books.[17]

9.2 Brand Stories in Public Relations

Let's consider the PR strategies and tactics most related to IMC. **Public relations** uses publicity and other nonpaid forms of promotion to influence the feelings, opinions, or beliefs about an organization, company, or product to buyers or other stakeholders.[18] **Publicity** is non-paid-for communication of information about a company, product, or service through media.[19] Despite declining trust, consumers still view media as a trusted source of information over a company's own published information and advertising (see Figure 9.1).[20]

Figure 9.1. Percent of people who believe each media source after seeing twice or less.

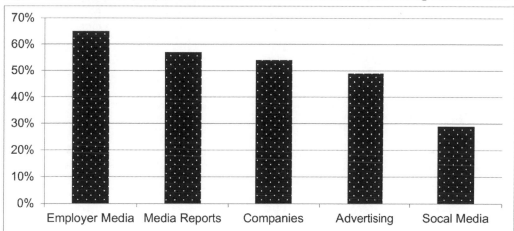

Source: "2022 Edelman Trust Barometer Global Report," Edelman.com (January 2022), pp, 28, https://www.edelman .com/sites/g/files/aatuss191/files/2022-01/2022%20Edelman%20Trust%20Barometer%20Global%20Report_Final.pdf

Some main tools of PR include press releases, custom pitches, and media relations.[21] PR also plans events, press conferences, and PR stunts to attract media coverage and build credibility.[22] The techniques most related to IMC are called **proactive public relations**, which involves initiating PR plans to achieve measurable results toward set marketing objectives.[23]

Public Relations Press Releases Have Evolved

A **press release** announces newsworthy events to share information about a company with the public. It is distributed via newswires and press release distribution services.[24] A **newswire** is an electronic news service that delivers breaking news to journalists.[25] The name came from news agencies that used to send news via telegraph wire.

Today, newswires, such as PR Newswire and Business Wire, distribute news via the internet to subscribing newsrooms and journalists. There are global, regional, and subject-focused wires. PR professionals pay newswires to distribute press releases to journalists.[26]

The number of press release distribution companies has increased, along with the services they offer. These services include search engine optimization (SEO), RSS feeds, media contact databases, media monitoring, and social media posting. Multimedia news releases are now created on custom landing pages that include images, videos, infographics, call-to-action buttons, and live social media feeds.[27]

A standard press release is written like a news article and follows Associated Press (AP) style. When writing a release, first, identify the target audience and write with their interests in mind. Consider tying the headline into a trending topic or current event. Write to elicit emotion, and include keywords throughout for SEO.[28] See Figure 9.2 for an AP style press release template worksheet.

To get the release out, use press release services, post on the company website, and share on social media and through media relations. **Media relations** is building trusted relationships with journalists and media outlets to tell an organization's story.[29] It includes seeking publicity for a company and responding to questions from journalists and requires up-to-date lists of media contacts, knowledge of media contact interests, and crafting custom media pitches.[30]

Figure 9.2. AP style press release template worksheet.

Company Logo

Contact Name *(press liaison)*   FOR IMMEDIATE RELEASE
Phone
Email
Website

Headline
(Attract attention and tell audience what release is about. Use 14-point bold common font like Times New Roman or Arial with Title Case. 65 to 80 characters long)

Subheading
(Builds upon headline with further description and explanation. Use 13-point same font italic with Title Case and around 120 characters.)

Lead Paragraph *(Start with dateline of bold location and date with city in all caps and state abbreviated. Body copy should give all the details starting with most important information first. First paragraph should summarize the entire release answering the five W questions of Who, What, When, Where, and Why.)*

Body Paragraphs *(The succeeding paragraphs provide supporting details of How.* This includes feature quotes under two sentences and list person title and company. Also add imbedded or linked media content with photos, audio, and videos. *Use 12-point same font with sentence case, third-person perspective, and do not use serial comma before last item in a series.)*

Feature Quotes *(*Include feature quotes to make the news more interesting and credible. List their title and company and ensure they are under two sentences.*)*

Media Content *(*Add media content with photos, audio, and videos to stand out. Imbed the content or link to a custom landing page if file size is too large.*)*

Boiler Plate *(The "about" section is a short description of the organization or company such as company background, awards, and time in business. Finish with an endnote like "For more information, contact us at [email]. Use 12-point same font with sentence case, third-person perspective, and should be less than 100 words.)*

Hash
(End with three-pound signs "###" signaling the end of the story.)

The Public Relations Pitch Gains Earned Media Coverage

A **PR pitch** is a short, personalized message outlining the value of a story and explaining why it should be published. Research indicates that journalists prefer pitches to be received via email and that they be short, engaging, and timely. Limit to two to three paragraphs and 150 to 400 words. Customize the pitch, knowing the stories the journalist writes, the focus of the news outlet, and the interests of readers.[31]

Lack of personalization is the main reason journalists reject pitches. Therefore, demonstrate that you put thought and effort into selecting to whom you sent it. Read each reporter's past articles, noting the point of view, style, and what they've covered. Pitch something new or a new angle, be timely, and tailor the pitch to the media. A pitch for TV should be different from a pitch for a podcast, print, or a website.

Create a compelling, direct email subject line that attracts attention but is not confusing or overdone. Write it like the title of an article.[32] An example of a PR pitch email subject line is "PITCH: 5 Alternative Valentine's Gifts to Chocolate and Flowers She'll Love." This could be a pitch for the Napa Valley Wine example presented in Chapter 8.

After the PR pitch subject line, be up front by telling the reporter that it's a pitch. Then immediately present a brief synopsis of the story idea, and follow up with information demonstrating that you understand the unique perspective and needs of the journalist, publication, and medium.[33]

When should you send pitches? Most journalists prefer pitches between 5:00 a.m. and 12:00 p.m. EST on Mondays. Should you follow up? Nearly 90 percent of journalists say they are okay with one follow-up email within a week.[34] If the journalist publishes the story, thank them, and share it. Reporters are evaluated on the success of their stories via views and shares. Helping them will build a relationship and trust for your next story pitch.[35]

Public Relations Events Make an Impression

A **PR event** is an event designed to showcase an organization, company, or product to the media and public. PR events also present an opportunity to listen and interact with customers as a form of experiential marketing.[36]

One form of PR event is a press conference. A **press conference** is an event by an organization to distribute information and answer inquiries from the media. It provides an opportunity for live dialogue where journalists ask questions. Press conferences are often scheduled to respond to positive or negative news or for a new product launch.[37] When planning a PR event, follow these steps:

1. Set a goal that drives all decisions.
2. Decide on the type of event.
3. Create a theme, event name, and hashtag.
4. Be strategic about location and timing.
5. Create promotional PR assets.
6. Promote the event and invite attendees.
7. Capture PR assets during the event.
8. Plan follow-up and recap.

First, set a goal by answering the question, "Why are we holding an event?" Is it to promote a new product; to reward, educate, or engage customers; to raise money for a cause; or to support the community?[38] The goal should guide all other decisions. You can also turn that general goal into a specific objective such as earning a certain number of media impressions.

Next, decide the type of event. Should it be an awards ceremony, dinner, lecture, tour, demonstration, concert, sponsorship, or fundraiser? Remember that the type of event should match the goal and appeal to the audience. An event to promote the Napa Valley Wine service example from Chapter 8 could be a Valentine's Day–themed wine tasting.

From the event type and goal, develop an overall message and create a memorable theme and name. Short, clever phrases work best. If it is an annual event, consider adding the year and turning the name or theme into an easy-to-share hashtag. The event name for Napa Valley Wines could be "Napa Valleytine's Day Tasting 2024," with the hashtag #NapaValleytinesTasting.

Based on event type, theme, and participants, select the location and timing. To make a grand, memorable statement, you need a grand, memorable venue. Consider high-profile landmarks, beautiful outdoor landscapes, or a strategic location such as the new factory at which an innovative product is being produced or the beautiful vineyard where wines are crafted.[39]

Timing may come from the theme or goal. A Valentine's Day wine tasting would occur near the holiday. For a new product launch, the press conference could be on the day of the release or days before. Don't plan for the same day as other high-profile events such as a sports game that may draw away attendance and attention.[40] Even a superior product will find it hard to draw attention if launched near the day of the Super Bowl.

Create and share PR assets, such as speakers and performers' pictures, previous event pictures, and event data infographics. Issue a press release, and reach out to individual media, focusing on local journalists most likely to attend. Create posters and ads, get on local events calendars, and use the company blog and email newsletter.[41] Promote your event on social media with the event hashtag before, during, and at the event. Encourage attendees to share updates and pictures live.[42]

When the event is over, don't end its promotion. Consider a press release announcing the number of attendees, money raised for a cause, or glasses of wine tasted. Continue monitoring social media for the event hashtag to thank attendees and to remind them to come back next year if it's an annual event.

Public Relations Stunts Can Spread via Social Media

A unique form of an event is a **PR stunt**, which is an event designed to attract public and media attention via unusual and often elaborate means. Unlike regular PR events, PR stunts need to be bold, unforgettable, fun, and unique.

A unique and memorable stunt was the ALS Ice Bucket Challenge, which became a social media viral sensation. The challenge even elicited celebrity participants dumping ice water on their heads to raise awareness and donations for the nonprofit organization.[43]

Another PR stunt is when Snapple attempted to make the world's largest ice pop. Unfortunately, the stunt failed when the 35,000-pound popsicle melted in the hot New York City summer sun, sending attendees running from the sticky mess. It did generate hundreds of news stories, but they focused on the mishap and not the quality of the ice

The ALS Ice Bucket Challenge PR stunt turned into a viral success that was voluntarily spread by consumers and celebrities. Getty Images: Rick Berkowitz.

pops. Snapple's PR manager said that despite the failure, the event did create broad brand awareness of the new product.[44]

In a more successful stunt, the International House of Pancakes (IHOP) switched its name to IHOB without revealing the reason. The company changed its website, social media accounts, Twitter handle, employee LinkedIn job titles, and even signage on one of its restaurants. After generating millions of impressions from media and consumers, it revealed that IHOB stood for International House of Burgers to introduce the new Ultimate Steakburger.[45]

When creating a PR stunt, ensure that the ideas are simple. An ice bucket, a giant popsicle, and an IHOB sign can easily be understood and shared. Ensure that it relates to the product it's promoting. A PR stunt may draw plenty of attention and media coverage, but if people don't remember the product and brand, it's a wasted effort.[46] Finally, don't forget brand and buyer social identity. What stunt will tell a story linking the two? For the Nappy Valley Wines example perhaps the Valentine's Day Tasting event can become a stunt by attempting to set the Guinness World Record for the largest wine toast.

Public Relations Is Evolving Its Method of Storytelling

While PR professionals pitch stories, there's a difference between a news story and a dramatic story. News is about what people have done, but stories are about people and who they are.[47] In the case study from Chapter 1, Steve Clayton, chief storyteller at Microsoft, reminded us that the secret to attracting attention is to "Start with a great story."[48] Instead of issuing standard press releases, he tells stories about real Microsoft employees doing interesting work on the Microsoft Stories blog.[49]

Combine what we learned from Clayton with what we've learned from Gini Dietrich. While PR professionals use traditional PR tactics, such as press releases, pitches, events, and stunts, they also take a more integrated approach. Public relations today goes beyond earned media to use an integrated mix of paid, earned, shared, and owned media.[50] In chapter 4 we learned about Dietrich's PESO media model that categorizes media based on the new realities of digital media and integration of disciplines (see Figure 4.3).

Even more traditional news-oriented press release and pitches have room for storytelling. Follow the standard of putting hard facts in the lead paragraph, but then look for opportunities where narrative can be a storytelling device. Or consider weaving the facts together in a narrative to pull the reader in with a story while delivering the news facts. A press release or pitch with just a few lines of a narrative story can help make information more dramatic and memorable.[51]

9.3 Brand Stories in Social Media

Social media has been one of the most disruptive new media channels impacting marketing communications. It's a major cause of marketers' having lost much of their control over their brand communications because consumers now have an equally powerful voice. No longer can marketers restrict the messages being sent out about their products and services because everyday consumers can talk back and share their own opinions with the company and with other consumers, sometimes reaching a mass scale.

Table 9.1. Main Components of Social Media Strategy

Tactics Used in Social Media Strategy				
Real-Time Brand Conversation	Scheduled Organic + Paid Brand Content	Curated Brand-Related Third-Party Content	Consumer-Generated Brand Content	Influencer Marketing
Types of Media Used per Social Media Tactics				
Shared + Owned Media	Owned + Paid Media	Earned Media	Shared Media	Paid Media

Differences between Social Media and Other Media

Other IMC channels involve planning and crafting visual and verbal messages. That is a part of social media, but it also involves listening and creating custom messages instantly in response to individual consumers. Real-time consumer discussions, scheduled owned and paid brand posts, curated related content from third parties, shared consumer-generated brand content, and paid influencer brand content combine into a social media strategy (see Table 9.1).

While marketers can't control the message, they can manage the conversation. If you simply treat social media as another one-way advertising medium, you will not succeed. Despite difficulties and even frustrations, marketers know that social media is important and are spending more money on it. The average percentage of marketing budgets spent on social media has increased from 3.5 percent in 2009 to 15 percent in 2021.[52]

What is social media? **Social media** facilitates the creation and sharing of information, ideas, and other forms of expression via virtual communities.[53] Companies use in-house or outsourced employees to manage their social media. **Social media marketing managers** oversee the creation and execution of an organization's social media strategy, including brand presence and specific campaigns.[54]

Social media marketing managers build brand communities on various social media platforms. A **brand community** is a group of people with social relations structured around being admirers of a brand.[55] When working on an IMC campaign, the brand may have an established brand community, or you could be tasked with building one.

Select Social Media Channels

For an IMC social media strategy, first, confirm that the brand is on the right social media channels. Compare the target audience in the creative brief and the user demographics of social media platforms. Ensure the brand is talking on the platforms where the target audience has accounts and is currently most active.

Look beyond monthly active users (MAUs) to see how active a demographic is on a social media platform each day via daily active users (DAUs) statistics. A teen may have a Facebook account to occasionally see what their parents and relatives post, but they're probably more active following influencers and communicating with friends on Snapchat, Instagram, or TikTok. If a client's target audience is active on a platform where the client doesn't have an account, one should be added. You have to go where the brand communication is happening, as we will see in the Crockpot case study at the end of the chapter. Crockpot didn't have a Twitter account, but when the brand showed up on Twitter Trends, the company created one. See Table 9.2 to consider the main social platforms by various categories.

Table 9.2. Social Media Channels by Category

Social Networks	
Facebook (2004)	A social network where users create profiles; connect to other users as "friends"; and exchange messages, photos, and videos.
LinkedIn (2003)	A business-focused social network where users create professional profiles of work experience and form connections with other professionals.
Media Sharing	
Instagram (2010)	A mobile social media service where users take photos and videos and share them on a variety of social networking platforms.
YouTube (2005)	A video-sharing social media service where users upload, view, and share user-generated and corporate media video.
Snapchat (2011)	A photo- and video-sharing social media messaging service where media and messages are available for a short time before disappearing.
Microblogs	
Twitter (2006)	A social network media service where users send short, character count–limited messages to other users.
Pinterest (2010)	A visual discovery social media service that enables collection and sharing of pictures linked to websites.
TikTok (2016)	A social media service based on a short-form video app for creating and sharing entertaining lip-sync, comedy, talent, and other videos.
Ratings and Reviews	
Yelp (2004)	A social media service that publishes crowdsourced ratings and reviews about local businesses.
TripAdvisor (2000)	A social media service providing ratings and reviews of travel-related content with travel forums and booking.
Google My Business (2014)	A social media listing that shows businesses in search including ratings and reviews, comments, photo sharing, and questions and answers.
Social Bookmarking/Knowledge	
Reddit (2005)	A social media news site and forum where content is shared in categories called subreddits and voted on by users.
Quora (2009)	A social media question-and-answer service where questions are submitted and answered by its community of users.
Blog (1999)	A website with reverse chronological posts featuring diary-type commentary articles on specific topics with comments and easy social media sharing.
Podcast (2005)	A series of episodes of audio content delivered digitally and often subscribed to through web syndication or streamed online.

Source: Keith Quesenberry, *Social Media Strategy: Marketing, Advertising and Public Relations in the Consumer Revolution,* 3rd ed. (Lanham, MD: Rowman & Littlefield, 2021).

Study Social Platform Communities for Story Insights

Once you identify the most important social media channels, consider the community, content, and interactions that occur on them. Each social platform is unique and comes with different expectations from users and for brands.

Content that performs well on Facebook is different from Instagram, TikTok, Twitter, YouTube, and Reddit. To understand the differences, conduct social media listening on each. **Social media listening** is collecting data from brand social media mentions and broader relevant conversations to improve strategy. Also, study social media platform algorithms.[56] **Algorithms** are formulas used to rank content and determine what appears in a person's social media feed.[57]

Most businesses today have low organic reach, meaning that a low percentage of what they post is seen by their followers. Average organic reach varies, but many companies must pay to reach an audience via social media advertising. **Social media advertising** uses social media platforms to create, target, and deliver paid marketing communications.[58]

Social media advertising is highly targetable and can reach very specific audiences. Targeting includes demographics, interests, behavior, and even competitor followers. You can also target people that "look like" the brand's followers. Or you can remarket to people who visited the brand's website but didn't make a purchase. This is how those new pair of shoes you looked at on a website appear in your newsfeed until you buy them. **Remarketing**, also known as retargeting, is serving ads to people who have already taken an action somewhere else, such as a website or app.[59]

Many social media advertising options include a direct call to action, making it a good direct marketing channel. This could send people to a website for more information, to view a video, to download an app, or to make a purchase. Options such as Instagram Shoppable Posts offer commerce built into the platform. The ability to make a purchase without leaving a social media platform is a form of social commerce (see Figure 9.3). **Social commerce** is the use of social media platforms for online buying and selling via e-commerce transactions.[60]

Figure 9.3. Social commerce sells products directly from posts.

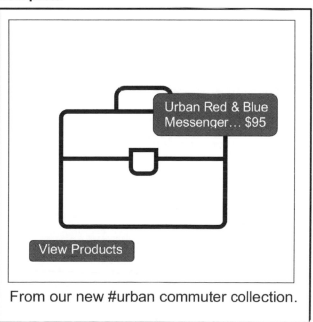

Social media is also a good IMC touchpoint for business-to-business products and services. Social media is an important part of personal sales today. Sales professionals using social media for prospecting and other parts of the selling process is called social selling. **Social selling** is a process of developing relationships through social media as part of the sales process.[61]

A strategy for increasing the reach of business-to-business and business-to-customer social media is to create content related to trending news, topics, or events. Brand-related content on a trending story can be a way to get into news feeds and to be shared. Also, consider content for events that draw live social media posts during the broadcast. This could be big events such as the Oscars and the Super Bowl, popular TV shows such as *Survivor* for B2B, or hot topics at a business conference such as South by Southwest (SXSW) for B2B.

For Super Bowl LVI, insurance company State Farm created a #TeamStateFarm TikTok challenge to engage a younger target audience. The campaign featured brand spokesperson Jake from State Farm acting as a talent scout. The winning videos were pinned at the top of Jake's TikTok page.[62]

Fill Social Feeds with Consumer and Third-Party Content

Not all social media brand content is created by the brand. **User-generated content (UGC)** is any brand-related photo, video, post, or comment published through a social media platform by an unpaid contributor. Content created by fans about the brand is a trusted source. Brands should monitor for user-generated content and ask permission to reshare on official brand accounts.

IMC plans can include contests to elicit brand social media content from fans. Honda did this on National Dog Day asking its fans to share pictures of their furry friends with their Hondas. Visit Mesa, which promotes living and vacationing in Mesa, Arizona, created a "For the Love of Mesa" contest, which asked people to share photos describing what Mesa meant to them. It got nearly 500 user-generated photos in two weeks.[63]

Brand accounts can also share content valuable to their audience created by other organizations. **Content curation** is gathering information relevant to a specific area of interest to present to others.[64] An example could be a car insurance company sharing an article from a car magazine on how to drive in the snow. Ben & Jerry's shares news articles about the causes the company supports that address issues such as climate change.[65] In Instagram you can do a collab post where both users can share the same post in their Feed or Reels as co-authors.

Earned media should be shared as well. An example is Turkey Hill ice cream retweeting a news article mentioning the company's clean water partnership on the PA Environment Digest blog.[66] The company also shared the History Channel's *Modern Marvels* episode that featured its factory showing how it makes ice cream.[67]

Sometimes, earned media can come from other brands. Wendy's has become famous for its sassy Twitter attitude. For #NationalRoastDay, other brands asked it for a roast. @Sun-Maid raisins tweeted "One roast, please." @Wendys replied, "Please stop ruining cookies."[68] Wendy's also uses its brand social media to promote events it sponsors, such as NCAA March Madness with @MarchMadnessMBB and #FinalFour.[69]

Another best practice in social media strategy is consistency. Create a consistent publishing schedule via a calendar. A **content calendar** plans how content will be distributed during a specified time period.[70] Planning a content calendar can also help spot opportunities to create relevant content. Consider common holidays, such as Valentine's Day, or national days, such as Bagel Day. Consider relevant content for weekly hashtags, such as

In social media, be sure to take advantage of target audience relevant hashtags as a way for the brand story to be found. Getty Images: Laurence Dutton.

#MotivationMonday or #TBT for Throwback Thursday.[71] Hashtags related to Valentine's Day for Nappy Valley Wines include #ValentineGift, #Valentinesday202X, #ValentineSeason, #ValentineLove, and #ValentinesEveryday.

Much of the content on brand social media channels is created in live two-way conversations. This happens through social media monitoring. **Social media monitoring** identifies and responds to brand mentions in social media to improve customer engagement. It is important to train frontline social media managers on the style and tone of the brand voice and the IMC campaign and to share key assets such as pictures, videos, and campaign hashtags. To measure the performance of social content and conversation, companies may measure engagement. **Engagement rate** is the total number of likes, shares, or comments across a social media campaign divided by either the number of account users or the number of generated impressions.[72]

Social Media Can Tell Stories in Many Ways

We learned in Chapter 2 how viral videos, such as Always #LikeAGirl, follow the five-act framework. Research has found that YouTube ad videos that tell a complete story receive

Table 9.3. Storytelling in Social Media Template Worksheet

Act 1 Introduction Provides background details, setting, previous events, characters, etc.	Consider sharing the organization's history, people, and mission or vision. Or establish the background of the protagonist as your typical customer.
Act 2 Rising Action Related incidents build toward a point of greatest interest—the climax.	Don't post the same promotion or main benefit over and over in different ways. Create posts that build toward a big action, reveal, or turning point.
Act 3 Climax The turning point changes a main character's fate—the brand or customer.	Present the brand or customer reaching a turning point and finding a solution or overcoming a challenge with product or service strengths.
Act 4 Falling Action Details of the consequences of the climax are revealed and played out.	If an obstacle was overcome, illustrate results for the brand or consumer. If an opportunity was seized, detail the outcomes pointing toward a final victory.
Act 5 Resolution Conflicts are resolved, releasing tension, and main characters are better off.	Show the brand or customer winning. Provide a glimpse of the ultimate goal of the brand and its customers—the happily ever after.

Source: Keith A. Quesenberry, "The Power of Storytelling in Social Media Marketing," SocialMediaToday.com (blog), April 8, 2015, http://www.socialmediatoday.com/marketing/2015-04-08/power-storytelling-social-media-marketing.

more shares and views.[73] Yet a lot of social media takes different forms, such as Instagram and Pinterest photos, 240-character tweets, and 15-second TikTok videos. For these platforms, think of each post as a small part of the larger story.[74]

Aim for a bigger brand story that leverages all five acts lived out in social media on a daily or weekly basis over a longer time. No matter the form or time, a series of social posts can take you on an emotional roller coaster where tension is created and then released, producing emotions consumers want to share with others. Table 9.3 provides a template worksheet with ideas on how to tell a story on social media.

How Does the Metaverse Impact IMC and Brand Storytelling?

One of the most talked about topics in marketing in recent years is the metaverse. Even Facebook changed its company name to Meta, signaling its focus on building virtual communities. The **metaverse** is immersive real-time digital environments built on virtual or augmented reality technology powered by a virtual economy, which is often built on cryptocurrency, NFTs, VR and AR.[75] **Virtual reality (VR)** is an artificial environment created with software that is presented to a user as a real environment.[76] **Augmented reality (AR)** is an integration of digital information with a user's environment in real time.[77] The metaverse enables people to have virtual identities, presence, and peer-to-peer relationships through interactions, transactions, user-generated content, and world building.[78] The metaverse is considered another component of Web3, which we discussed in Chapter 8.

What does the metaverse mean for IMC and brand storytelling? Some shoppers will walk to stores in a virtual mall as digital avatars looking at 3D furniture or trying on a virtual pair of pants while interacting with AI-powered virtual salespeople. But at a basic level, the metaverse offers a new way to connect the brand story with the customer through consumer touchpoint. Creativity will play a big role in imaging immersive virtual interactions that deliver brand experiences and products and entice engagement to build brand communities.[79]

Mark Zuckerberg may have generated a lot of press when he announced Facebook was rebranding itself as Meta in December 2021, but there is a lot more to the metaverse than Meta's efforts to create a metaverse. The metaverse includes gaming companies, such as Epic Games, the maker of Fortnite, and Microsoft's acquisition of Activision to build the metaverse. Epic Games formed a partnership with LEGO to build a metaverse for kids.[80]

Early metaverse platforms include Roblox, Fortnite, Decentraland, Minecraft, and Meta's Horizon Worlds. Gucci created a brand activation on Roblox by creating a metaverse version of its real-world Gucci Garden, which attracted 19.9 million visitors in two weeks. Vans also partnered with Roblox to create a virtual interactive skate park, Vans World. It allowed brand fans to virtually visit skate parks with friends, earning points through game play to spend on virtual Vans sneakers and apparel and to build customized skateboards in a virtual skate shop. Vans World attracted over 48 million visitors in a couple of months.[81]

Some other examples of brands telling stories in the metaverse include Warner Bros., the US Golf Association, and Nike. Warner Bros. created a digital launch party for the movie *In the Heights* where fans could play games, create a community mural, and dance with people around the world in a virtual flash mob. The US Golf Association created an AR-powered app that allowed fans to explore the 2021 US Open and US Women's Open courses.[82]

Nike created Nikeland metaverse in Roblox for its fans to meet and socialize, plus engage in brand experiences and promotions. In a couple of months, 7 million people visited Nikeland to enjoy brand experiences, such as celebrity appearances by LeBron James, games with rewards, and ownership of their own "yard" or personal space to show off their collectibles. Exclusive branded digital products can be worn on fans' avatars around other Roblox environments to create digital brand ambassadors.[83]

Other brands have created merged digital and real-life experiences through the metaverse. During New York Fashion Week, Puma launched an integrated physical and digital experience called "Black Station." Visitors to the website interacted with the brand's Fashion Week show as if they were there in person. Digital exhibits featured 3D sneakers, and NFT holders could redeem tokens for physical pairs of shoes.

Marketers call these hybrid digital and physical efforts a "phygital" experience. **Phygital marketing** blends digital metaverse and physical real-life brand experiences. Instead of jumping completely into the virtual world, phygital experiences combine physical and digital consumers may be more comfortable with including AR/VR and 3D modeling or metaverse experiences that reflect a physical one.[84]

Samsung's New York flagship store sustainability fashion show was simultaneously created in the brand metaverse space in Decentraland as a "simulverse." **Simulverse** is when a physical event is simultaneously played out in the metaverse. Related, **Twinning** is crafting digital experiences that mimic a physical one, or vice versa. Examples of twinning are when Gucci created physical figurines of its SuperGucci NFTs or when Prada added NFTs to its limited-edition physical clothes.

Another brand strategy for the metaverse is tokenization. **Tokenization** is when physical items are reformatted into NFTs on a blockchain. Tommy Hilfiger created NFTs of luxury and exclusive physical merchandise on the Boston Portal marketplace in Decentraland. The company's release was timed with physical fashion week hosted in the fashion district of this 3D virtual world.[85]

9.4 Brand Stories in Influencer Marketing

We began Chapter 1 with Michelle Phan, the first influencer, saying, "Platforms—they come and go, but storytelling is forever."[86] It's fitting we end on the last category of IMC consumer touchpoints with influencer marketing. **Influencer marketing** leverages key leaders to advocate on behalf of a brand to reach the larger market. **Influencers**, sometimes called creators, are people who bring expertise to a specific area, have a sizable number of engaged followers, and share brand messages for compensation.[87]

Influencers have become important to marketers not only because of their importance in reaching audiences but also because of their influence on purchase decisions. Over 51 percent of consumers say they get ideas for product purchases from celebrities and creators, and 45 percent say they want to buy products directly from creators on social media.[88]

If social media marketing represented a loss of control for the marketer, influencer marketing is no different. Marketers pay influencers to promote a brand, yet the ultimate control is retained by the influencer to maintain authenticity and credibility with their audience. Influencer marketing isn't simply an influencer sharing brand-created posts.

As we learned with Michelle Phan, the success of influencers is their ability to tell stories that resonate with their followers. Brands need to find the right influencers to reach their target audience. Then look for a natural match between the stories the influencer tells with the story the brand is telling. It was a natural fit with Phan and Lancôme.

Influencer marketing is one of the fastest growing IMC strategies as it is often more trusted than brand messages. Getty Images: Vadym Pastukh.

Table 9.4. Influencers Come in Different Forms and Followings

Mega-Influencers	More than 1 million followers and often considered celebrities who may be more famous than influential.
Macro-Influencers	Between 100,000 and 1 million followers and usually gained their fame through the internet.
Micro-Influencers	Between 1,000 and 100,000 followers and focus on a specific niche as an industry expert or topic specialist.
Nano-Influencers	Less than 1,000 followers and have influence within their community.
Brand Ambassadors	Influencers who are rewarded or hired by the brand for long-term relationships.
Advocates	Brand loyalists who engage with a brand because they love it but may not have a large influence.

Source: Keith A. Quesenberry, "The Power of Storytelling in Social Media Marketing," SocialMediaToday.com (blog), April 8, 2015, http://www.socialmediatoday.com/marketing/2015-04-08/power-storytelling-social-media-marketing.

Influencers can be found by the brand searching on social media platforms where the target audience spends the most time. Then use a general search for keywords and hashtags associated with the industry and brand. Also, look through the brand's followers. Followers already have an interest in the brand, and some may have considerable influence. After you have identified influencers, reach out to form a relationship.[89]

Another way to find influencers is to use an influencer platform or network. An **influencer marketing platform** provides influencer search within a database of vetted influencers via categories and interests. These platforms provide follower and engagement statistics and can help with relationship and content management, analytics, and payment.[90] When selecting influencers, no matter the methods, consider the type and size of their influence (see Table 9.4).

Don't assume that a brand needs a high-profile celebrity to succeed in influencer marketing. Research by Edelman indicates that only 18 percent of respondents were attracted to influencers for their larger following. Relatability was nearly two times as important as popularity in attracting people to influencers.[91]

It's natural to think mega- or macro-influencers are best because of their mass reach, but micro-influencers can be more effective.[92] *Adweek* reports that average micro-influencer engagement is 60 percent higher and can drive 22 times more conversions.[93] A survey of national advertisers reveals that more than half use mid-level (66 percent) or micro-influencers (59 percent) compared to less than half who use macro-influencers (44 percent).[94]

Once you have the right influencers, determine how content will be created. Certain influencers or influencer networks may have standards for what they will or will not do. Consider various ways to create influencer content that is best for the brand and influencer and their audience. Forms of influencer brand content include the following:

- Influencer created brand content
- Influencer shared brand content
- Product and service reviews and mentions
- Influencer brand account takeovers

- Brand guest content contributions
- Collaboration on contests or giveaways
- Repurposed influencer content in other channels[95]

Some influencers, such as advocates or brand ambassadors, may post for the brand by receiving response, gratitude, and rewards. This is different from influencers who are paid for shorter-term campaigns or even individual posts. Some influencers may post for sending gifts such as free products. Others may post with affiliate marketing where they are paid based on sales generated.

Pura Vida's brand ambassador program #PuraVidaCrew combines methods. These fans tell friends, family, and followers about Pura Vida, weaving the product into their lifestyle. Unique ambassador codes give new customers 20 percent off purchases, and ambassadors earn commission and free products, plus have access to sneak peeks, exclusive content, and VIP giveaways.[96] The result is an army of Pura Vida marketers sharing authentic lifestyle images.[97]

9.5 CASE

Crockpot Firestorm

A final consideration for PR and IMC is crisis communications. This is more of the reactive part of PR, but it can greatly impact an IMC plan. **Crisis communications** attempt to mitigate damage to the company's or organization's reputation by third-party sources.[98] An example of a crisis affecting IMC is what happened to the appliance brand Crockpot.

In 2018, the NBC show *This Is Us* aired an episode with a story line of Jack Pearson dying in a house fire. To the mortification of the brand, the story was that the fire was caused by a faulty Crockpot, killing a beloved character in the popular TV show.

People all over social media spread the story of Crockpots being unsafe. Many were afraid they would burn their houses down and kill their families. Some even shared pictures and videos on social media of them throwing away their Crockpots. Was there a real product defect and fire risk? No. It was a fictional story not based on a real safety crisis.[99]

Fortunately, Crockpot had a crisis communications plan. Its public relations firm Edelman turned the story around by reacting quickly and compassionately. Edelman presented an alternative story line that engaged the consumer to change the conversation in the communication channels where consumers were reacting rather than just through an official statement in a traditional press release.[100] The PR firm opened a new Twitter account @CrockPotCares and used the trending #Crockpot hashtag to get its voice into the conversation where it was happening.[101] Edelman used the account to comfort fans over the loss of Jack and share facts about the product's safety.

On Facebook, Crockpot fans created a trending hashtag #CrockPotIsInnocent to stick up for the brand. The brand's marketers and Edelman took that story further by getting the actor who plays Jack Pearson to do a TV ad and TV news appearances to tell the public that Crockpots are safe and that he enjoys using them.

Partnering with NBC, one ad ran just before the Super Bowl showing Jack ladling a bowl of chili out of a Crockpot saying, "find the ability to forgive."[102] In the end, Pearson became the ultimate influencer to market the brand. The PR agency spun the story but spun it in the direction of truth. Instead of a disaster, a month later, Crockpot sales had increased from the brand exposure.[103]

In this chapter, we explored the discipline of public relations, how it has changed, and its important role in marketing communications and storytelling for brands. We also looked at how storytelling is important in the digital media disciplines of social media and influencer marketing. These areas complete our look at the different media or consumer touchpoints IMC plans use to tell their brand stories and deliver a campaign to meet marketing objectives. Yet we are not done with story. In the next chapter, we will look at how to get the plans off paper and into the world. As you will see, storytelling has a role to play in creating your final IMC plan and pitching it to the client.

QUESTIONS

1. With the concept of spin sucks in your mind, find a recent example of a brand that doesn't understand the new rules of PR and is still trying to be spin doctors and using propaganda in a negative way.
2. Do you feel influencer marketing is and will always be effective? Is there a saturation limit to the number of products influencers sell or the number of influencers that can sell?

EXERCISES

1. With the evolving landscape of digital media and social media, it seems like there is a blurring between the disciplines and practices of advertising, public relations, and digital or interactive marketing. Review the definitions of each professional practice, and categorize specific marketing communications tactics under each. How do you see these disciplines as separate and how do you see them as merging? How does Gini Dietrich's PESO media model fit with each?
2. Explore the IMC consumer touchpoint of influencers further. If you are working on a campaign plan, what role will influencers play? Is it better for the brand to find and manage itself or to use an influencer network? Or find examples of a current brand and its current influencers. Then consider how those influencers can help the brand to tell full five-act stories. Should they create full stories as videos or tell parts over multiple posts? Who are the main characters and protagonist and what is the setting? What is the inciting moment, rising action, climax, falling action, and resolve?

KEY CONCEPTS

Advocates

Algorithms

Augmented reality (AR)

Blog

Brand ambassadors

Brand community

Content calendar

Content curation

Crisis communications

Engagement rate

Facebook

Google My Business

Influencer marketing

Influencer marketing platform

Influencers

Instagram

LinkedIn
Macro-influencers
Media relations
Mega-influencers
Metaverse
Micro-influencers
Nano-influencers
Newswire
Phygital marketing
Pinterest
Podcasts
PR event
PR pitch
PR stunt
Press conference
Press release
Proactive public relations
Propaganda
Public relations
Publicity
Quora

Reddit
Remarketing
Simulverse
Snapchat
Social commerce
Social media
Social media advertising
Social media listening
Social media marketing managers
Social media monitoring
Social selling
TikTok
Tokenization
TripAdvisor
Twinning
Twitter
User-generated content
Virtual reality (VR)
Yelp
YouTube

PART

IV

Getting the Story into the World

Selling the Drama

Final Plans and Pitches

PREVIEW

We're entering the final part of our storytelling journey as we turn to getting the brand story out into the world. In this chapter, we'll learn to sell integrated marketing communications (IMC) strategy recommendations as stories in plan books and pitches. First, we'll consider two famous speeches and their elements of story. Then we'll look at creating an IMC plan book, outline, and pitch. Ad agency veteran Jon Steel has witnessed four decades of both good and bad pitches selling IMC campaigns to agency marketing clients. He has learned, "You need a compelling story. A story that brings your message to life and enables audience members to relate to it, be moved by it."[1] We'll end the chapter with our main case study breaking down the organization and presentation of an IMC plan into the five-act story framework.

CHAPTER 10 LEARNING OBJECTIVES

1. Explore some of the best speeches and their elements of storytelling.
2. Learn the importance of an IMC plan book, pitch and how they're different from IMC strategy.
3. Comprehend how to put together an IMC plan outline and book.
4. Know how to create a compelling IMC pitch.
5. Understand the IMC plan as a five-act story itself.

10.1 Lincoln and King Jr.

In this chapter, we will bring everything together as we compile all the components of IMC into a final plan strategy and creative campaign recommendations for the marketing client. This consists of a complete written report of the plan and a presentation, often called a pitch.

These plans and pitches can occur with current clients where you are presenting a new plan to be approved or presented with a potential client to try to win a new account against competing marketing communications agencies. In either situation, there is a lot of time and money riding on the decisions. You must put as much work into how you communicate recommendations as you did in coming up with them.

First, we will look at two great storytellers who led audiences and their country through great problems into solutions and victory through story. *Time* magazine's list of the Top 10 Greatest Speeches includes speeches from Abraham Lincoln and Martin Luther King Jr.[2] What do these speeches have in common and how do they apply story?

Abraham Lincoln's Gettysburg Address Is a Story to Remember

In 1863 at the site of one of the Civil War's deadliest and most pivotal battles, Edward Evert was the featured speaker to dedicate the Gettysburg Civil War Cemetery, where there were 51,000 casualties.[3] More than a dedication, the speakers wanted to help end the war. Evert spoke first delivering a two-hour speech beginning with "It was appointed by law in Athens, that the obsequies of the citizens who fell in battle should be performed at the public expense, and in the most honorable manner." You probably don't remember Evert, these words, or his speech.

Then Abraham Lincoln spoke for two minutes beginning with "Fourscore and seven years ago our fathers brought forth, on this continent, a new nation, conceived in liberty, and dedicated to the proposition that all men are created equal."[4] Unlike Evert's speech, Lincoln's words probably sound familiar, and you remember them as part of the Gettysburg Address. Even Edward Everett realized that Lincoln's speech was more effective. After the event, he wrote to Lincoln saying, "I should be glad, if I could flatter myself that I came as near to the central idea of the occasion, in two hours, as you did in two minutes."[5]

What can we learn from the two speeches? In Evert's speech, he communicated a long list of rational arguments, going back to the ancient Greeks, and directly criticized the South. In contrast, Lincoln knew his audience and used the opportunity to call everyone, the North and South, back into a unified country through the power of story. See Table 10.1 for how the Gettysburg Address follows the five-act story framework to engage and motivate a nation.

Martin Luther King Jr.'s Speech Is a Story to Inspire

One hundred years after Lincoln's Gettysburg Address, Martin Luther King Jr. delivered the "I Have a Dream" speech from the steps of the Lincoln Memorial in Washington, DC. It was a defining movement for the American civil rights movement. In what is known as one of the best speeches in history, King told a story of American racial harmony. The following year, he became the youngest man to win the Nobel Peace Prize. Catherine Carr in *Fast Company* points out key reasons why it is a powerful speech. The following are key strengths of King's "I Have a Dream" speech:

- *It's in a symbolic location.* King begins echoing Lincoln's speech: "Five score years ago" on the steps of the Lincoln Memorial upon which Lincoln's Gettysburg Address is etched in stone.

Table 10.1. Lincoln's Gettysburg Address Applied to Freytag's Story Framework

Story Act	Speech Text	Story Act Development
Act 1 Exposition Characters, setting, basic conflict are established leading to tension. An inciting moment begins rising action of complications.	"Four score and seven years ago our fathers brought forth on this continent, a new nation, conceived in Liberty, and dedicated to the proposition that all men are created equal. Now we are engaged in a great civil war, testing whether that nation or any nation so conceived and so dedicated, can long endure."	Characters are introduced as the founding fathers of the United States and citizens of the nation in this land seeking liberty. The inciting moment is introduced as the Civil War begins rising complications.
Act 2 Complication Tension mounts as the main character's efforts to reach a goal meet conflicts and obstacles. Frustration builds as opposing forces intensify.	"We are met on a great battlefield of that war. We have come to dedicate a portion of that field, as a final resting place for those who here gave their lives so that that nation might live. It is altogether fitting and proper that we should do this. But, in a larger sense, we cannot dedicate— we cannot consecrate—we cannot hallow—this ground."	The story becomes more complex as Lincoln brings up the clashing interests and tension mounts as the audience are reminded that the soldiers gave their lives so that the nation may live. They are reminded that they have not reached that goal and therefore cannot truly dedicate that ground. There is more to accomplish.
Act 3 Climax Conflict reaches a high turning point that could lead to victory or defeat for the main character, resulting in good or bad consequences.	"The brave men, living and dead, who struggled here, have consecrated it, far above our poor power to add or detract. The world will little note, nor long remember what we say here, but it can never forget what they did here. It is for us the living, rather, to be dedicated here to the unfinished work which they who fought here have thus far so nobly advanced."	The conflict reaches a high point. The turning point signals that this battle could lead to victory or defeat depending on the actions of all who hear the message in person or shared in print. Lincoln calls on them to finish the work begun by those who lost their lives.
Act 4 Reversal Events play out in falling actions from the reversal in the climax. Momentum slows as the characters head toward a final resolution.	"It is rather for us to be here dedicated to the great task remaining before us—that from these honored dead we take increased devotion to that cause for which they gave the last full measure of devotion—that we here highly resolve that these dead shall not have died in vain . . ."	The result of the conflict plays out in falling actions based on the audience dedicating themselves to continue the great task ahead. Lincoln says that these falling actions of the continued fight must be carried out so those who have died have not died in vain.
Act 5 Denouement Conflict is resolved and tension is released, creating normalcy where the main characters are better off.	". . . that this nation, under God, shall have a new birth of freedom—and that government of the people, by the people, for the people, shall not perish from the earth."	The conflict is resolved by depicting a picture of the final victory where tension will be released and a return to normalcy of a united nation. A resolution where the main characters, citizens of the United States, are better off.

- *It speaks to the head and heart.* He uses rational arguments from the Declaration of Independence and the Constitution while evoking emotion from Bible passages and African American spirituals.
- *It uses vivid metaphors.* He paints a picture using metaphors such as coming to the capital to cash a check, which has come back with insufficient funds.
- *It conveys ideas through contrast.* King contrasts "what is" against "what could be" through problem/solution, past/present, and ideal/reality examples.
- *It repeats key points.* He repeats phrases, such as "Now is the time," and "I have a dream," to create a rhythm, structure, and flow, making the message memorable.
- *It delivers a clear call to action.* The purpose of the presentation is clear. King wanted listeners to take action now with dignity and discipline.[6]

In Chapter 3, we learned the value of inside-out marketing thinking via Simon Sinek and his "start with why" concept. Sinek's inspiration for this concept came from studying influential people who accomplished their goals, such as Dr. King. Sinek adds to our knowledge of the effectiveness of King's message by saying, "Dr. King didn't tell people what needed to change in America. He went around and told people what he believed. I believe, I believe, I believe." He told people. And people who believed what he believed took his cause, made it their own, and told people. Dr. King started with the why, then moved on to the how and the what to make the dream become a reality.[7]

Selling dreams of a better future can be a powerful story. A recent example was Nike's Dream Crazier TV commercial narrated by Serena Williams. The ad tells the story of women in sports and moments that may have been considered "crazy" by some but that have helped

The Lincoln Memorial represents two speeches that moved people and an entire country to help achieve goals. Getty Images: Marc Dozier.

advance women's participation, performance, and accomplishments in sport.[8] In chapter 5 we learned how Carol Williams took a similar approach with her famous tagline for Secret deodorant "Strong enough for a man but made for a woman."

Serena highlights some of the contradictions between standards for men and women in sport, such as "If we show emotion, we're called dramatic" and "If we get angry, we're hysterical, irrational or just plain crazy."[9] These are examples of cultural tensions that Luke Sullivan talked about in Chapter 1. He suggested studying a client's product category and looking for conflicts or cultural tensions that can be turned into stories.[10]

That's what Nike did. The company knows its female target audience and understands the contradictions and tensions they face. Nike highlights them but then flips the narrative, turning the negative stereotypes into a positive. Serena continues saying, "a woman running a marathon was crazy"; "a woman dunking was crazy"; "a woman winning 23 grand slams, having a baby, and then coming back for more . . . crazy." The narration is over powerful images of women accomplishing great feats in sports. The commercial ends with the line "It's only crazy until you do it." That fades into Nike's tagline "Just Do It."[11]

The Dream Crazier TV commercial premiered during the Oscars and quickly went viral. After just one day, it had over 6 million earned media views on YouTube and more than 28 million on Twitter. Sentiment analysis of social media comments was overwhelmingly positive. The mention of Nike's tagline hashtag #justdoit increased by over 2,000 percent, reaching over 600 million people on the internet.[12] That is the power of brand storytelling from a brand that knows its target audience's story and perspective.

But before Dream Crazier could deliver those amazing marketing results, the idea first had to be pitched by the ad agency Wieden+Kennedy to the marketing department at Nike to be approved by the client.

While an IMC plan and pitch may not have the enormous implications of a civil war or civil rights movement, they serve a similar purpose: to propose a specific plan of action to overcome a challenge and convince an audience to support and implement that plan. There can be a lot riding on IMC recommendations. Nike spent $3.8 billion on advertising and promotion in 2022.[13]

10.2 IMC Plan Book

A complete IMC plan needs to be pitched to the marketing client. It represents a new direction for the company with a significant investment of time and money. Therefore, a special pitch meeting is scheduled, and a special report document is created called a plan book. A plan book is more than the IMC strategy. It is a selling document designed to convince the client your solution addresses their IMC problem and will meet their marketing objectives.

IMC Strategies Need to Be Sold in Plan Books and Pitches

An **IMC plan book** is a document used in a presentation or to sell an IMC strategy or campaign to a current marketing client or to win a new client. The plan book is the written portion of a pitch to your client with your IMC recommendations. It provides the details, whereas your presentation hits the highlights. A plan book is often given to the client after a presentation and therefore is sometimes also called a "leave behind."

Table 10.2. Phrases That Don't Portray Confidence and What to Say Instead

Words or Phrases to Avoid	What to Say Instead
"I think this would . . ."	Begin with what you were going to say next.
"In my opinion . . ."	Nothing
"I'm not sure, but . . ."	Begin with what you were going to say after *but*.
"In our research, we found . . ."	"Research revealed that"
"We feel the design looks better."	"Whitespace is less cluttered and more engaging."
"It's important to note that . . ."	Begin with what you were going to say next.
"Needless to say . . ."	Nothing
"Maybe you should try . . ."	"It is recommended that the brand . . ."
"It makes sense to . . ."	Begin with what you were going to say next.
"I just believe . . ."	"It is recommended that the brand . . ."
"For what it's worth . . ."	Nothing
"It actually performed better."	"It performed better."
"Hopefully . . ."	Nothing

Source: Kathy Petros and Ross Petros, "Want to Sound More Confident? Avoid These 11 Words and Phrases That Make You Look 'Weak,' Say Grammar Experts," CNBC.com, November 7, 2021, https://www.cnbc.com/2021/11/07/overused-words-and-phrases-that-make-you-sound-weak-less-confident-according-to-grammar-experts.html.

As a student, young professional, or even seasoned veteran, it can be scary to present a plan where millions of dollars will be invested based on your recommendations. Yet remember the weeks of research you've invested in your client, their market, competitors, target audience and creative thinking to arrive at your solution. You are the communications expert, and that is why they hired you. Therefore, you must write and present with confidence.

How do you present with confidence? Start with the language you use. See Table 10.2 for a list of words and phrases grammar experts say to avoid and what to say or not say to portray confidence. This applies to pitches but also everyday business interactions. Another consideration in your writing is to use a third-person perspective versus the first person. It can be perceived as a stronger presentation in an objective marketing communications document.such as "The research shows consumers favor . . ." vs. "We believe that the research shows . . ."

An IMC plan book should set up and showcase your recommendations. Don't confuse the plan book with the strategic process. As Parente and Straugsbaurgh–Hutchinson (2014) say in *Advertising Campaign Strategy*, "Never confuse what you need to know to produce a campaign with what you need to report to the client." Visuals also play an important role. A picture is often worth a thousand words. See Table 10.3 for a list of visual formats and suggested uses to help make your IMC plan book more concise and convincing.

The scale and scope of the plan book will vary. The outline in this chapter is for a complete IMC plan. For your specific client or assignment, you may need to add or subtract sections. The IMC plan book outline template worksheet in Table 10.4 can be modified for your specific client project or student assignment.

Table 10.3. Graphic Elements to Use for Concise and Convincing Communication

Bar Graphs	Use to compare data for competitors, the market, and consumer trends.
Pie Charts	Use for percentages of a whole, such as market share, media spending, product usage, consumer preferences, and budgets.
Line Graphs	Use for illustrating spending and sales trends over time.
Tables	Use when summarizing long lists of numbers or words in context, such as a SWOT analysis graph with four quadrants and bulleted information.
Pictures	Use to show current marketing communications for the company and competitors and to present examples of creative executions in context.
Illustrations	Use to show ideas for which you don't have a photo from stock images or your own photography, such as in storyboards.
Infographics	Use to visually explain a complex subject, process, or a large data set into an easily digestible graphic.
Subheadings	Use to break up long blocks of text into sections with descriptive headings and subheadings organized in a table of contents.
Table of Contents	Use to list the main headings and subheadings with corresponding page numbers for readers to easily find information.
Paragraphs	Use paragraphs to break up dense blocks of type focusing on one topic in 4-5 sentences or 100-200 words per paragraph.
Bulleted Lists	Use to highlight important information or key points in short phrases.
Box/Quotes	Use to highlight important information for support or transition such as a pull quote. Use quotes when the way something was said is important.

The following are types of projects or assignments for IMC plan books:

- A new brand or rebrand
- A new product launch
- A sales promotion campaign
- A business-to-business or trade campaign
- A nonprofit or cause campaign
- A new business pitch or request for proposal
- A student class project
- A student client project
- A student plan competition
- A student run agency

Plan Books and Pitches Require Multiple People and Processes

Creating an IMC plan report or book involves unique activities that require different skills. These skills need to be worked on at the same time. Various people should be assigned different tasks to complete the plan on time. **Project management** is the planning and organizing of a company's resources over a specific task, event, or project toward completion.[14] Today, there are many software tools that facilitate and organize project management, such

Don't underestimate the importance of project management as a key element to creating a successful IMC plan book and pitch. Getty Images: FG Trade.

as Basecamp, Monday.com, Trello, and Asana. These tools also help in communication and collaboration with remote employee or student team members.

An IMC agency has many team members involved in the process. Account managers handle client relations and strategy. Researchers collect and conduct client, competitor, market, and consumer research. Account planners or account managers work on creative briefs and overall creative strategy. Media planners research target audience media use and calculate the most efficient and effective media mix. Creative directors, copywriters, and art directors work on creative concepts and creative executions. Public relations (PR), digital marketing, and social media experts complete their important specialized aspects of the plan. A project manager keeps all these people organized and accountable in assigning tasks, setting up schedules, and checking on progress.

In selling a new approach, you may have to critique past efforts that were wrong or not very good. Don't shy away from this but do it with tact. **Tact** is the sense of what to say without offending when delivering difficult information.[15] This is an important skill in business. Don't say that the client's current advertising is horrible, sucks, or is stupid. The person reading your plan may have created or at least approved it. Instead, point out why it may not be performing well and that the new recommendations will be better for specific reasons. An exception is if customers are saying it. Direct quotes of customers on social media or in focus groups saying the client's previous ads suck may be just what they need to hear.

The final IMC plan book presents the entire picture of the project following a progression of the problem, analysis, and strategic and tactical recommendations. Explain where the client has been, where they want to go, and how and why your plan will get them there. Provide ample reasoning and support for why your plan isn't just creative ideas but rather, a focused solution through an IMC effort. Table 10.4 is an example of an IMC plan book outline template worksheet that takes the client through this process.

Table 10.4. IMC Plan Book Outline Template Worksheet

Executive Summary
Table of Contents
Introduction
Situation Analysis
    Company Overview (Mission, Current Users, Marketing, and Product/Service)
    Market Overview (Industry and Consumer Research)
    Competitive Assessment (Sales and Marketing Communications)
SWOT Analysis
    SWOT (Graphic Summary)
    Problems and Opportunities
Target Market (Definition and Profile)
Objectives
    Marketing Objectives (Follow SMART guidelines)
    Communications Objectives (Follow SMART guidelines)
Budget and Timeline
IMC Communications Strategy (Message and Rationale)
    Creative Brief
    Creative Concept (Big Idea and Rationale)
IMC Creative Executions
    Advertising
    Public Relations
    Digital Marketing
    Social Media
    Direct Marketing
    Sales Promotion
    Personal Sales
Media Strategy
    Media Mix (Objective and Budget)
    Media Schedule
Evaluation Plan
Conclusion
References
Appendix (Research, Budget, Media Details)

10.3 IMC Plan Outline

An IMC plan should begin with an executive summary. This appears first in the document but should be written last. An **executive summary** is an overview of the main points of a strategic plan for someone who doesn't have time to review the entire document to help them make a quick decision and stay informed. An executive summary can be two to four paragraphs but should be no more than one page.

The table of contents helps readers easily find a specific topic or more details. This could be for the executive who only reads the summary but wants more details on a specific area or for the person who was in your pitch presentation who wants more details on a topic of importance to them. A **table of contents** lists the main heading and subheading sections with corresponding page numbers for readers to easily find information. Each heading and subheading section should be a significant portion of the plan with multiple paragraphs focused on a topic—too many headings and the plan will feel complicated and choppy; not enough and it will feel dense and difficult to process.

After the table of contents and before the first main section, provide a brief introduction paragraph. An introduction is different from an executive summary. It doesn't provide a complete summary or provide the solution. It establishes the premise of the plan. An **introduction** is a brief description of the purpose of a document, letting the reader know what they will read and why it is important.

Situation Analysis Sets the Stage

The first two sections of the IMC plan book can be confused but are separate and serve different purposes. A **situation analysis** is an analysis of internal and external environmental factors that influence business performance in the context of past performance and future objectives.[16] Also called a situation assessment, it is the first step in strategic thinking to highlight key issues affecting client performance. The SWOT analysis is part of the situation analysis that summarizes and categorizes information and insights uncovered. A **SWOT analysis** is a framework to evaluate a company's competitive position by assessing internal strengths and weaknesses with external opportunities and threats.[17]

The type and amount of information you need to collect to create an IMC plan is not the same as you need for the IMC plan book. The client knows their business, competitors, and industry well. Don't simply tell them everything they already know. Instead, highlight key information, letting them know you took the time to know their business and know what is important to them. Clients look for signs that you "did your homework."

Begin with a company overview. Draw attention to the relevant parts of brand history, mission, current customers, current marketing, products, and services. At the point of writing the plan book, you'll know what information led to the creative strategy and the creative concepts that you're recommending. Highlight insights most relevant to setting up the solutions you're providing. Don't leave out the company's mission or vision. Let the client know that you know what is important to them. An IMC plan pitch to Patagonia wouldn't begin well if it didn't mention Patagonia's 1 percent for the planet pledge and its commitment to supporting the environment.

If one creative concept features the founder of the company, be sure to include some of that history in the company overview. If another concept hinges upon a key customer insight, mention it in the situation analysis. When explaining creative concepts later in the plan, refer to that key information in the situation analysis as support.

Market Overview Explains the Challenge

Discuss some of the most relevant research and insights beyond internal information about the company. Let the client know you understand the key challenges and opportunities that everyone in their industry faces. What matters most to consumers in the market? How do they currently feel about the brand? What most inspired your understanding of their problem and your proposed solutions? Include consumer surveys, trend reports, and competitor insights.

Present key data in graphs, tables, charts, or infographics. Data visualized is easier to understand and interpret so conclusions can be reached more quickly. Problems and opportunities can be seen more clearly through graphics.[18] Using visual elements throughout will make your plan more concise while still conveying important information.

When adding visual elements, reference the visual in the text and let the reader know why it is there and what it shows. Don't place all visuals at the end (making your reader flip or scroll back and forth)—place them in the text where they are relevant.

Competitive Assessment Identifies the Foes

Next, present key information about the client's main competitors. Think Ben & Jerry's and Haagen-Daz ice cream or Delta and American Airlines. Who tends to be in the consumer consideration set, along with your client's brand, or closest in market share?

Did you uncover insights as to why competitors are performing better or worse? What is their latest marketing campaign? Do they have a tagline, spokesperson, or new promotional effort? Show examples of ads, social posts, and websites to contrast your proposed creative strategy, concepts, and executions differentiating your client in the mind of their target consumers.

If relevant, bring up substitute products outside the market category that require a shift in message. For example, in the last recession, casual dining restaurants such as Applebee's competed more with fast-food restaurants such as McDonald's as discretionary income declined. Applebee's switched to a value message to convince people of the affordability of a date night. An Applebee's PR release said, "As America's purse strings tighten . . . Applebee's 2 for $20 menu gives guests a choice of sharable appetizer and two full size meals."[19]

SWOT Analysis Summarizes the Situation

The SWOT analysis summarizes everything found in the situation analysis and categorizes it into key factors visually expressed as a four-quadrant graphic (see Figure 10.1). The purpose

Figure 10.1. SWOT analysis graphic template worksheet.

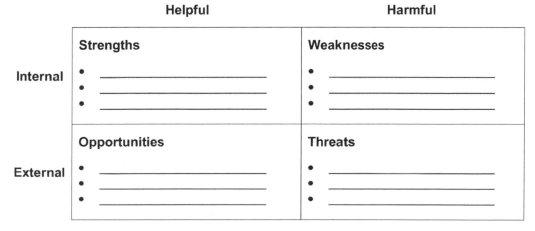

of a SWOT is to link where the client has been to where they want to go by visually high-lighting internal strengths and weaknesses and external threats and opportunities.

After the SWOT analysis graphic, look to describe the client's main problems from internal weaknesses and external threats. Then find and describe some key opportunities where the client's internal strengths match external opportunities. These connections help lead the way toward potential solutions. The problems should highlight the need for a new IMC plan, and the opportunities should lead to meeting the marketing objectives. Sometimes, problems can be turned into opportunities.

Talk only about problems and opportunities that marketing communications can help solve. If a client has a poor store location, don't recommend moving the store. That's outside the scale and scope of IMC. But you could recommend a clever creative message that tells customers the poor location is worth it for better selection and better prices. Solve the problem with their current product, place, and place offerings through new marketing communications.

Target Market Identifies the Audiences

Clearly define the group that will be the focus of the IMC plan with relevant demographic, psychographic, behavioral, and geographic variables (see Chapter 4). Highlight any key insights you discovered about this segment of the market while thinking ahead to your creative and media strategies. Is there anything about the target market that is key to your recommendations that needs to be set up first?

Also, include secondary target markets. These could be people who influence the main purchasers of the product or service. Parents may be the main grocery shopper for a household, but kids influence what is bought. Cliff Bar Kids' target market is parents, but they may also have a secondary target market of kids. The message to parents is that the bar is healthy, whereas the message to kids is that it tastes great. For years, the cereal brand Kix has used the tagline, "Kid-Tested. Parent-Approved" as a message to both target audiences.[20]

Another example could be a consumer and trade target for a new product launch. If Kix or Cliff Bar came out with a new flavor, they would target consumers to drive demand but also need it to be in stores. Shelf space is a premium, and trade campaigns convince a business-to-business secondary target audience to stock new products. Buyers in supermarket chains would be defined via firmographics, such as job titles, company name, size, or members of professional organizations.

Most IMC agencies also create a profile of a typical customer. A **target market profile** is a description of your ideal customer describing demographic, psychographic, and behavioral traits, along with core needs, purchase decisions, and media habits. Profiles can be a descriptive bulleted list, a paragraph narrative, or a graphic including images and logos.[21] Profiles help you picture a group of people as one ideal customer, including their needs, wants, problems, and personality. A target market profile may include the stages customers go through when making a purchase. Profiles may also describe the type of media channels, TV shows, and brands they prefer.[22]

A version of the target market profile that is popular in digital marketing is a **persona**, which is a fictional character created to identify similar patterns of behavior and common goals that represent a target audience. Personas include an illustrative picture and fictional name to describe common behaviors, preferences, motivations, and goals of ideal customers.[23]

Consider the following information when creating a target market profile or persona:

- Profile name
- Demographic description
- Psychographic description
- Behavioral characteristics
- Geographic considerations
- Goals and frustrations
- Personality and motivations
- Favorite media and shows
- Favorite brands and influencers
- Stages of the buyer's journey

The software and data media planners' use for media strategies often provide insights into creating audience profiles. Tools such as SRDS, MRI-Simmons, comScore, and Nielson have custom and syndicated audience segments with demographic, psychographic, behavioral, purchase-based, and media consumption information to get a more complete picture of the target consumer.[24]

Objectives Establish the Finish Line

Marketing clients typically come to IMC agencies with marketing objectives, so reiterate to them that you know that the IMC plan must return marketing results. Make it clear that you know what those results are—the ones that are most important to the client. For a smaller business, you may need to help in this area by estimating or setting some sales or marketing share objectives for them.

In Chapter 4, we learned that **marketing objectives** focus on a direct return on the firm's marketing investment, such as reaching a specific level of sales, revenue, or market share.

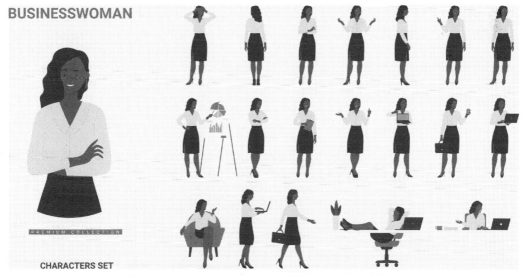

A target market profile or persona portrays a typical persona in your target audience including an illustrative picture of someone in the target. Getty Images: Flash Vector.

The marketing objective is usually tied to an annual objective that must be met within the yearly marketing budget and that justifies the marketing spend with a return on investment.

Include the marketing objective or objectives in your IMC plan, but you may also need objectives to measure communications effectiveness. **Communications objectives** focus on effective communication, such as a specific level of advertising recall or brand or product awareness or a measurable change in attitudes, brand image, or reputation. There may be overall communications objectives or specific marketing communications objectives for significant parts of the plan, such as awareness for TV or engagement for social media.

Marketing and communications objectives should meet SMART guidelines. **SMART** is specific (quantified such as X% or $X), measurable (data you can access), achievable (not too high), relevant (support vision/mission and address problem/opportunity), and timely (due date such as X months or in 20XX year). Demonstrate that you understand the relationship between your IMC plan recommendations and their purpose to support real objectives you and the client must meet.

Budget and Timeline Set the Rules

In many cases, the overall budget and timeline are provided by the client during the initial project briefing or request for a new business pitch. But you want to restate them in your IMC plan book to let the client know you are aware of the parameters within which you are working. Like the objectives, the budget and timeline are a good reminder of the scale, scope, and purpose of the strategies, tactics, and concepts being recommended.

For smaller clients, you may need to estimate the budget and timeline. They may not have the resources or time to create them. Seek to answer the question, What money will be spent to meet marketing objectives within what time frame? Chapter 4 provides a further explanation of the main methods for determining a marketing budget. The timeline tends to correlate with the marketing budget based on a calendar year. This can vary for movie releases, elections, events, or fundraising campaigns that have a specific end date.[25]

IMC Communications Strategy Sells Your Big Idea

Before the creative brief, concepts, and executions, provide a brief overview of your approach. Present a road map for how the various tactics and touchpoints will help achieve the objectives. For example, explain how TV ads will deliver broad awareness combined with highly targeted digital marketing via YouTube and remarketing via email and social media. Describe PR as filling in early for general awareness and later for brand advocacy. Tell how a sales promotion will drive trial and repeat purchases during the high season. Explain how the sales team will use promotional materials at the point of sale to emphasize the key message.

Don't give away creative concepts, such as your tagline or big idea, yet. Provide short rationales for each broad aspect of your creative strategy and link back to the key problems, opportunities, objectives, and insights you have already stated. Paint a picture with broad strokes as statements, a narrative, or a graphic showing how elements work together.

Next present the creative brief—a key link between background and research to creative concepts and executions. Remember that the **creative brief** is the strategic document used to develop creative content for IMC plans and campaigns. The creative brief should already have been approved by the client, yet it is important to include it to remind everyone. The brief will set up your creative concepts and be used to determine if they are on strategy.

Sometimes, IMC agencies present a client with just one creative concept recommendation, and other times, the client or agency will want more options (two or three). In that case, the other sections of the plan, before and after, remain the same, but one, two, or three big creative concept ideas and example executions will be explained and presented after the creative brief.

Now, it is time for the reveal of your creative concepts and creative executions. The creative concept is often called "the big idea." Don't underestimate the value of making a big deal out of a big idea. Dedicate a page in a plan book and a slide in a presentation to introduce the creative concept first presented as the campaign tagline. Then explain the premise behind the big idea, the promise it delivers to the target audience, and how it will move them from "what they currently think–feel–do" to "what you want them to think–feel–do."

Remember that the client has not spent the weeks you have, immersed in research and brainstorming. Briefly connect the dots for them by going back to the challenge, promise, and key consumer insight that inspired the big idea, such as women in sport being misunder-stood–the basis of Nike's Dream Crazy example in Chapter 9. Explain how your big idea has legs as a basis for a variety of media and executions for a long time. Discuss how it is relevant, compelling, and original. Describe the specific look and feel and how they're important to the idea, such as black and white photos, a spokesperson, or a witty tone.

Often, agencies create a concept board as a single visual or collage of images to represent the big idea. Some will create a narrative video to introduce and explain the creative concept behind each the big idea. No matter what form you use, the important part is to set the stage for the creative executions you're about to present and how they are the perfect solution to change the target audience's perceptions and actions to meet the client's marketing objectives.

IMC Creative Executions Show Your Idea Has Legs

Demonstrate how the campaign will look to the target audience in various media to prove that the idea is big and has legs for any medium and tactic. Bring the campaign to life for the client through visual examples and well-crafted copy for print ads, scripts, and posts.

Make a big deal out of your big idea and tagline, such as "I LOVE COFFEE" on an individual slide, in a concept board or narrative video. Getty Images: Indigolotus.

Mock-up ideas to appear as real as possible to make it easy for the client to imagine. Read and act out radio scripts. Create storyboards for TV scripts. Design billboards in pictures of real billboards on highways and city streets. Mock-up social media posts the size and shape of each social platform. Make it clear how the idea can be delivered in a variety of verbal and visual ways and vehicles.

The creative executions depicted from advertising, PR, digital marketing, social media, direct marketing, sales promotions, and personal sales will depend on the specific client, market, target, objectives, and media mix recommendations. Present creative executions in an order that flows best for the big idea.

Some agencies begin with print ads, work up to TV, and then show PR and social media. Other times, they'll begin with TV as the full expression of the idea and demonstrate how it also works with visuals and words in print, audio-only radio, short copy on billboards, and as consumer-generated content on social media.

Another option is to present creative executions in the order in which the target consumer may experience them. If you're launching a new product, PR may begin with news stories or a publicity stunt. Then social media and influencer marketing spread the buzz. Later, traditional advertising appears to move the consumer to the point of sale and a new in-store experience.

Mock-up creative executions in realistic visual environments so that clients can image what the ads will really look like. Meves "White blank billboards in the subway tunnel." Creative #495697483. Getty Images, http://www.gettyimages.com/detail/495697483.

Media Strategy Shows How You'll Reach the Audience

The media strategy is about delivering the most efficient and effective spend of the budget. As we learned in Chapter 4, **media planning** determines the types of advertising media used, the amount of budget allocated to each (media mix), and the specific time schedule for each media vehicle.[26] Restate the target audience and mention any insights learned in the situation analysis that informed the media strategy. Your target market profile or persona may have indicated media habits you can highlight.

Mention the overall budget, time period, and media objectives. Media objectives are set to expose a percentage of the target audience to the message a number of times through reach and frequency. Emphasize reaching a minimum number of the target audience a minimum number of times without overexposing them and wasting media dollars.

Then present the recommended media mix with spending allocations. A pie chart can show the media mix with percentages of the budget devoted to each media vehicle. But keep in mind that spending on different media doesn't mean equal exposure. Some media is more expensive to reach the target than others (see Chapter 4). This is where cost per mille (CPM) becomes a useful comparison metric. Network TV ads average $20 CPM, whereas Google Display Ads average only $3 CPM, but each medium serves different strategic purposes.

The paid media planning template in Chapter 4 provides an example of how to show the media mix recommendations, CPM, and budget allocation. You also want to include a media calendar or flow chart to show how different touchpoints and tactics will be used at different times. Be sure to explain the rationale behind scheduling, such as early spending for a product launch or increased spending during certain periods for seasonal products. Also, explain flighting or pulsing strategies used to stretch the media budget.

A media calendar or flow chart shows how each medium and tactic will be deployed across the plan period and the weight behind each. A media flow chart includes media type in the first column and columns for each month during the plan period, typically a budget year from January through December. Different sales promotions can be indicated in a row beneath the months each promotion will run. Some media flow charts also include measurements such as gross ratings points (GRPs) for each media and period. Table 10.5 presents an example media calendar flow chart template worksheet.

Evaluation Plan Explains How You'll Measure Success

Last but not least, detail how you will measure IMC plan results and when you will assess them. Once again, this tells the client you know that you will be held accountable for the return on investment of implementing your IMC plan recommendations. Connect specific marketing and communications objectives to each media tactic explaining what will be measured, how, and when. Most likely you'll need the client to provide sales and market share results from internal sources. That is fine, but mention it, and set an expectation for when or how often the numbers will be provided and evaluated.

For broad communications objectives such as brand perception, awareness, or recall you may need focus groups or surveys halfway through and/or at the end of the plan period. For digital marketing such as social media ads, real-time measurement is possible, but manage expectations by setting monthly or quarterly social media or digital media reports. These more frequent check-ins can be early indicators the plan is working. If not, media, message, and creative executions can be adjusted. Build into the budget research and software needed to measure results and deliver reports.

Table 10.5. Media Calendar Flow Chart Template Worksheet

Media	Jan.	Feb.	Mar.	Apr.	May	June	July	Aug.	Sept.	Oct.	Nov.	Dec.
Promo												
TV												
Radio												
Print												
Billboard												
Social												
Display												
Video												
Search												

10.4 IMC Plan Pitch

Congratulations—you have made it to the presentation pitch! Half your work is about to begin. Frankly, it doesn't matter how many weeks of hard work you spent on the IMC plan; if your presentation falls flat, it could all be wasted effort. Even the best ideas won't see the light of day if they can't be sold in a presentation.

This may sound dramatic, but in a new business situation, you could not win the account with a flat pitch. With an existing client, the best ideas often feel the riskiest, so your best pitch is needed to get them accepted and approved. The presentation offers exciting creative opportunities to have your recommendations and creative concepts really shine.

The last thing you want to do is think of the presentation as an afterthought or something you throw together at the last minute. It doesn't matter how well the IMC pitch book is written; an effective presentation is much more than creating bullet point slides from the pitch book and simply holding up the ads.

A typical pitch book can be 30 pages or even 70 pages long. It takes planning to know what to highlight and how to fit that information into a 20- to 30-minute presentation. If you are lucky, the client may give you 45 minutes to an hour, but even then, you want to save plenty of time for questions.

Know Your Objective and Your Audience

The objective of the plan pitch is to sell your ideas in a live presentation. Your target audience for the pitch is your client. You need to convince the client that your plan will solve their marketing problem and meet their objectives. Sadly, the best idea doesn't always win. A poor idea professionally presented will typically beat out the best idea poorly presented. Clients will not buy a creative idea simply for its creativity. You must convince them that creativity is the best way to achieve their marketing objectives.

In the plan pitch, you most likely will be presenting to multiple people from the marketing department or other departments. Do your homework—research the people who will be in the room. Know each person's background and role to determine what criteria they care about most. Then ensure that you highlight those criteria in the presentation to address each person's perspective. You can't cover everything, but you can cover the things you know people in the room will be looking for and feel are important.

Know How to Sell an Idea

Ideas don't sell themselves. Clients will not automatically recognize the wisdom of your recommendations. Work hard to ensure that they see the brilliance behind them. This often requires taking them through your thought process while highlighting key research and insights. They have not been in the brainstorming sessions with you where and when your ideas first emerged.

Sometimes, you must explain what seems obvious from your perspective. To you, an uncluttered layout obviously looks better than one cluttered with information. Remember what we learned from Carol Williams in Chapter 5 about the value of seeing through other people's eyes? A client may see a cluttered layout as conveying more information and therefore, more effective. To help them see your perspective, explain how white, or negative, space between elements focuses attention for more effective communication. Similarly, don't just show a graph or data and assume they will get the main point. Make it clear what the graph, chart, or table told you and why it is important.

Let the Creative Concept Drive the Pitch

One purpose of the pitch book is to prove that your big idea is big enough to be executed in multiple ways in multiple media showing that the idea has legs. The presentation provides an opportunity to prove this even further. Concept some more creative executions, except this time the medium is the pitch and the people in the pitch.

In what ways outside of the ads can you apply the concept? Think about what your pitch team will wear, drink, and eat. If the client sells hiking gear, can you have the pitch at a park instead of the office? Can the pitch team present in hiking gear instead of business attire? If your idea is about dogs, can you bring a dog to the pitch? If it revolves around a song, can you perform it live?

What You Say and Show Matters

What you say should be the main form of information delivery. Slides should highlight and reinforce your verbal message through visuals and minimal words. You don't want the audience reading the slides instead of listening to you. And you shouldn't read them either! Plan out general points you want to make with bulleted note cards to jog your memory. Don't write out your presentation in full sentences on note cards and read them. This isn't an acceptance speech. Know the material and present it conversationally and naturally.

It is better to have 10 slides with one image, statistic, and point on each than to have one slide with all 10. Jon Steel, group planning director of WPP, recommends starting with sticky notes and writing one idea with one visual and six to seven words on each. Then move them around to plan out the progression.

The order of what you show and say matters. Build up to a reveal of the big idea considering story and five acts. Remember that the pitch book is known as the leave behind for a reason. Don't hand out the pitch book until you're done with the presentation. You don't want the client reading instead of listening to you and you don't want to spoil the story before you tell it.

Scout the Room and Rehearse the Pitch

If you can, visit the presentation room or ask for details and pictures. You want to know the size of the room, the furniture, and the equipment. Large posters of creative ads will not work to present in a small room. Small posters of ads or screens will not work in a big room. Make sure you know how to work the audiovisual equipment and that your tech is compatible. Have multiple backups in case it doesn't work. You don't want two to three weeks of work and a possible trip across the country to not go as planned because of a $10 adapter or faulty USB drive.

Plan your pitch on paper but rehearse the presentation aloud. What sounds good on paper doesn't always sound good said aloud. Also, what you plan to say tends to take longer than you expect. A full team presentation run-through a day before the client pitch is a great opportunity to obtain feedback for last-minute tweaks. Practice acting out the radio, video, and TV scripts with character voices and sound effects. Read your print copy with emphasis.

Know ahead of time the type of room you will be presenting in to avoid last minute complications and potential disastrous results. Getty Images: Simonkr.

Plan for Objections and Questions

If you know the client well and have done research on the people in the room, you can plan for objections and questions. For example, any client on a food brand will bring up the question, "What about appetite appeal?" They expect good photography or video footage of their food. Therefore, include it in your creative concepts, or be prepared to explain why you haven't. You can even raise the objection and answer it yourself, such as "I know that you are looking for appetite appeal. We plan to hire a food photographer and place amazing food shots next to the logo."

Be sure to leave time for questions. This takes away from what you can present, but leaving without asked-and-resolved questions will put doubt in the client's mind. There are always questions, so get them addressed before you leave. To prepare, brainstorm possible questions each person in the room might ask, and draft good responses. If they catch you off guard with one question you don't know the answer to, don't make something up. Say you don't know but will get back to them with a response.

Ad professional Jon Steel has been in and seen many presentations over his career. He shares further tips on what he feels creates the kind of presentation that makes you like the presenter, engage with them, and embrace their ideas:

- Create active participants, not passive subjects.
- Engage the person not just their job title.
- Lead them to make the connections themselves.
- Use conversational language and avoid jargon.
- Facts alone don't persuade. Tell a compelling story.
- Present with conviction, confidence, and passion.[27]

10.5 CASE

IMC Plan as a Story

Does your IMC plan tell a story? An IMC plan is a strategy document but also a selling document that takes the form of a written report and a presentation. As we have learned, one of the most effective forms of written and oral communication is story. Before an IMC plan can help a client sell, it must be sold.

The following is an outline of the main parts of the IMC plan placed on a dramatic arc to ensure you are telling a compelling story to your client. Take them on a journey of discovery of how your solution will help them overcome their problem and take advantage of an opportunity. Make their brand the hero against competitors to meet their marketing objectives. Show them the path from where they are to where they want to be.

Act 1 Provides the Introduction and Exposition

Introduce the background of the brand, its history, and its mission. The client obviously knows this, but you are letting them know that you know and making sure you are all starting from the same setting, such as "Open on a hundred-year-old company founded on values of . . ."

Additional context comes in explaining the industry, including the latest trends and main competitors. Identifying the main competitor establishes the antagonist. Most businesses have someone they are trying to catch up to or keep from catching them.

Complete the exposition of the story by describing who the brand is trying to reach. A well-defined target audience is a key to success. Even the biggest brands with the largest budgets don't have the resources to reach everyone, and messages to everyone motivates no one. Understanding the perspective and motivations of the target is important because most clients personally are not members of their own target market. Again, help them see the world through their target's eyes like Carol Williams.

Act 2 Conveys the Conflict Leading to Rising Action

This is where you spell out the conflict of the story. There is usually an inciting situation—the reason the client needs a new strategy. Often, the incitement is something getting in the way of marketing objectives or something that can help the brand reach those objectives.

Clearly identifying the problem or opportunity ensures that you and the client are working toward the same end goal. Making this a specific, measurable, attainable, realistic, and time-bound marketing objective (SMART) ensures from the beginning that your plan will be able to be measured for success against what the client cares about most.

Don't be afraid to tactfully explain insights found in your research that conflict with the client's current beliefs and/or strategies. Delivering a hard truth can raise tensions and anxieties as anticipation builds for a solution. Help them see the world through their target's eyes like Carol Williams.

Act 3 Delivers the Climax and Turning Point

The high point of the written plan and your presentation should be the reveal of the big idea that is going to solve the problem and seize an opportunity against the competitor. Don't just reveal it—sell it. Explain how the idea is more than creative. Point out how it is also a strategic solution.

Describe how the research insights from everything before this part of the plan led to the big idea as the solution. This is the turning point because the solution has been revealed and everything after this is the result of that solution.

Act 4 Explains the Falling Actions and Results

This is where the results of the research and insights and the big idea play out in specific IMC actions. Recommend how the brand's advertising, PR, digital, social, direct marketing, sales promotion, and personal sales should change. How does each play a role in the big idea and creative solution?

Explain how the big idea integrates with each form of traditional and digital media and tactic. Show the full potential of the idea by explaining how it can translate across disciplines of advertising, PR ,digital marketing, and social media management.

The last action of the big idea should be examples. Paint a picture of what the strategy will really look like. Show the client creative executions in each of the selected media channels. Prove the solution works with a multichannel strategy.

Act 5 Provides the Resolution and Denouement

In Act 5, the conflict is resolved. The client can now see the victory over the competitor. The final resolution is given, and any remaining tension of not knowing how to solve the problem is released with a tying up of loose ends.

The final outcome includes your media strategy, budget, schedule, and evaluation plan. The media mix is explained, and the media calendar shows when, where, and how the plan will take place across the various IMC consumer touchpoints. Reassure the client that you know the client's budget and that you will spend it effectively and efficiently to obtain the objectives.

The last loose end is return on investment. Complete the path to where the client wants to be by explaining how success will be measured. This is demonstrated through your evaluation plan, which clearly links each tactic and media vehicle to marketing objectives established at the beginning of the plan. The solution is made clear, and you have told the story of their future success.

Note that these five acts of a story shouldn't appear in the actual plan document and presentation as subheadings or defined titled sections. They merely guide what you cover, in what order, and why to ensure you tell a story. A book or movie doesn't stop in the middle of the action to alert the reader or viewer with subtitles such as "Conflict," "Climax," and "Resolution."[28] Still follow the IMC Plan Book Outline Template Worksheet in Table 10.4.

In this chapter, we looked at the importance of an IMC plan book and pitch. These are different than the IMC strategy you have developed. We also considered the importance of storytelling in the plan book and pitch, with your audience being the marketing client. A strategy that is not well told will not get sold and out into the world. In the next chapter, we take a pause between selling strategies and executing concepts to consider important legal and ethical standards for marketing communication. Before your plan gets out in the world ensure you know what you can and can't do and what you should and shouldn't do.

QUESTIONS

1. Project management is an important role and discipline. What examples can you give from projects you worked on where the project was managed well and when it was managed poorly?
2. Did you ever make the mistake of not planning out the way you would present an idea, project, or recommendation in a meeting or class? What was the result?

EXERCISES

1. Review Chapter 4 on IMC plan strategies and compare it to the IMC pitch outline in this chapter. What are the similarities and what are the differences? Do you agree that the pitch book should be different from an IMC plan? Is there a situation where an IMC plan would be more appropriate? Specifically compare Figure 4.2 and Figure 4.4 with Table 10.4.
2. Think back to the last presentation you experienced that was really good. Make a list of the key characteristics that made it engaging and convincing. Now think back to the last presentation you attended that was really bad. Make a list of the key characteristics that made it boring and uninspiring. From the two lists, put together your own list of tips for an effective presentation pitch. Alternatively, find videos of good presentations online such as a TED Talk, and create your list from there.

KEY CONCEPTS

Bar graphs
Box/quotes
Bulleted lists
Communications objectives
Executive summary
Illustrations
Introduction
IMC plan book
Line graphs
Marketing objectives
Media planning
Paragraphs

Persona
Pictures
Pie charts
Project management
Situation analysis
SMART creative brief
Subheadings
SWOT analysis
Table
Table of contents
Tact
Target market profile

Stories Well Told

Legal and Ethical Marketing Communications

PREVIEW

Our journey into brand storytelling continues as we consider marketing communication's impact on consumers and society. It can be positive or negative as Bill Bernbach says: "All of us who professionally use the mass media are the shapers of society. We can vulgarize that society. We can brutalize it. Or we can help lift it onto a higher level."[1] We'll begin with a look at John F. Kennedy's Consumer Bill of Rights, which called businesses to higher standards, and the more recent hearings in Congress over the negative impacts of social media. Then we'll learn the legal standards to follow in executing your integrated marketing communications (IMC) plan, ethical situations you may face, and the code of ethics for IMC professionals. Our case study looks at false cereal claim cases brought by the Federal Trade Commission (FTC) against Kellogg's.

CHAPTER 11 LEARNING OBJECTIVES

1. Discover the basis of consumer rights and consider consumer rights on social media.
2. Learn the laws and regulations that apply to marketing communications.
3. Consider ethical standards and situations you may face in the profession.
4. Understand the professional code of ethics for application in IMC plans.

11.1 Kennedy's Consumer Bill of Rights
and Haugen's Call for Regulation

The 35th President of the United States, John F. Kennedy, is often referred to by his initials JFK. In 1962, he delivered a special message to Congress on protecting consumer interests:

> If consumers are offered inferior products, if prices are exorbitant, if drugs are unsafe or worthless, if the consumer is unable to choose on an informed basis, then his dollar is wasted, his health and safety may be threatened, and the national interest suffers. The march of technology . . . has increased the difficulties of the consumer along with his opportunities; and it has outmoded many of the old laws and regulations and made new legislation necessary.[2]

Nearly 60 years later, former Facebook employee Frances Haugen testified before a congressional subcommittee on consumer protection, product safety, and data security. Haugen echoed Kennedy's call for updates to outmoded laws and regulations because the march of technology has not stopped. The technology Haugen spoke about was social media:

> I am here today because I believe that Facebook's products harm children, stoke division, weaken our democracy and much more. The company's leadership knows ways to make Facebook and Instagram safer and won't make the necessary changes because they have put their immense profits before people. Congressional action is needed.[3]

What has happened between these two events to protect consumers? What legislation has passed and what regulations have been put into place? Who oversees and enforces them? As marketing communications professionals, we need to be aware of how to practice our profession both legally and ethically to do no harm and foster trust in the marketing system. Will your IMC campaign be lawful and ethical?

JFK's Consumer Bill of Rights
JFK presented the four basic rights of consumers in a speech to Congress. These consumer rights—to choose freely, to be heard, to be informed, and to be safe—formed the foundation of federal protection for US consumers.

The **Consumer Bill of Rights** is a set of regulations that protect consumers from both the hazards in the products they purchase and misleading information about those products. In the years that followed, numerous laws were passed to expand support for the interests of consumers in issues concerning the advertising, financing, labeling, and packaging of products.[4] See Table 11.1 for the six pillars of the Consumer Bill of Rights.

Frances Haugen's Call for Social Media Regulation
It's been more than 25 years since Congress enacted regulations for the internet. Facebook whistleblower Frances Haugen brought this up in her testimony to a congressional subcommittee in the fall of 2021. From her experience and internal documents collected when she was an employee, she claimed Facebook knows it can reduce misinformation and hate speech

Table 11.1. Consumer Bill of Rights First Introduced by President John F. Kennedy

Right to safety	The right to be protected against the marketing of products and services that are hazardous to health or to life.
Right to be informed	The right to be protected against fraudulent, deceitful, or grossly misleading information, advertising, labeling, or other practices, and to be given the facts needed to make informed choices.
Right to choose	The right to have available a variety of products and services at competitive prices.
Right to be heard	The right to be assured that consumer interests will receive full and sympathetic consideration in making government policy, both through the laws passed by legislatures and through regulations passed by administrative bodies.
Righht to education	The right to have access to programs and information that help consumers make better marketplace decisions.
Right to redress	The right to work with established mechanisms to have problems corrected and to receive compensation for poor service or for products that do not function properly.

Source: "Consumer Bill of Rights," Commonwealth of Massachusetts, accessed April 14, 2022, https://www.mass.gov/service-details/consumer-bill-of-rights.

but chooses not to because it is driven more by metrics that increase profit and less by concern for reducing human harm.[5]

Her suggestions include displaying posts in chronological order instead of using algorithms based on engagement. She also suggested adding an additional click before users share content to reduce misinformation and hate speech. Haugen claims these changes wouldn't make Facebook unprofitable but says "it just won't be a ludicrously profitable company."[6]

In Chapter 9, we learned that 46 percent of consumers view media as a divisive force using disinformation for commercial gain, yet 58 percent say they'll buy or advocate for a brand based on brand beliefs and values.[7] Knowing this, some marketers have come out against Facebook, now called Meta, and its practices.[8]

In May 2020, George Floyd's murder in Minneapolis set off the largest racial justice protests in the United States since the civil rights movement. In June a coalition of nonprofits, including the Anti-Defamation League, NAACP, NHMC, and Mozilla, called on companies to pause advertising on Facebook and Instagram during the month of July for a "long history of allowing racist, violent, antisemitic, and verifiably false content to run rampant."[9]

Patagonia joined more than 1,200 companies, including REI, Ben & Jerry's, Puma, Honda, Coca-Cola, Unilever, Hershey, Starbucks, Best Buy, Levi's, Bayer, VW, and Verizon, in the #StopHateForProfit campaign. After Haugen's testimony in 2021, Patagonia reaffirmed its Facebook ad boycott alleging that the platform continues to spread hate speech and misinformation about climate change.[10]

Other companies have shifted their IMC strategies away from some social media channels. British cosmetics company Lush stopped posting on Facebook, Instagram, TikTok, and Snapchat in the fall of 2021 due to revelations about the negative impact social media algorithms have on users' mental health—something relevant to the brand's target audience of young girls. Lush's chief digital officer Jack Constantine explained, "And if there are changes to these social media platforms, we will go back to them. We would need to see them move away from the purposeful, addictive algorithms they use and follow the advice of their own research."[11]

The Facebook and Instagram advertising boycott was symbolically important but did not hurt Facebook financially. Most of Facebook's ad revenue comes from small businesses that have become dependent on the platform for promotion. Many of the small businesses that joined the ban in July 2020 returned a month or two later. Facebook reported that ad revenue grew 10 percent during the ban compared to July of the previous year. Mark Zuckerberg said during an earnings call, "some seem to wrongly assume that our business is depended on a few large advertisers."[12]

The legal framework that protects Facebook, Twitter, Google, and internet service providers such as Verizon from what they publish is Section 230. **Section 230** is part of the 1996 Communications Decency Act, which says online intermediaries that host or republish speech are protected against laws that would be used to hold them legally responsible for what others say. At the time, lawmakers determined that it would not be feasible for internet companies to prevent objectionable content from appearing on their websites. Without this provision, the internet would not have grown as fast as it has.[13]

Internet providers such as social networks are left to regulate themselves, yet some believe self-regulation is an impossible task. In response to Haugen's testimony, Nick Clegg, Facebook vice president of global affairs, said, "We're not saying this is a substitution of our own responsibilities, but there are a whole bunch of things that only regulators and lawmakers can do. I don't think anyone wants a private company to adjudicate on these difficult trade-offs between free expression on one hand and moderating or removing content on the other."[14]

Section 230 shields the third party from liability but not the creator of online content. Marketers, advertisers and PR professionals must publish truthful information and cannot use

Online privacy and data security are key issues today that marketing communications professionals must consider. Getty Images: Juststock.

misinformation or "fake news" to sell their products and services. Free speech rights do not apply to commercial speech. IMC professionals today must also consider what information we are collecting about consumers and how we protect and use that data. As Bill Bernbach implies in the quote at the beginning of the chapter, we should not vulgarize society in order to make a sale.

We began this chapter with stories of people fighting for the rights of consumers. In the rest of the chapter, we'll take a story approach to the laws and ethical considerations that apply to the practice of integrated marketing communications. We will learn from an IMC professional's perspective about the way you might encounter these considerations in the development of an IMC campaign. This should prepare you to know what to look for in developing and executing an IMC plan.

11.2 Keeping Brand Stories Legal

You have just been put on a new account, and as an agency or an individual, the client is tasking you with creating a new IMC plan. Your objective is to overcome some challenges they're facing or take advantage of some opportunity to meet specific marketing objectives. The client is paying you a sizable amount of money, and much rides on these results and the client relationship. Despite these very real pressures, you can't ignore laws to get results or to keep the client happy. You also don't want to take advantage of a customer. You may get a quick sale, but that sale could hurt the client and your agency in the long run.

From the beginning of the development of an IMC plan, you want to ensure you approach it from the right perspective. There are a few key facts you need to keep in mind:

1. You don't need to break laws or ethical standards to meet marketing objectives.
2. Don't assume everyone knows the law and has thought through ethical consequences.
3. Just because the client or your coworkers have done it in the past, doesn't mean it was legal or ethical.
4. As the communications agency, you can be held liable for illegal ad claims and practices, along with your marketing client.

Keeping the Client Agency Relationship Legal

Let's begin with the basis and inception of any IMC plan, the client–agency relationship. As an agency, there are duties you have to the client. For one, you can't create IMC campaigns for two competing companies without getting both of their permission. Let's say Starbucks comes to you to create a new campaign. If you're currently creating ads for Dunkin Donuts, you need to disclose the financial relationship and get permission from both companies.[15]

It is unlikely that Starbucks would hire you to create its IMC campaign if you are already working on one for Dunkin Donuts. The two companies are in direct competition, and it would be perceived as a conflict of interest. However, if a small regional coffee chain from the Southeast approaches you to create an IMC campaign, the client may be fine with your having another client that's a regional coffee chain in the Pacific Northwest because the two companies do not directly compete in the same market. In fact, your experience with a similar business may be perceived as a benefit.[16]

Some IMC agencies become experts in specific types of business as their specialty. They serve multiple banks, health insurance, or prescription drug clients as long as they are not in direct competition. The key is disclosure and obtaining permission before work begins.[17]

Agencies also need to disclose financial relationships with suppliers. IMC agencies will contract for services to other businesses on behalf of the marketing client, such as a market research firm, photographer, or video production company. If the agency owns, partially owns, or gets a commission for recommending a specific supplier it needs to disclose that to the client. Clients want to be assured they are getting the best provider for the job, not the one most financially beneficial to your agency.[18]

Sometimes, companies or agencies will get ideas for advertising and promotions from people not employed by either. If the ideas get used, those people may expect compensation. Yet those ideas or similar ones could have already been under development by internal employees. Be sure to keep records of ideas and when they have been submitted. On the other hand, if outsiders submit ideas that you or the client want to use, be sure to make agreements before they're published.[19]

Finally, when it comes to client–agency relationships, not knowing isn't an acceptable defense. Under the law, IMC agencies can be jointly held accountable for misleading claims, copyright infringement, and violation of privacy and publicity rights.[20] You should make independent checks on the information. Agencies cannot claim that they were only doing what their clients told them to do.[21] It's your responsibility to question and ask for evidence of product claims, ownership of copyrights, and permission for use of likenesses and creative work.

Following Standards for Truth in Advertising

You and your agency are responsible for creating truthful advertising. What rules need to be followed? The main governing body over truth in advertising in the United States is the **Federal Trade Commission (FTC)**, which is responsible for protecting consumers from unfair trade practices, including deceptive advertising.[22]

The FTC judges whether an ad is truthful based on guidelines set by the Federal Trade Commission Act. The rule is set in the Act, and clarifications are stated in the FTC's Deception Policy Statement and Unfairness Policy Statement. These have been summarized in Table 11.2.

How does the FTC apply these standards? It looks at an ad from the point of view of a "reasonable consumer." Determining whether an ad is deceptive isn't based on specific words but on the overall context. What do all the words, phrases, and pictures together convey to consumers? This can include both "express" and "implied" claims.

An **express claim** is literally made in an ad. A supplement that says it prevents colds is an express claim. An **implied claim** is one made indirectly or by inference. A supplement that says it boosts the immune system to prevent colds is an implied claim. Both must have evidence that taking the supplement substantially prevents colds or significantly boosts the immune system resulting in fewer people getting colds versus those who don't take the supplement.[23]

Another example would be a car battery ad claiming that the battery is durable and works in tough conditions combined with a visual of a car starting in cold, snowy weather. A reasonable consumer would expect the battery to work in bad winter weather. In both examples, advertisers should obtain objective evidence to support the claim—something experts in each field would deem reasonable. Evidence required varies by product or service. Health and safety claims require a higher level of substantiation supported by competent, reliable scientific evidence.[24]

Table 11.2. FTC Truth-in-Advertising Rules for Deceptive and Unfair Ads

Federal Trade Commission Act	FTC Deception Policy Statement	FTC Unfairness Policy Statement
Advertising must be truthful and non-deceptive;	An ad is deceptive if it contains a statement or omits information that:	An ad or business practice is unfair if:
Advertisers must have evidence to back up their claims; and	Is likely to mislead consumers acting reasonably under the circumstances; and	It causes or is likely to cause substantial consumer injury which a consumer could not reasonably avoid; and
Advertisements cannot be unfair.	Is "material" or important to a consumer's decision to buy or use the product.	It is not outweighed by the benefit to consumers.

Source: "Advertising FAQs: A Guide for Small Business," FTC.gov, April 2001, https://www.ftc.gov/tips-advice/business-center/guidance/advertising-faqs-guide-small-business; and Dean K. Fueroghne, *Law & Advertising: A Guide to Current Legal Issues*, (4th ed., Lanham, MD: Rowman & Littlefield, 2017).

Advertisers are expected to have evidence to support claims before an ad runs. In deciding truthfulness, the FTC also considers what the ad does not say. Not including information can't leave consumers with a mistaken impression about the product. For an ad to be false, the claim must also be pertinent to a consumer's decision to buy or use the product.[25]

The FTC pays the closest attention to ads that make claims about health and safety or claims that people have trouble evaluating themselves. Statements from satisfied customers are

The Federal Trade Commission is the main regulatory body for advertising that judges whether an ad is deceptive, false or unfair. River North Photography, "Federal Trade Commission." Creative # 530746609. Getty Images, http://www.gettyimages.com/detail/530746609.

typically not sufficient to support health or safety claims. On the other hand, ads that make subjective claims or claims people can judge themselves receive less scrutiny, such as "Our coffee tastes great."[26]

Additional laws apply to ads for specialized products, such as drugs and supplements, financial products, and products sold through mail or online. Each state also has consumer protection laws that govern ads. Depending on the client, product, and service, you should consult those laws and seek legal advice from an attorney specializing in these areas who knows the details of your client's specific situation. These are simply guidelines and should not be considered legal advice.

How the FTC Enforces False Advertising Violations

These laws and regulations are enforced in multiple ways with possible penalties depending on the nature of the violation. The remedies that the FTC or the courts have imposed in past cases include the following:

- *Cease and desist orders.* The FTC can order a company to stop running the ads, add substantiation in future ads, and pay $46,000 a day if it violates the law again.
- *Civil penalties.* Civil penalties range from thousands to millions of dollars, and advertisers can be required to give full or partial refunds to consumers who purchased.
- *Corrective advertising.* Advertisers may have to run new ads to correct misinformation, notify purchasers about deceptive claims, and include specific disclosures in future ads.[27]

FTC staff cannot clear ads before they run, but they publish information on their website (FTC.gov) providing guidance to help comply with the law. Companies and agencies should also obtain advice from attorneys specializing in these areas. How does the FTC police the laws? Typically, consumers or competitors report suspected ads to the FTC for it to investigate.[28]

In an extreme example of a civil case, Russell Christoff was a model whose image unknowingly appeared on jars of Taster's Choice instant coffee and in ads in 18 different countries. A Canadian, Christoff originally posed for an image in 1986 and was paid $250. He was told that if Nestlé Canada used the picture on a label for brick coffee in Canada, he would be paid another $2,000.[29]

Christoff was never contacted, assumed the image was not used, and forgot about it. In 2002 when on a shopping trip in California, he noticed his face on a Taster's Choice jar label. He filed a civil lawsuit, and the court ruled that he was not informed of his photo being on eight different labels from 1997 to 2003. A jury awarded him more than $15 million in damages.[30]

Special Circumstances in Advertising Claims

In addition to the overall standards for deceptive advertising, substantiation, and truth in ad claims, there are specific techniques that the FTC addresses. Table 11.3 provides a summary of these special circumstances and situations.

Table 11.3.   FTC Summary of Specific Types of Claims and Wording in Ads

Bait and switch advertising	It is illegal to advertise a product the company has no intention of selling only to sell a consumer something else at a higher price.
Comparative advertising	It is legal to compare a product to competitor products as long as the ad claims are truthful.
Sweepstakes	Sweepstakes that require a purchase are illegal, alternative methods of entry must be provided, and specific disclosures vary by state.
Contests	Contests must be awarded based on skill not by chance, official rules must include judging standards, and specific disclosures vary by state.
Disclosures and disclaimers	A disclosure must be clear and conspicuous so consumers notice it and understand it, and it cannot contradict other statements in the ad.
Endorsements and testimonials	Consumer, celebrity, and expert endorsements must reflect their honest experience or opinion and may not be deceptive or unsubstantiated.
Environmental advertising	Words like biodegradable, recyclable, and environmentally friendly can't be used if a product doesn't meet standards which can vary by state.
"Free" claims	When "free" offers are tied to purchase, that price cannot be increased from its regular price, and ads must clearly disclose the terms of the offer.
Guarantees	Ads with guarantees must clearly disclose how to get details, conditions, or limits, and copies of warranties must be available before the sale.
"New" claims	Avoid calling a product "new" that has been on the market for six months. Products like fabric and tires have specific "new" regulations.
Sales	You can't advertise a "sale" price if the former price wasn't offered for a substantial time, and "sale" can't be used if the reduction is meaningless.

Source: "Advertising FAQ's: A Guide for Small Business," FTC.gov, April 2001, https://www.ftc.gov/tips-advice/business-center/guidance/advertising-faqs-guide-small-business.

What are some examples of these additional standards and guidelines? An ad for a diet program may claim in the headline that you can "Lose 10 pounds in one week without dieting." But the fine print can't simply contradict that statement by saying something like "Diet and exercise are required." A car dealer can't advertise a very low price for a new car model to "bait" a consumer, luring them onto the car lot, only to be told that the model is not available and then sold on "switching" to a higher-priced vehicle.[31]

An investigation in Canada found the use of stripped-down bait vehicles with few options built in very limited quantities. The Automobile Protection Association said, "In four years of looking for a Honda Fit (DX), advertised according to the Honda promotion around $16,000 and up, we never found one in a showroom that you could get for the advertised price."[32]

In an environmental advertising claim, the FTC acted against Kohl's and Walmart for falsely marketing rayon textile products as bamboo and making deceptive environmental claims, touting that the "bamboo" was made using eco-friendly processes. Converting bamboo into rayon requires the use of toxic chemicals that produce hazardous pollutants. The FTC asked the court to order Kohl's and Walmart to stop making deceptive green claims in ads and pay penalties of $2.5 million and $3 million.[33]

Watch out for bait-and-switch advertising for products, such as low-priced new cars that dealers have no intent on selling. Getty Images: Alan Schein Photography.

The FTC states that consumer endorsements must reflect the typical experience, not just a few satisfied customers. Saying "Your results may vary" is not enough. Celebrity endorsement must reflect the celebrity's honest opinion, and if the ad represents that the celebrity uses the product, then the celebrity must actually use it. Expert endorsements must be made by a person with sufficient qualifications to be an expert in the field and must be supported by an evaluation, examination, or testing.[34]

Advertisers must also disclose material connections between a person endorsing a product and the company selling it. If an endorser is an employee or relative of the advertiser, that fact must be disclosed. An advertiser must also disclose if a consumer has been paid for giving an endorsement. Celebrities must disclose if they have a financial interest in a company they are endorsing. This applies to part owners, such as Ryan Reynolds with Aviation Gin, Rihanna with Fenty, and Kate Hudson with Fabletics.[35]

In 2022, TurboTax's use of the word *free* in its ads was challenged by the FTC and the Bureau of Consumer Protection. They allege that TurboTax's ads touting free products mislead consumers claiming that most tax filers can't use the company's free service. The FTC cites that in 2020, approximately two-thirds of tax filers could not use TurboTax's free product.[36]

Despite the small percentage of filers who qualify for the free product, the ads repeat the word *free*. In one ad, an announcer says, "That's right, TurboTax Free is free. Free, free, free, free." Samuel Levine, director of the Bureau of Consumer Protection said, "TurboTax is bombarding consumers with ads for 'free' tax filing services, and then hitting them with charges when it's time to file." The case has not been settled, and the company maintains that it has been transparent with its advertising practices.[37]

Businesses within highly regulated industries, such as pharmaceuticals, medical devices, financial, gambling, tobacco, alcohol, and firearms, have additional restrictions and are monitored by the FCC (Federal Communications Commission), the FDA (US Food and Drug Administration), the ATC (Bureau of Alcohol, Tobacco, Firearms, and Explosives), and the SEC (US Securities and Exchange Commission). For example, the SEC charged Kim Kardashian for unlawfully touting the security of Crypto EMAX tokens on social media and not disclosing the payment she received. In the health care industry, marketers must follow the HIPPA (Health Insurance Portability and Accountability Act guidelines).

Specific Regulations for Digital and Social Media Marketing

Ad claims on the internet must also be truthful and substantiated. Companies must give consumers notice of a website's information practices, offer them a choice as to how their personally identifying information is used, provide access to the information collected about them, and ensure the security of the information collected. The Children's Online Privacy Protection Act requires websites to obtain verifiable parental consent before collecting, using, or disclosing personal information from children under 13.[38]

In 2020, a landmark privacy law took effect in the United States. The **California Consumer Protection Act (CCPA)** grants consumers the right to know what information companies collect about them and to opt out of having their data shared or sold.[39] For a summary of the five new rights granted, see Table 11.4. Even though the CCPA only applies to California citizens, most companies have applied the standard everywhere, and other states have begun to pass similar laws.[40]

The FTC has additional endorsement guidelines for bloggers and social media influencers. They require influencers and brands to clearly disclose material connections that affect the credibility consumers give to an endorsement on social media. Influencers can be consumers, celebrities, spokespersons, or employees. Material connections include monetary payment, free product gifts, or a business and family relationship.[41]

The FTC suggests wording such as "Company X gave me this product to try" or "Some of the products I'm going to use in this video were sent to me by their manufacturers." It is not enough to have a general disclosure on a home page or in the description of a video. Disclosures must be prominent at the beginning, close to claims, and not hidden behind hyperlinks. Special consideration is given to microblogs. The FTC suggests starting tweets with "#sponsored," "#promotion," and "#ad" or for a contest or sweepstakes, "#contest" or "#sweepstakes."[42]

Table 11.4 Five Rights Granted by the California Consumer Privacy Act (CCPA)

1. **Right to request disclosure of business' data collection and sales practices**
2. **Right to request specific personal Information collected previous 12 months**
3. **Right to have this information deleted (with some exceptions)**
4. **Right to request personal information not be sold to third parties**
5. **Right to not be discriminated against for exercising these new rights**

Source: Catherine D. Meyer, James R. Franco, Fusae Nara, "Countdown to CCPA #3: Updating Your Privacy Policy," PillsburyLaw.com, July 8, 2019, https://www.pillsburylaw.com/en/news-and-insights/ccpa-privacy-policy.html.

Influencers must disclose financial connections to products and businesses that they promote on social media. Getty Images: Hispanolistic.

You can ask for reviews, but if the person receives a form of value in return, such as a free product or a discount, it must be disclosed. Brands also must provide training about claim and disclosure requirements to influencers and monitor for compliance. If employees post about an employer's products, they must disclose the relationship. This also applies to advertising agency or public relations firm employees who are endorsing a client's product or service.[43]

With native advertising and sponsored content online, the FTC states, "An advertisement or promotional message shouldn't suggest or imply to consumers that it's anything other than an ad." Also, avoid using "deceptive door openers." Ensure native ads are identified as ads before consumers click on a link to advertising content. And those disclosures must be clear and prominent.[44]

The FTC Consumer Review Fairness Act protects consumers' ability to share honest opinions about a business's products and services. Businesses are not allowed to create terms and conditions that prohibit honest reviews or threaten legal action for posting negative reviews. Businesses can prohibit or remove reviews that contain confidential or private information or that are clearly false, misleading, or inappropriate.[45]

Photos and videos have different regulations. If you took the photo or created the video yourself, or if the brand bought stock photos or rights from a photographer, you don't need attribution. Yet don't assume a photo or video found in a brand folder was purchased by the company and that it has the right to use it forever in all circumstances—remember Russell Christoff and his $15 million Taster's Choice photo.

Not all photos used online are purchased. Alternatives include free stock photo resources and Creative Commons. **Creative Commons** provides licenses as an alternative way for creators to retain copyright while allowing others to copy, distribute, and make some use of their work. There are multiple levels, from attribution commercial use to non-commercial attribution.[46]

Just because a photo is on the internet doesn't mean that it is free. Check each photo's copyright notice and seek permission from the owner. In social media, brands use consumer-generated content. Many monitor for brand mentions and engage with consumers. If you want to reshare consumer brand posts, seek permission. A direct message and response often work, but companies should have formal consumer-generated content policies and keep a record of all permissions granted.

Permission applies to celebrity photos on social media. Actress Katherine Heigl sued Duane Reade over posting a paparazzi photo of her carrying Duane Reade shopping bags on its Twitter and Facebook accounts with "Even @KatieHeigl can't resist shopping #NYC's favorite drugstore." While she did not own the photo, she claimed the drugstore misappropriated the photo for its own commercial advertising.[47]

Keep in mind that these are general guidelines and do not imply legal advice. Brands should consult their own lawyers and directly reference the law. Many requirements come from the **Digital Millennium Copyright Act**, which updated US copyright law to apply to the development of electronic commerce, distribution of digital works, and protection of copyright owners' rights.[48] Also consider AI as a jump start for ideas not an end. Chatbot ChatGPT will answer questions and write an ad from data from the Internet. DALLE-E 2 will draw anything. But they lack human nuance, insight, and refinement, can be wrong, biased and pose copyright issues.

11.3 Keeping Brand Stories Ethical

With the emphasis on brand storytelling, let's begin this section on ethics with several stories. Imagine that you were put into these situations; consider what you would do.

1. You joined a new agency and are assigned a radio campaign that previously used celebrity names. The client extended it, so you write new commercials using other celebrity names. Your boss loves them! But when you ask about permissions, he says the celebrities won't hear the ads and if they do, we'll stop running them.
2. You created ads for a family-run business that used innocent flirtation between brand characters. The client loved them, and they were successful so they want more. Your boss wants you to make them more overtly sexual. The creative director wants more shocking sexual innuendo in the ads thinking that it will win a creative award.
3. You are working on ads for a new client that sells herbal supplements. The creative brief makes some bold weight loss claims. You will be writing headlines and copy and creating images of what the supplement can do for consumers. You ask the account executive about the claims, and they say that the client says they are legitimate.
4. You're creating an ad for your biggest client to announce a new product. The time-frame is short, so you must use a stock photo for the first ad. After that, you plan to

have a photo shoot to cast diverse people. The only stock photos you find with the activity you need are of white models. The client wants to make the photo more diverse and suggests darkening the skin of some people.

5. You are working on a new video project for a client and are bidding the project out to several video production companies. You have one that you feel is best for the job, but your boss asks you to recommend a different company. You ask a coworker about it and they say your boss owns part of the company.

6. You have been working at an agency for years and have never had any issues. You get a new client, and your boss asks you to work on it. The company sells a legal tobacco product, but you feel uncomfortable helping to promote it because you had a family member die from a disease related to smoking.

7. You work for a cosmetics company and love the product, your coworkers, and your boss. One day, you receive an email from the company president. It was sent to all employees asking them to create email addresses with made-up names and to go on social media review sites to give your products five-star positive reviews.

What Makes Something Ethical or Unethical?

What would you do in each of the preceding situations? Did you get a sense that they may be wrong? How did you know? Your decisions of what to do in situations like these will be based on a combination of morals and ethics. **Morals** are what you personally feel is right or wrong. **Ethics** are standards that determine which behaviors are right or wrong.[49] The first step is simply to acknowledge that these situations do happen and may happen to you.

Surveys indicate close to one in four employees feel pressure to act unethically. Table 11.5 lists the main causes of pressure to perform unethical acts at work. Unethical actions have real personal and professional consequences for employees and real financial consequences for businesses.

For example, Wells Fargo paid a $3 billion settlement after employees opened millions of accounts without customer consent. The employees performed the actions, but most said they felt pressure from management to open fake accounts to meet aggressive new account goals.[50]

You can't control the story you are placed in, but you can control how you react. The key is to know the standards and be prepared. First, consider the factors that may be at play in these stories and others you may face. Figure 11.1 illustrates the various factors at play in any ethical or legal situation within your company or with a client.

Table 11.5. Root Causes of Employees Being Asked to Act Unethically

Root Cause	Example
Make company look better	Cheat the system to make results look higher.
Time pressures	Shortcut a project to complete it before a deadline.
Productivity goals	Sell products customers don't need to achieve a sales goal.

Source: Zorana Ivcevic, Jochen I. Menges, and Anna Miller, "How Common Is Unethical Behavior in U.S. Organizations?" HBR.org, March 20, 2020, https://hbr.org/2020/03/how-common-is-unethical-behavior-in-u-s-organizations.

Figure 11.1. Factors at play in an ethical or legal situation with coworkers, management, or clients.

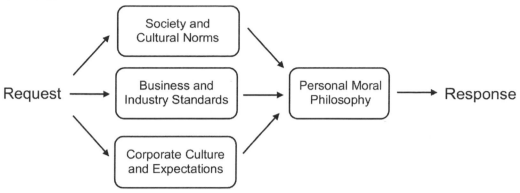

In any request or task, you filter it through various standards, which are depicted in Figure 11.1. **Social or cultural norms** are unwritten rules or expectations of behavior that are considered acceptable in a specific cultural or social group.[51] These norms would be basic guidelines that most of us know are right or wrong based on living in a specific country or culture. For example, most of us know that taking a bribe is unethical. However, in some societies, bribes may be expected and a standard way of conducting business.

For business and industry standards, you look to professional organizations. Most have written codes of conduct A **code of ethics** is a guide of principles designed to help professionals conduct business honestly and with integrity.[52] For IMC, several organizations may apply, including the AMA (American Marketing Association), the 4A's (American Association of Advertising Agencies), the AAF (American Advertising Federation), the IAE (Institute for Advertising Ethics), and the PRSA (Public Relations Society of America). In the next section, we'll consider the American Association of Advertising Agencies' Member Code of Conduct.

For corporate culture and expectations, look to the IMC agency you work for and the client you are working on. **Corporate culture** is the beliefs and behaviors that determine how a company's employees and management interact and handle outside business transactions.[53] Some agencies and marketing clients may have more conservative standards, while others may be more relaxed. An agency may push employees to take risks and create controversial concepts to gain attention and win awards. A client may be a family-run business that emphasizes family values and would not want to be controversial in its messaging and images.

Finally, you have your own personal moral philosophy. A **personal moral code** is an unwritten set of rules we create for ourselves to live by.[54] This could come from how and where you were raised, your family, and the schools you attended. It can come from friends, mentors, and life experiences. Religious beliefs also come into play. Your personal faith will determine how you behave in certain circumstances.

While most people don't have a written personal moral code, it is important to think through your personal beliefs and determine ahead of time what you are and are not willing to do. This can then drive the decisions you make about where to work, with what clients you work, and how you react in a specific situation. If you don't know ahead of time, you could find yourself going along with something you may regret later.

Know your personal moral values so that you are prepared before you face a tough situation with your coworkers, a boss, or client. Getty Images: 7713 Photograpy.

Much of what comes into play in ethical situations is based on what society, professions, organizations, and a person value. **Values** are the worth or importance you place on something that can guide your behavior.[55] If you value honesty and integrity, you will place those above achievements and success. On the other hand, if you value achievement and success, you may place that over honesty and integrity. Of course, these values are not mutually exclusive. Most people would agree that the ideal way to achieve success is through honesty and integrity.[56]

11.4 Professional Ethics

Businesses and industries have professional codes of conduct and ethical standards. One of the main professional organizations that applies to IMC is the American Association of Advertising Agencies (4A's). While IMC involves more than advertising, the 4A's represent the advertising agencies that have long offered more than advertising to their marketing clients including public relations, direct, digital and social media marketing. The 4A's has more than 600 member advertising and marketing agencies across 1,200 offices, which direct more than 85 percent of the total US advertising spend.[57]

American Association of Advertising Agencies Code of Ethics

The 4A's sets standards to ensure citizen rights are observed and protected while minimizing government intervention. Agencies should recognize these obligations to their clients, other agencies, the media, and the public at large.[58]

Table 11.6. Summary of 4A's Member Code of Conduct

The 4A's Member Code of Conduct sets forth core principles, best practices, and guidelines to which 4A's members agree and adhere.
In addition to obeying the predominant laws and legal regulations pertaining to advertising, members agree to extend and broaden the application of high ethical standards that benefit the public, the advertiser, the media, and 4A's members themselves.
4A's members will not knowingly create, place, or distribute: (1) Statements, suggestions, or pictures offensive to public decency or minority segments of the population; (2) Marketing messages that are intentionally discriminatory, offensive, false, or stereotypical.
Comparative messaging shall be governed by the same standards of truthfulness, claim substantiation, etc. that apply to other forms of advertising.
Members must take reasonable steps to employ third-party vendors who abide by the 4A's Member Code of Conduct and engage only with reputable suppliers and media platforms.
4A's members are called upon to avoid employing known advertising formats that are particularly annoying, interruptive, or obstructive to consumers.
Where marketing messages are placed by a 4A's member in a medium that is able to identify a consumer's personal behavior for the purpose of maximizing engagement, the consumer shall be provided an opportunity to "opt out" or decline the messaging.
4A's member agencies must be transparent with their clients to build trust in the relationship collaborating to ensure contractual provisions are mutually understood.
In addition to not discriminating against groups in employment, 4A's members should actively seek to diversify their workforce at all levels across race, gender, sexual orientation, gender identity, age, religion, disability status, and nationality.

Source: "The 4A's Member Code of Conduct," AAAA.org, March 16, 2018, https://www.aaaa.org/4as-member-code-conduct/.

Table 11.6 provides a summary of the 4A's Member Code of Conduct that explains core principles, best practices, and guidelines that 4A's members follow. The Code of Conduct was created with the belief that sound, ethical, and transparent business practices act as an assurance to marketing clients that 4A's member agencies can be trusted as valued partners. The 4A's states that unethical practices lead to "false representations; dilution of service; diversion and erosion of talent; loss of prestige; and a weakening of public confidence, both in marketing messages and the institutions of marketing and advertising."[59]

New Ethical Considerations with New Media

Other ad practices to consider have emerged with digital media. An example is **behavioral targeting**, which is used by advertisers to customize messages based on web-browsing behavior, such as web pages visited or searches made.[60] This improves the relevance and effectiveness of ads but is considered by some consumers as an invasion of privacy. Some have complained that Facebook listens to their conversations to place customized ads in their feed. Facebook denies using this technique.[61] As an advertiser, you need to decide what data and techniques you are willing to use. Just because you can doesn't always mean that you should.

An example of an ethical situation was a controversy that emerged from a Peloton ad. Peloton and its advertising agency faced an ethical pushback over a holiday TV ad they created. The ad showed a woman's yearlong fitness journey after her husband gives her a Peloton bike for Christmas. At the end of the year, she shares a compilation of her video diary with her husband.[62]

Critics said that the woman was already healthy and trim and that the husband was forcing her to exercise. Peloton claimed that the ad was misinterpreted. The actress who played the woman in the spot said, "I think that it was my fault. My eyebrows looked worried, I guess? People were like, 'She looks scared!'"[63]

The ad went viral on social media via criticism that it sent a sexist message. The backlash was so prominent that Peloton's stock price dropped as much as 10 percent. One social media user tweeted that they should "jail everyone involved in the pitching, scripting, acting, shooting, and approval of the Peloton ad."[64]

Another ethical situation came from a Pepsi TV ad. The ad showed attractive young people protesting and holding signs such as "Join the conversation" while smiling, laughing, clapping, and high-fiving. The story ends when celebrity Kendall Jenner offers a police officer a can of Pepsi. He accepts and smiles. The crowd cheers. The ad aired in early 2017 after nationwide protests in 2016 following police shootings of Americans around the Black Lives Matter movement.[65]

After the ad was posted on YouTube, criticism erupted saying that Pepsi misappropriated imagery from serious protests to sell its product. Critics also said the ad minimized the danger protestors encounter and the frustrations that they feel. Many saw the ad as tone-deaf, including Bernice King, the daughter of Martin Luther King Jr., who tweeted, "If only Daddy would have known about the power of #Pepsi."[66]

In the Peloton and Pepsi examples, the clients and IMC agencies may have benefited by seeking additional opinions on their messages and meaning. Having diverse client and agency employees and/or outside communications partners or consumer panels or focus groups share their unique perspectives could have helped.

As we learned from Advertising Hall of Fame member Carol Williams in Chapter 5, understanding your audience's perspective matters. When seeking consumer insight, her agency reminds us to ask, "Whose eyes are you looking through when you view the world?"[67]

We have just just touched the surface of marketing communication law and ethics. For formal legal advice, consult organization lawyers, official documents, and more in-depth resources. What you put out into the public helps to shape society. As Bill Bernbach said, you can choose to vulgarize and brutalize society, or you can choose to help lift it to a higher level. You don't need to break or bend laws and ethical standards to meet marketing objectives.

11.5 CASE

Kellogg's False Cereal Ad Claims

You may expect deceptive ads to come from small companies, "shady" fly-by-night operations, or scams, yet Kellogg's, the world's leading producer of cereal, has had its fair share of dealings with the FTC over ad claims. In 2009, the FTC settled charges against Kellogg's over claims in ads. The FTC determined the claim that Frosted Mini Wheats were "clinically shown to improve kids' attentiveness by nearly 20%" was false and violated the law.[68]

Kellogg's claimed in a national ad campaign of television, print, and internet ads that a breakfast of Frosted Mini Wheats improved children's attentiveness by nearly 20 percent. The FTC alleged that only about half the children who ate Frosted Mini Wheats for breakfast showed any improvement in attentiveness, and only about one in nine improved by 20 percent or more.[69]

More importantly, the results were achieved in comparison to eating no breakfast. One TV ad featured small print saying, "Based upon independent clinical research, kids who had Frosted Mini Wheats cereal for breakfast had up to 18% better attentiveness 3 hours after breakfast than kids who ate no breakfast."[70]

FTC Chairman Jon Leibowitz said, "We tell consumers that they should deal with trusted national brands. So, it's especially important that America's leading companies are more 'attentive' to the truthfulness of their ads and don't exaggerate the results of tests or research." The settlement barred deceptive or misleading cognitive health claims for Kellogg's breakfast and snack foods and barred the company from misrepresenting tests or studies. Kellogg's was also required to pay $4 million in refunds to customers who purchased the products.[71]

Ten years later, Kellogg's was in the news again about ad claims. Under another settlement, it agreed to stop using certain phrases with Frosted Mini Wheats, Raisin Bran, Smart Start, and other cereals. It can no longer advertise products where added sugars are at least 10 percent of calories as "healthy," "wholesome," "nutritious," or "beneficial." The words can only describe a specific ingredient, such as "contains nutritious whole grain wheat." Certain cereals also can no longer be advertised as "lightly sweetened." Kellogg's set aside $12 million in cash and $8 million in vouchers to pay back to consumers who bought the products.[72]

In this chapter, we began with JFK's Consumer Bill of Rights and Frances Haugen's call for social media regulation to protect consumers. The lesson in this chapter is that the strategies and techniques we've learned can have a great influence on consumer behavior and society. With that great power comes great responsibility. While we have a responsibility to clients to meet their marketing objectives, we must also take responsibility for the brand stories that we put out into the world. Thus, we learned key considerations in creating legal, ethical, and professional IMC plans and marketing comunication. In the next chapter, we return to where we began—the research behind marketing to know what works and what doesn't.

QUESTIONS

1. Think of an ethical situation you have faced in a job. What was asked of you and how did you react?
2. Look at the influencers you follow on social media. Are they using the proper disclosures that we learned about in this chapter?

EXERCISES

1. Find a recent ad that is making product or service claims. Compare it to the FTC's Truth-in-Advertising Rules for Deceptive and Unfair Ads (Table 11.2). Does the ad meet the standards of truthfulness? Does it contain a statement or omit information that is likely to mislead consumers acting reasonably under the circumstances? Is the information or omission of information important to their decision to buy the product or use the service?
2. Would you rather create a campaign for JUUL (www.juul.com) or Truth (truthinitiative.org)? What ethical and/or legal considerations would you consider? If asked by your boss to work on one or the other, what society and cultural norms would you consider? Do professional ethical standards apply to the 4A's Code of Conduct (Table 11.6)? What about your own personal moral philosophy?

KEY CONCEPTS

Bait and switch advertising
Behavioral targeting
California Consumer Protection Act (CCPA)
Cease and desist orders
Civil penalties
Code of ethics
Comparative advertising
Consumer Bill of Rights
Contests Corrective advertising
Corporate culture
Creative commons
Digital Millennium Copyright Act
Disclosures and declaimers
Endorsements and testimonials
Environmental advertising
Ethics
Express claim
Federal Trade Commission (FTC)
"Free" claims

FTC Deception Policy Statement
FTC Trade Commission Act
FTC Unfairness Policy Statement
Guarantees
Implied claim
Morals
"New" claims
Personal moral code
Right to be heard
Right to be informed
Right to choose
Right to education
Right to redress
Right to safety
Sales
Section 230
Social and cultural norms
Sweepstakes
Values

Stories That Work

Marketing Research and Analytics for Communications

PREVIEW

This is the final chapter in our journey through brand storytelling in integrated marketing communications (IMC). We now look at market research and analytics. We'll explore the origins of the popular platform Google Analytics and market research expert Bernard Marr's concept of KPQs versus KPIs. Then, we learn descriptive, predictive, and prescriptive analytics methods of research for IMC. Great marketing communications is built upon data, but not everyone is open to it. As Stuart McDonald, former chief marketing officer at Expedia.com, says, "Tracking marketing is a cultural thing. . . . Either you're analytical and data-driven, or you go by what you think works. People who go by gut are wrong."[1] We conclude with a case study on the power of research by telling the story of the research that led to the creation of this book at its unique approach to IMC from a brand storytelling perspective.

CHAPTER 12 LEARNING OBJECTIVES

1. Discover the origins of Google Analytics and the concept of KPQs.
2. Learn the purpose and methods of descriptive analytics for IMC.
3. Discover the value and methods of predictive analytics for IMC.
4. Explore the opportunities and methods of prescriptive analytics for IMC.

12.1 Urchin Software, Google Analytics, and Marr's KPQs

Your IMC campaign *looks* great, but is it *really* great? In this chapter, we cover the most prominent marketing analytic data techniques. They help measure and evaluate the effectiveness and return on investment of the various marketing communications strategies, techniques, and tools we've gone over throughout this book. But first, let's look at the early inception of Google Analytics, which has helpedrevolutionized marketing communications from its early intuitive roots to its data-driven present.

In Chapter 4, we learned the importance of understanding your client's marketing mix. As part of that, we included knowing the history and backstory of the company and brand. For context, it is important to discover the company's human side of founders starting in a garage, making a childhood dream come true, an event that put a cause on their heart, or something they needed but couldn't get. We learned that even big companies can benefit from showcasing their humble roots.

In Chapter 3, we also learned about the value of Simon Sinek's Golden Circle. Through his research on the most influential people, he discovered that they begin with why and how when other people start with what. Most of us today take software tools such as Google Analytics for granted, but did you ever pause to think why and how it began before it became what you use today? Any good story and protagonist or hero (Google Analytics) must have an origin story. An **origin story** is a backstory that establishes the background narrative that informs the identity and motivations of the main characters in a story.[2]

Google Analytics Began as Urchin Software Corp.

Most people know the origin story of Google. Sanford University graduates Larry Page and Sergey Brin rented a garage from their friend Susan Wojcicki in 1998. They worked day and night for months developing what would come to be known as Google. Their why was to create a website that organized and maintained links to all kinds of information, on one platform, accessible to common people around the world.[3] What is the origin story for one of the most widely used web analytics services on the web?

In 1995, Brett Scrosby, Scott Crosby, Paul Muret, and Jack Ancone founded Quantified Systems in San Diego, California, to create and host websites for their clients. While they didn't start in a garage, the two original founders and college roommates, Paul Muret and Scott Crosby, began with a desk in a corner of Scott's uncle's office.[4]

They grew to add clients and additional business partners. They also quickly began to realize that to more accurately track and charge their customers, they had to create their own software to generate diagnostic statistics. Customers would pay more if they knew exactly how much traffic their website was generating and from where that traffic was coming.[5]

This early version of Quantified Systems web-driven analytics software was created out of necessity to support the company's main service of hosting websites, yet it soon blossomed to replace and become the new core service that they offered. Because of the foresight of the value their new analytics platform created, Quantified Systems became Urchin Software Corporation in just a few years.[6]

The new Urchin software developed the UTM code. **UTM** stands for "Urchin Traffic Monitor" code and provides the ability for the website to track where the traffic to that site originally came from on the internet.[7] Fast-forward to 2005, when Google, fresh off its initial

UTM "Urchin Tracking Module" is the basis of Google Analytics first created in the 1990s by Urchin Software. Getty Images: SpiffyJ.

2004 public stock launch, acquired the Urchin Software Corporation and essentially used and renamed the analytics software platform to what the world now knows as Google Analytics.[8]

Many Focus on KPIs, But Bernard Marr Says to Start with KPQs

Anyone who has used Google Analytics will tell you that it is a powerful tool. The amount of data you can get from Google Analytics is massive. It lets marketers track more than 200 metrics that span the marketing funnel from acquisition to conversion. They will also tell you that the massive amount of data that you can get from Google Analytics is overwhelming. Big data is too big to be practically useful. As an IMC manager, you need to narrow down the data to the metrics that are most important to your business, plan, and client.[9]

Narrowing down the enormous amount of data and metrics available to the modern marketing manager often gets expressed through key performance indicators. **Key performance indicators (KPIs)** are a set of quantifiable measurements used to gauge a company's performance against a set of objectives. Your key marketing and communications objectives should guide the KPIs that you measure and analyze to gauge the success of your marketing and IMC plans.[10]

Yet most market researchers will tell you that any good research begins with questions, not data and metrics. In fact, big data expert Bernard Marr says that instead of beginning with metrics often identified as KPIs, you should begin with key performance questions (KPQs). KPQs identify the questions managers need answers to before finding the KPIs that will help answer those questions. As Bernard Marr says, "In business, we often focus too much time on finding answers without asking the right questions."[11] In some ways this is like Simon Sinek's perspective from Chapter 3. Research should first begin with why you are collecting it, not with what you are collecting.

A **key performance question (KPQ)** is a management question that captures exactly what managers need to know when it comes to each of their strategic objectives. While big data presents enormous possibilities, often the problem is that the data is too big. Starting with KPQs ensures that your performance indicators, or key measurement data, are most relevant to key business, marketing, and communications objectives. Even Google has realized this. Google's former CEO, Eric Schmidt, says, "We run the company by questions, not by answers."[12]

In 2022, the CMO Survey reported that digital marketing investments increased over the previous year and that data analytics skyrocketed to become the top priority. Data-related activities experienced the largest growth in spending. Data analytics, specifically, grew 37.2 percent from 57 percent of companies investing in 2021 to 78 percent of companies investing in 2022. Larger companies were seen investing the most in data analytics, with 92 percent of companies with more than 10,000 employees investing in data analytics. With data collection and purchasing becoming more complex, companies are also increasing their investments in capabilities to analyze, store, manage, and automate their data through marketing technology systems or platforms (see Figure 12.1).[13]

A useful framework for any IMC manager to consider when attempting to evaluate the effectiveness and return on investment of various strategic communications elements is to first reflect on the purpose that your chosen analytic will serve. Do you want to present a story about what has happened in the past? Do you want to try to predict what will happen in the future given your current course of action? Or do you want to differentiate the relative effectiveness of a range of strategic element options at your disposal? The answers to these questions will guide you in your choice of analytics to utilize.

Figure 12.1. Data analytics investments have become a top priority for CMOs.

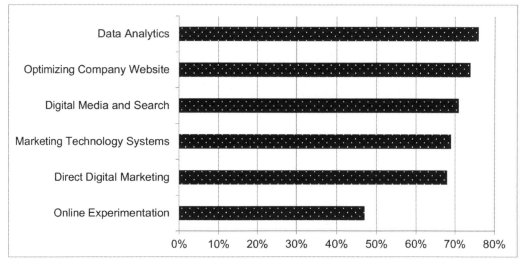

Source: Christine Moorman, "The Highlights and Insights Report February 2022," CMOSurvey.org, February 2022, https://cmosurvey.org/wp-content/uploads/2022/02/The_CMO_Survey-Highlights_and_Insights_Report-February_2022.pdf.

Research should begin with asking a few vital questions, or Bernard Marr's KPQs before you consider KPIs. Getty Images: Claud Nakaguawa.

In academic research, you learn the scientific method. First, you define a research question and then determine the research method and the data needed to be collected to answer it. Another way to think about it is to start with why you are researching and then determine how you will research and what you will measure. Bernard Marr suggests keeping key objectives, questions, and metrics to "a vital few." Aim for one to three key marketing and communications objectives, one to three KPQs for each objective, and then one to three KPIs for each question.[14] We will now expand on the three broad analytics categories of descriptive, predictive, and prescriptive.

12.2 Descriptive Analytics for IMC

This first level of analytics helps to paint the picture of "what happened" regarding your particular IMC element and its effectiveness. In other words, you want to present a story about what has happened in the past. Remember back in Chapter 4 that the marketing plan's specified marketing objectives are important and initial drivers of the IMC plan—what numbers such as sales, market share, leads, awareness, volunteers, or donations must be met?

What Are Descriptive Analytics and How Can We Use Them?
Descriptive analytics can be used to describe the basic results of an IMC campaign. Basic textbooks in marketing research and statistics review both the calculation/coding and reporting/visualization of these forms of descriptive analytics. Descriptive analytics typically include three broad statistical categories:

1. **Frequency distributions** are raw counts and percentages for a particular variable of interest, such as brand followers.
2. **Central tendency/location measures** include the mean, or average result in a range of observations, and mode, or the most frequent result in a range of observations.
3. **Variability measures** include standard deviation, or how close the distribution of values for a variable congregates around the mean value and range, or the difference between the smallest and largest value in a range of observations.[15]

Earlier in this chapter, we learned about how Google Analytics began. Many marketers rely on Google Analytics for its extensive descriptive analytics, such as visits/new visits, page views, pages per visit, session duration, bounce rate, visitor demographics, and goal completions/conversions. These descriptive analytics can provide valuation indictors. For example, **bounce rate** is the percentage of visitors that left your site immediately after visiting it.[16] If your website or a specific page on your website has a high bounce rate, then you know something is wrong. This could be the poor content or design of the web page. Or it could be the message of the ad driving them to the page sets up the wrong expectation.

These descriptive analytics are often arranged and visualized in a marketing dashboard design. A **marketing dashboard** is a visual representation of the most relevant measures, or KPIs, in one display to enable data-driven decision marketing. Marketing dashboards such as those used in Google Analytics can display real-time results of users currently on the website, regularly scheduled snapshots, or more in-depth data downloads.[17]

Marketing dashboards visually display the most relevant IMC measures often described as key performance indicators (KPIs). Getty Images: Andrey Popov.

How Descriptive Analytics Have Been Used in Previous Chapters

In Chapter 4, we highlighted the importance of such descriptive metrics as reach, frequency, and impressions associated with advertising campaigns. These basic descriptive metrics can tell the company what happened in terms of the number of households reached by the ad campaign, how frequently those households were exposed to the ads, and ultimately how many impressions were created by the campaign.

In Chapter 5, we learned that if a brand story resonates with its target audience, a "sweet spot" of engagement among its customers will be achieved. These engaged and loyal customers will then attempt to spread the brand's story to others, such as through brand advocates. How might you measure the level of resonance an IMC campaign has built around a brand's story?

You could start by looking at the number of likes, shares, and positive comments via sentiment analysis surrounding that campaign on social media sites such as YouTube, Twitter, and Facebook. **Sentiment analysis** uses natural language processing to identify the emotional tone behind a body of text, such as social media posts.[18] These types of KPIs for resonance might also be used to describe how a campaign is or is not a "big idea that has legs."

Other examples of descriptive analytics include consumer reactions to specific types of media. In Chapter 7, we learned that 46 percent of adults searched online for a brand or product after they first saw an out-of-home ad, such as a billboard or transit ad. We also learned that consumers are 48 percent more likely to click on a mobile ad after first seeing the brand in an out-of-home ad.[19]

More descriptive analytics were described in Chapter 8. We learned that average response rates for an internal direct mail list are 9 percent and for external lists, nearly 5 percent, while average email response rates are under 2 percent.[20] We also learned that the most direct behavior to assess the effectiveness of a direct marketing promotion and/or message was to track the number, or percentage, of customers that click through to your custom landing page.

In Chapter 9, descriptive analytics informed us that 46 percent of consumers view media as a divisive force using disinformation for commercial gain, yet 58 percent say they'll buy or advocate for a brand based on brand beliefs and values.[21] All of these IMC results are types of descriptive analytics because they simply restate what has already happened in the marketplace. Table 12.1 provides a more comprehensive list of the various examples of descriptive analytics that were highlighted in previous chapters.

There Are Additional Descriptive Analytics in IMC

In addition to these chapter examples, there are other popular descriptive analytics involving IMC strategies. Brand and message awareness or brand liking, loyalty, and equity can be gauged by survey questionnaires and competitive intelligence research studies. They can describe a brand's awareness through aided rather than unaided recognition/recall percentages for the brand.

You can also measure liking levels, such as the percentage of consumers that indicate a criteria level of liking for the brand. You could measure loyalty levels through a percentage of repeat buyers. Equity levels can be measured with market share, awareness, and preference in the product category. Some of these descriptive analytics, such as awareness and liking levels, can be used to evaluate the message of an IMC campaign.

Table 12.1. Examples of Descriptive Analytics by Chapter

Chapter	Example of Descriptive Analytics
Chapter 1	**Google Search Results** "157 million results"; **Marketing Budget Spends** "digital marketing spending rose 15.8 percent"; **Revenue Growth** "from $300 million to $1.2 billion in revenue"
Chapter 2	**Viewership** "44 percent of all viewership"; **Market Share** "over 8 percent market share by 2007"; **Sales Increase** "12.5 percent in the year"; **Earned-Media Attention** "distributed through 280 digital partners drawing 52 million views"; **Video Virality** "was watched more than 90 million times"; **Sentiment** "96 percent positive sentiment for the campaign"
Chapter 3	**Agreement Level** "62 percent of frozen treat buyers agree"; **Compound Growth** "the company's compound growth of 140 percent from 2017 to 2020"
Chapter 4	**Customer Segment Size** "this customer segment is only 14 percent of the US population"; **Reach/Frequency/Impressions** "to reach 70 percent three times a month requires 2.3 billion impressions"; **Gross Rating Point** "the top-rated TV series in 2021 was *Sunday Night Football* with a 4.8 rating"; **Cost per Impression/ Cost per Click/Cost per Acquisition/Cost per Mille** "the average CPM was $3.12"
Chapter 5	**Subscription Retention Rate** "1.67 million monthly subscribers with an annual retention rate of 92 percent"; **Usage Rate** "Airbnb users in the United States and Europe rose 17 percent"
Chapter 6	**Call-to-Action Effectiveness** "adding the words 'please post this' or 'copy and paste' makes a meme twice as likely to be shared"; **Website Visits** "YouTube is the second most visited website behind Google"; **Ad Skip Rate** "because 76 percent of people report they automatically skip ads"; **Radio Listening** "Spotify is the largest with 83.1 million US listeners"
Chapter 7	**Audience Growth** "print and digital magazine audiences grew from 210 million in 2012 to 222 million in 2020"; **Brand Website Visits** "68 percent take further action such as visiting the brand website"; **Daily Newspaper Circulation** "US daily newspaper circulation print and digital combined was 24.3 million"; **Subscription Pass-Along Rate** "newspaper subscribers will pass along the paper to two other people"; **Purchase Decision Influence** "65 percent of adults say newspaper ads are influential in making purchase decisions"; **OOH Ad Effectiveness** "46 percent of adults searched online for a brand or product they first saw in an OOH ad"
Chapter 8	**Direct Mail Response Rate** "average response rates for an internal direct mail list are 9 percent"; **Consumer Trust Level** "consumer trust in direct mail is higher (76 percent) than other forms of marketing"; **Clickthrough Rate** "a percentage of people shown an ad who click on it often calculated as link clicks divided by impressions"; **Conversion Rate** "a percentage of people who visited a website landing page and took an action"
Chapter 9	**Media Trust** "Percentage of people who believe each media source after seeing twice or less." **Micro-Influencer Engagement/Conversions** "*Adweek* reports that average micro-influencer engagement is 60 percent higher and can drive 22 times more conversions"
Chapter 10	**CPM** "Network TV ads cost $20 cost per mille and Google Display Ads are only $3 cost per mille"; **GRP** "some media flow charts also include measurements such as gross ratings points (GRPs) for each media and period"

Other measures include cost per level. **Cost per acquisition (CPA)** is the total cost of acquiring a customer based on dividing the dollar amount spent on an IMC campaign by the number of new customers after the campaign's launch.[22] **Cost per lead (CPL)** is the total cost of acquiring an interested potential new customer based on dividing the dollar amount spent on an IMC campaign by the number of new customer leads generated after the campaign's launch.[23] And **cost per attendee** is used to let you know whether your event is cost effective based on how many people it reached.[24]

In many social media efforts, communication objectives focus on the engagement of the brand community. **Engagement rate** is the total number of likes, shares, or comments across a social media campaign divided by either the number of account users or the number of generated impressions.[25] Another descriptive analytic related to social media is online buzz. **Buzz score** is the rate or frequency with which a brand is mentioned, particularly on the internet and social media tools.[26] Other marketers measure this as a **share of voice (SOV)**, which is the share of conversations generated around a brand online compared to direct competitors.[27]

In direct digital marketing, an important metric measure how much each customer spends per order. Average **order value (AOV)** is the average dollar amount spent on every order placed on a website or application.[28] An opposite measure of AOV is the percentage of people who leave items in their online shopping carts without making a purchase, which is the **abandonment rate**.[29]

When it comes to advertising, many marketers like to see the return that they are getting for their advertising spend. **Return on advertising spend (ROAS)** measures the efficacy of an advertising campaign and helps businesses evaluate which methods are working and how they can improve future advertising efforts.[30] For website optimization, a key descriptive analytic has to do with search. **Search traffic** includes website total visits, unique visitors, organic traffic, website visitors, page views per session, top pages, dwell rate/time, and other measures.[31]

Descriptive Analytics Also Include Multivariate Techniques

Beyond typical single-variable techniques to generate descriptive analytics, we can also employ more advanced multivariate modeling techniques. These advanced techniques look at more than one variable at a time to provide rich descriptive analytic information about IMC campaign elements.

Cluster analysis is a popular descriptive modeling technique that can be used to discover distinct segments of the population based on combinations of attitudes, interests, opinions, and behaviors related to a company's product offering. Once collected in this type of descriptive modeling analysis, these formed population segments can be profiled by descriptive statistics for each segment's demographic, psychographic, and behavioral tendencies. These descriptive profiles can form the basis for developing tailored marketing communications for each segment. In Chapter 8, we learned about audience segmentation for digital marketing with the example of the amusement park segmenting its CRM list.

Similar in scope to cluster analysis is **perceptual mapping**, which is an advanced multidimensional scaling descriptive technique that creates a visual representation of customers' perceptions of brands in a product category and their performance on key product attributes.

Figure 12.2. An example of perceptual mapping of cluster analysis of various market segments.

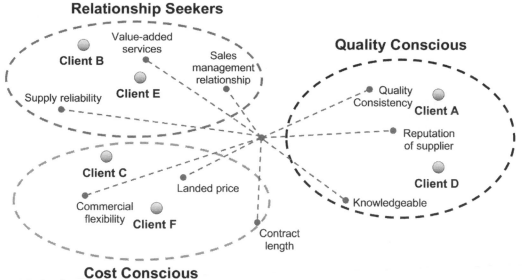

Source: Modified from Ashok Charan, Marketing Analytics Practitioner's Guide to Marketing Analytics and Research Methods, MarketingMind, accessed May 17, 2022, https://www.ashokcharan.com/Marketing-Analytics/~sg -segmentation-analysis.php, Ashok © Charan.

Perceptual mapping is based on marketing research survey methods. This advanced descriptive analytic technique is very useful to understand where a brand resides in the minds of its consumers. This has substantial implications for how the message strategy and creative briefs in an IMC plan book are created. See Figure 12.2 for a visual example that combines cluster analysis with perceptual mapping.

In the example in Figure 12.2, sets of product attributes are mapped together in specific locations in the multidimensional scaling space of commercial flexibility, landed price, and contract length under the "Cost Conscious" space on the map. This is toward where specific cluster segments tend to gravitate for "Client C" and "Client F" customer segments.[32]

Another more advanced descriptive analytic technique involves the use of **social network analysis**, which can identify influencers among a target market segment, typically one that uses a social media tool, such as Instagram, to connect with each other via posts, likes, shares, comments, and follows. After influencers are identified with this technique, a brand can tailor marketing communications to reach these influencers.

Through the influencers, the brand can communicate to and persuade the influencer's vast social media networks of consumers. A network graph of Instagram users can be used to determine the strength and frequency of specific influencers and their various ties and links to specific brand communities.[33]

In this section, we introduced the concept of using descriptive statistics to establish what has happened in the past. Descriptive statistics are useful for a company to "paint a picture," from which that company can plan and build its IMC strategies. From a pitch presentation point of view, descriptive statistics are useful at the beginning of a presentation to establish a baseline of comparison against which IMC strategy recommendations will follow in the pitch.

From a storytelling perspective, descriptive statistics serve to establish a set of facts surrounding the key "characters," or major competitors, and "plot," or share of market, mind, and heart that often involves tension for the company's future gains and losses.

In both a pitch and a story, the exposition of descriptive analytics sets the stage (Act 1) for a course of rising action (Act 2) in which newly recommended IMC strategic elements are offered to win the battle for market share (Act 3) and ultimately achieve successful resolution and thriving normalcy (Acts 4 and 5) for company stakeholders.

12.3 Predictive Analytics for IMC

If descriptive analytics set the stage for the pitch or brand story, then predictive analytics offer the company a glimpse into the future given a current or recommended set of IMC strategy elements. In other words, you want to try to predict what will happen in the future given your current course of action. But we're not talking about Nostradamus type of predictions— we use data, research, and managerial experience.

Companies use **predictive analytics** to forecast what an important metric goal will look like. That metric can be whatever they deem to be important, such as product sales. Generally, predictive analytics in marketing and IMC contexts involve market demand functions.

Market Demand Functions in Predictive Analytics

Market demand functions involve the demanded quantity of a product as a function of the total amount of expenditures that an industry allocates for its marketing communications and strategies. Such demand curves paint a broad picture involving potential market share that a specific company might enjoy if and when it decides to spend certain budget levels on its marketing campaigns.[34]

It is also important to note that companies have discovered that marketing spending in proportion to company revenue that is needed to generate sales varies depending on the specific industry. As can be seen in Figure 12.3, consumer services (14 percent) tend to spend the highest percentage of company revenues on marketing, while energy companies tend to invest the least in marketing (0.5 percent).[35]

Figure 12.3. Marketing spending as percent of company revenues by industry.

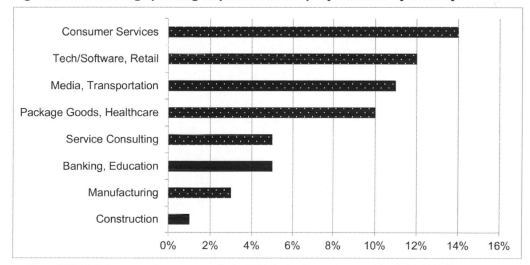

Source: "Which industry spends most on marketing?" Marketing-Interactive.com, March 16, 2017, https://www.marketing-interactive.com/which-industry-spends-most-on-marketing.

Forecasting Methods in Predictive Analytics

Predictive analytics employ various **forecasting methods** to estimate potential future demand for both an industry and a particular company. Winer and Dhar have grouped the various forecasting methods into four types:

1. Judgment
2. Counting
3. Time series
4. Association/causal[36]

Judgment methods are simply based on what they sound like—mere judgmental opinions from company managers, sales force staff, executives, and industry experts that involve minimal quantitative methods. This method is also known as naïve extrapolation. Some marketing managers have years of experience with a specific company or in a specific industry and have learned to estimate demand. These intuitive estimates are not specifically data driven but should not be discounted. They can be significantly accurate, and you will most likely work with clients used to using this method.

Counting methods employ typical marketing research methods, such as focus groups, market testing, and survey questionnaires. We covered many of these methods in Chapter 4 when we discussed understanding the marketing mix, identifying IMC touchpoints, and planning the media mix. Counting methods were also considered in Chapter 5 to understand the IMC campaign target audience. Focus groups and survey questionnaires are often employed to uncover consumer insights highlighted in the creative brief and that lead to the development of the creative idea. Consumer research often inspires a big idea such as Snickers' "You're Not You When You're Hungry."

Time-series methods use a company's historical sales data to estimate future demand, including exponential smoothing. One particular application of time-series methods is in predicting the seasonality of product and service demands and thus IMC timing and spending. For example, a product such as iced tea or ice cream can have year-round sales, but based on historical sales data, it is predicted that the heaviest sales of the year occur during the summer months.

Knowing that iced tea tends to be consumed more in the summer, how would that affect your IMC strategy? Imagine that you are working on an IMC plan for iced tea brands Gold Peak or Turkey Hill. How would time-series research predict a seasonality of higher summer sales affecting your recommendations in the key areas of the marketing mix, IMC touchpoints, media mix, consumer insights, creative brief, and creative idea? See Table 12.2 for seasonality considerations possibly affecting IMC strategy for an iced tea brand.

Association/causal methods merge historical sales data with IMC element expenditures to determine the association of sales with specified IMC strategy elements, such as correlation/regression. As an example, a stronger positive correlation that approaches the statistical value of +1 of unit sales with the number of in-store promotions per week would suggest future sales are heavily dependent on how much a company spends on in-store promotions.

In the iced tea example that we just discussed, association and causal methods could be used to test the strategies developed with the time-series methods. After implementing the IMC strategy recommendation, depicted in Table 12.2, association/causal research could be used to test whether the predictions were accurate. For example, perhaps television was cut

Table 12.2. Seasonality Considerations in IMC Strategy for an Iced Tea Brand

	Possible IMC Strategy Implications Due to Time-Series Research That Estimates a Summertime Seasonal Spike in Iced Tea Sales
Marketing Mix	The marketing client may increase production during the summer months and emphasize single-serve bottles versus gallon size.
IMC Touchpoints	Public Relations may plan events related to spring and summer that can make thirst-quenching iced tea newsworthy for earned media.
Media Mix	Media may emphasize outdoor exposure, such as billboards, transit, radio, sports sponsorship, and social media versus television ads.
Consumer Insights	During the hot summer months, consumers are looking more for cold thirst-quenching beverages than for flavor or hot beverages.
Creative Brief	The main message in the creative brief may emphasize that Turkey Hill Iced Tea is bottled cold, shipped cold, and sold cold.
Creative Idea	The creative idea may play off of Turkey Hill's Lancaster County country image with cold thirst-quenching "Cold-Fashioned Refreshment."

from the IMC touchpoints and media mix to shift money into outdoor and summer sports sponsorship. However, such a shift might be shown in association and causal methods not to have increased sales as intended.

The idea of spending more on media experienced outdoors makes sense, but consumers still watch TV in the summer and may need that larger brand awareness to help the other IMC touchpoints and media deliver sales results. Single-variable regression models

Causal research can help you know if different IMC tactics are effective including if in-store promotions drive sales. Getty Images: Karl Tapales.

Figure 12.4. A single-variable regression model prediction for sales of ice cream.

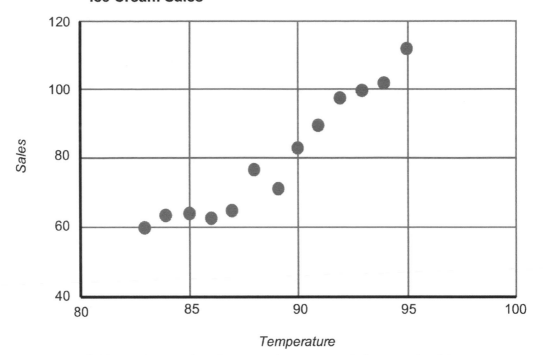

Source: Modified from Lenke Harmath, "A focus on visualizations: Scatter plot" Sweetspot by ClickDimensions, May 30, 2014, https://www.sweetspot.com/en/2014/05/30/focus-visualizations-scatter-plot/ © Sweetspot.

can be used by IMC managers to estimate unit sales of a company's product using different IMC campaign element expenditure levels. **Single-variable regression models** use linear regression to predict continuous variable outcomes given previous data that generally reflects a linear shape.[37]

Figure 12.4 shows a very simplistic single-variable regression model predicting ice cream sales using outside temperature. In the scatterplot of data points, you can see an obvious and strong linear association between sales with increasing temperature. The statistical results that this single-variable regression model generates can then be used to generally predict how much ice cream a company will sell given a specific outside temperature.[38]

12.4 Prescriptive Analytics for IMC

Prescriptive analytics are an advanced form of analytics that examine data to answer the questions of "What should be done?" or "What can be done to make _____ happen?"[39] If our research chapter were a story, prescriptive analytics would offer the best plot device to get us to Act 5 of the journey. The client wants a course of action to achieve success and end "happily ever after."

Prescriptive analytics take what we've learned from what has happened in the past via descriptive analytics. They also consider where the current course of action is taking us via predictive analytics and then attempt to answer the question, "Which IMC strategic elements would offer the best path to success?"

Multiple Linear Regression Models in Prescriptive Analytics

Prescriptive analytics use multiple linear regression models. A **multiple linear regression model** is a statistical technique that uses several variables to predict the outcome of a response variable. It estimates the relationship between a quantitative dependent variable and a set of two or more independent variables.

A multiple linear regression model could be used to determine how strong the relationship is between two or more independent variables and one dependent variable. For example, you might want to know how TV, search ads, and social media advertising spending affect sales.[40]

Multiple linear regression models are also known as marketing mix models. In the context of the IMC framework, they are useful in comparing the relative effectiveness of more than one IMC strategy element at a time. In other words, you want to differentiate the relative effectiveness of a range of strategic element options in your IMC plan.

This third type of analytics, prescriptive analytics, can be used to predict future important outcomes such as brand sales, awareness, and preferences. They also can be used to simultaneously test and compare the relative and unique contributions of each IMC campaign element. Prescriptive analytics in marketing and IMC strategy give the marketing manager an idea of the size and direction of potential cause-and-effect relationships between the company's marketing goals and the IMC strategy elements designed to achieve those goals (see Figure 12.5).

Figure 12.5. Prescriptive analytics could be used to choose IMC strategy elements.

Using historical internal company data sets, IMC managers can build marketing mix models to simultaneously test the unique contributions of each and every type of promotion run in a particular week or month to that month's total unit sales. For example, if your company runs advertisements across different media (connected TV, email, search ads, social media), along with consumer sales promotions (coupons, promotional items, samples) each week or month, you can input that data into a linear regression model that predicts unit weekly or monthly sales from these various inputs.

Not only can you use this regression modeling to predict future demand; you can also use it to compare the relative sizes and directions of each input variable's effect. This model might show you that your social media and connected TV ads substantially outperform your email and search ads, whereas your promotional items outperform all your various ads regardless of the medium. Variations of this regression prescriptive analytics (such as logistic regression) can test your various IMC strategy elements for other desirable outcomes, such as customer retention.

Prescriptive Analytics Include Various Testing Methods

Another popular type of prescriptive analytic technique involves the use of marketing experiments to test the effectiveness of campaigns. A common form of marketing experiments in IMC is A/B testing. **A/B testing** compares two versions of a marketing campaign or versions of an element in a specific ad. It is used in measurable media, typically digital, where users are divided randomly into a control group and a variation group.[41]

For IMC campaign tests, this design attempts to control as many alternative factors as possible in the marketing environment in order to isolate the unique and true effect of the newly created IMC campaign. Comparing the newly created campaign against an existing or old campaign, marketing experiments can be used to gauge the relative effectiveness of a campaign before it is launched on a bigger scale in the marketplace.

On a larger scale, test markets can be used to help predict the success of an IMC campaign before it is fully launched nationwide. A **test market** is a representative location selected to test a company's new product, service, or promotion.[42] Test markets are typically

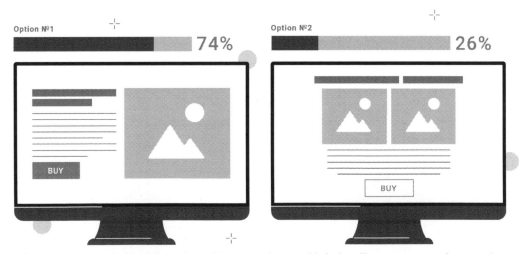

A/B testing can help determine things such as which landing page version performs better. Getty Images: Nadezhda Fedrunova.

chosen in representative locations that have the typical makeup of the larger market to gain greater insights into the viability and scalability of newly created campaigns.

An example of a test market is the fast-food restaurant chain Wendy's. Before launching a new product nationally, the company tested its new plant-based Spicy Black Bean Burgers in Columbus, Ohio; Jacksonville, Florida; and Pittsburgh, Pennsylvania.[43] McDonald's used test markets to predict national success of its version of a plant-based burger the McPlant. After testing in 600 stores for six months, McDonald's decided to discontinue the product offering due to low demand.[44]

In chapter 1 we learned about Paul Zak's neuroscience research on story. His research firm Immersion offers marketers a SaaS platform to send brand fans a link to watch content while wearing a smartwatch. The software connects subtle changes in heartbeat to predict neurochemicals in the brain producing data that pinpoints the moments of emotional connection or disengagement while watching your story (GetImmersion.com).

The future of research and analytics in IMC is heading into more of an agile marketing framework. **Agile marketing** is executing marketing at a pace and scale to take advantage of shortened product life cycles, short-lived technology advantages, new trends, and new consumer behaviors.[45] McKinsey & Company calls it "modern marketing," where markers and their strategic partners must revamp capabilities to meet marketing's new rhythms and demands. McKinsey recommends a set of capabilities and mindsets for modern marketing. See Table 12.3 for a highlight of some of those key elements.[46]

Table 12.3. Some Key Elements Needed for a More Agile "Modern" Marketing

Key Elements	From	To
Strategy and Insights	Limited insights and lagging indicators	Brand vision and strategy informed by real-time insights that are integrated into operations and the front lines
Creative and Content	Periodic and intuition-driven campaigns	Always on content driven by analytics and data, dynamically curated, and augmented by AI tools
Media and Channel Activation	Channel activation plans are managed in silos and optimized episodically	Rapidly iterated activity utilizing unique attributes of each channel, tied to a 360-degree view of the customer journey
Customer Experience and Personalization	Several broad offerings across large customer segments	Customer experience that is data driven and personalized, leveraging unified customer data across all interactions to allow for purposeful communications
Measurement and Marketing Return on Investment	Limited ability to measure the impact	Holistic, customer-level ability to measure all or most components of marketing investments

Source: Modified from Sarah Armstrong, Dianne Esber, Jason Heller, and Bjorn Timelin, "Modern Marketing: What It Is, What It Isn't, and How to Do It," McKinsey.com, March 2, 2020, https://www.mckinsey.com/business-functions/marketing-and-sales/our-insights/modern-marketing-what-it-is-what-it-isnt-and-how-to-do-it.

12.5 CASE

Dramatic Effects of Storytelling in Super Bowl Ads and Viral Ad Videos

We began this book in Chapter 1 by emphasizing the power of storytelling as an effective IMC strategy. This storytelling focus was initially inspired by our own research that investigated the unique contribution of the five-act dramatic plot leading to an increase in favorable attitudes toward Super Bowl commercials.

Michael Coolsen, a marketing professor, was teaching a sports marketing course in 2010 when during the week after the Super Bowl was played, he showed his students the "winning" TV ad in class—"Fence" by Budweiser.[47] In SpotBowl.com's consumer favorability poll, the "Fence" ad garnered the highest average score with a 4.07 on a five-point "helmet" rating scale (1 = a fumble and 5 = a touchdown). "Fence" additionally scored very highly with an average score of 7.82 on a 0–10 rating scale for USA Today's Ad Meter.

After he showed "Fence" to his students, he asked them to discuss their hypotheses to explain why this particular ad would be rated so highly among consumers. A wide range of responses ensued. The ad was mildly amusing but not too exciting or "laugh-out-loud" funny. The ad had animals in it and an orchestrated score, and the brand (Budweiser/Anheuser-Busch) was very well known. Other responses included that the ad features a common and relatable theme of deep friendship and that it "tugs on your heartstrings." Needless to say, many different variables can potentially contribute to the rise and fall of the overall favorability of a TV ad.

Michael then told Keith Quesenberry about his experiences in class that day discussing the various reasons to explain why the "Fence" ad "broke through the clutter" of Super Bowl TV spots. Michael voiced his own opinion that this ad felt very much like a mini-movie told in just 60 seconds. As we describe how the idea came about, see if you can recognize James Webb Young's creative process from Chapter 5.

Keith worked at the advertising agency that created SpotBowl.com and wrote the descriptions of the ads as they ran live to get them up on the website for voting (*Gather Raw Material*). Keith had an extensive ad agency creative background, including writing TV commercials for many clients. Drawing from his previous training and experience, he tried to match the inputs with the outcomes (*Play Matchmaker*). Then, he stopped working and went to bed to "sleep on the problem" (*Forget About It*). His subconscious mind kept working, pulling in raw material from studying Shakespeare in high school English. Keith had a eureka moment when he awoke (*Birth of the Idea*)—thinking "five-act Shakespearian play." The "Fence" ad contained all the elements of a complete five-act dramatic arc.

Long-lost animal friends (the protagonists) stumble upon each other only to find that a fence (the antagonist) separates them from their intentional reunion. In the climactic moment of the dramatic arc, the bull rushes and breaks through the fence to be with his childhood friend, a glorious Budweiser Clydesdale horse. The ad ends in fantastic resolution with the bull in full stride right beside the Budweiser Clydesdale, with two farmers proclaiming that "nothing comes between friends . . . especially fences."[48]

The descriptive analytics of the strong consumer favorability poll ratings for the "Fence" ad gave way to Quesenberry and Coolsen's hypothesis for a more prescriptive analytic test involving a potential cause-and-effect relationship (*Optimize the Idea*). Super Bowl ads that attempted to incorporate more of a dramatic story arc might be more favorably received than Super Bowl ads that fell short of any substantial dramatic plotline.

Figure 12.6. Aggregate measure of mean ad favorability rating increased as the number of acts present in the ad increased.

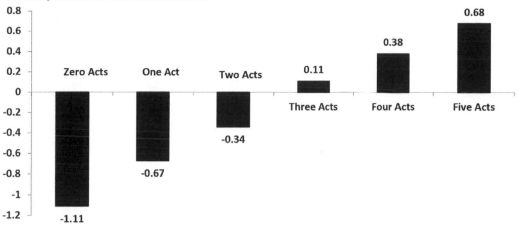

Source: Keith A. Quesenberry and Michael K. Coolsen, What makes a Super Bowl ad super? Five-act dramatic form impacts consumer Super Bowl advertising ratings. *Journal of Marketing Theory and Practice*, 2014, 22 (4), 437–454.

They then used a quantitative research design, coding over two years' worth of Super Bowl TV ads for the number of dramatic acts and the two Super Bowl ad ratings polls to test their hypothesis that ads with a full dramatic five-act story would be associated with significantly higher favorability ratings compared to ads without drama (or with less dramatic acts).

Employing a linear regression model, they pitted the number of dramatic acts in each Super Bowl TV ad against the simple duration of the TV ads by inserting both of these inputs into the model to predict consumer favorability ratings of the ads. The linear regression analysis displayed that an increase in the number of dramatic acts in the TV ads strongly predicted a clear and substantial rise in their favorability ratings. See Figure 12.6 for the combined SpotBowl.com and USA Today Ad Meter ratings results for each story act.

The average rating of ads with very few to no dramatic acts was significantly lower than the average rating of ads that contained higher levels of dramatic acts. The linear regression analytic was prescriptive in nature in that it suggests to companies that they should create TV ads with dramatic arc story lines if they want the audience to favor them more.

Their published research findings attracted the attention of various media outlets (*The New York Times, Forbes, TIME, The New Yorker, Harvard Business Review*) and large corporations (Ipsos, Saatchi & Saatchi, Microsoft, Vodafone) over the subsequent years, and they have even been interviewed on TV for MSNBC.[49] They went on to generalize this prescribed dramatic story line arc effect in viral advertising videos on YouTube.[50] The more acts a viral ad video told the higher the number of views and shares it earned. Now this brand storytelling IMC book has pulled in many more research studies, industry best practices, and case study examples supporting and expanding upon the dramatic story framework across consumer touchpoints and diverse traditional and digital media.

This chapter has explored the exciting area of research and data analytics. First, we learned about the origins of digital data with Google Analytics and the value of starting with the right research questions to narrow data collection and method. Then, we learned about the three main types of research and the measures most related to IMC plan management. We closed the chapter with a case study of the research that inspired this book.

QUESTIONS

1. What do you think of Bernard Marr's key performance questions (KPQs)? Do you think that it is a valuable approach compared to starting with key performance indicators (KPIs)? Can you see the relation of Marr's concept with Simon Sinek's Start with Why?
2. Which of the three types of research methods discussed in this chapter (descriptive, predictive, prescriptive) do you feel is the most valuable in developing an IMC plan?

EXERCISES

1. Descriptive analytics are effective in painting a picture of what has happened in the past. Pick a favorite brand of yours and use Google search engine and/or Google Analytics to collect an assortment of descriptive analytics. After you have collected a sizable amount of descriptive analytics for your chosen brand, create a narrative story around them. Can you create a five-act dramatic arc around these statistics that introduces tension? If so, can you create an IMC strategy recommendation to resolve this narrative tension for your chosen brand? If you cannot introduce tension in your story based on your collected statistics, attempt to find additional descriptive analytics that might suggest tension for your chosen brand.
2. Predictive analytics attempt to predict demand in the future. Forecasting methods based on judgment do not typically necessitate quantitative methods. Thus, imagine yourself as an expert or executive in an industry of your choice, such as fashion or entertainment, and speculate on the future revenue growth or decline of that industry. Do you believe that some brands in your chosen industry will see substantial gains in market share, whereas other brands will remain stagnant or incur major losses? Explain your rationale for your forecasting judgments.

KEY CONCEPTS

A/B testing
Abandonment rate
Agile marketing
Association/causal methods
Average order value (AOV)
Bounce rate
Buzz score
Central tendency/location measures
Cluster analysis
Cost per acquisition (CPA)
Cost per attendee (CPA)
Cost per lead (CPL)
Counting methods
Descriptive analytics
Engagement rate
Forecasting methods
Frequency distributions
Judgment methods
Key performance indicators (KPIs)

Key performance question (KPQ)
Market demand functions
Marketing dashboard
Multiple linear regression model
Origin story
Perceptual mapping
Predictive analytics
Prescriptive analytics
Return on advertising spend (ROAS)
Search traffic
Sentiment analysis
Share of voice (SOV)
Single-variable regression models
Social network analysis
Test market
Time-series methods
UTM
Variability measures

Glossary

15-Second bookends are TV ads that run at the beginning and end of a commercial break or are run in different dayparts.

Abandonment rate is the percentage of created website shopping carts that are abandoned versus purchased.

A/B testing compares two versions of a marketing campaign or versions of an element in a specific ad.

Account executives serve as the main contact with marketing clients in a marketing communication firm.

Account planners are strategists who bring the consumer's perspective into the process of developing marketing communications.

Actionable insight is a true understanding of people in the target audience and situations related to the product that can be used to meet marketing objectives.

Advertainment is a form of entertainment created with the purpose of advertising something.

Advertising impressions are an estimate of the audience for a media insertion (one ad) or campaign.

Advocates are brand loyalists who engage with a brand because they love it but may not have a large influence.

Agile marketing is executing marketing at a pace and scale to take advantage of shortened product life cycles, short-lived technology advantages, new trends, and new consumer behaviors.

Alt text is the alternative text used in HTML code to describe an image on a web page so it can be "seen" by a search engine.

Algorithms are formulas used to rank content and determine what appears in a person's social media feed.

Animated GIF is a single file that contains a number of images or frames presented in a specific order.

Announcer (ANNCR) is seen and heard on camera delivering a brand, product message.

Archetype is a character in a story created based on a set of qualities identifiable to readers or audiences.

Art directors are designers who coordinate ad type, photos, and illustrations.

Association/causal methods merge historical sales data with IMC element expenditures to determine the association of sales with specified IMC strategy elements, such as correlation/regression.

Attention is the process by which a consumer selects information to interpret and when they are aware of stimuli in an environment.

Audience segmentation is dividing a target market into subsets based on demographics, needs, priorities, common interests, and other criteria to better understand and communicate to a target audience.

Augmented reality (AR) is an integration of digital information with a user's environment in real time.

Average order value (AOV) is the average dollar amount spent on every order placed on a website or application.

Bait-and-switch advertising is the illegal practice of advertising a product the company has no intention of selling only to sell a consumer something else at a higher price.

Banner ads are hyperlinked, image-based ads in the shape of a banner (horizontal rectangle) that appear at the top, middle, or bottom of websites or mobile apps, also sold as squares or vertical rectangles.

Banner blindness refers to the tendency of internet users to ignore banner ads.

Bar graphs are used in IMC plan books to compare data for competitors, the market, and consumer trends.

Behavior breakthrough is level 2 of the creative effectiveness ladder where creativity changes consumer behavior relevant to the success of the brand.

Behavioral targeting is used by advertisers to customize messages based on web-browsing behavior, such as web pages visited or searches made.

Binge-watching is watching many or all episodes of a TV series in rapid succession.

Big idea is a driving, unifying force behind brand marketing efforts.

Blockchain is a distributed database shared among nodes of a computer network that maintains a secure decentralized record of transactions.

Blog is a website with reverse chronological posts featuring diary-type commentary articles on specific topics with comments and easy social media sharing.

Body copy is the main text of an ad, which provides more detailed information, such as product features.

BOGO is a buy one, get one offer to purchase one item at regular price and receive another free or at a discount.

Bounce rate is the percentage of visitors that left your site immediately after visiting it.

Box/quotes are used in IMC plan books to highlight important information for support or transition, such as a pull quote. Use quotes when the way something was said is important.

Brand ambassadors are influencers who are rewarded or hired by the brand for long-term relationships.

Brand builder is level 4 of the creative effectiveness ladder where creativity improves brand measures of awareness, consideration, preference, or purchase intent.

Brand community is a group of people with social relations structured around being admirers of a brand.

Bulleted lists are used in IMC plan to highlight important information or key points in short phrases.

Bull's-eye is the center of a target, which is the precise point to achieve the desired results.

Bundles encourage customers to try more of a company's products by selling them together for a discount.

Buyer is the person who handles the actual purchase.

Buzz score is the rate or frequency with which a brand is mentioned, particularly on the internet and social media tools.

California Consumer Protection Act (CCPA) is a landmark privacy law that took effect in the United States in 2020, which grants consumers the right to know what information companies collect about them and to opt out of having their data shared or sold.

Campaign is a set of coordinated activities based on a common theme to promote a product through different media.

Call to action (CTA) is the next step a marketer wants the audience to take and how.

Catchphrase is a phrase often repeated and connected to a particular organization or business.

Cease and desist orders can be issued by the FTC to order a company to stop running the ads, add substantiation in future ads, and pay over $46,000 a day if it violates the law again.

Central tendency/location measures include the mean, or average result in a range of observations, and mode, or the most frequent result in a range of observations.

Chief storyteller is an employee of an organization tasked with telling the brand's story to both internal and external audiences.

Civil penalties can range from thousands to millions of dollars, and advertisers can be required to give full or partial refunds to all consumers who purchased.

Classical drama is a chronologically organized plot that draws an audience into recognizing the feelings of the characters (sympathy) and sharing in them (empathy).

Clickthrough rate (CTR) is a percentage of people shown an ad who click on it; often calculated as link clicks divided by impressions.

Climax is the third act of a story where the plot takes a turning point for the better or for the worse.

Close-up tightly frames an actor's face, making their emotional reaction the focus.

Cluster analysis is a popular descriptive modeling technique in marketing that can be used to discover distinct segments of the population based on combinations of attitudes, interests, opinions, and behaviors related to a company's product offering.

Code of ethics is a guide of principles designed to help professionals conduct business honestly and with integrity.

Commercial triumph is level 5 of the creative effectiveness ladder where creativity increases sales and market share beyond a single quarter or campaign period.

Communications objectives focus on effective communication, such as a specific level of advertising recall or brand or product awareness or a measurable change in attitudes, brand image, or reputation.

Comparative advertising is the legal practice of comparing a product to competitor products as long as the ad claims are truthful.

Comparative mythology studies myths of various cultures and identifies common themes or underlying similarities.

Compiled lists are lists of people built from proprietary and publicly available data. They are less expensive than response lists and typically focus on targeting geographic areas or demographic characteristics.

Complication is the second act of a story, which begins with an inciting moment that creates conflict-producing tension.

Connected TV (CTV) advertising combines the technical capabilities of digital advertising with the user experience of television.

Consumer is the ultimate user of products, services, or ideas.

Consumer Bill of Rights is a set of regulations that protect consumers from both the hazards in the products they purchase and misleading information about those products.

Content calendar plans how content will be distributed during a specified time period.

Content curation is gathering information relevant to a specific area of interest to present to others.

Content marketing, also known as inbound marketing, is the publishing and distribution of text, video, or audio materials to consumers online.

Conversion rate is a percentage of people who visited a website landing page and took an action, such as buying a product, downloading an app, or subscribing to an email newsletter.

Cookie is a small amount of data generated by a website and saved by your web browser to remember information about you.

Cooperative advertising (co-op advertising) is when national manufacturers partially pay for local ads placed by retail stores that feature their product.

Copywriters are writers of advertising or publicity copy.

Corrective advertising is when advertisers may have to run new ads to correct misinformation, notify purchasers about deceptive claims, and include specific disclosures in future ads.

Corporate culture is the beliefs and behaviors that determine how a company's employees and management interact and handle outside business transactions.

Cost per acquisition (CPA) is the total cost of acquiring a customer based on dividing the dollar amount spent.

Cost per attendee is used to let you know whether your event is cost effective based on how many people it reached.

Cost per click (CPC) is an internet advertising metric that is the amount spent to get an advertisement clicked.

Cost per impression (CPI) is an internet advertising metric that defines cost according to the number of impressions.

Cost per lead (CPL) is the total cost of acquiring an interested potential new customer based on dividing the dollar amount spent.

Cost per mille (CPM) is the cost to reach 1,000 people or households; it is widely used to compare the cost effectiveness of two or more alternative media vehicles.

Counting methods employ typical marketing research methods, such as focus groups, market testing, and survey questionnaires.

Coupons are printed certificates offering price reductions for specific products for a specific period.

Creative brief is a strategic document used to develop creative content for integrated marketing communications plans and campaigns.

Creative Commons provides licenses as an alternative way for creators to retain copyright while allowing others to copy, distribute, and make some use of their work.

Creative effectiveness ladder is a hierarchy of the main types of effects that creative marketing produces, from least to most commercially effective.

Creative revolution era is the advertising era (1950–2000) led by Bill Bernbach that added humor, irony, wit, and emotion to ads that respected the intelligence of the consumer.

Creative work is the visual and verbal combination that informs and persuades an audience about a product.

Creator is someone who brings something new or original into being.

Crisis communications attempt to mitigate damage to the company's or organization's reputation by third-party sources.

Cross fade is an edit that gradually fades one seen out and another gradually fades in.

Cryptocurrency is a virtual currency secured by cryptography based on blockchain technology that makes it nearly impossible to counterfeit or double spend.

Customer centric means understanding who your most valuable customers are and delivering the most value to them.

Customer relationship management (CRM) combines database computer technology with customer service and marketing communications to provide meaningful one-on-one communications with customers.

Database marketing is using computer databases to design, create, and manage customer data lists for locating, selecting, targeting, servicing, and establishing relationships with customers to enhance long-term value.

Decider is the person who ultimately determines whether, what, where, and how to buy.

Denouement is the fifth act in a story where the conflict or complication is resolved and tension is released.

Descriptive analytics can be used to describe the basic results of an IMC campaign.

Dialogue is a conversation between two or more characters.

Digital disruption era is the advertising era (2000–2015) that brought digital data tools that made new connections between people and brands.

Digital marketing is the promotion of products and services to reach customers via digital media on computers and mobile devices.

Digital marketing specialists develop online media, such as websites, online ads, and paid search.

Digital Millennium Copyright Act updated US copyright law to apply to the development of electronic commerce, distribution of digital works, and protection of copyright owners' rights.

Direct marketing, also known as direct response advertising, is using one or more forms of media, such as mail, email, and phone, to solicit a direct response from a customer making a purchase.

Display advertising is a graphic image, animation, or video displayed on a website, mobile app, or social network for advertising purposes.

Display advertising networks serve as an intermediary between advertisers and publishers.

Dolly zoom moves the camera on a track closer to magnify a subject.

Drama is a state, situation, or series of events involving an interesting or intense conflict of forces.

Dramatic structure is the structure of dramatic works, such as books, plays, and films, with a beginning, middle, and end that follows the journey of characters.

Earned media refers to getting media to talk about the brand in newspaper and trade articles, on broadcast news and podcasts, or in blogs, without payment.

Elaboration likelihood model is a theory of dual processing where persuasion happens through a rational central route and an emotional peripheral route.

Empathy is the ability to understand and share the feelings of another person.

End cap is a branded point-of-purchase display at the end of a shopping aisle in a store.

Enduring icon is level 6 of the creative effectiveness ladder where creativity drives brand sales growth consistently with the same strategy or creative work over a long time (three or more years).

Engagement rate is the total number of likes, shares, or comments across a social media campaign divided by either the number of account users or the number of generated impressions.

Ethics are standards that determine which behaviors are right or wrong.

Executive summary is an overview of the main points of a strategic plan for someone who doesn't have time to review the entire document to help them make a quick decision and stay informed.

Exposition is the first act of a story that sets the stage by introducing character and setting.

Experiential marketing is a marketing approach that directly engages consumers and invites them to participate in a branded experience.

Experiments are observations performed to answer a question or solve a problem.

Express claim is literally made in an ad. A supplement that says it prevents colds is an express claim.

Facebook is a social network where users create profiles; connect to other users as "friends"; and exchange messages, photos, and videos.

Fade-in is a dissolve edit from a blank screen to a picture.

Fade-out is a dissolve edit from a picture to a blank screen.

Federal Trade Commission (FTC) is responsible for protecting consumers from unfair trade practices, including deceptive advertising.

Firmographics are data used to segment companies into meaningful categories for business-to-business marketing.

Flash sales create a sense of urgency because they usually run for only one day or several hours.

Flighting alternates between running an advertising schedule and stopping ads.

Free gift with purchase entices customers to purchase more for a gift such as spending over $50 for a free bag.

Free samples are products offered in a small size or for a limited time and are often used to get people to try new products.

Focus groups involve a small group of 6 to 10 people who participate in a discussion led by a moderator.

Forecasting methods estimate potential future demand for both an industry and a particular company.

Free shipping can boost online sales for a certain time or for orders over a certain amount year-round.

Free standing inserts (FSIs) are loose papers, which contain ads or coupons, often in color, added separately to a newspaper.

Frequency is the average number of exposures received by a portion of a defined population that was reached.

Frequency distributions are raw counts and percentages for a particular variable of interest, such as brand followers.

Freytag's Pyramid a sequence of five structural phases in drama.

Gatekeeper is the person who controls access to the decision-makers and influencers.

Giveaways entice people to enter for a chance to win something, such as a gift or a trip.

Golden Circle is a model to explain how legendary leaders achieve what others just as smart, hardworking, and funded do not.

Google My Business is a social media listing that shows businesses in searches and includes ratings and reviews, comments, photo sharing, and questions and answers.

Gross rating point (GRP) measures the size of an audience reached by a specific traditional media vehicle or schedule during a specific time.

GRP (%) = Reach (%) × Average frequency (#).

Having legs means a campaign theme can be created for many different media, for a long period of time.

Headline is the part of an ad designed to attract the reader's attention.

Help is making it easier for someone to do something by giving them something they need.

Hero is the protagonist of a narrative who displays characteristics of courage, perseverance, and sacrifice.

High-/low-angle shot looks down on a subject for a sense of superiority or up for inferiority.

Holiday promotions try to capture sales at times when consumers tend to spend more, such as Christmas, Halloween, or Valentine's Day.

Hype is extravagant or intensive publicity or promotion.

Idea is nothing more or less than a new combination of old elements.

Identity is the experiences, relationships, and values that create one's sense of self.

Illustrations are used to show ideas for which you don't have a photo from stock images or your own photography, such as in storyboards.

IMC plan book is a document used in a presentation or to sell an IMC strategy or campaign to a current marketing client or to win a new client.

Immersion is creating emotionally resonant experiences that lead to a higher likelihood of immediate action and easier recall later.

Implied claim is one made indirectly or by inference.

Impressions are each time an ad is shown and are often calculated as reach times frequency.

Influencers, also called creators, are people who bring expertise to a specific area, have a sizable number of engaged followers, and share brand messages for compensation.

Influencer marketing leverages key leaders to advocate on behalf of a brand to reach the larger market.

Influencer marketing platform provides influencer search within a database of vetted influencers via categories and interests.

Influential idea is level 1 of the creative effectiveness ladder where creativity maximizes engagement and sharing to overachieve in campaign metrics and media efficiency.

Infographics are used to visually explain a complex subject, process, or a large data set into an easily digestible graphic.

Instagram is a mobile social media service where users take photos and videos and share them on a variety of social networking platforms.

Integrated marketing communications align and coordinate all marketing communications from the consumers' perspective to present a cohesive whole that persuades them to purchase.

Internal database lists are lists of a company's qualified leads and current customers, also known as CRM lists.

Internet impressions are a single display of online content to a user's web-enabled device.

Interstitial ads take up an entire screen and appear as a separate web page before the user is directed to the page they want to visit.

Initiator is the person who first thinks of buying a product or service.

In-store advertising includes any advertising messages inside a store that sells a product.

Introduction is a brief description of the purpose of a document, letting the reader know what they will read and why it is important.

Inverted pyramid structure is a news story form that places the most important information in the lead paragraph, then details like the background in the remaining paragraphs from most to least important.

Judgment methods, also known as naïve extrapolation, are mere judgmental opinions from company managers, sales force staff, executives, and industry experts that involve minimal quantitative methods.

Jump cut is an edit that cuts between two sequential shots where the subjects move.

Kerning is the space between letters and words.

Key performance indicators (KPIs) are a set of quantifiable measurements used to gauge a company's performance against a set of objectives.

Key performance question (KPQ) is a management question that captures exactly what managers need to know when it comes to each of their strategic objectives.

Keyword is a word or a combination of words, known as a key phrase, that people use in search queries.

Landing page is the webpage a user is sent to after clicking on any link or CTA and should match closely with the previous message.

Layout indicates where the component parts of an ad, such as image, headline, subhead, body copy, and logo, are to be placed.

Lifestyle discounts provide discounts to certain types of customers, such as senior citizens, teachers, military, or full-time students.

Line graphs are used in IMC plan books for illustrating spending and sales trends over time.

Line spacing is the space between lines of type. If letters or lines are too far apart, it is hard to tell if they are part of the same word or paragraph. If they are too close, they become hard to read.

LinkedIn is a business-focused social network where users create professional profiles of work experience and form connections with other professionals.

Logo is a graphic design element used as a consistent symbol for a company, organization, or brand.

Long shot shows a subject in surrounding environment sometimes from a crane or drone.

Loyalty programs invite customers to sign up to receive reward points for repeat purchases.

Lovemarks are brands that recognize that the heart rules the head in decision-making.

Macro-influencers have between 100,000 and 1 million followers and usually gained their fame through the internet.

Main visual is the photograph, illustration, or graphic in an ad used to gain audience interest.

Market is a collection of people who wish to buy a specific product, known as an industry or business sector.

Marketing dashboard is a visual representation of the most relevant measures, or KPIs, in one display to enable data-driven decision marketing.

Market demand functions involve the demanded quantity of a product as a function of the total amount of expenditures that an industry allocates for its marketing communications and strategies.

Marketing mix is the combination of controllable marketing variables a firm uses to achieve sales objectives in the target market.

Marketing objectives focus on a direct return on the firm's marketing investment, such as reaching a specific level of sales, revenue, or market share.

Media planning determines the types of advertising media used, the amount of budget allocated to each (media mix), and the specific time schedule for each media vehicle.

Media relations is building trusted relationships with journalists and media outlets to tell an organization's story.

Medium shot features a subject from the waist up to show its surroundings.

Mega-influencers have more than 1 million followers and are often considered celebrities who may be more famous than influential.

Memes are ideas expressed as visuals, words, and/or videos that spread on the internet from person to person.

Metadata is information entered about a web page to provide context and information to search engines.

Metaverse is immersive real-time digital environments built on virtual or augmented reality technology powered by a virtual economy, which is often built on cryptocurrency and NFTs.

Micro-influencers have between 100,000 and 1 million followers and usually gained their fame through the internet.

Modern marketing refers to moving goods from producer to consumer through advertising and sales.

Morals are what you personally feel is right or wrong.

Multiple linear regression model is a statistical technique that uses several variables to predict the outcome of a response variable.

Music is used to set a mood and evoke emotion to aid in telling a story.

Myth is a traditional story of ostensibly historical events that serves to explain a practice, belief, or natural phenomenon.

Noble purpose is being in service of something bigger than yourself and adding value for your customers.

Nano-influencers have less than 1,000 followers and have influence within their community.

Native advertising is the blending of marketing materials into a news media to provide valuable content but also a marketing message.

Neuromarketing maps participants' brains using magnetic resonance imaging (MRI) to record conscious and subconscious responses to brands, products, and advertising.

Newswire is an electronic news service that delivers breaking news to journalists.

Non-fungible tokens (NFTs) are cryptographic assets based on a blockchain with unique identification codes that distinguish them from others.

Observation is a form of qualitative research that collects data using multiple senses to examine people in natural settings and situations.

Origin story is a backstory that establishes the background narrative that informs the identity and motivations of the main characters in a story.

Out-of-home (OOH) advertising is any advertising media found outside of the home but not inside a store.

Owned media is content created by the brand on platforms it owns and controls, such as websites, corporate blogs, videos, webinars, and brand podcasts.

Pack shot (or product shot) is a close-up photo or video showing a product and its package.

Paid media is anything where the brand pays for its message to appear in front of any audience.

Paid search advertising, sometimes called pay per click (PPC), refers to paying for a website to appear on search results.

Pan is the camera moving horizontally left or right from a fixed location.

Paragraphs are used in IMC plan books to break up dense blocks of type focusing on one topic in four or five sentences or 100–200 words per paragraph.

Perceptual map is a marketing research technique that plots consumers' views about a brand or product on horizontal and vertical axes of different attributes.

Perceptual mapping is an advanced multidimensional scaling descriptive technique that creates a visual representation of customers' perceptions of brands in a product category and their performance on key product attributes.

Persona is a fictional character created to identify similar patterns of behavior and common goals that represent a target audience.

Personal moral code is an unwritten set of rules we create for ourselves to live by.

Phygital marketing blends digital metaverse and physical real-life brand experiences.

Pictures are used to show current marketing communications for the company and competitors and to present examples of creative executions in context.

Pie charts are used in IMC plan books for percentages of a whole, such as market share, media spending, product usage, consumer preferences, and budgets.

Pinterest is a visual discovery social network service that enables collection and sharing of pictures linked to websites.

Place (distribution) refers to carrying the products to consumers and the extent of market coverage.

Podcast is a series of episodes of audio content delivered digitally and often subscribed to through web syndication or streamed online.

Point of purchase is a special in-store exhibit placed where the product is sold.

Points of differentiation are the attributes that make the brand distinctive from competitors'.

Points of parity are the elements of a product that make it similar to products in a category.

Positioning is the way consumers view competitive brands or products in a market.

Predictive analytics are used to forecast what an important metric goal will look like in the future.

Press conference is an event by an organization to distribute information and answer inquiries from the media.

Press release announces newsworthy events to share information about a company with the public.

Preview pane is the window in an email program where you can read part of an email without opening it.

Price is the amount a customer must pay to acquire a product.

Price promotions are when products are offered at a discounted price.

Price war is repeated cutting of prices below those of competitors.

Proactive public relations involves initiating PR plans to achieve measurable results toward set marketing objectives.

Product is a bundle of features, functions, benefits, and uses capable of exchange.

Product discounts typically offer a percentage off the price or reduce the price to a specific dollar amount for a limited time.

Project management is the planning and organizing of a company's resources over a specific task, event, or project toward completion.

Promotion is marketing communications, or the promotional messages and media used to communicate to a target market.

Propaganda is messages designed to shape perceptions or motivate actions that an organization wants.

PR event is an event designed to showcase an organization, company, or product to the media and public.

PR pitch is a short, personalized message outlining the value of a story and explaining why it should be published.

PR stunt is an event designed to attract public and media attention via unusual and often elaborate means.

Publicity is the non-paid-for communication of information about a company, product, or service through media.

Public relations uses publicity and other nonpaid forms of promotion to influence the feelings, opinions, or beliefs about an organization, company, or product to buyers or other stakeholders.

Public relations executives develop strategies for nonpaid forms of brand communication.

Public service announcements (PSAs) are promotional messages carried by the media at no cost as a public service.

Pulsing combines continuous advertising with intermittent planned spikes in ad runs.

Primary research is new research conducted to answer specific questions.

Prescriptive analytics are an advanced form of analytics that examine data to answer the questions of "What should be done?" or "What can be done to make _____ happen?"

Qualitative research collects exploratory data that are not initially quantified to further understand a problem.

Quantitative research collects statistically large samples of empirical data, often to support findings from qualitative research.

Quora is a social network question-and-answer service where questions are submitted and answered by its community of users.

Reach is the number or percentage of people or households of a defined population exposed to a particular advertising media vehicle or media schedule during a specific time.

Reddit is a social network news site and forum where content is shared in categories called subreddits and voted on by users.

Relevance is sharing stories relevant to your business and industry—what is pertinent to the market.

Remarketing, also known as retargeting, is serving ads to people who have already taken an action somewhere else, such as a website or app.

Research and repetition era is the advertising era (1935–1950) dominated by Gallup's market research, Rosser Reeves's USP, and media repetition.

Resonance is engagement generated through the prolonging of a message by reflection and amplification.

Resound is fans' echoing messages to widely celebrate a brand.

Response lists are lists of people who have responded to another company's offers, belong to certain organizations, or have indicated special interests through subscriptions to publications.

Retail advertising is local stores or merchants advertising national brands using sale ads in local media to entice customers to visit stores.

Reversal is the fourth act in a story where results of the climax as a series of events or falling action move the plot toward a resolution.

Rich media ads look like traditional banner ads but add interactive elements beyond static images, such as video, audio, and clickable elements, to make them engaging.

Right to be heard is the right from the Consumer Bill of Rights to be assured that consumer interests will receive full and sympathetic consideration in making government policy, both through the laws passed by legislatures and through regulations passed by administrative bodies.

Right to be informed is the right from the Consumer Bill of Rights to be protected against fraudulent, deceitful, or grossly misleading information, advertising, labeling, or other practices, and to be given the facts needed to make informed choices.

Right to choose is the right from the Consumer Bill of Rights to have available a variety of products and services at competitive prices.

Right to education is the right from the Consumer Bill of Rights to have access to programs and information that help consumers make better marketplace decisions.

Right to redress is the right from the Consumer Bill of Rights to work with established mechanisms to have problems corrected and to receive compensation for poor service or for products that do not function properly.

Right to safety is the right from the Consumer Bill of Rights to be protected against the marketing of products and services that are hazardous to health or to life.

Return on advertising spend (ROAS) measures the efficacy of an advertising campaign and helps businesses evaluate which methods are working and how they can improve future advertising efforts.

Rough (or thumbnail) is a preliminary sketch of an ad layout.

Rule of thirds is a principle that divides an image or layout into thirds horizontally and vertically to place elements in an appealing, balanced way.

Sales promotions are direct inducements that provide extra value or incentive for the product to create an immediate sale.

Sales spike is level 3 of the creative effectiveness ladder where creativity creates a short-term growth in brand sales, market share, or profitability.

Search engine optimization (SEO) is a process of improving website rankings on search engine results pages.

Search traffic includes website total visits, unique visitors, organic traffic, website visitors, page views per session, top pages, dwell rate/time, and other measures.

Secondary research discovers information previously collected for other purposes that is publicly available.

Section 230 is part of the 1996 Communications Decency Act, which says online intermediaries that host or republish speech are protected against laws that would be used to hold them legally responsible for what others say.

Sentiment analysis uses natural language processing to identify the emotional tone behind a body of text, such as social media posts.

Shared media are nonpaid forms of social media where the brand talks about itself, consumers talk about the brand, and both talk directly through social networks, reviews, forums, and consumer blogs.

Share of voice (SOV) is the share of conversations generated around a brand online compared to direct competitors.

Simulverse is when a physical event is simultaneously played out in the metaverse.

Situation analysis is an analysis of internal and external environmental factors that influence business performance in the context of past performance and future objectives.

Single-variable regression models use linear regression to predict continuous variable outcomes given previous data that generally reflects a linear shape.

SMART is a guideline for writing objectives that stands for specific, measurable, achievable, relevant, and timely.

Snapchat is a photo- and video-sharing social media messaging service where media and messages are available for a short time before disappearing.

Social commerce is the use of social media platforms for online buying and selling via e-commerce transactions.

Social identity is the collection of group memberships that help define the individual.

Social media advertising uses social media platforms to create, target, and deliver paid marketing communications.

Social media facilitates the creation and sharing of information, ideas, and other forms of expression via virtual communities.

Social media listening is collecting data from brand social media mentions and broader relevant conversations to improve strategy.

Social media marketing managers oversee the creation and execution of an organization's social media strategy, including brand presence and specific campaigns.

Social media monitoring identifies and responds to brand mentions in social media to improve customer engagement.

Social media strategists plan brand social media connecting it to marketing objectives and advertising and public relations.

Social network analysis can identify influencers among a target market segment, typically one that uses a social media tool, such as Instagram, to connect with each other via posts, likes, shares, comments, and follows.

Social or cultural norms are unwritten rules or expectations of behavior that are considered acceptable in a specific cultural or social group.

Social selling is a process of developing relationships through social media as part of the sales process.

Sound effect (SFX) is a specific sound added to a movement or scene.

Sponsored content is a popular form of native advertising where a brand writes an article and pays for it to appear on another website.

Sponsorship is a fee paid for a property or an event in return for associated marketable resources.

Storyboard is a visual blueprint or outline of a TV script or video showing a series of images.

Story Circle is a simplified narrative arc adapted from The Hero's Journey.

Story grammar is a rule system describing parts of a well-formed story and the order in which they are presented.

Story map is story grammar presented as an outline. Carl B. Smith suggests an outline for teaching students about the characteristics of literature through a story map of setting, plot, mood, and theme.

Subhead conveys specific details about the product while guiding the reader's attention to the body copy.

Subheadings are used in an IMC plan book to break up long blocks of text into sections with descriptive headings and subheadings organized in a table of contents.

Superimpose (SUPER) places one image, graphic, or text over another.

Surveys collect participant responses on facts, opinions, and attitudes through questionnaires with statistically representative samples of the larger population.

Sympathy is a feeling of concern for someone else.

SWOT analysis is a framework to evaluate a company's competitive position by assessing internal strengths and weaknesses with external opportunities and threats.

Tables are used in IMC plan books when summarizing long lists of numbers or words in context, such as a SWOT analysis graph, with four quadrants and bulleted information.

Table of contents is used in IMC plan books to list the main headings and subheadings with corresponding page numbers for readers to easily find information.

Tact is the sense of what to say without offending when delivering difficult information.

Tagline (or slogan) summarizes the main idea of a marketing campaign in a few memorable words.

Target audience is the specific group of consumers most likely to want a product or service and the group who should see marketing communications.

Target market is a specific portion of the total population most likely to purchase a particular company's products or services.

Target market profile is a description of your ideal customer describing demographic, psychographic, and behavioral traits, along with core needs, purchase decisions, and media habits.

Technographics are data used to segment companies based on the technology they use such as hardware, software, tools and applications.

Television or video script is a written blueprint or outline of a TV or video ad including both video and audio descriptions.

Tension is an emotion of inner striving, unrest, or imbalance.

Test market is a representative location selected to test a company's new product, service, or promotion.

TikTok is a social media service based on a short-form video app for creating and sharing entertaining lip-sync, comedy, talent videos, and other videos.

The Hero's Journey is a common heroic narrative where a protagonist sets out, has transformative adventures, and returns home.

Theory of new page states that you should create a completely new-looking page, in the same shape, using the same old elements, with every campaign.

Tilt is the camera moving vertically up or down from a fixed location.

Time-series methods use a company's historical sales data to estimate future demand, including exponential smoothing.

Tokenization is when physical items are reformatted into NFTs on a blockchain.

Tracking shot moves the camera sideways, forward, or backward on a dolly.

Trade association is a trade group founded by businesses in a specific industry to promote their common interests.

Transportation theory is a mechanism to affect beliefs whereby an audience is drawn into the world of a narrative by becoming involved with the characters through conflict and an identifiable beginning, middle, and end story line.

TripAdvisor is a social media service providing ratings and reviews of travel-related content with travel forums and booking.

Twinning is crafting digital experiences that mimic a physical one, or vice versa.

Twitter is a social media service where users send short, character count–limited messages to other users.

Two shot includes two subjects in a frame often in dialogue.

Typography is using type and its principles to arrange text in a visually appealing way that best conveys a message.

Ultimate revelation era is the advertising era (2015–present) that takes what was learned in the creative revolution about emotional storytelling and combines it with the technology and data of the digital disruption.

Unique selling proposition (USP) is a benefit that prospects want that is unique from what competitors offer.

User is the person or persons who use the product or service.

User-generated content (UGC) is any brand–related photo, video, post, or comment published through a social media platform by an unpaid contributor.

UTM stands for "Urchin Traffic Monitor" code and provides the ability for the website to track where the traffic to that site originally came from on the internet.

Values are the worth or importance you place on something that can guide your behavior.

Variability measures include standard deviation, or how close the distribution of values for a variable congregates around the mean value and range, or the difference between the smallest and largest value in a range of observations.

Video ads are like TV ads placed in banner ads on websites and on social networks. Usually, they are played with the sound off with an option to turn the sound on.

Viral advertising videos are branded videos produced for the internet that facilitate and encourage people to pass along a marketing message.

Virtual reality (VR) is an artificial environment created with software that is presented to a user as a real environment.

Voice-over (VO) is heard off camera narrating or delivering a brand product message.

Web3 is a decentralized version of the World Wide Web built on blockchain technology and cryptocurrencies, which make the internet more assessable, secure, and private.

White space (negative space) is the area found between design elements that enables them to stand out.

Yelp is a social media service that publishes crowdsourced ratings and reviews about local businesses.

Youtility is marketing that is so useful that people would pay for it.

YouTube is a video-sharing social media service where users upload, view, and share user-generated and corporate media video.

YouTube bumper ads are six-second nonskippable ads that run on YouTube videos pre-, mid-, and postroll.

Zoom shot uses the camera lens to move closer, magnifying the subject.

Notes

Chapter 1. Point of View: Storytelling Perspectives

1. Michelle Castillo, "Michelle Phan Is Ready to Reach Beyond YouTube With Her New Icon Network," Adweek.com, April 7, 2015, https://www.adweek.com/convergent-tv/michelle -phan-plans-reach-beyond-youtube-icon-network-163918/.

2. Kathleen Hou, "Michelle Phan Was YouTube's Biggest Beauty Star. Then She Vanished." The Cut, July 2019, https://www.thecut.com/2019/09/michelle-phan-youtube-beauty-star-on-why-she -left.html.

3. "Creator," Merriam-Webster.com, accessed September 23, 2021, https://www.merriam-web ster.com/dictionary/creator.

4. Brennan Kilbane, "Michelle Phan on Influence (and How to Use It)," *Allure*, February 20, 2021, https://www.allure.com/story/michelle-phan-the-original-beauty-vlogger-interview.

5. Kilbane, "Michelle Phan on Influence."

6. Castillo, "Michelle Phan Is Ready to Reach Beyond YouTube."

7. Michelle Phan, "Why I Left," YouTube.com, June 1, 2017, https://youtu.be/UuGpm01SPcA.

8. Phan, "Why I Left."

9. Celinne Da Costa, "3 Reasons Why Brand Storytelling Is the Future of Marketing," Forbes.com, January 31, 2019, https://www.forbes.com/sites/celinnedacosta/2019/01/31/3-reasons -why-brand-storytelling-is-the-future-of-marketing/.

10. Billee Howard, "Storytelling: The New Strategic Imperative of Business," Forbes.com, April 4, 2016, https://www.forbes.com/sites/billeehoward/2016/04/04/storytelling-the-new-strategic -imperative-of-business/.

11. Harrison Monarth, "The Irresistible Power of Storytelling as a Strategic Business Tool," *Harvard Business Review*, March 11, 2014, https://hbr.org/2014/03/the-irresistible-power-of-story telling-as-a-strategic-business-tool.

12. Alina Tugend, "From Bedtime to the Boardroom: Why Storytelling Matters in Business," Entrepreneur.com, April 11, 2015, https://www.entrepreneur.com/article/243414.

13. Michael Plummer, "How Great Storytelling Can Make Your Business Stand Out," Forbes .com, August 26, 2021, https://www.forbes.com/sites/forbestechcouncil/2021/08/26/how-great -storytelling-can-make-your-business-stand-out/.

14. Alina Tugend, "Storytelling Your Way to a Better Job or a Stronger Startup," *New York Times*, December 12, 2014, https://www.nytimes.com/2014/12/13/your-money/storytelling-to-find-a -job-or-build-a-business.html.

15. Matt Bertram, "How to Use Storytelling in Digital Marketing to Transform Your Business," Forbes.com, July 19, 2021, https://www.forbes.com/sites/theyec/2021/07/19/how-to-use-story telling-in-digital-marketing-to-transform-your-business/.

16. Henry DeVries, "How to Win More Business with the Art of Storytelling," Forbes.com, February 12, 2021, https://www.forbes.com/sites/henrydevries/2021/02/12/how-to-win-more-business-with-the-art-of-storytelling/.

17. Sam Del Rowe, "Marketing Needs a Story to Tell," *CRM Magazine*, February 1, 2017, https://www.destinationcrm.com/Articles/Editorial/Magazine-Features/Marketing-Needs-a-Story-to-Tell-116079.aspx.

18. Jonathan Godtschall, "The Science of Storytelling: How Narrative Cuts through Distraction Like Nothing Else," FastCompany.com, October 16, 2013, https://www.fastcompany.com/3020044/the-science-of-storytelling-how-narrative-cuts-through-distraction.

19. Alina Tugend, "The Tales We Tell," *Entrepreneur*, April 2015.

20. Keith A. Quesenberry and Michael K. Coolsen, "Drama Goes Viral: Effects of Story Development on Shares and Views of Online Advertising Videos," *Journal of Interactive Marketing* 48 (2019, November): 1–16; and Keith A. Quesenberry and Michael K. Coolsen, "What Makes a Super Bowl Ad Super for Word-of-Mouth Buzz? Five-Act Dramatic Form Impacts Super Bowl Ad Ratings," *Journal of Marketing Theory and Practice* 22, no. 4 (2014): 437–54.

21. "3 Brilliant Brands Telling Stories—A Case Study," AllGoodTales.com, accessed July 5, 2022, https://allgoodtales.com/3-brilliant-brands-telling-stories-a-case-study/.

22. "Attention," Common Language Marketing Dictionary, accessed September 21, 2021, https://marketing-dictionary.org/a/attention/.

23. Allison Matyus, "Why Too Many Streaming Services Will Make Us Go Back to Cable," Life Wire.com, July 14, 2021, https://www.lifewire.com/why-too-many-streaming-services-will-make-us-go-back-to-cable-5192602.

24. Laurel Wentz, "Cannes Swept by PR, Integrated, Internet Winners," AdAge.com, June 29, 2009, http://adage.com/print?article_id=137630.

25. Nicola Kemp, "'Long Live the Prince': The Brands Re-Writing History to Highlight Knife-Crime," CreativeBrief.com, May 18, 2021, https://www.creativebrief.com/bite/long-live-prince-brands-re-writing-history-highlight-knife-crime; and "Titanium 2022," Cannes Lions, LoveTheWork.com, accessed July 5, 2022, https://www.lovethework.com/en-GB/awards/titanium-192?year=2022.

26. Fred Bertino, "Telling the Stories of Its Clients' Brands," *Advertising Age* 69, no. 50 (1998): c10–c11.

27. Sam Del Rowe, "Marketing Needs a Story to Tell," *CRM Magazine*, February 1, 2017, https://www.destinationcrm.com/Articles/Editorial/Magazine-Features/Marketing-Needs-a-Story-to-Tell-116079.aspx.

28. "The Evolving Customer Experience: Perspectives from the Industry," Facebook.com, June 24, 2021, https://www.facebook.com/business/news/insights/the-evolving-customer-experience-perspectives-from-the-industry.

29. Christine Moorman, "The CMO Survey: Managing and Measuring Marketing Spending for Growth and Returns," August 2021, https://cmosurvey.org/wp-content/uploads/2021/08/The_CMO_Survey-Highlights_and_Insights_Report-August_2021.pdf.

30. "The Evolving Customer Experience: Perspectives from the Industry."

31. "The Evolving Customer Experience: Perspectives from the Industry," Facebook.com, June 24, 2021, https://www.facebook.com/business/news/insights/the-evolving-customer-experience-perspectives-from-the-industry.

32. "Influencer," Common Language Marketing Dictionary, accessed September 24, 2021, https://marketing-dictionary.org/i/influencer/.

33. Vangie Beal, "User Generated Content (UGC)," Webopedia.com, May 24, 2021, https://www.webopedia.com/definitions/ugc/.

34. Pamela Bump, "What Is YouTube Shorts and Why Marketers Are Already Using It [+5 Brand Examples]," HubSpot.com, September 10, 2021, https://blog.hubspot.com/marketing/youtube-shorts.

35. "Pro Skateboarder Ishod Wair Finds Balance in the Midst of a Hectic Career. #shorts," Nike, YouTube.com, January 22, 2022, https://youtu.be/1kzFofBfZwQ.

36. "Convexity Meningioma: A Hollywood Stuntwoman's Story," Johns Hopkins Medicine, You Tube.com, February 10, 2016, https://youtu.be/LXD3QRPYDvc.

37. Jennifer Edson Escalas and Barbara B. Stern, "Antecedents and Consequences of Emotional Responses to Advertising," *Advances in Consumer Research* 30, no. 1 (2003, January): 85–90.

38. Tiffany Hsu, "The Advertising Industry Has a Problem: People Hate Ads," NYTimes.com, October 28, 2019, https://www.nytimes.com/2019/10/28/business/media/advertising-industry-research.html.

39. Jennifer Edson Escalas, Marian Chapman Moore, and Julie Edell Britton, "Fishing for Feelings? Hooking Viewers Helps!" *Journal of Consumer Psychology* 14, no. 1/2 (2004): 105–14.

40. Escalas and Stern, "Antecedents and Consequences of Emotional Responses to Advertising."

41. Tchiki Davis, "Sympathy vs. Empathy," *Psychology Today*, July 14, 2020, https://www.psychologytoday.com/us/basics/empathy.

42. "Empathy," *Psychology Today*, accessed September 18, 2021, https://www.psychologytoday.com/us/basics/empathy.

43. Julie A. Edell and Marian Chapman Burke, "The Power of Feelings in Understanding Advertising Effects," *Journal of Consumer Research* 14, no. 3 (1987): 421–33.

44. Gregory W. Boller and Jerry C. Olson, "Experiencing Ad Meanings: Crucial Aspects of Narrative/Drama Processing," *Advances in Consumer Research* 18, no. 1 (1991): 172–75.

45. Escalas and Stern, "Antecedents and Consequences of Emotional Responses to Advertising."

46. Melanie C. Green and Timothy C. Brock, "The Role of Transportation in the Persuasiveness of Public Narratives," *Journal of Personality and Social Psychology* 79, no. 5 (2000): 701–21; and Quesenberry and Coolsen, "Drama Goes Viral."

47. Melanie C. Green and Jenna L. Clark, "Transportation into Narrative Worlds: Implications for Entertainment Media Influences on Tobacco Use," *Addiction* 108, no. 3 (2013), 477–84.

48. Escalas, Chapman Moore, and Edell Britton, "Fishing For Feelings? Hooking Viewers Helps!"

49. Paul J. Zak, "Why Your Brain Loves Good Storytelling," *Harvard Business Review* (2014, October): 2–4; and Paul J. Zak, "At Attention," *TD: Talent Development* 74, no. 9 (2020): 42–47.

50. "Tension," Merriam-Webster.com, accessed September 24, 2021, https://www.merriam-webster.com/dictionary/tension.

51. Zak, "Why Your Brain Loves Good Storytelling."

52. Paul J. Zak, "How Stories Change the Brain," *Greater Good Magazine*, December 17, 2013, https://greatergood.berkeley.edu/article/item/how_stories_change_brain.

53. Zak, "How Stories Change the Brain."

54. Jonathan Godtschall, "Infecting an Audience: Why Great Stories Spread," FastCompany.com, October 20, 2013, https://www.fastcompany.com/3020046/infecting-an-audience-why-great-stories-spread.

55. Zak, "At Attention."

56. Quesenberry and Coolsen, "What Makes a Super Bowl Ad Super for Word-of-Mouth Buzz?"

57. Quesenberry and Coolsen, "Drama Goes Viral."

58. Ibid.

59. Chuck Ross, "Integrated Marketing: The Brand-New 60-Year-Old Idea," *Television Week* 27 (2008, April): 2.

60. Ross, "Integrated Marketing."

61. "Hill, Holliday, Connors, Cosmopulos," AdAge Encyclopedia, published September 15, 2003, https://adage.com/article/adage-encyclopedia/hill-holliday-connors-cosmopulos/98697.

62. Bernice Kanner, "Slices of Life: Selling Reality," *New York Magazine*, February 17, 1986; and Chris Amorosino, "John Hancock Mutual Life Insurance Company: Real Life, Real Answers Campaign," accessed September 21, 2021, https://www.warc.com/content/paywall/article/gale-emmc/john-hancock-mutual-life-insurance-company-real-life-real-answers-campaign/84445.

63. Bertino, "Telling the Stories of Its Clients' Brands."

64. "Frederick Bertino," Adforum.com, accessed September 21, 2021, https://www.adforum.com/talent/1647-frederick-bertino.

65. "Advertainment," Merriam-Webster.com, accessed September 24, 2021, https://www.merriam-webster.com/dictionary/advertainment.

66. Elefthera Parapis, "Now Playing," *Brandweek* 45, no. 20 (2004): 38–39.

67. Parapis, "Now Playing."

68. Rance Crain, "Byron Lewis on Advertising: It's Always Been about Storytelling," *Advertising Age* 84, no. 30 (2013): 23.

69. Crain, "Byron Lewis on Advertising."

70. E. J. Schultz, "Mascots Are Brands' Best Social-Media Accessories," *Advertising Age* 83, no. 13 (2012): 2–25.

71. "Luke Sullivan—Tensions," Stan Talks, YouTube.com, April 8, 2019, https://www.youtube.com/watch?v=gSrXAAFX6rg.

72. "Publicity," Common Language Marketing Dictionary, accessed September 22, 2021, https://marketing-dictionary.org/p/public-relations/.

73. Baith Waite, "Edward Bernays and Why We Eat Bacon for Breakfast," GoBraithWaite.com, https://gobraithwaite.com/thinking/edward-bernays-and-why-we-eat-bacon-for-breakfast/.

74. Richard Etchison, "5 'Founding Fathers' of PR," Crenshaw Communications, accessed September 22, 2021, https://crenshawcomm.com/blogs/5-founding-fathers-pr/.

75. "Our History," Edelman.com, accessed September 21, 2021, https://www.edelman.com/about-us/our-history.

76. Richard Edelman, "One on One," Edelman.com, October 4, 2016, https://www.edelman.com/insights/one-on-one-prweek-conference.

77. Donna Talarico, "What We're Not Talking About When We Talk About News," OHO.com, April 2, 2019, https://www.oho.com/blog/news-vs-stories-whats-difference.

78. "The Inverted Pyramid Structure," Purdue Online Writing Lab, accessed September 22, 2021, https://owl.purdue.edu/owl/subject_specific_writing/journalism_and_journalistic_writing/the_inverted_pyramid.html.

79. "The Inverted Pyramid Structure."

80. "Characteristics of a Dramatic Work," BBC Bitesize Guides, accessed September 21, 2021, https://www.bbc.co.uk/bitesize/guides/z6vwcqt/revision/3.

81. "Kerrygold TV Spot, 'First Day' Song by Gregory Alan Isakov," iSpot.tv, accessed March 1, 2022, https://www.ispot.tv/ad/tqgb/kerrygold-first-day-song-by-gregory-alan-isakov.

82. Matt Charles, "Increasing Your Media Coverage through Storytelling," PRSay.PRSA.com, January 8, 2019, https://prsay.prsa.org/2019/01/08/how-to-increase-your-media-coverage-through-storytelling/.

83. Michelle Dziuban, "The Power of Storytelling in PR," Cision.com, March 14, 2016, https://www.cision.com/2016/03/the-power-of-storytelling-in-pr/.

84. Mario Juarez, "The Unlikely Story of Microsoft's Chief Storyteller," Mario-Juarez.com, April 2, 2019, https://mario-juarez.com/new-blog/2019/4/2/the-unlikely-story-of-microsofts-chief-storyteller.

85. Juarez, "The Unlikely Story of Microsoft's Chief Storyteller."

86. Ibid.

87. Athima Chansanchai, "The People Behind Windows 11: Listening, Solving Problems and Designing with Purpose," Blogs.Windows.com, August 5, 2021, https://blogs.windows.com/windows experience/2021/08/05/the-people-behind-windows-11-listening-solving-problems-and-designing -with-purpose/.

88. Lauren McMenemy, "What Is a Chief Storyteller?" SkyWord, March 22, 2018, https://www .skyword.com/contentstandard/what-is-a-chief-storyteller-five-business-leaders-share-their-stories/.

89. "Chief Storyteller," WhatIs.com, TechTarget, accessed September 22, 2021, https://whatis .techtarget.com/definition/chief-storyteller.v

Chapter 2. Plays to Pyramids: Aristotle, Shakespeare, and Freytag

1. "$100 Contest!" Antartic-circle.org, November 13, 2016, http://www.antarctic-circle.org /advert.htm.

2. "$100 Contest!"

3. Colin Schultz, "Shackleton Probably Never Took Out an Ad Seeking Men for a Hazardous Journey: The Famous Tale of How Ernest Shackleton Put Together His Antarctic Expedition Is Probably a Myth," Smithsonian.com, September 10, 2013, http://www.smithsonian mag.com/smart-news/shackleton-probably-never-took-out-an-ad-seeking-men-for-a-hazardous -journey-5552379/.

4. "Myth," Merriam-Webster.com, accessed July 6, 2017, https://www.merriam-webster.com /dictionary/myth.

5. "Drama," Merriam-Webster.com, accessed October 2, 2021, https://www.merriam-webster .com/dictionary/drama.

6. Andrew Webster, "Nielsen: Dramas Most Popular Primetime TV, But Reality Shows Win on Product Placement," TheVerge.com, April 19, 2012, https://www.theverge.com/2012/4/19/2960515 /nielsen-report-drama-most-popular-primetime-genre.

7. "Tops of 2016: TV," Nielsen.com, December 13, 2016, http://www.nielsen.com/us/en /insights/news/2016/tops-of-2016-tv.html.

8. "List of Longest-Running Scripted U.S. Television Series," Wikipedia.com, July 6, 2017, https://en.wikipedia.org/wiki/List_of_longest-running_scripted_U.S._primetime_television_series.

9. "List of Longest-Running UK Television Series," Wikipedia.com, June 15, 2017, https:// en.wikipedia.org/wiki/List_of_longest-running_UK_television_series.

10. "Curse of the Billy Goat," Wikipedia.com, June 26, 2017, https://en.wikipedia.org/wiki /Curse_of_the_Billy_Goat.

11. "Big Brother (U.S. TV series)," Wikipedia.com, July 7, 2017, https://en.wikipedia.org/wiki /Big_Brother_(U.S._TV_series).

12. "Binge-watch," Merriam-Webster.com, accessed October 2, 2021, https://www.merriam -webster.com/dictionary/binge-watch.

13. Barbara B. Stern, "'What's in a Name?' Aristotelian Criticism and Drama Research Abstract," *Advances in Consumer Research* 19, no. 1 (1992): 452–54.

14. "Poetics by Aristotle," The Internet Classics Archive, accessed September 13, 2022, http:// classics.mit.edu/Aristotle/poetics.1.1.html.

15. Lily Carroll, "Aristotelian Narrative Structures," penandthepad.com, accessed March 6, 2022, https://penandthepad.com/structure-shakespearean-play-6173760.html.

16. Carroll, "Aristotelian Narrative Structures."

17. "Lessons from Ancient Greece—Aristotle on Storytelling," Presspage.com, accessed March 6, 2022, https://www.presspage.com/news/lessons-from-ancient-greece-aristotle-on-storytelling/.

18. "Titanium 2022," Cannes Lions, LoveTheWork.com, accessed July 5, 2022, https://www.lovethework.com/en-GB/awards/titanium-192?year=2022.

19. "Google—Black-Owned Friday—Case Study," AgencyCompile.com, accessed July 6, 2022, https://www.agencycompile.com/agencies/bbh-new-york/content/google---black-owned-friday---case-study.

20. Joshua J. Mark, "Aristotle," WordHistory.com, May 22, 2019, https://www.worldhistory.org/aristotle/.

21. Will Gompertz, "Why Is Shakespeare More Popular than Ever?" BBC News Magazine, April 23, 2016, http://www.bbc.com/news/magazine-36114485.

22. Dan Kopt, "What Is Shakespeare's Most Popular Play?" Pricenomics.com, September 22, 2016, http://www.bbc.com/news/magazine-36114485.

23. "William Shakespeare," Biography.com, 2017, https://www.biography.com/people/william-shakespeare-9480323.

24. "Art for Art's Sake." *Encyclopedia Britannica*, January 23, 2015. https://www.britannica.com/topic/art-for-arts-sake

25. "Critical Essays Shakespeare's Tragedy," Cliffnotes.com, 2016, https://www.cliffsnotes.com/literature/o/othello/critical-essays/shakespeares-tragedy.

26. Rebecca Ray, "The Five Act Play (Dramatic Structure)," StoryboardThat.com, 2016, http://www.storyboardthat.com/articles/e/five-act-structure.

27. "Freytag, Gustav German Writer," Britannica.com, 2017, https://www.britannica.com/biography/Gustav-Freytag.

28. "Freytag's Pyramid," OxfordReference.com, accessed October 4, 2021, https://www.oxfordreference.com/view/10.1093/oi/authority.20110803095835564.

29. Gustav Freytag, *Technique of the Drama: An Exposition of Dramatic Composition and Art*, trans. Elias J. MacEwan from the sixth German ed., [1863] 1895, Chicago: Griggs.

30. Jerome Stern, *Making Shapely Fiction* (New York: W.W. Norton & Company, 2000).

31. Boris Trbic, "Scripting Short Films," *Screen Education* 58 (Winter 2010): 72–77.

32. Sondra B. Willobee, *The Write Stuff: Crafting Sermons That Capture and Convince* (Louisville, KY: Westminster John Knox Press, 2009).

33. Ali Taghizadeh, "A Theory of Literary Structuralism (in Henry James)," *Theory & Practice in Language Studies* 3, no. 2 (2013): 285–92.

34. David Bordwell, *Poetics of Cinema* (New York: Routledge, 2017).

35. Bordwell, *Poetics of Cinema*.

36. Ibid.

37. Kristin Thompson, *Storytelling in Film and Television* (Cambridge, MA: Harvard University Press, 2003).

38. Joshua Patrick, "Shakespeare's Five Act Structure: Learn It, Live It, Love It," Owlcation.com, July 27, 2019, https://owlcation.com/humanities/Shakespeares-5-Act-Structure-Learn-It-Live-It-Love-It.

39. John B. Black, "An Evaluation of Story Grammars," *Cognitive Science: A Multidisciplinary Journal* 3 (1979): 213–29.

40. Fran Lehr, "ERIC/RCS: Story Grammar," *The Reading Teacher* 40, no. 6 (1987): 550–52.

41. Neil Cohn, "Visual Narrative Structure," *Cognitive Science* 37 (2013): 413–52.

42. Carl B. Smith, "Story Map: Setting, Plot, Mood, Theme (ERIC/RCS)," *Reading Teacher* 44, no. 2 (1990): 178–79.

43. C. Scott Littleton, *The New Comparative Mythology: An Anthropological Assessment of the Theories of Georges Dumezil* (Berkeley: University of California Press, 1982).

44. "Monomyth: Hero's Journey Project," Berkeley ORIAS, accessed October 2, 2021, https://orias.berkeley.edu/resources-teachers/monomyth-heros-journey-project.

45. "What Do Star Wars, The Matrix, and Lion King Have in Common?" Wired.com, March 2, 2012, https://www.wired.com/2012/03/what-do-star-wars-the-matrix-and-lion-king-have-in-common/.

46. "The Dan Harmon Story Circle: What Authors Can Learn from Rick and Morty," ReedsyBlog, March 25, 2021, https://blog.reedsy.com/guide/story-structure/dan-harmon-story-circle/.

47. "The Story Circle: Elevate Your Narrative with a Simple Eight-Step Guide and Worksheet," StudioBinder.com, accessed October 1, 2021, https://www.studiobinder.com/blog/downloads/story-circle-template/.

48. Dan Harmon, "Story Structure 103: Let's Simplify Before Moving On," Channel 101, 2017, https://channel101.fandom.com/wiki/Story_Structure_103:_Let%27s_Simplify_Before_Moving_On.

49. "Congratulations to the Commercial Stars of 2022!" USA Today Ad Meter, accessed July 6, 2022, https://admeter.usatoday.com.

50. "Robo Dog: The All-Electric Kia EV6," Kia America, YouTube.com, February 3, 2022, https://youtu.be/HoNMz_OV_dI.

51. Joseph Campbell, *The Hero with a Thousand Faces*, 3rd ed. (New World Library, 2014).

52. "Top Ad Campaigns of the 21st Century," Adage.com, 2017, http://adage.com/lp/top15/#intro.

53. Surya Solanki, "History of BMW Films," BMWBlog.com, November 11, 2016, http://www.bmwblog.com/2016/11/11/history-bmw-films/.

54. "Titanium Lions," CannesLions.com, accessed July 6, 2022, https://www.canneslions.com/enter/awards/lions-categories/titanium-lions#/

55. "BMW Films: The Escape," YouTube.com, October 23, 2016, https://www.youtube.com/watch?v=jzUFCQ-P1Zg.

56. "Top Ad Campaigns of the 21st Century."

57. Jack Neff, "Ten Years In, Dove's 'Real Beauty' Seems to Be Aging Well," Adage.com, January 22, 2014, http://adage.com/article/news/ten-years-dove-s-real-beauty-aging/291216/.

58. "Top Ad Campaigns of the 21st Century."

59. "Top Ad Campaigns of the 21st Century."

60. "Case Study: Always #LikeAGirl," Campaign, October 12, 2015, http://www.campaignlive.co.uk/article/1366870/case-study-always-likeagirl#0Xqg8M2WYzb37OFI.99.

61. "Case Study: Always #LikeAGirl."

62. "Mac vs PC Commercial—Viruses," YouTube.com, November 19, 2007, https://www.youtube.com/watch?v=ZwQpPqPKbAw.

63. Jim Dalrymple, "Apple Desktop Market Share on the Rise; Will the Mac Mini, iPod Help?" Macworld.com, March 21, 2005, http://www.macworld.com/article/1043741/marketshare.html.

64. Katie Marsal, "Apple's U.S. Mac Marketing Share Rises to 8.1 Percent in Q3," Appleinsider.com, October 17, 2007, http://appleinsider.com/articles/07/10/17/apples_u_s_mac_market_share_rises_to_8_1_percent_in_q3.

65. Stern, "What's in a Name?"

Chapter 3. Dramatic Brands: From Form to Function

1. Simon Sinek, "How Great Leaders Inspire Action," TEDx Puget Sound, September 2009, https://www.ted.com/talks/simon_sinek_how_great_leaders_inspire_action/transcript?language=en.

2. Sinek, "How Great Leaders Inspire Action."

3. Sinek, "How Great Leaders Inspire Action."

4. "Golden Circle for Organizations," SimonSinek.com, accessed June 1, 2022, https://simon sinek.com/product/golden-circle-for-organizations/.

5. Sinek, "How Great Leaders Inspire Action"; and Dave Chaffey, "Golden Circle Model: Simon Sinek's Theory of Value Proposition, Start with Why," SmartInsights.com, June 11, 2021, https://www.smartinsights.com/digital-marketing-strategy/online-value-proposition /start-with-why-creating-a-value-proposition-with-the-golden-circle-model/.

6. Mark Gurman, "Read Tim Cook's Staff Memo on 10th Anniversary of Job's Death," Bloomberg.com, October 5, 2021, https://www.bloomberg.com/news/articles/2021-10-05 /read-tim-cook-s-staff-memo-on-10th-anniversary-of-jobs-s-death.

7. Natasha Daily, "Apple Now Has the Most Valuable Brand in the World at More than $260 Billion, Surpassing Amazon and Google," BusinessInsider.com, January 27, 2021, https://www.business insider.com/apple-surpasses-amazon-as-worlds-most-valuable-brand-2021-1.

8. Jason Snell, "Steve Jobs: Making a Dent in the Universe," Macworld.com, October 5, 2011, https://www.macworld.com/article/214642/steve-jobs-making-a-dent-in-the-universe.html.

9. Ben & Jerry's, "Our Values and Mission," BenJerry.com, accessed October 6, 2021, https://www .benjerry.com/values.

10. Halo Top, "About Us," HaloTop.com, accessed October 6, 2021, https://halotop.com/ about-us.

11. Amrita Khalid, "How Noom Won 2020, a Banner Year for Wellness and Weight-Loss Apps," Inc., May 18, 2021, https://www.inc.com/amrita-khalid/noom-saeju-jeong-weight-loss-app.html.

12. "About Us. Hi, We're Noom," Noom.com, accessed March 2, 2022, https://web.noom.com /ABOUT-US/.

13. "Parity Product," Investopedia.com, accessed October 8, 2021, https://www.investopedia .com/terms/p/parity-product.asp.

14. "Price Promotions," Knowledge@Wharton, June 4, 2012, https://kwhs.wharton.upenn.edu /term/price-promotions/.

15. "Price War," Merriam-Webster.com, accessed October 8, 2021, https://www.merriam-web ster.com/dictionary/price%20war.

16. R. Rao Akshay, Mark E. Bergen, and Scott Davis, "How to Fight a Price War," *Harvard Business Review*, March–April 2000, https://hbr.org/2000/03/how-to-fight-a-price-war.

17. "Apple iPhone 13 Pro TV Commercial, 'Hollywood in Your Pocket,' Song by Labrinth," Commercial Hub, YouTube.com, September 21, 2021, https://www.youtube.com/ watch?v=dNaPQ1SMbCs.

18. Keith A. Quesenberry and Michael K. Coolsen, "Drama Goes Viral: Effects of Story Development on Shares and Views of Online Advertising Videos," *Journal of Interactive Marketing* 48 (2019): 1–16.

19. "The Leading Ice Cream Brands of the United States in 2020, Based on Sales (in Million U.S. Dollars)," Statista, December 21, 2020, accessed October 6, 2021, https://www.statista.com /statistics/190426/top-ice-cream-brands-in-the-united-states/.

20. Kathie Canning, "Retail Ice Cream Sales Tumble," DiaryFoods.com, January 22, 2020, https://www.dairyfoods.com/articles/94067-retail-ice-cream-sales-tumble.

21. Kaitlin Kamp, "Ice Cream and Frozen Novelties—US—April 2021," Mintel, April 2021, https://reports.mintel.com/display/1045097/.

22. Kamp, "Ice Cream and Frozen Novelties."

23. Lisa Earle McLeod, "Why I Believe in Noble Purpose," Forbes.com, May 5, 2014, https://www .forbes.com/sites/lisaearlemcleod/2014/05/05/why-i-believe-in-noble-purpose/?sh=745afde270ef.

24. Lisa Earle McLeod, "McLeod & More website homepage" McLeodAndMore.com, accessed October 6, 2021, https://www.mcleodandmore.com/.

25. Earle Mcleod, "Why I Believe in Noble Purpose."

26. Earle McLeod, "Why I Believe in Noble Purpose."

27. "The Persuaders Interviews," *Frontline*, PBS.org, December 15, 2003, https://www.pbs.org/wgbh/pages/frontline/shows/persuaders/interviews/.

28. "The World's First All-Electric Supertrucks GMC Hummer EV Pickup and SUV," GMC.com, accessed October 6, 2021, https://www.gmc.com/electric/hummer-ev.

29. Paul J. Zak, "Why Your Brain Loves Good Storytelling," *Harvard Business Review*, 2014, October, 2–4.

30. Chaffey, "Golden Circle Model: Simon Sinek's Theory of Value Proposition."

31. Peter Fader, "Customer Centricity: Focus on the Right Customers for Strategic Advantage," Wharton School Press, accessed September 14, 2022, https://wsp.wharton.upenn.edu/book/customer-centricity/.

32. "Grand American Touring 2022 Road King," Harley-Davidson.com, accessed October 8, 2021, https://www.harley-davidson.com/us/en/motorcycles/road-king.html.

33. "Vespa Homepage," Vespa.com, accessed October 8, 2021, https://www.vespa.com/us_EN/.

34. "Carl Jung Swiss Psychologist," Britannica.com, accessed September 30, 2021, https://www.britannica.com/biography/Carl-Jung.

35. "Definition of Archetype," Literarydevices.net, accessed September 30, 2021, https://literarydevices.net/archetype/.

36. "Definition of Archetype."

37. Ibid.

38. Conor Neill, "Understanding Personality: The 12 Jungian Archetypes," Conorneill.com, April 21, 2018, https://conorneill.com/2018/04/21/understanding-personality-the-12-jungian-archetypes/.

39. Margaret Mark and Carol S. Pearson, *The Hero and the Outlaw: Building Extraordinary Brands Through the Power of Archetypes* (New York: McGraw-Hill, 2001).

40. Michael K. Coolsen and Madoka Kumashiro, "Self-Image Congruence Models Conceptualized as a Product Affirmation Process," *Advances in Consumer Research* 36 (2009, January): 980–81.

41. "Beyond Limits," Nike, accessed October 10, 2021, https://www.nike.com/gb/running/breaking2.

42. "Factbox: Nike's Vaporfly Running Shoes and Tumbling Records," Reuters.com, January 24, 2020, https://www.reuters.com/article/us-athletics-shoe-factbox/factbox-nikes-vaporfly-running-shoes-and-tumbling-records-idUSKBN1ZN0NH.

43. Coolsen and Kumashiro, "Self-Image Congruence Models Conceptualized as a Product Affirmation Process."

44. "Identity," *Psychology Today*, accessed October 10, 2021, https://www.psychologytoday.com/us/basics/identity.

45. "Identity."

46. Albert M. Muniz Jr. and Thomas C. O'Guinn, "Brand Community," *Journal of Consumer Research* 27, no. 4 (2001): 412–32.

47. "Our Story," yeti.com, accessed October 14, 2021, https://stories.yeti.com/story/our-story.

48. Stephen Read and Lynn Miller, "Stories Are Fundamental to Meaning and Memory: For Social Creatures, Could It Be Otherwise?" in *Knowledge and Memory: The Real Story*, ed. Robert S. Wyer, Jr., 139–52 (New York: Lawrence Erlbaum Associates, 1995).

49. Kevin Roberts, "Brand Loyalty Reloaded," Saatchi & Saatchi, 2015, https://www.saatchikevin.com/wp-content/uploads/2014/09/Loyalty-Beyond-Reason-Red-Paper-Jan-2015.pdf.

50. Saul McLeod, "Social Identity Theory," SimplyPsychology.org, 2019, https://www.simplypsychology.org/social-identity-theory.html.

51. "Belief," Merriam-Webster.com, accessed October 14, 2021, https://www.merriam-webster.com/dictionary/belief.

52. "Quality," Merriam-Webster.com, accessed October 14, 2021, https://www.merriam-webster.com/dictionary/qualities.

53. "Personality," Merriam-Webster.com, accessed October 14, 2021, https://www.merriam-webster.com/dictionary/personality.

54. "Look," Merriam-Webster.com, accessed October 14, 2021, https://www.merriam-webster.com/dictionary/look.

55. "Expression," Merriam-Webster.com, accessed October 14, 2021, https://www.merriam-webster.com/dictionary/expression.

56. "Offer," Merriam-Webster.com, accessed October 14, 2021, https://www.merriam-webster.com/dictionary/offers.

57. Keith A. Quesenberry, "How to Avoid a Social Media Brand Identity Crisis (Social Brand ID Template)," PostControlMarketing.com, December 14, 2016, https://www.postcontrolmarketing.com/how-to-avoid-a-social-media-brand-identity-crisis/.

58. "Our Story."

59. Roberts, "Brand Loyalty Reloaded."

60. "About Us. Hi, We're Noom."

61. Wang, "Noom Topped $400M Revenue in 2020."

62. Amrita Khalid, "How Noom Won 2020, a Banner Year for Wellness and Weight-Loss Apps" Inc., May 18, 2021, https://www.inc.com/amrita-khalid/noom-saeju-jeong-weight-loss-app.html.

63. "Consumer," Common Language Marketing Dictionary, accessed September 19, 2021, https://marketing-dictionary.org/c/consumer/.

64. Oscar Wang, "How Gatorade Fueled Its Business Growth with Customer Insights," Prophet.com, August 2018, https://www.prophet.com/2018/08/gatorade-digital-business-growth-strategy/.

65. Robert Williams, "Gatorade Boosts UGC with New App for Teen Athlete Videos," MarketingDive.com, May 31, 2019, https://www.marketingdive.com/news/gatorade-boosts-ugc-with-new-app-for-teen-athlete-videos/555894/.

66. "Public Service Announcement," Common Language Marketing Dictionary, accessed September 19, 2021, https://marketing-dictionary.org/p/public-service-announcement/.

Chapter 4. Set the Stage: Marketing, IMC, and Media

1. "Philip Kotler Quotes," pkotler.org, accessed October 19, 2021, https://www.pkotler.org/quotes-from-pk.

2. "Philip Kotler," Marketing Kellogg.Northwestern.edu, https://www.kellogg.northwestern.edu/faculty/directory/kotler_philip.aspx.

3. "Marketing Mix," Marketing-Dictionary.org, accessed October 19, 2021, https://marketing-dictionary.org/m/marketing-mix/.

4. "Target Market," Marketing-Dictionary.org, accessed October 19, 2021, https://marketing-dictionary.org/t/target-market/.

5. "Market," Investopedia.com, accessed October 20, 2021, https://www.investopedia.com/terms/m/market.asp.

6. Annmarie Hanlon, "The Segmentation, Targeting, Positioning (STP) Marketing Model," SmartInsights.com, June 3, 2021, https://www.smartinsights.com/digital-marketing-strategy/customer-segmentation-targeting/segmentation-targeting-and-positioning/.

7. "Brand Positioning," Marketing-Dictionary.org, accessed October 20, 2021, https://marketing-dictionary.org/b/brand-positioning/.

8. "Product," Marketing-Dictionary.org, accessed October 19, 2021, https://marketing-dictionary.org/t/target-market/.

9. "Price," Marketing-Dictionary.org, accessed October 19, 2021, https://marketing-dictionary.org/p/price/.

10. "Distribution," Marketing-Dictionary.org, accessed October 19, 2021, https://marketing-dictionary.org/d/distribution/.

11. "Marketing Communications," Marketing-Dictionary.org, https://marketing-dictionary.org/m/marketing-communications/.

12. "Medill Professor Emeritus Don Schultz Dies, Leaves Legacy in Integrated Marketing Communications: Shultz Had International Reputation as 'Father of IMC,'" Medill.Northwestern.edu, June 5, 2020, https://www.medill.northwestern.edu/news/2020/medill-professor-emeritus-don-schultz-dies-leaves-legacy-in-integrated-marketing-communications.html.

13. Don Schultz, Charles H. Patti, and Philip J. Kitchen, *The Evolution of Integrated Marketing Communications* (Abingdon, Oxon: Routledge, 2013).

14. "Brand Positioning Statements," Association of National Advertisers, ANA.net, May 28, 2020, https://www.ana.net/miccontent/show/id/aa-brand-positioning-statements.

15. Keith A. Quesenberry, "Visualize Your Marketing Strategy to Form a Solid Foundation for All Marketing Communication," PostControlMarketing.com, October 12, 2016, https://www.postcontrolmarketing.com/visualize-your-marketing-strategy-to-form-a-solid-foundation-for-all-marketing-communication/.

16. Richard Edelman, "One on One," Edelman.com, October 4, 2016, https://www.edelman.com/insights/one-on-one-prweek-conference.

17. "Steps to Find Your Target Audience," Marketing Evolution.com, accessed October 20, 2021, https://www.marketingevolution.com/marketing-essentials/target-audience.

18. "Buying Roles," Common Language Marketing Dictionary, accessed September 19, 2021, https://marketing-dictionary.org/b/buying-roles/.

19. Margaret Rouse, "Firmographic Data," WhatIs.TechTarget.com, September 2016, https://whatis.techtarget.com/definition/firmographic-data.

20. Mark Schaefer and Brooke Sellas, "Key Takeaways on the Future of Marketing—Episode 174," BusinessGrow.com, Marketing Companion Podcast, accessed October 20, 2021, https://businessesgrow.com/podcast-the-marketing-companion-2/.

21. Jason Feifer, "How Gatorade Redefined Its Audience and a Flagging Brand," FastCoCreate.com, May 22, 2012, http://www.fastcocreate.com/1680819/how-gatorade-redefined-its-audience-and-a-flagging-brand/.

22. "Old Spice Campaign Is Not Only Great, It Sells—Now #1 in U.S. in Both Dollar and Volume Share," CampaignBrief.com, July 16, 2010, http://www.campaignbrief.com/2010/07/old-spice-campaign-is-not-onl.html.

23. Chris Isidore, "Ford's Mustang Mach-E Is Eating into Tesla's US Sales," March 5, 2021, *CNN Business*, https://www.cnn.com/2021/03/04/business/ford-mustang-mach-e-tesla-market share/index.html.

24. "2009 Institutional Brand and Parental Influence on College Choice: A Noel-Levitz Benchmark Psychographic Study," Noel-Levitz, 2009, https://files.eric.ed.gov/fulltext/ED541569.pdf.

25. Nicole Lyn Pesce, "How That Devastating 'This Is Us' Fire Actually Boosted Crock-Pot Sales," MarketWatch.com, May 10, 2018, https://www.marketwatch.com/story/how-that-devastating-this-is-us-fire-actually-boosted-crock-pot-sales-2018-05-10.

26. Gini Dietrich, "Why Communicators Must (Finally) Embrace the PESO Model," Spinsucks.com, January 5, 2021, https://spinsucks.com/communication/pr-pros-must-embrace-the-peso-model/.

27. Dietrich, "Why Communicators Must (Finally) Embrace the PESO Model."

28. "Media Planning," Marketing-Dictionary.org, accessed October 21, 2021, https://market ing-dictionary.org/m/media-planning/.

29. "Five Questions to Answer before You Finalize Your Media Plan," McKinsey.com, November 18, 2020, https://www.mckinsey.com/capabilities/growth-marketing-and-sales/our-insights /five-questions-to-answer-before-you-finalize-your-media-plan.

30. Donald E. Parente and Kristen L. Stausbaugh-Hutchinson, *Advertising Campaign Straegy: A Guide to Marketing Communications Plans*, 5th ed. (Boston, MA: Cengage Learning, 2015).

31. "Resident Population of the United States by Sex and Age as of July 1, 2020 (in Millions)," Statista .com, July 2021, https://www.statista.com/statistics/241488/population-of-the-us-by-sex-and-age/.

32. "Reach," Marketing-Dictionary.org, accessed October 25, 2021, https://marketing-dictionary .org/r/reach/.

33. "Frequency," Marketing-Dictionary.org, accessed October, 25, 2021, https://marketing-dictio nary.org/f/frequency/.

34. "Reach."

35. "Reach."

36. "Advertising Impression," Marketing-Dictionary.org, accessed October 25, 2021, https://mar keting-dictionary.org/a/advertising-impression/.

37. "Impression (Internet)," Marketing-Dictionary.org, accessed October 25, 2021, https://mar keting-dictionary.org/i/impression/.

38. "Gross Rating Point (GRP)," Marketing-Dictionary.org, accessed October 21, 2021, https:// marketing-dictionary.org/g/gross-rating-point/.

39. Rick Porter, "TV Long View: A Guide to the Every-Expanding World of Ratings Data," HollywoodReporter.com, October 5, 2019, https://www.hollywoodreporter.com/tv/tv-news /tv-ratings-explained-a-guide-what-data-all-means-1245591/.

40. "Gross Rating Point (GRP)," Marketing Dictionary.org, accessed October 25, 2021, https:// marketing-dictionary.org/g/gross-rating-point/.

41. Michael Schneider, "100 Most-Watched TV Shows of 2020-2021: Winners and Losers," Variety.com, May 25, 2021, https://variety.com/2021/tv/news/most-popular-tv-shows -highest-rated-2020-2021-season-1234980743/.

42. Jeanie Poggi, "What It Costs to Advertise in TV's Biggest Shows in 2020-2021 Season," AdAge.com, October 30, 2020, https://adage.com/article/media/tvs-most-expensive-shows -advertisers-season/2281176.

43. "Cost per Impression," Marketing-Dictionary.org, accessed October 21, 2021, https://market ing-dictionary.org/c/cost-per-impression/.

44. "Cost per Click (CPC)," Marketing-Dictionary.org, accessed October 21, 2021, https://mar keting-dictionary.org/c/cost-per-click/.

45. Amine Rahal, "Measuring Success: Six Digital Marketing Metrics and KPIs for 2021," Forbes .com, December 10, 2021, https://www.forbes.com/sites/forbescommunicationscouncil/2021/04/28 /measuring-success-six-digital-marketing-metrics-and-kpis-for-2021/?sh=2df332aa6172.

46. "Cost per Thousand (CPT)," Marketing-Dictionary.org, accessed October 21, 2021, https:// marketing-dictionary.org/c/cost-per-thousand-impressions/.

47. "What Is the Average CPM on Each Social Platform?" WebFX.com, https://www.webfx .com/tools/cpm-calculator/#table; David Doty, "It's All About Pricing: Digital Is Winning Simply Because It's a Cheaper Way for Advertisers to Reach Consumers: A 101 Course," Forbes.com, October 29, 2019, https://www.forbes.com/sites/daviddoty/2019/10/29/its-all-about-pricing-digital-is -winning-simply-because-its-a-cheaper-way-for-advertisers-to-reach-consumers-a-101-course/?sh =6f75a3ff3275; and "Online Advertising Costs in 2021," TopDraw.com, March 26, 2021, https:// www.topdraw.com/insights/is-online-advertising-expensive/.

48. "Banner Blindness," Marketing-Dictionary.org, accessed October 30, 2021, https://marketing-dictionary.org/b/banner-blindness/.

49. Tim Edmundson, "Your Guide to Connected TV Advertising," Mountain.com, accessed November 14, 2021, https://mountain.com/blog/your-guide-to-connected-tv-advertising/.

50. Jack Neff, "Why Brands Like P&G And L'oreal Are Investing More In CTV With Help From Retail Media Networks," Agage.com, Nobember 28, 2022, https://adage.com/article/media/why-brands-pg-and-loreal-are-investing-more-ctv-help-retail-media-networks/2454241?utm_source=ad-age-wake-up-call&utm_medium=email&utm_campaign=20221128&utm_content=hero-headline

51. "What Is Flighting?" Investopedia.com, June 14, 2021, https://www.investopedia.com/terms/f/flighting.asp.

52. Feifer, "How Gatorade Redefined Its Audience and a Flagging Brand."

53. Feifer, "How Gatorade Redefined Its Audience and a Flagging Brand."

54. Caroline Beuley, "The Digital Strategy Driving Gatorade's Growth," Prophet.co, August 9, 2016, https://medium.com/@ProphetBrand/the-digital-strategy-driving-gatorades-growth-f1909c778bc7.

55. Beuley, "The Digital Strategy Driving Gatorade's Growth."

56. "Advertising Spending of Selected Beverage Brands in the United States in 2019 (in Million U.S. Dollars), Statista, July 13, 2020, https://www.statista.com/statistics/264985/ad-spend-of-selected-beverage-brands-in-the-us/.

Chapter 5. Point of View: Consumer Insight and Creative Brief

1. Carol Williams, "Carol Williams—Developing Strategic Advertising Insights," Stan Talks, YouTube.com, April 10, 2018, https://youtu.be/faxWScOQyF8.

2. Sapna Maheshwari, "An Ad Woman at the Top of an Industry That She Thinks Still Has Far to Go," *New York Times*, April 24, 2017, https://www.nytimes.com/2017/04/24/business/carol-williams-advertising-hall-of-fame.htmlk.

3. Williams, "Carol Williams—Developing Strategic Advertising Insights."

4. Maheshwari, "An Ad Woman at the Top of an Industry That She Thinks Still Has Far to Go."

5. Williams, "Carol Williams—Developing Strategic Advertising Insights."

6. "Luke Sullivan—Tensions," Stan Talks, YouTube.com, April 8, 2019, https://www.youtube.com/watch?v=gSrXAAFX6rg.

7. "Carol H. Williams," carolhwilliams.com, accessed November 1, 2021, https://carolhwilliams.com/.

8. Christina Newberry, "Influencer Marketing Guide: How to Work with Social Media Influencers," August 10, 2021, Blog.Hootsuite.com, https://blog.hootsuite.com/influencer-marketing/; and Mark Schaefer and Jay Acunzo, "How Does Content Work in the World Today?" October 27, 2021, BusinessGrow.com, https://businessesgrow.com/2021/10/27/how-does-content-work/.

9. Keith A. Quesenberry, "Why You Need to Be an Influencer Brand and the 3 Rs of Becoming One," Entrepreneur.com, June 22, 2022, https://www.entrepreneur.com/article/428086.

10. "Relevant," Dictionary.com, accessed October 27, 2021, https://www.dictionary.com/browse/relevant; and Schaefer and Acunzo, "How Does Content Work in the World Today?"

11. "Reach," Marketing-Dictionary.org, accessed October 25, 2021, https://marketing-dictionary.org/r/reach/.

12. "Resonance," Dictionary.com, accessed October 27, 2021, https://www.dictionary.com/browse/resonance; and Schaefer and Acunzo, "How Does Content Work in the World Today?"

13. "Resound," Dictionary.com, accessed May 20, 2022, https://www.dictionary.com/browse/resound.

14. "Bull's-eye," Dictionary.com, accessed October 27, 2021, https://www.dictionary.com/browse/bull-s-eye.

15. OnePeloton.com homepage, accessed November 3, 2021, https://www.onepeloton.com.

16. Brian Dean, "Peloton Subscriber and Revenue Statistics (2021)," BackLinko.com, March 15, 2021, https://backlinko.com/peloton-users.

17. Ann-Christine Diaz, "Airbnb Asks, 'Why Vacation Somewhere When You Can Live There?'" AdAge.com, April 19, 2016, https://adage.com/creativity/work/dont-go-there-live-there/46533?.

18. "Number of Airbnb Users in the United States from 2016 to 2022 (in Millions)," Statista, June 6, 2018, accessed November 3, 2021, https://www.statista.com/statistics/346589/number-of-us-airbnb-users/.

19. "Advertising Message (Creative Work)," Marketing-Dictionary.org, accessed November 3, 2021, https://marketing-dictionary.org/a/advertising-message/.

20. "Campaign," Marketing-Dictionary.org, accessed November 3, 2021, https://marketing-dictionary.org/c/campaign/.

21. "Actionable Insight," Techopedia.com, accessed November 1, 2021, https://www.techopedia.com/definition/31721/actionable-insight.

22. Rob Hernandez, "Big Ideas: Research Can Make a Big Difference," MillwardBrown.com, accessed November 1, 2021, http://www.millwardbrown.com/docs/default-source/insight-documents/points-of-view/Millward_Brown_POV_Big_Ideas.pdf.

23. "Have Legs," Cambridge Dictionary, accessed November 1, 2021, http://dictionary.cambridge.org/us/dictionary/british/have-legs.

24. Philip Kotler, Hermawan Kartajaya, and Iwan Setiawan, *Marketing 4.0: Moving from Traditional to Digital* (Hoboken, NJ: Wiley, 2017), 128–29.

25. Cenk Bulbul and Netta Gross, "4 Steps to Finding a True Human Insight about Your Audience," ThinkWithGoogle.com, https://www.thinkwithgoogle.com/marketing-strategies/search/human-insights-audience-strategy/.

26. Joei Chan, "How to Find Consumer Insights on Social Media: The Expert Guide," accessed November 8, 2021, Linkfluence, https://www.linkfluence.com/blog/consumer-insights-social-media-guide.

27. David Stafford, "3 Questions You Need to Answer Before Writing Your Next Story," TheWritingPractice.com, 2021, https://thewritepractice.com/questions-writing-book/.

28. "Business Case Studies," Businesscasestudies.co.uk, accessed September 15, 2017, http://businesscasestudies.co.uk/food-standards-agency/market-research-and-consumer-protection/primary-and-secondary-research.html#ixzz3IgNvWPPI.

29. Kathleen Sampey, "Neiman Debuts Anti-Smoking Ads," *Adweek* 43, no. 46 (2002): 6.

30. "Surveys," InsightAssociation.org, accessed November 8, 2021, https://www.insightsassociation.org/issues-policies/glossary.

31. "Surveys."

32. "Observation," Robert Wood Johnson Foundation, accessed September 27, 2019, http://www.qualres.org/HomeObse-3594.html.

33. Douglas B. Holt, "got milk?" AEF.com, 2002, https://aef.com/classroom-resources/case-histories/got-milk/.

34. Jeff Manning and Kevin Lane Keller, "Got Advertising That Works?" *Marketing Management* 13, no. 1 (2004): 16–20.

35. Holt, "got milk?"; and Manning and Keller, "Got Advertising That Works?"

36. "Surveys," InsightAssociation.org, accessed November 8, 2021, https://www.insightsassociation.org/issues-policies/glossary.

37. "Surveys."

38. "Grand Ogilvy Winner: 'Mischievous Fun with Cheetos,'" TheARF.org, 2009, https://cdn .thearf.org/ARF_Knowledgebase/ARF%20Ogilvy%20Award%20Case%20Studies/2009%20 ARF%20David%20Ogilvy%20Award%20CS/Ogilvy-09-CS-Cheetos.pdf; and Carmen Nobel, "Neuromarketing: Tapping into the 'Pleasure Center' of Consumers," Forbes.com, February 1, 2013, https://www.forbes.com/sites/hbsworkingknowledge/2013/02/01/neuromarketing-tap ping-into-the-pleasure-center-of-consumers/?sh=5145a6932745.

39. Geschreven Door Diede, "5 Neuromarketing Advertising Examples That Will Help Make Better Commercials," UnravelResearch.com, May 24, 2019, https://www.unravelresearch.com/en /blog/5-neuromarketing-advertising-examples-that-will-help-you-make-better-commercials.

40. "Trade Association," Dictionary.com, accessed November 8, 2021, https://www.dictionary .com/browse/trade-association.

41. "Research," Convenience.org, accessed November 8, 2021, https://www.convenience.org /Research.

42. Chan, "How to Find Consumer Insights on Social Media: The Expert Guide."

43. "What's the Difference Between Social Monitoring and Social Listening?" Sprinklr.com, April 1, 2021, https://www.sprinklr.com/blog/social-monitoring-vs-social-listening/.

44. Chan, "How to Find Consumer Insights on Social Media: The Expert Guide."

45. Gareth Price, "Ask an Expert: How Do You Identify an Insight?" Brandwatch.com, Septem- ber 15, 2016, https://www.brandwatch.com/blog/gareth-price-how-do-you-identify-an-insight/.

46. Erica Sweeney, "Fruit or Vegetable? Heinz Brings Age-Old Debate around Tomatoes to Digital," MarketingDive.com, April 6, 2018, https://www.marketingdive.com/news/fruit-or -vegetable-heinz-brings-age-old-debate-around-tomatoes-to-digital/520767/.

47. Price, "Ask an Expert: How Do You Identify an Insight?"

48. "What Is Planning?" Apg.org.uk, accessed November 8, 2021, http://www. https://www.apg .org.uk/knowledge-whatisplanning.

49. "Account Executive," Marketing-Dictionary.org, accessed November 8, 2021, https://market ing-dictionary.org/a/account-executive/.

50. "Copywriter," Merriam-Webster.com, accessed November 7, 2021, http://www.merriam -webster.com/dictionary/copywriter.

51. "Art Director," Merriam-Webster.com, accessed November 7, 2021, http://www.merriam -webster.com/dictionary/art%20director.

52. "Career Overview: Public Relations," WetFeet.com, accessed November 7, 2021, https:// www.wetfeet.com/articles/career-overview-public-relations.

53. What Is a Digital Marketing Specialist?" Sokanu.com, accessed November 7, 2021, https:// www.sokanu.com/careers/digital-marketing-specialist/.

54. Maxwell Gollin, "10 Social Media Job Titles (and What They Actually Mean)," Fal con.io, March 5, 2019, https://www.falcon.io/insights-hub/case-stories/cs-social-media-manage ment/10-social-media-job-titlesand-what-they-actually-mean/.

55. "Perceptual Mapping," BusinessDictionary.com, accessed October 1, 2019, http://www .businessdictionary.com/definition/perceptual-mapping.html.

56. Jim Joseph, "Move Your Business Forward by Drawing a Perceptual Map," Entrepreneur.com, June 3, 2015, https://www.entreprencur.com/article/246813.

57. H. Allen White, "Elaboration Likelihood Model," Oxford Bibliographies, February 23, 2011, https://www.oxfordbibliographies.com/view/document/obo-9780199756841/obo-9780199 756841-0053.xml.

58. Roger Dooley, "Emotional Ads Work Best," NeuroscienceMarketing.com, accessed Novem- ber 3, 2021, https://www.neurosciencemarketing.com/blog/articles/emotional-ads-work-best.htm.

59. Dooley, "Emotional Ads Work Best."

60. Carly Carmanna, "Pepsi Super Bowl Commercials, Ranked," Mashed.com, February 5, 2021, https://www.mashed.com/323980/pepsi-super-bowl-commercials-ranked/.

61. "Bubly 2019 Superbowl Campaign," ShortyAwards.com, accessed November 8, 2021, https://shortyawards.com/12th/bubly-2019-superbowl-campaign.

62. Jeff Suess, "Our History: Odorono Ads Made Us Realize We Needed Deodorant," February 14, 2017, Cincinnati.com, https://www.cincinnati.com/story/news/2017/02/14/odorono-ads-made-us-realize-we-needed-deodorant/97922010/.

63. James Webb Young, *A Technique for Producing Ideas* (New York: McGraw-Hill Education, 2003). (Originally published 1940).

64. James Clear, "Book Summary: A Technique for Producing Ideas by James Webb Young," accessed November 9, 2021, https://jamesclear.com/book-summaries/a-technique-for-producing-ideas.

65. Young, *A Technique for Producing Ideas.*

66. Paul Sloane, "Why Are Children So Much More Creative than Adults?" Destination-Innovation.com, accessed November 9, 2021, https://www.destination-innovation.com/why-are-children-so-much-more-creative-than-adults/.

67. "Evian Roller Babies," ViralVideoChart, Evian, YouTube.com, July 3, 2009, https://www.youtube.com/watch?v=Lb1IUHXoljE.

68. E. J. Schultz, "Evian Drops Its Babies in Favor of New U.S. Ad Approach," AgAge.com, July 9, 2018, https://adage.com/article/cmo-strategy/evian-throws-babies-favor-ad-approach/314122.

69. Steven Whiteside, "Effectiveness Insights from Ten Years of Snickers' 'You're Not You When You're Hungry,'" WARC, October 29, 2020, https://www.warc.com/newsandopinion/opinion/effectiveness-insights-from-ten-years-of-snickers-youre-not-you-when-youre-hungry/3892.

70. James Miller, "Case Study: How Fame Made Snickers' 'You're Not You When You're Hungry' Campaign a Success," CampaignLive.com, October 26, 2016, https://www.campaignlive.com/article/case-study-fame-made-snickers-youre-not-when-youre-hungry-campaign-success/1413554.

71. Miller, "Case Study: How Fame Made Snickers."

72. Ibid.

73. Ibid.

74. Whiteside, "Effectiveness Insights from Ten Years of Snickers."

75. Curtis Newbold, "How to Conduct Observations for Research," TheVisualCommunicationsGuy.com, January 30, 2018, https://thevisualcommunicationguy.com/2018/01/30/how-to-conduct-observations-for-research/.

Chapter 6. Sound and Motion: TV Ads, Online Video, and Radio

1. "What Bill Said: William Bernbach Quotes from DDB," BrainBlaze.com, accessed July 7, 2022, https://brainblaze.com/bill-said-william-bernbach-quotes-ddb/.

2. "What Bill Said."

3. Tyson Quick, "Advertising Evolution: How Personalization Has Improved over Time," Instagpage.com, June 11, 2021, https://instapage.com/blog/evolution-of-advertising.

4. Quick, "Advertising Evolution."

5. Ibid.

6. "David Ogilvy: British Advertising Executive," Encyclopedia Britannica, accessed November 15, 2021, https://www.britannica.com/biography/David-Ogilvy.

7. "I Am Legend: Rosser Reeves," Adweek.com, November 12, 2008, https://www.adweek.com/agencyspy/i-am-legend-rosser-reeves/3212/.

8. Lawrence R. Samuel, *The American Dream: A Cultural History* (Syracuse, NY: Syracuse University Press, 2012), 202.

9. Mark Hamilton, "The Ad That Changed Advertising. The Story Behind Volkswagen's Think Small Campaign," Medium.com/TheAgency.com, March 20, 2015, https://medium.com/theagency/the-ad-that-changed-advertising-18291a67488c.

10. Hamilton, "The Ad That Changed Advertising."

11. Avi Dan, "The Man Who Saw Creativity as the Last Unfair Advantage Legally Allowed in Marketing," Forbes.com, January 10, 2019, https://www.forbes.com/sites/avidan/2019/06/10/when-advertising-was-transformed-forever-and-became-the-art-of-persuasion/?sh=3afe8ce85ef7.

12. Dan, "The Man Who Saw Creativity as the Last Unfair Advantage Legally Allowed In Marketing."

13. "Ogilvy on Advertising Quotes," GoodReads.com, accessed November 15, 2021, https://www.goodreads.com/work/quotes/627791-ogilvy-on-advertising.

14. "David Ogilvy: British Advertising Executive."

15. "Beetle Overtakes Model T as World's Best-Selling Car," A&E Television Networks, February 13, 2020, https://www.history.com/this-day-in-history/beetle-overtakes-model-t-as-worlds-best-selling-car.

16. "Beetle Overtakes Model T."

17. Hamilton, "The Ad That Changed Advertising."

18. Hamilton, "The Ad That Changed Advertising."

19. "Beetle Overtakes Model T."

20. Keith Reinhard, "Advertising Today," Stan Talks, YouTube.com, March 29, 2018, https://youtu.be/WIgXU2Z7700.

21. Reinhard, "Advertising Today."

22. Mark Dominiak, "A Good Yarn Can Sell Your Message," *Television Week* 23, no. 51 (2004): 27, https://search.ebscohost.com/login.aspx?direct=true&db=buh&AN=15589490&site=ehost-live&scope=site.

23. Jean Marie Brechman and Scott C. Purvis, "Narrative, Transportation and Advertising," *International Journal of Advertising* 34, no. 2 (2015): 366–81.

24. Matthias Glaser and Heribert Reisinger, "Don't Lose Your Product in Story Translation: How Product–Story Link in Narrative Advertisements Increases Persuasion," *Journal of Advertising* (2021, September): 1–18.

25. Glaser and Reisinger, "Don't Lose Your Product in Story Translation."

26. "What Is a Teleplay? A Guide to Understanding the TV Script Format," MasterClass.com, August 30, 2021, https://www.masterclass.com/articles/what-is-a-teleplay-a-guide-to-understanding-the-tv-script-format.

27. David Ciccarelli, "What Is the Most Effective Length for a TV Commercial?" Voices.com, November 9, 2021, https://www.voices.com/blog/effective_length_for_tv_commercials/.

28. Joe Johnson, "Increasing Your TV Buy with 15-Second 'Bookends,'" LinkedIn.com, February 13, 2015, https://www.linkedin.com/pulse/increasing-tv-buy-15-second-bookends-joe-johnson.

29. "Film Terms Glossary: Guide to 95 Film Terms," Masterclass.com, June 24, 2021, https://www.masterclass.com/articles/film-terms-guide#a-glossary-of-95-film-terms.

30. "Viral Marketing," Marketing-Dictionary.org, accessed November 22, 2021, https://marketing-dictionary.org/v/viral-marketing/.

31. Kristen Baker, "The Ultimate Guide to Viral Campaigns," Blog.HubSpot.com, May 13, 2021, https://blog.hubspot.com/marketing/viral-campaigns.

32. Keith A. Quesenberry and Michael K. Coolsen, "Drama Goes Viral: Effects of Story Development on Shares and Views of Online Advertising Videos," *Journal of Interactive Marketing* 48 (2019, November): 1–16.

33. Quesenberry and Coolsen, "Drama Goes Viral."

34. Abigail Posner, "The Engagement Project: Finding the Meaning in Memes," *Think with Google* Newsletter, June 2013, https://www.thinkwithgoogle.com/articles/memes-with-meaning.html.

35. Posner, "The Engagement Project."

36. Rodney Ho, "How Tag Team's Geico 'Scoop! There It Is' Became Adweek's 2021 Ad of the Year," *The Atlanta Journal-Constitution*, December 30, 2021, https://www.ajc.com/life /radiotvtalk-blog/how-tag-teams-geico-scoop-there-it-is-became-adweeks-2021-ad-of-the-year /U5D2Q7MHLZAZHFCOJXDVN5HFHM/.

37. "The New Tag Team GEICO Commercial Is the Brand's Most-Seen Ad in America Right Now," PRNewsWire.com, February 4, 2021, https://www.prnewswire.com/news-releases/the -new-tag-team-geico-commercial-is-the-brands-most-seen-ad-in-america-right-now-301222598 .html; and Brett Molina, "Remember the 'Scoop! There It IS!' Geico Ad with Tag Team? It's Now an Actual Ice Cream." *USA Today*, September 13, 2021, https://www.usatoday.com/story/money /food/2021/09/13/geico-tag-team-scoop-ice-cream-whoomp-there-it-is-ad/8314525002/.

38. Derek Thompson, *Hit Makers: How to Succeed in an Age of Distraction* (New York: Penguin, 2017), 57.

39. Lada Adamic, Thomas Lento, Eytan Adar, and Pauline Ng, "The Evolution of Memes on Face-book," Facebook.com, January 8, 2014, https://www.facebook.com/notes/facebook-data-science/ the-evolution-of-memes-on-facebook/10151988334203859.

40. Baker, "The Ultimate Guide to Viral Campaigns."

41. "10 Agency Tips for Creating Professional CTV Videos," C-IStudios.com, February 20, 2021, https://c-istudios.com/creating-professional-ctv-videos/.

42. "10 Agency Tips for Creating Professional CTV Videos."

43. "The Fundamentals of Connected TV Advertising," Innovid.com, accessed November 19, 2021, https://www.innovid.com/resources/fundamentals-of-ctv-advertising/.

44. "The Most Enhanced Ad Products on TV," Brighline.tv, accessed November 19, 2021, https://www.brightline.tv/what-we-do.

45. Will Richmond, "Survey: 90% of Advertisers and Agencies Plan to Increase CTV Ad Budgets," VideoNuze.com, April 14, 2021, https://www.videonuze.com/article/survey-90-of -advertisers-and-agencies-plan-to-increase-ctv-ad-budgets.

46. Parker Herren, "Netflix Reveals Ad Plan Price, Nielsen Partnership and More 'Basic with Ads' Details," AdAge.com, October 13, 2022, https://adage.com/article/media/netflix-reveals-ad -plan-price-nielsen-partnership-and-more-basic-ads-details/2442666.

47. Christina Newberry, "25 YouTube Statistics That May Surprise You: 2021 Edition," Blog .Hoostuite.com, February 2021, https://blog.hootsuite.com/youtube-stats-marketers/.

48. Paige Cooper, "The Complete Guide to YouTube Ads for Marketers," June 11, 2020, Blog .Hootsuite.com, https://blog.hootsuite.com/youtube-advertising/.

49. Theodor Arhio, "Tips from the Field," Academy for Ads, February 13, 2018, https://youtu .be/hD3LsJTP8b0.

50. Arhio, "Tips from the Field."

51. Ben Jones and Matt Lindley, "Building for Bumpers," Academy for Ads, February 13, 2018, https://youtu.be/8gKMn2TbRsw.

52. Ross Benes, "US Audio Advertising Forecast 2021," eMarketer.com, October 11, 2021, https://www.emarketer.com/content/us-audio-advertising-forecast-2021.

53. "Why Radio FAQs," RAB.com, accessed November 22, 2021, https://www.rab.com/why radio/WRnew/faq/faq.cfm.

54. Stan Freberg, "Stretching the Imagination," originally recorded for the Radio Advertis-ing Bureau 1965, Dick Williams, YouTube.com, accessed November 22, 2021, https://youtu.be /PoQk0olAgPk.

55. "Results of 4A's 2011 Television Production Cost Survey," AAAA.org, January 24, 2013, https://www.aaaa.org/index.php?checkfileaccess=/wp-content/uploads/2013/01/7480.pdf &access_pid=20131

56. Joyce Bragg, "A Quick Guide to Radio Advertising Costs," SearchKaralo.com, November 7, 2021, https://searchkarlo.com/a-quick-guide-to-radio-advertising-costs/.

57. "Why Radio FAQs."

58. Tammy Greenberg, "Six Ingredients That Make Motel 6 a Successful Brand," ANA. net, December 10, 2018, https://www.ana.net/blogs/show/id/mm-blog-2018-12-rab-ingredients -for-motel6-success.

59. Ryan Faughnder, "Top Super Bowl Radio Ads? Motel 6 Turns Lights On," BaltimoreSun .com, February 3, 2014, https://www.baltimoresun.com/entertainment/la-et-ct-top-super-bowl-ra dio-ads-motel-6-20140203-story.html.

60. Greenberg, "Six Ingredients That Make Motel 6 a Successful Brand."

Chapter 7. The New Page: Magazine, Newspaper, and Out-of-Home Advertising

1. Gary Bellafante, "A Pioneer in a Mad Men's World," NYTimes.com, June 8, 2012, https://www.brainyquote.com/quotes/william_bernbach_103347.

2. "Mary Wells Lawrence," Britannica.com, accessed November 29, 2021, https://www.britan nica.com/biography/Mary-Wells-Lawrence.

3. "Famous Advertisers in History: Mary Wells Lawrence," ProofIsInTheWriting.com, March 23, 2018, https://proofisinthewriting.com/2018/03/23/advertising-legend-mary-wells-lawrence/.

4. "Famous Advertisers in History."

5. Ibid.

6. Ibid.

7. Mark Hamilton, "The Ad That Changed Advertising. The Story Behind Volkswagen's Think Small Campaign," Medium.com/TheAgency.com, March 20, 2015, https://medium.com/theagency /the-ad-that-changed-advertising-18291a67488c.

8. Hamilton, "The Ad That Changed Advertising."

9. Ibid.

10. Abigail Posner, "The Engagement Project: Finding the Meaning in Memes," *Think with Goo-gle* Newsletter, June 2013, https://www.thinkwithgoogle.com/articles/memes-with-meaning.html.

11. Helmut Krone, "The New Page," DDB Worldwide, YouTube.com, April 14, 2015, https://www.youtube.com/watch?v=yDmLQ5zQjRs&t=572s.

12. Katie Sullivan Porter, "The Best Display Ads of 2022, and Why They Work," Marin Software.com, April 22, 2022, https://www.marinsoftware.com/blog/the-best-display-ads-of-2022 -and-why-they-work.

13. "Magazine Media Factbook," Association of Magazine Media, 2021, https://designobserver .com/feature/helmut-krone-period/4657.

14. "Magazine Media Factbook."

15. Tom Neveril, "Consumers Ignore Ads That Aren't Telling Their Stories," *Advertising Age* 79, no. 10 (2008): 16.

16. Jeff Manning and Kevin Lane Keller, "Got Advertising That Works?" *Marketing Manage-ment*, 13, no. 1 (2004): 16–20, https://search-ebscohost-com.ezproxy.messiah.edu/login.aspx?direct =true&db=buh&AN=12123042&site=ehost-live&scope=site.

17. Manning and Keller, "Got Advertising That Works?"

18. Ibid.

19. "Tide-Stain," 2008Super Bowl, YouTube.com, February 5, 2008, https://youtu.be/TGg hswQgAzE; "Tide: My Talking Stain," Adage.com, February 4, 2008, https://adage.com/creativity /work/my-talking-stain/2312; and Manning and Keller, "Got Advertising That Works?"

20. Chingching Chang, "Imagery Fluency and Narrative Advertising Effects," *Journal of Advertising* 42, no. 1 (2013): 54–68.

21. "Magazine Media Factbook."

22. "Headline," Marketing-Dictionary.org, accessed November 30, 2021, https://marketing-dic tionary.org/h/headline/.

23. Jim Aitchison, *Cutting Edge Advertising: How to Create the World's Best Print for Brands in the 21st Century* (Singapore: Prentice Hall, 1999).

24. "Subhead," Marketing-Dictionary.org, accessed November 30, 2021, https://marketing-dic tionary.org/s/subhead/.

25. "Body Copy," Marketing-Dictionary.org, accessed November 30, 2021, https://market ing-dictionary.org/b/body-copy/.

26. "Pack Shot," Collinsdictionary.com, accessed December 8, 2021, https://www.collinsdictio nary.com/us/dictionary/english/pack-shot.

27. Will Keyton, "Call to Action," Investopedia.com, March 29, 2020, https://www.investopedia .com/terms/c/call-action-cta.asp.

28. "Logo," Marketing-Dictionary.org, accessed December 8, 2021, https://marketing-dictionary. org/l/logo/.

29. "Tagline," Marketing-Dictionary.org, accessed November 30, 2021, https://marketing-dictio nary.org/t/tagline/.

30. "Catchphrase," Dictionary.Cambridge.org, accessed November 30, 2021, https://dictionary .cambridge.org/us/dictionary/english/catchphrase.

31. Bonnie Mills, "'Think Different' or 'Think Differently,'" QuickAndDirtyTips.com, October 7, 2010, https://www.quickanddirtytips.com/education/grammar/think-different-or-think-differently.

32. Edward Boches, "How Volkswagen Just Squandered 55 Years of Great Advertising: Emissions Deception Flushes Decades of Hard-Earned Goodwill," Adweek.com, September 29, 2015, https://www.adweek.com/brand-marketing/how-volkswagen-just-squandered-55-years-great -advertising-167239/.

33. "Layout," Marketing-Dictionary.org, accessed November 30, 2021, https://marketing-dictio nary.org/l/layout/.

34. Thumbnail," Marketing-Dictionary.org, accessed November 30, 2021, https://marketing -dictionary.org/t/thumbnail/.

35. Hamilton, "The Ad That Changed Advertising."

36. Alice Jackson, "10 Ways to Use Typography Principles Creatively," DesignHill.com, June 9, 2020, https://www.designhill.com/design-blog/ways-to-use-typography-principles-creatively/.

37. Jackson, "10 Ways to Use Typography Principles Creatively."

38. Kara Holmstrom, "The Importance of Typography in Advertising," DigglesCreative .com, accessed November 30, 2021, https://www.digglescreative.com/blog/importance-of-typog raphy-in-advertising.html.

39. Holmstrom, "The Importance of Typography in Advertising."

40. Ibid.

41. Mads Soegaard, "The Power of White Space," Interaction-Design.org, February 2019, https://www.interaction-design.org/literature/article/the-power-of-white-space.

42. Darren Rose, "Rule of Thirds," Digital-Photography-School.com, accessed November 30, 2021, https://digital-photography-school.com/rule-of-thirds/.

43. Michael Barthel and Kristen Worden, "Newspapers Fact Sheet," PewReseach.org, June 29, 2021, https://www.pewresearch.org/journalism/fact-sheet/newspapers/.

44. "Community Newspaper Facts & Figures," NNAWeb.org, accessed November 30, 2021, https://nnaweb.org/article?articleCategory=community-facts-figures.

45. "Community Newspaper Facts & Figures."

46. "2017 Print & Digital Specs The Inquire Daily News Philly.com," 2017.

47. "Coupon," Marketing-Dictionary.org, accessed December 9, 2021, https://marketing-dictionary.org/c/coupon/.

48. "Free-standing Insert," Dictionary.Cambridge.org, accessed December 9, 2021, https://dictionary.cambridge.org/us/dictionary/english/free-standing-insert.

49. "Retail Advertising," AdAge Encyclopedia, September 15, 2003, https://adage.com/article/adage-encyclopedia/retail-advertising/98854.

50. "Cooperative Advertising," Marketing-Dictionary.org, accessed December 9, 2021, https://marketing-dictionary.org/c/cooperative-advertising/.

51. "Out-of-Home (OOH) Advertising," Marketing-Dictionary.org, accessed November 30, 2021, https://marketing-dictionary.org/o/out-of-home-ooh-advertising/.

52. "OOH Creative Best Practices," Out of Home Advertising Association of America, OAAA.org, September 2021, https://thoughtleadership.oaaa.org/wp-content/uploads/2021/09/OAAA-Creative-Best-Practices-.pdf; and Mary Lister, "Get Started with Out-of-Home Advertising: Here's How," WordStream.com, August 13, 2020, https://www.wordstream.com/blog/ws/2020/02/26/out-of-home-advertising.

53. "Everything You Need to Know about Out-of-Home Advertising," Broadsign.com, November 9, 2018, https://broadsign.com/blog/out-of-home-advertising/.

54. "OOH Creative Best Practices."

55. "Creativity Drives Data Drives Creativity for Spotify Ads," CNBC International, YouTube.com, November 2, 2018, https://www.youtube.com/watch?v=cshKKhKnSgY.

56. "OOH Creative Best Practices."

57. Lina Miranda, "How to Design Effective Out-of-Home Ads," AdQuick.com, June 21, 2021, https://www.adquick.com/blog/how-to-design-effective-out-of-home-ads/.

58. "OOH Creative Best Practices."

59. Miranda, "How to Design Effective Out-of-Home Ads," AdQuick.com, June 21, 2021, https://www.adquick.com/blog/how-to-design-effective-out-of-home-ads/.

60. "OOH Creative Best Practices."

61. "OOH Media Formats," OAAA.org, accessed December 9, 2021, https://oaaa.org/AboutOOH/OOHBasics/OOHMediaFormats/King-SizeBusPosters.aspx.

62. "Chick-fil-A Cows Recognized for Sustained Success," QSRweb.com, June 7, 2009, https://www.qsrweb.com/news/chick-fil-a-cows-recognized-for-sustained-success/.

63. "Chick-fil-A Cows Recognized for Sustained Success."

64. Ellen Meyers, "Chick-fil-A Ends 22-Year Relationship with Cow Campaign Ad Creator, The Richards Group," DallasNews.com, July 21, 2016, https://www.dallasnews.com/business/local-companies/2016/07/21/chick-fil-a-ends-22-year-relationship-with-cow-campaign-ad-creator-the-richards-group/.

65. Bellafante, "A Pioneer in a Mad Men's World."

Chapter 8. Connecting with the Audience: Direct, Digital, and Experiential Marketing

1. Jay Baer, "Jay Baer Quotes and Sayings," InspiringQuotes.us, assessed December 23, 2021, https://www.inspiringquotes.us/author/8531-jay-baer.

2. Robert D. McFadden, "Lester Wunderman, Father of Direct Marketing, Dies at 98," *The New York Times*, January 14, 2019, https://www.nytimes.com/2019/01/14/business/lester-wunderman-dead.html.

3. McFadden, "Lester Wunderman, Father of Direct Marketing, Dies at 98."

4. Ibid.

5. Emily Langer, "Lester Wunderman, Advertising Executive Perfected Direct Marketing, Dies at 98," WashingtonPost.com, January 15, 2019, https://www.washingtonpost.com/local/obituaries /lester-wunderman-advertising-executive-who-perfected-direct-marketing-dies-at-98/2019/01/15 /f84ac918-17b0-11e9-88fe-f9f77a3bcb6c_story.html.

6. Rob Stokes, *eMarketing—The Essential Guide to Marketing in a Digital World* (Quirk (Pty) Ltd., 2021).

7. Mark Tungate, "Ten Things Lester Wunderman Taught Us," AdForum, January 14, 2019, https://www.adforum.com/tribune/ten-things-lester-wunderman-taught-us.

8. "About Us," WundermanThompson.com, accessed January 14, 2022, https://www.wunder manthompson.com/about-us.

9. "Hellmann's See More in Your Fridge," WundermanThompson.com, accessed July 11, 2022, https://www.wundermanthompson.com/work/hellmanns-more-in-your-fridge.

10. Jon Springer, "Why Hellman's Is Boasting About No One Responding to Its Ad: A Giveaway with No Entrants Makes a Point About Overlooked Food Waste," AdAge.com, April 27, 2022, https://adage.com/article/marketing-news-strategy/hellmanns-boasting-about-no-one-responding -ad/2414486.

11. Jay Bear, "Youtility: Why Smart Marketing Is about Help Not Hype," Amazon.com, accessed January 14, 2022, https://www.amazon.com/Youtility-Smart-Marketing-about-Help /dp/1591846668.

12. "Hype," OxfordLearnersDictionaries.com, accessed January 19, 2022, https://www.oxford learnersdictionaries.com/us/definition/english/hype_1.

13. "Help," OxfordLearnersDictionaries.com, accessed January 19, 2022, https://www.oxford learnersdictionaries.com/us/definition/english/help_1?q=help.

14. Jay Baer, "Youtility: Why Smart Marketing Is about Help, not Hype," YouTube.com, May 3, 2013, https://youtu.be/a8x0K9pPOSI.

15. Jonah Berger, "Arousal Increases Social Transmission of Information," *Psychological Science* 22, no. 7 (2011): 891–93, https://doi.org/10.1177/0956797611413294.

16. Kerry Jones, Kelsey Libert, and Kristin Tynski, "The Emotional Combinations That Make Stories Go Viral," *Harvard Business Review*, May 23, 2016, https://hbr.org/2016/05/research -the-link-between-feeling-in-control-and-viral-content.

17. "Direct Marketing," Marketing-Dictionary.org, accessed December 23, 2021, https://market ing-dictionary.org/d/direct-marketing/.

18. "Database Marketing," Marketing-Dictionary.org, accessed December 23, 2021, https://mar keting-dictionary.org/d/database-marketing/.

19. "Direct Mail Response Rates in 2021," Simplynoted.com, accessed January 14, 2022, https:// simplynoted.com/blogs/news/direct-mail-response-rates.

20. Dennis Kelly, "Why Consumers Trust Direct Mail Marketing," Postalytics.com, May 2, 2019, https://www.postalytics.com/blog/why-consumers-trust-direct-mail-marketing/.

21. Dennis Kelly, "The Ultimate Guide to Direct Mailing List Selection and Testing," Postalytics .com, June 13, 2019, https://www.postalytics.com/blog/direct-mailing-list/.

22. Kelly, "The Ultimate Guide to Direct Mailing List Selection and Testing."

23. "How Much Does Buying a Mailing List Cost?" CostOwl.com, accessed January 19, 2022, https://www.costowl.com/b2b/marketing-buy-mailing-list-cost.html.

24. Kelly, "The Ultimate Guide to Direct Mailing List Selection and Testing."

25. "Mailing Lists," Experian.com, accessed January 14, 2022, https://www.experian.com /small-business/mailing-lists.

26. "Direct Marketing Best Practices," CRMTRends.com, accessed January 15, 2022, http://www.crmtrends.com/directmarketing.html.

27. Bob Stone, *Successful Direct Marketing Methods*, 8th ed. (New York: McGraw-Hill, 2008).

28. Stone, *Successful Direct Marketing Methods*.

29. "Sales Promotion Meaning," Economicsdiscussion.net, accessed January 15, 2022, https://www.economicsdiscussion.net/marketing-management/sales-promotion-meaning/31948.

30. "Sales Promotion," Inc.com Encyclopedia, accessed January 15, 2022, https://www.inc.com/encyclopedia/sales-promotion.html.

31. Rob Stokes, *eMarketing—The Essential Guide to Marketing in a Digital World* (Quirk (Pty) Ltd., 2021).

32. Stokes, *eMarketing*.

33. Ibid.

34. "What Is Digital Marketing?" AMA.org, accessed December 23, 2021, https://www.ama.org/pages/what-is-digital-marketing/.

35. "What Is Digital Marketing?"

36. Ibid.

37. Stokes, *eMarketing*.

38. Ibid.

39. Ibid.

40. Ibid.

41. "Share of Desktop Search Traffic Originating from Google in Selected Countries as of April 2021," Statista, May 10, 2021, accessed January 16, 2022, https://www-statista-com.ezproxy.messiah.edu/statistics/220534/googles-share-of-search-market-in-selected-countries/.

42. Stokes, *eMarketing*.

43. "Branded vs. Non-Branded Keywords," WebFX.com, accessed January 30, 2022, https://www.webfx.com/digital-marketing/learn/branded-vs-non-branded-keywords/.

44. Stokes, *eMarketing*.

45. Ibid.

46. "The 10 Best Display Advertising Networks," WebFX.com, accessed January 16, 2022, https://www.webfx.com/digital-advertising/learn/top-display-ad-networks/.

47. Baer, "Jay Baer Quotes and Sayings."

48. "What Does Animated GIF Mean?" Techopedia.com, August 25, 2016), https://www.techopedia.com/definition/1948/animated-gif

49. "Market Segmentation: Definition, Types, Benefits, and Best Practice," Qualtrics.com, accessed January 14, 2022, https://www.qualtrics.com/experience-management/brand/what-is-market-segmentation/.

50. Keith A. Quesenberry, "Segment Your Target Audience for More Effective Digital and Social Media Marketing," PostControlMarketing.com, February 13, 2021, https://www.postcontrolmarketing.com/segment-your-target-audience-for-more-effective-digital-and-social-media-marketing/.

51. "New Report: The Need for Hyper-individualization," accessed January 16, 2022, https://formation.ai/brand-loyalty-2020 the-need-for-hyper-individualization/.

52. Abby Fields, "What Is Web3 and Why Is It Important to the Future of Marketing?" WebFX.com, https://www.webfx.com/blog/marketing/what-is-web3/.

53. Adam Hayes, "What Is a Blockchain?" Investopedia.com, June 24, 2022, https://www.investopedia.com/terms/b/blockchain.asp.

54. Jake Frankenfield, "Cryptocurrency," Investopedia.com, May 28, 2022, https://www.investopedia.com/terms/c/cryptocurrency.asp.

55. Rakesh Sharma, "Non-Fungible Token (NFT)," Investopedia.com, June 22, 2022, https://www.investopedia.com/non-fungible-tokens-nft-5115211.

56. Fields, "What Is Web3 and Why Is It Important to the Future of Marketing?"

57. Pamela Bump, "How Your Audience Could Shift in Web 3," BlogHubSpot.com, May 16, 2022, https://blog.hubspot.com/marketing/how-the-business-landscape-could-change-in-web-3.

58. "Cookies," Techterms.com, accessed July 13, 2022, https://techterms.com/definition/cookie.

59. Caroline Forsey, "How Marketers Are Preparing for Google's Third-Party Cookie Phaseout," Blog.HubSpot.com, June 13, 2022, https://blog.hubspot.com/marketing/marketers-prepare-third-party-cookie-phaseout.

60. "Introducing NFT Cloud: Mint and Sell NFTS on a Trusted, Sustainable Platform," Salesforce.com, accessed July 13, 2022, https://www.salesforce.com/products/web3/nft/.

61. Eric Hazen, Greg Kelly, Hamza Khan, Dennis Spillecke, and Lareina Yee, "Marketing in the Metaverse: An Opportunity for Innovation and Experimentation," McKinsey.com, May 24, 2022, https://www.mckinsey.com/business-functions/growth-marketing-and-sales/our-insights/marketing-in-the-metaverse-an-opportunity-for-innovation-and-experimentation.

62. Forsey, "How Marketers Are Preparing for Google's Third-Party Cookie Phaseout."

63. Ibid.

64. Bernard Marr, "The Amazing Ways Nike Is Using the Metaverse, Web3 and NFTs," Forbes.com, June 1, 2022, https://www.forbes.com/sites/bernardmarr/2022/06/01/the-amazing-ways-nike-is-using-the-metaverse-web3-and-nfts/?sh=3abcd9a756e9.

65. Alan Cook, "Marketing in the Metaverse: Imagination Is the Limit," CMO Today by Deloitte, WSJ.com, April 1, 2022, https://deloitte.wsj.com/articles/marketing-in-the-metaverse-imagination-is-the-limit-01648764698.

66. Sarah Perez, "Starbucks Details Its Blockchain-Based Loyalty Platform and NFT Community, Starbucks Odyssey," September 12, 2022, https://techcrunch.com/2022/09/12/starbucks-unveils-its-blockchain-based-loyalty-platform-and-nft-community-starbucks-odyssey/.

67. "Experiential Marketing," Marketing-Dictionary.org, accessed December 23, 2021, https://marketing-dictionary.org/e/experiential-marketing/.

68. "Sponsorship," Marketing-Dictionary.org, accessed January 16, 2022, https://marketing-dictionary.org/s/sponsorship/.

69. Justin Lofranco, "Reebok Reintegrates Commitment to CrossFit Community," MorningChalkUp.com, https://morningchalkup.com/2021/03/06/reebok-reiterates-commitment-to-crossfit-community/.

70. "Stadiums of NFL Football," accessed January 16, 2022, https://www.stadiumsofprofootball.com.

71. "Sponsors," BAA.org, accessed January 16, 2022, https://www.baa.org/partners/sponsors.

72. Adam Bittner, "Heinz Field Has a New Name, and Steelers Fans Hate It," Post-Gazette.com, July 11, 2022, https://www.post-gazette.com/sports/steelers/2022/07/11/heinz-field-naming-rights-deal-acrisure-stadium/stories/202207110054.

73. Bittner, "Heinz Field Has a New Name."

74. Ibid.

75. Noah Strackbein, "Steelers Fans Start Petition to Remove Acrisure Stadium," FanNation, Sports Illustrated, July 14, 2022, https://www.si.com/nfl/steelers/news/pittsburgh-steelers-fans-petition-remove-acrisure-stadium.

76. "In-Store Advertising," Marketing-Dictionary.org, accessed November 30, 2021, https://marketing-dictionary.org/i/in-store-advertising/.

77. "In Store Advertising," OAAA.org, accessed January 16, 2022, https://oaaa.org/AboutOOH/OOHBasics/OOHMediaFormats/InStoreAdvertising.aspx.

78. "End Cap," Marketing-Dictionary.org, accessed January 16, 2022, https://marketing-dictionary.org/e/end-cap/.

79. "Reimagining Coffee for Starbucks at Safeway," Catman.Global, accessed January 16, 2022, https://www.catman.global/wp-content/uploads/2021/04/Starbucks-Case-Study_compressed.pdf.

80. "Reimagining Coffee for Starbucks at Safeway."

81. "Runner Up Service Design Award Core77 Design Awards 2018," Designawards.Core7 .com, accessed January 16, 2022, https://designawards.core77.com/Service-Design/76119 /Southwest-Airlines-Digital-Wayfinding-Design-Prototype.

82. Lydia Schrandt, "10 Best Laughs at Southwest Airline Humor," 10Best.com, https:// www.10best.com/interests/travel-tips/10best-laughs-at-southwest-airline-humor/.

83. Risto Moisio and Eric J. Arnould, "Extending the Dramaturgical Framework in Marketing: Drama Structure, Drama Interaction and Drama Content in Shopping Experiences," *Journal of Consumer Behavior* 4, no. 4 (2005): 246–56.

84. Moisio and Arnould, "Extending the Dramaturgical Framework in Marketing."

85. Ibid.

86. Jessica Heasley, "2020 Grand EX Award: Taco Bell, Edelman, UEG and the Best Campaign of the Year," EventMarketer.com, June 23, 2020, https://www.eventmarketer.com /article/2020-grand-ex-award-taco-bell/.

87. Amelia Lucas, "Reservations for Taco Bell's Hotel Sell Out in 2 Minutes," CNBC.com, June 27, 2019, https://www.cnbc.com/2019/06/27/taco-bell-hotel-reservations-sell-out-in-2-min utes.html.

88. Lucas, "Reservations for Taco Bell's Hotel Sell Out in 2 Minutes."

89. Peter Adams, "Campaign of the Year: Taco Bell's 'The Bell,'" MarketingDive.com, December 9, 2019, https://www.marketingdive.com/news/taco-bell-hotel-dive-awards/566217/; and "Here's Your Inside Look at the Bell Hotel—Taco Bell," Taco Bell, YouTube.com, August 12, 2019, https:// youtu.be/xjkUxcQquXc.

90. Adams, "Campaign of the Year: Taco Bell's 'The Bell.'"

91. Heasley, "2020 Grand EX Award"; and Adams, "Campaign of the Year."

Chapter 9. New Model for Newsworthy: Public Relations, Social Media, and Influencer Marketing

1. Gini Dietrich, *Spin Sucks: Communication and Reputation Management in the Digital Age* (Seattle: Pearson Education, 2014), 4.

2. Lisa Held, "Psychoanalysis Shapes Consumer Culture: Or How Sigmund Freud, His Nephew and a Box of Cigars Forever Changed American Marketing," American Psychological Association, APA.org, December 2009, https://www.apa.org/monitor/2009/12/consumer.

3. Iris Mostegel, "The Original Influencer," HistoryToday.com, February 6, 2019, https:// www.historytoday.com/miscellanies/original-influencer.

4. Mostegel, "The Original Influencer."

5. Robert McNamara, "Edward Bernays, Father of Public Relations and Propaganda," ThoughtCo.com, April 30, 2019, https://www.thoughtco.com/edward-bernays-4685459.

6. "Edward Bernays," *Encyclopedia Britannica*, November 18, 2021, https://www.britannica .com/biography/Edward-Bernays.

7. Mostegel, "The Original Influencer"; and Held, "Psychoanalysis Shapes Consumer Culture."

8. Paul Farhl, "The Original Spin Doctor," WashtingonPost.com, November 23, 1991, https://www.washingtonpost.com/archive/lifestyle/1991/11/23/the-original-spin-doctor /109f782a-5964-4d99-94f7-b4b666bc1f74/.

9. "LEGO Imagination Engine Chatbot," Edelman.com, accessed July 11, 2022, https:// www.edelman.com/expertise/digital/our-work/imagination-engine-chatbot.

10. "LEGO Imagination Engine Chatbot."

11. Dietrich, *Spin Sucks.*

12. Gini Dietrich, "Arment Dietrich Is No Longer a PR Firm?" SpinSucks.com, January 4, 2010, https://spinsucks.com/communication/arment-dietrich-is-no-longer-a-pr-firm/.

13. Dietrich, *Spin Sucks*.

14. Dietrich, *Spin Sucks*.

15. "Glossary of Terms," PRSA.org, accessed January 24, 2022, https://www.prsa.org/about/all-about-pr/glossary-of-terms.

16. "Societally Leadership Is Now a Core Function of Business," Edelman.com, accessed January 21, 2022, https://www.edelman.com/news-awards/2022-edelman-trust-barometer-reveals-even-greater-expectations-business-lead-government-trust.

17. Roger Dooley, "Spin Sucks by Gini Dietrich," NeuroscienceMarketing.com, accessed July 11, 2022, https://www.neurosciencemarketing.com/blog/articles/spin-sucks.htm.

18. "Public Relations," Marketing-Dictionary.org, accessed January 22, 2021, https://marketing-dictionary.org/p/public-relations/.

19. "Publicity," Marketing-Dictioinary.org, accessed January 22, 2022, https://marketing-dictionary.org/p/public-relations/.

20. "2022 Edelman Trust Barometer Global Report," Edelman.com, January 2022, 28 https://www.edelman.com/sites/g/files/aatuss191/files/2022-01/2022%20Edelman%20Trust%20Barometer%20Global%20Report_Final.pdf.

21. Ramya Priya, Hanin Dita, and Ramil M. Del Rosario, "18 Recommended Newswire and Press Release Distribution Services," ContentGrip.com, July 5, 2022, https://www.contentgrip.com/best-press-release-distribution-services/.

22. Ben Sailer, "29 Examples of Basic PR Disciplines, Tactics, and Campaigns You Can Follow," CoSchedule.com, accessed January 24, 2022, https://coschedule.com/blog/public-relations-examples#8.

23. "Glossary of Terms."

24. Lucas Downey, "Press Release," Investopedia.com, October 13, 2020, https://www.investopedia.com/terms/p/pressrelease.asp.

25. "Newswire," CollinsDictionary.com, accessed January 24, 2022, https://www.collinsdictionary.com/us/dictionary/english/newswire.

26. "Newswires 101: Everything You've Ever Wanted to Know," AgilityPR.com, accessed January 24, 2022, https://www.agilitypr.com/newswires-101/.

27. Daria Nartya, "How to Write a Press Release AP Style," PRNews.io, February 25, 2021, https://prnews.io/blog/how-to-write-a-press-release-ap-style.html.

28. Priya, Dita, and Del Rosario, "18 Recommended Newswire and Press Release Distribution Services"; and Nartya, "How to Write a Press Release AP Style."

29. "Public Relations and Media Relations: What's the Difference?" ShiftComm.com, accessed January 24, 2022, https://www.shiftcomm.com/insights/public-relations-media-relations-whats-difference/.

30. "Glossary of Terms."

31. "How to Craft a Winning Media Pitch in 2022," Info.MuckRack.com, accessed February 24, 2022, https://info.muckrack.com/guide-to-pr-pitching-2020.

32. "How to Craft a Winning Media Pitch in 2022."

33. Ibid.

34. Mike Schneider, "New Muck Rack Survey: The State of Journalism 2021," MuckRack.com, March 15, 2021, https://muckrack.com/blog/2021/03/15/state-of-journalism-2021.

35. "How to Craft a Winning Media Pitch in 2022."

36. "10 Steps to Build a Successful Event PR Strategy," EventBright.com, November 2, 2017, https://www.eventbrite.com/blog/event-pr-ds00/; and "Glossary of Terms."

37. James Chen, "Press Conference," Investopedia.com, March 26, 2021, https://www.investopedia.com/terms/p/press-conference.asp.

38. "PR Event Planning: 6 Ways to Get the Word Out," SocialTables.com, accessed January 24, 2022, https://www.socialtables.com/blog/event-planning/pr-event/.

39. Chen, "Press Conference."

40. Chen, "Press Conference."

41. Ibid.

42. Ibid.; and "10 Steps to Build a Successful Event PR Strategy."

43. "Ice Bucket Challenge Dramatically Accelerated the Fight Against ALS," ALS.org, June 4, 2019, https://www.als.org/stories-news/ice-bucket-challenge-dramatically-accelerated-fight-against-als.

44. "Snapple PR Stunt Washed Away in Summer Heat," PRWeek.com, June 22, 2005, https://www.prweek.com/article/1242879/snapple-pr-stunt-washes-away-summer-heat.

45. "How Do You Get the World to Care about Burgers from a Pancake House?" Droga5.com, accessed January 24, 2022, https://droga5.com/work/ihob/.

46. Daney Parker, "How to Create a Brilliant PR Stunt," PRmoment.com, February 7, 2019, https://www.prmoment.com/pr-insight/how-to-create-a-brilliant-pr-stunt.

47. Donna Talarico, "What We're Not Talking About When We Talk About News," OHO.com, April 2, 2019, https://www.oho.com/blog/news-vs-stories-whats-difference.

48. Michelle Dziuban, "The Power of Storytelling in PR," Cision.com, March 14, 2016, https://www.cision.com/2016/03/the-power-of-storytelling-in-pr/.

49. Mario Juarez, "The Unlikely Story of Microsoft's Chief Storyteller," Mario-Juarez.com, April 2, 2019, https://mario-juarez.com/new-blog/2019/4/2/the-unlikely-story-of-microsofts-chief-storyteller.

50. Gini Dietrich, "Why Communicators Must (Finally) Embrace the PESO Model," Spinsucks.com, January 5, 2021, https://spinsucks.com/communication/pr-pros-must-embrace-the-peso-model/.

51. Brooklyn Pratt, "Day-to-Day Storytelling: How to Include Narrative in Hard News Stories," TheGroundTruthProject.org, May 12, 2021, https://thegroundtruthproject.org/day-to-day-storytelling-how-to-include-narrative-in-hard-news-stories/.

52. "The CMO Survey Highlights and Insights February 2010," CMOSurvey.com, February 2010, https://cmosurvey.org/wp-content/uploads/2017/04/cmo-survey-highlights-and-insights-february-2010.pdf; and "The CMO Survey Highlights and Insights August 2021," CMOSurvey.com, August 2021, https://cmosurvey.org/wp-content/uploads/2021/08/The_CMO_Survey-Highlights_and_Insights_Report-August_2021.pdf.

53. Keith A. Quesenberry, *Social Media Strategy: Marketing, Advertising and Public Relations in the Consumer Revolution*, third ed. (Lanham, MD: Rowman & Littlefield, 2021).

54. Quesenberry, *Social Media Strategy.*

55. Ibid.

56. Ibid.

57. Ibid.

58. Ibid.

59. Zach Brooke, "Understanding the What and Why of Ad Retargeting," AMA.org, March 1, 2016, https://www.ama.org/marketing-news/understanding-the-what-and-why-of-ad-retargeting/.

60. Quesenberry, *Social Media Strategy.*

61. Quesenberry, *Social Media Strategy.*

62. Jason Notte, "State Farm Picks TikTok over TV in Super Bowl Ad Shuffle," Adweek.com, January 22, 2022, https://www.adweek.com/brand-marketing/state-farm-tiktok-challenge-super-bowl-ad/.

63. Julia Manoukian, "10 User-Generated Content Examples That Stand Out Right Now," CrowdRiff.com, accessed January 30, 2022, https://crowdriff.com/resources/blog/ugc-marketing-campaigns.

64. Quesenberry, *Social Media Strategy*.

65. "We Use Our Position to Influence Change," Benjerry.com, accessed January 30, 2022, https://www.benjerry.com/values/issues-we-care-about.

66. "Turkey Hill Clean Water Partnership—Three Scoops of Water Pollution Reduction," Twitter.com, May 3, 2021, https://twitter.com/paenvirodigest/status/1389155678225375232?cxt=HHwWgIC5pdbuoscmAAAA.

67. "Check It Out!" Twitter.com, May 5, 2021, https://twitter.com/TurkeyHillDairy/status/1367884048492814336?cxt=HHwWgICzxe7S2fslAAAA.

68. "Please stop ruining cookies. #NationalRoastDay," Twitter.com, February 11, 2021, https://twitter.com/Wendys/status/1359932399870738433?cxt=HHwWgoC4zf_Tud8lAAAA.

69. "#FinalFour Twitter Live presented by @Wendys," Twitter.com, April 5, 2021, https://twitter.com/i/broadcasts/1dRJZNgprmDJB.

70. Quesenberry, *Social Media Strategy*.

71. Michelle Lee, "Recurring Twitter hashtags for every day of the week," Business.Twitter.com, accessed January 30, 2022), https://business.twitter.com/en/blog/recurring-twitter-hashtags-for-every-day-of-the-week.html.

72. Amine Rahal, "Measuring Success: Six Digital Marketing Metrics and KPIs for 2021," Forbes.com, December 10, 2021, https://www.forbes.com/sites/forbescommunicationscouncil/2021/04/28/measuring-success-six-digital-marketing-metrics-and-kpis-for-2021/?sh=2df332aa6172.

73. Keith A. Quesenberry and Michael K. Coolsen, "Drama Goes Viral: Effects of Story Development on Shares and Views of Online Advertising Videos," *Journal of Interactive Marketing* 48 (2019, November): 1–16.

74. Philip Kotler, Hermawan Kartajaya, and Iwan Setiawan, *Marketing 4.0: Moving from Traditional to Digital* (Hoboken, NJ: John Wiley & Sons, 2017), 128–29.

75. Eric Hazen, Greg Kelly, Hamza Khan, Dennis Spillecke, and Lareina Yee, "Marketing in the Metaverse: An Opportunity for Innovation and Experimentation," McKinsey.com, May 24, 2022, https://www.mckinsey.com/business-functions/growth-marketing-and-sales/our-insights/marketing-in-the-metaverse-an-opportunity-for-innovation-and-experimentation.

76. "Virtual reality (VR)," TechTarget.com, May 2015, https://www.techtarget.com/whatis/definition/virtual-reality.

77. Alexander S. Gillis, "Augmented reality (AR)," TechTarget.com, July 2022, https://www.techtarget.com/whatis/definition/augmented-reality-AR.

78. Hazen et al., "Marketing in the Metaverse.

79. Alan Cook, "Marketing in the Metaverse: Imagination Is the Limit," CMO Today by Deloitte, WSJ.com, April 1, 2022, https://deloitte.wsj.com/articles/marketing-in-the-metaverse-imagination-is-the-limit-01648764698.

80. Hazen et al., "Marketing in the Metaverse.

81. Hazen et al., "Marketing in the Metaverse.

82. Cook, "Marketing in the Metaverse."

83. Bernard Marr, "The Amazing Ways Nike Is Using the Metaverse, Web3 and NFTs," Forbes.com, June 1, 2022, https://www.forbes.com/sites/bernardmarr/2022/06/01/the-amazing-ways-nike-is-using-the-metaverse-web3-and-nfts/?sh=3abcd9a756e9.

84. Asa Hiken, "Phygital Marketing in the Metaverse: How Brands Are Merging Digital and Real-Life Experiences," AdAge.com, October 17, 2022, https://adage.com/article/digital-marketing-ad-tech-news/phygital-marketing-metaverse-how-brands-are-merging-digital-and-real-life-experiences/2442281.

85. Hiken, "Phygital Marketing in the Metaverse."

86. Michelle Castillo, "Michelle Phan Is Ready to Reach Beyond YouTube with Her New Icon Network," Adweek.com, April 7, 2015, https://www.adweek.com/convergent-tv/michelle -phan-plans-reach-beyond-youtube-icon-network-163918/.

87. Quesenberry, *Social Media Strategy*.

88. "The Evolving Customer Experience: Perspectives from the Industry," Facebook.com, June 24, 2021, https://www.facebook.com/business/news/insights/the-evolving-customer-exper ience-perspectives-from-the-industry.

89. "The Ultimate Guide to Influencer Marketing," Izea.com, accessed February 1, 2022, https://izea.com/influencer-marketing/.

90. Werner Geyser, "Top Influencer Marketing Platforms to Boost Your Campaigns for 2022," InfluencerMarketingHub.com, January 21, 2022, https://influencermarketinghub.com/top -influencer-marketing-platforms/.

91. Richard Edelman, "In Brands We Trust? 2019 Edelman Trust Barometer Special Report," 2019, Edelman.com, https://www.edelman.com/research/trust-barometer-special -report-in-brands-we-trust.

92. Keith Quesenberry, "A Simple Guide to Influencer Marketing in Social Media," Post-ControlMarketing.com, August 23, 2018, https://www.postcontrolmarketing.com/simple-guide -influencer-marketing/.

93. Sami Main, "Micro-Influencers Are More Effective with Marketing Campaigns than Highly Popular Accounts," Adweek.com, March 30, 2017, https://www.adweek.com/digital /micro-influencers-are-more-effective-with-marketing-campaigns-than-highly-popular-accounts/.

94. "Advertisers Love Influencer Marketing: ANA Study," ANA.net, April 3, 2018, https:// www.ana.net/content/show/id/48437.

95. Josephine Hardy, "6 Ways to Repurpose Influencer Content," AcornInfluence.com, June 21, 2018, https://acorninfluence.com/blog/6-ways-to-repurpose-influencer-content/.

96. "Become a Brand Ambassador," PuraVidaBracelets.com, accessed November 2, 2019, https://www.puravidabracelets.com/pages/brand-ambassadors.

97. Griffin Thall, Jay Baer, and Adam Brown, "Is This the Best Business on Instagram?" Social-Pros Podcast, ConvinceAndConvert.com, September 13, 2019, https://www.puravidabracelets.com /pages/brand-ambassadors.

98. "What Is Crisis Communications?" ShiftComm.com, accessed January 24, 2022, https:// www.shiftcomm.com/insights/what-is-crisis-communications/.

99. Priya Krishna, "How 'This Is Us' Unwittingly Reinvented the Humble Crock-Pot," NewYorker.com, February 21, 2018, https://www.newyorker.com/culture/annals-of-gastronomy /how-this-is-us-unwittingly-reinvented-the-humble-crock-pot.

100. Nicole Lyn Pesce, "How That Devastating 'This Is Us' Fire Actually Boosted Crock-Pot Sales," MarketWatch.com, May 10, 2018, https://www.marketwatch.com/story/how-that -devastating-this-is-us-fire-actually-boosted-crock-pot-sales-2018-05-10.

101. Melissa Agnes, "Baffling Proof That Issues Can Strangely Emerge from Any-where," MellissaAgnes.com, February 1, 2019, https://melissaagnes.com/baffling-proof-issues -can-strangely-emerge-anywhere/.

102. Krishna, "How 'This Is Us' Unwittingly Reinvented the Humble Crock-Pot."

103. Pesce, "How That Devastating 'This Is Us' Fire Actually Boosted Crock-Pot Sales."

Chapter 10. Selling the Drama: Final Plans and Pitches

1. Jon Steel, "Jon Steel—Making Effective Presentations," Stan Talks, YouTube.com, July 24, 2018, https://youtu.be/5KldwSafeD4.

2. "Top 10 Greatest Speeches," TIME.com, accessed February 7, 2022, http://content.time .com/time/specials/packages/completelist/0,29569,1841228,00.html.

3. "Gettysburg Address," NationalGeographic.org, accessed February 7, 2022, https://voicesof democracy.umd.edu/everett-gettysburg-address-speech-text/.

4. Edward Everett, "'Gettysburg Address' (19 November 1863)," VoicesOfDemocracy.umd .edu, accessed February 7, 2022, https://voicesofdemocracy.umd.edu/everett-gettysburg-address -speech-text/.

5. "The Gettysburg Address," AbrahamLincolnOnline.com, accessed February 7, 2022, http:// www.abrahamlincolnonline.org/lincoln/speeches/gettysburg.htm.

6. Catherine Carr, "What Made 'I Have a Dream' Such a Perfect Speech," January 19, 2015, FastCompany.com, https://www.fastcompany.com/3040976/what-made-i-have-a-dream -such-a-perfect-speech.

7. Guy Raz, "Simon Sinek: How Do Great Leaders Inspire Us to Take Action?" TED Radio Hour, NPR.org, May 18, 2018, https://www.npr.org/transcripts/612154435.

8. Ian Anušić, "Dream Crazier: How Nike Thrives on Social Issues Based Marketing," MediaTool-Kit.com, February 3, 2022, https://www.mediatoolkit.com/blog/nike-social-issues-based-marketing/.

9. "Nike—Dream Crazier #JustDoIt" Nike, Campaigns of the World, YouTube.com, January 11, 2020, https://youtu.be/zWfX5jeF6k4.

10. "Luke Sullivan—Tensions," Stan Talks, YouTube.com, April 8, 2019, https://www.youtube .com/watch?v=gSrXAAFX6rg.

11. "Nike—Dream Crazier #JustDoIt."

12. Anušić, "Dream Crazier: How Nike Thrives on Social Issues Based Marketing."

13. D. Tighe, "Nike's Marketing Expenses Worldwide from 2014 to 2022," Statista.com, August 15, 2022, https://www.statista.com/statistics/685734/nike-ad-spend/.

14. "Project Management," Investopedia.com, accessed April 6, 2022, https://www.investopedia .com/terms/p/project-management.asp.

15. "Tact," CollinsDictionary.com, accessed July 12, 2022, https://www.collinsdictionary.com /us/dictionary/english/tact.

16. Adaptive Planning," Marketing-Dictionary.org, accessed March 31, 2022, https://market ing-dictionary.org/a/adaptive-planning/.

17. W. Kenton, "Strength, Weakness, Opportunity, and Threat (SWOT) Analysis," Investopedia. com, March 29, 2021, https://www.investopedia.com/terms/s/swot.asp.

18. Mathieu Start, "Why Data Visualization Is Important," Analyticks.co, June 10, 2020, https:// analytiks.co/importance-of-data-visualization/.

19. Derek Farley, "Applebee's 2 for $20 Is Back with Fresh Flavors from the Neigh-borhood," Applebees.com, 2011, https://www.applebees.com/en/news/2011/applebeesr-2-for-20 -is-back-with-fresh-flavors-from-the-neighborhood.

20. Kixcereal.com, accessed April 4, 2022, https://www.kixcereal.com/products/.

21. M. T. Wroblewski, "How to Create a Target Market Profile and Positioning Statement," SmallBusiness.Chron.com, September 22, 2020, https://smallbusiness.chron.com/create-target-mar ket-profile-positioning-statement-40517.html.

22. Wroblewski, "How to Create a Target Market Profile and Positioning Statement."

23. Heather Pemberton Levy, "What's in a Name? Creating Personas for Digital Mar-keting," Gartner.com, July 30, 2015, https://www.gartner.com/en/marketing/insights/articles /whats-in-a-name-creating-personas-for-digital-marketing.

24. "Audience Segments," Nielsen.com, accessed April 4, 2022, https://www.nielsen.com /solutions/media-planning/audience-segments/.

25. Keith A. Quesenberry, "Visualize Your Marketing Strategy to Form a Solid Foundation for All Marketing Communication," PostControlMarketing.com, October 12, 2016, https://www.postcontrolmarketing.com/visualize-your-marketing-strategy-to-form-a-solid-foundation-for-all-marketing-communication/.

26. "Media Planning," Marketing-Dictionary.org, accessed October 21, 2021, https://marketing-dictionary.org/m/media-planning/.

27. Steel, "Jon Steel—Making Effective Presentations."

28. Keith A. Quesenberry, "Does Your Social Media Plan Tell a Story?" PostControlMarketing.com, October 25, 2018, https://www.postcontrolmarketing.com/social-media-plan-tell-story/.

Chapter 11. Stories Well Told: Legal and Ethical Marketing Communications

1. Mitch Stoller, "Content Marketing as Bernbach and Ogilvy Would Have Done It," Adage.com, December 19, 2014, https://adage.com/article/digitalnext/content-marketing-bernbach-ogilvy/296336.

2. John F. Kennedy, Special Message to the Congress on Protecting the Consumer Interest, online by Gerhard Peters and John T. Woolley, the American Presidency Project, accessed July 11, 2022, https://www.presidency.ucsb.edu/node/237009.

3. Frances Haugen, "Statement of Frances Haugen," U.S. Senate Committee on Commerce, October 4, 2021, https://www.commerce.senate.gov/services/files/FC8A558E-824E-4914-BEDB-3A7B1190BD49.

4. "Consumer Bill of Rights," Encyclopedia.com, accessed April 14, 2022, https://www.encyclopedia.com/finance/encyclopedias-almanacs-transcripts-and-maps/consumer-bill-rights.

5. Barbara Ortutay and David Klepper, "Facebook Whistleblower Testifies: Five Highlights," APNews.com, October 5, 2021, https://apnews.com/article/facebook-frances-haugen-congress-testimony-af86188337d25b179153b973754b71a4.

6. Ortutay and Klepper, "Facebook Whistleblower Testifies."

7. "2022 Edelman Trust Barometer Global Report," Edelman.com, January 2022, 28, https://www.edelman.com/sites/g/files/aatuss191/files/2022-.

8. Luis Andres Henao, Nomaan Merchang, Juan Lozano, and Adam Geller, "For George Floyd, A Complicated Life and Consequential Death," APNews.com, https://apnews.com/article/george-floyd-profile-66163bbd94239afa16d706bd6479c613.

9. Shirin Ali, "Patagonia Doubles Down on Facebook Boycott in Wake of Whistleblower Leaks," TheHill.com, October 29, 2021, https://thehill.com/changing-america/enrichment/arts-culture/579111-patagonia-is-boycotting-facebook-and-urges-others-to/; and "#StopHateForProfit," ShortyAwards.com, accessed October 17, 2022, https://shortyawards.com/13th/stop-hate-for-profit-social-campaign.

10. Ali, "Patagonia Doubles Down on Facebook Boycott in Wake of Whistleblower Leaks."

11. Bella Webb, "Lush Is Quitting Social Media, the Start of a Trend?" VogueBusiness.com, November 22, 2021, https://www.voguebusiness.com/consumers/lush-is-quitting-social-media-the-start-of-a-trend-facebook-instagram-snapchat-tiktok.

12. Tiffany Hsu and Eleanor Lutz, "More than 1,000 Companies Boycotted Facebook. Did It Work?" *New York Times*, August 1, 2020, https://www.nytimes.com/2020/08/01/business/media/facebook-boycott.html.

13. "Section 230 of the Communications Decency Act," Electronic Frontier Foundation, accessed July 11, 2022, https://www.eff.org/issues/cda230.

14. Richard Luscombe, "Facebook: Nick Clegg Avoids Questions on Whistleblower Haugen's Testimony," TheGuardian.com, October 10, 2021, https://www.theguardian.com/technology/2021/oct/10/facebook-nick-clegg-frances-haugen-us-capitol-attack?CMP=Share_iOSApp_Other.

15. Dean K. Fueroghne, *Law & Advertising: A Guide to Current Legal Issues*, fourth ed. (Lanham, MD: Rowman & Littlefield, 2017).

16. Fueroghne, *Law & Advertising*.

17. Ibid.

18. Ibid.

19. Ibid.

20. Ibid.

21. Ibid.

22. "Advertising FAQ's: A Guide for Small Business," FTC.gov, April 2001, https://www.ftc.gov/tips-advice/business-center/guidance/advertising-faqs-guide-small-business.

23. "Advertising FAQ's."

24. "Dietary Supplements: An Advertising Guide for Industry," FTC.gov, April 2001, https://www.ftc.gov/business-guidance/resources/dietary-supplements-advertising-guide-industry.

25. "Advertising FAQ's."

26. Ibid.

27. Ibid.

28. Ibid.

29. Ashby Jones, "A Man, a Coffee Label, and a Lawsuit," August 17, 2009, WSJ.com, https://www.wsj.com/articles/BL-LB-17600.

30. Jones, "A Man, a Coffee Label, and a Lawsuit."

31. "Advertising FAQ's."

32. Brian Mellersh, "Annual Auto Industry Investigation Finds Bait-and-Switch Ads, Additional Fees a Perennial Problem," CTVNews.ca, April 4, 2018, https://www.ctvnews.ca/w5/annual-auto-industry-investigation-finds-bait-and-switch-ads-additional-fees-a-perennial-problem-1.3884034?cache=%2F7.482702%2F7.608529.

33. "FTC Uses Penalty Offense Authority to Seek Largest-Ever Civil Penalty for Bogus Bamboo Marketing from Kohl's and Walmart," FTC.gov, April 8, 2022, https://www.ftc.gov/news-events/news/press-releases/2022/04/ftc-uses-penalty-offense-authority-seek-largest-ever-civil-penalty-bogus-bamboo-marketing-kohls.

34. "Advertising FAQ's."

35. Ibid.

36. "FTC Sues Intuit for Its Deceptive TurboTax "Free" Filing Campaign," FTC.gov, March 29, 2022, https://www.ftc.gov/news-events/news/press-releases/2022/03/ftc-sues-intuit-its-deceptive-turbotax-free-filing-campaign; and Jonathan Stempel, "U.S. Judge Will Not Block Intuit TurboTax Ads That FTC Found Deceptive," Reuters.com, April 22, 2022, https://www.reuters.com/technology/us-judge-will-not-block-intuit-turbotax-ads-that-ftc-found-deceptive-2022-04-22/.

37. "FTC Sues Intuit for Its Deceptive TurboTax "Free" Filing Campaign"; and Stempel, "U.S. Judge Will Not Block Intuit TurboTax Ads That FTC Found Deceptive."

38. "Advertising FAQ's."

39. Adam Janofsky, "California Lawmakers Pass Only Minor Changes to Privacy Measure," WSJ.com, September 16, 2019, https://www.wsj.com/articles/california-lawmakers-pass-only-minor-changes-to-privacy-measure-11568626204.

40. Jeff John Roberts, "Here Comes America's First Privacy Law: What the CCPA Means for Business and Consumers," September 13, 2019, https://fortune.com/2019/09/13/what-is-ccpa-compliance-california-data-privacy-law/.

41. Mitchell J. Katz, Michael Ostheimer, and Mamie Kresses, "FTC Staff Reminds Influencers and Brands to Clearly Disclose Relationship: Commission Aims to Improve Disclosures in Social Media

Endorsements," FTC.gov, April 19, 2017, https://www.ftc.gov/news events/press-releases/2017/04/ftc-staff-reminds-influencers-brands-clearly-disclose.

42. "The FTC's Endorsement Guides: What People Are Asking," FTC.gov, May 2015, https://www.ftc.gov/tips-advice/business-center/guidance/ftcs-endorsement-guides-what-people-are-asking#intro.

43. "The FTC's Endorsement Guides."

44. "Native Advertising: A Guide for Business," FTC.gov, December 2015, https://www.ftc.gov/tips-advice/business-center/guidance/native-advertising-guide-businesses.

45. "Consumer Review Fairness Act: What Businesses Need to Know," FTC.org, February 2017, https://www.ftc.gov/tips-advice/business-center/guidance/consumer-review-fairness-act-what-businesses-need-know.

46. "About the Licenses," CreativeCommons.org, accessed November 19, 2019, https://creativecommons.org/licenses/.

47. Nancy Gray, "Katherine Heigl Settles with Walgreens Over Use of Photo," GrayFirm.com, November 5, 2018, https://grayfirm.com/blog/katherine-heigl-settles-walgreens-over-use-photo/.

48. "Executive Summary Digital Millennium Copyright Act Section 104 Report," Copyright.gov, accessed August 15, 2017, https://www.copyright.gov/reports/studies/dmca/dmca_executive.html.

49. Jennifer Gunner, "What's the Difference Between Ethics, Morals and Values?" YourDictionary.com, https://examples.yourdictionary.com/difference-between-ethics-morals-and-values.html.

50. Zorana Ivcevic, Jochen I. Menges, and Anna Miller, "How Common Is Unethical Behavior in U.S. Organizations?" HBR.org, March 20, 2020, https://hbr.org/2020/03/how-common-is-unethical-behavior-in-u-s-organizations.

51. Saul McLeod, "Social Roles," SimplyPsychology.org, 2008, https://www.simplypsychology.org/social-roles.html.

52. Adam Hayes, "Code of Ethics," Investopedia.com, August 1, 2021, https://www.investopedia.com/terms/c/code-of-ethics.asp.

53. Evan Tarver, "Corporate Culture," Investopedia.com, September 1, 2021, https://www.investopedia.com/terms/c/corporate-culture.asp.

54. "Moral-code," YourDictionary.com, accessed May 5, 2022, https://www.yourdictionary.com/moral-code.

55. "Value," OxfordLearnersDictionaries.com, accessed May 5, 2022, https://www.oxfordlearnersdictionaries.com/us/definition/english/value_1.

56. Gunner, "What's the Difference Between Ethics, Morals and Values?"

57. "Making Agencies Matter in 2022 and Beyond," AAAA.org, accessed May 5, 2022, https://www.aaaa.org/about-the-4as/.

58. "The 4A's Member Code of Conduct," AAAA.org, March 16, 2018, https://www.aaaa.org/4as-member-code-conduct/.

59. "The 4A's Member Code of Conduct."

60. "Behavioral Targeting," BlueFountainMedia.com, accessed November 19, 2019, https://www.bluefountainmedia.com/glossary/behavioral-targeting/.

61. Amit Chowdhry, "Facebook Reiterates That It Does Not Listen to Conversations through Your Phone for Ad Targeting," Forbes.com, October 31, 2017, https://www.forbes.com/sites/amitchowdhry/2017/10/31/facebook-ads-microphone/#e123b34534d3.

62. Scott Stump, "Peloton Responds to Backlash over Holiday Commercial, Says It Was 'Misinterpreted,'" Today.com, December 3, 2019, https://www.today.com/news/peloton-faces-backlash-ridicule-over-new-holiday-commercial-t169080.

63. Christi Carras, "Peloton Actress Blames Her Face for Viral Ad Controversy," LATimes.com, December 12, 2019, https://www.latimes.com/entertainment-arts/tv/story/2019-12-12/peloton-bike-commercial-actress-monica-ruiz.

64. Carras, "Peloton Actress Blames Her Face for Viral Ad Controversy."

65. Daniel Victor, "Pepsi Pulls Ad Accused of Trivializing Black Lives Matter," NYTimes.com, April 5, 2017, https://www.nytimes.com/2017/04/05/business/kendall-jenner-pepsi-ad.html.

66. Victor, "Pepsi Pulls Ad Accused of Trivializing Black Lives Matter."

67. "Carol H. Williams," carolhwilliams.com, accessed November 1, 2021, https://carolhwilliams.com/.

68. "Kellogg to Pay $4 Million for False Advertisements," ZDRLawFirm.com, July 10, 2013, https://www.zdrlawfirm.com/kellogg-to-pay-4-million-for-false-advertisements/.

69. "Kellogg to Pay $4 Million for False Advertisements."

70. "Noah Munch—Frosted Mini Wheats Commercial (2009)," Kids Commercials Rock, YouTube.com, August 19, 2010, https://youtu.be/uXQKM7gxxo8.

71. "Kellogg to Pay $4 Million for False Advertisements"; and "Kellogg Settles FTC Charges That Ads for Frosted Mini-Wheats Were False," FTC.org, April 20, 2009, https://www.ftc.gov/news-events/news/press-releases/2009/04/kellogg-settles-ftc-charges-ads-frosted-mini-wheats-were-false.

72. Sam Bloch, "Kellogg Agrees to Stop Marketing Sugary Cereals as 'Healthy,'" TheCounter.com, October 24, 2019, https://thecounter.org/kellogg-sugary-cereal-healthy-label/.

Chapter 12. Stories That Work: Research and Analytics for Communications

1. "48 Analytics Quotes from the Experts," Scuba.io, accessed May 6, 2022, https://www.scuba.io/blog/48-analytics-quotes-experts.

2. "Origin Story," Dictionary.com, accessed May 6, 2022, https://www.dictionary.com/browse/origin-story.

3. Drew Hendricks, "6 $25 Billion Companies That Started in a Garage," Inc.com, accessed May 6, 2022, https://www.inc.com/drew-hendricks/6-25-billion-companies-that-started-in-a-garage.html.

4. Haran Huang, "Google Analytics History (Until 2023)," BBCCSS.com, November 19, 2019, https://www.bbccss.com/the-history-of-google-analytics.html.

5. Huang, "Google Analytics History (Until 2023)."

6. Scott Crosby, "Urchin Software Corp.: The Unlikely Origin Story of Google Analytics, 1996-2005-ish," Urchin Software Corp. Vault, https://urchin.biz/urchin-software-corp-89a1f5292999.

7. Aaron Dinin, "The Founder of Google Analytics Taught Me How to Choose the Perfect Name for a Startup," Entreneurshandbook.co, December 21, 2020, https://entrepreneurshandbook.co/the-founder-of-google-analytics-taught-me-how-to-choose-the-perfect-name-for-a-startup-9d456b0c3278.

8. Luis Franco and Mayra Valdes, "History of Google Analytics," Justia, February 23, 2021, https://onward.justia.com/history-of-google-analytics/.

9. John Bonini, "The 10 Most-Tracked Google Analytics Metrics [Original Data]," Databox.com, https://databox.com/the-most-tracked-google-analytics-metrics.

10. Alexandra Twin, "Key Performance Indicators (KPIs)," Investopedia.com, July 6, 2021, https://databox.com/the-most-tracked-google-analytics-metrics.

11. Bernard Marr, "What Are Key Performance Questions (KPQs)?" BernardMarr.com, accessed July 13, 2022, https://bernardmarr.com/what-are-key-performance-questions-kpqs/.

12. Marr, "What Are Key Performance Questions (KPQs)?"

13. Christine Moorman, "The Highlights and Insights Report February 2022" CMOSurvey. org, February 2022, https://cmosurvey.org/wp-content/uploads/2022/02/The_CMO_Survey-High lights_and_Insights_Report-February_2022.pdf.

14. Marr, "What Are Key Performance Questions (KPQs)?"

15. Naresh K. Malhorta, *Essentials of Marketing Research: A Hands-On Orientation* (New York, NY: Pearson Prentice Hall, 2014).

16. Mike Hodgdan, "Where Can I See My Google Analytics Statistics?" Infront Webworks, July 10, 2013, https://www.infront.com/blog/where-can-i-see-my-google-analytics-statistics/; "7 Key Stats You Should Be Checking on Google Analytics Every Month," SMPerth.com, September 8, 2017, https://www.smperth.com/resources/google/7-key-stats-google-analytics/; and Wesley Chai, "Google Analytics," Techtarget.com, April 2021, https://www.techtarget.com/searchbusinessanalytics /definition/Google-Analytics.

17. Ibid.

18. "Sentiment Analysis (Opinion Mining)," TechTarget.com, accessed May 6, 2022, https:// www.techtarget.com/searchbusinessanalytics/definition/opinion-mining-sentiment-mining.

19. "Everything You Need to Know about Out-of-Home Advertising," Broadsign.com, November 9, 2018, https://broadsign.com/blog/out-of-home-advertising/.

20. "Direct Mail Response Rates in 2021," Simplynoted.com, accessed January 14, 2022, https:// simplynoted.com/blogs/news/direct-mail-response-rates.

21. "2022 Edelman Trust Barometer Global Report," Edelman.com, January 2022, 28, https:// www.edelman.com/sites/g/files/aatuss191/files/2022-.

22. Amine Rahal, "Measuring Success: Six Digital Marketing Metrics and KPIs for 2021," Forbes .com, December 10, 2021, https://www.forbes.com/sites/forbescommunicationscouncil/2021/04/28 /measuring-success-six-digital-marketing-metrics-and-kpis-for-2021/?sh=2df332aa6172.

23. "Cost per Lead," Klipfolio.com. accessed April 20, 2022, https://www.klipfolio.com /resources/kpi-examples/digital-marketing/cost-per-lead.

24. "Six Event Metrics Every Management Professional Should Understand," Everwall.com, October 7, 2021, https://everwall.com/blog/six-event-metrics-every-management-professional -understand/.

25. Rahal, "Measuring Success."

26. Kenneth E. Clow and Donald Baack, *Integrated Advertising, Promotion, & Marketing Communications*, ninth ed. (New York: Pearson, 2021).

27. "Share of Voice Guide for Marketers," Talkwalter.com, April 21, 2022, https://www.talk walker.com/blog/measure-share-voice.

28. "Average Order Value (AOV)," Corporate Finance Institute, January 20, 2022, https:// corporatefinanceinstitute.com/resources/knowledge/ecommerce-saas/average-order-value-aov/.

29. Rajkumar Venkatesan, Paul Farris, and Ronald Wilcox, *Marketing Analytics: Essential Tools for Data-Driven Decisions* (University of Virginia Press/Darden Business Publishing, 2021).

30. "What Is ROAS? Calculating Return on Ad Spend," BigCommerce.com, April 19, 2022, https://www.bigcommerce.com/ecommerce-answers/what-is-roas-calculating-return-on-ad-spend/.

31. "Digital Marketing KPIs and Metrics: The Ultimate Guide," DashThis.com, accessed April 20, 2022, https://dashthis.com/blog/digital-marketing-kpis-and-metrics-ultimate-guide/.

32. Ashok Charan, "Marketing Analytics Practitioner's Guide to Marketing Analytics and Research Methods," MarketingMind, accessed May 17, 2022, https://www.ashokcharan.com/Mar keting-Analytics/~sg-segmentation-analysis.php.

33. James Phoenix, "Instagram # Community Detection with Machine Learning," Under Standingdata.com, March 18, 2020, https://understandingdata.com/instagram-community-detec tion-with-machine-learning/.

34. Philip Kotler and Kevin Lane Keller, *Framework for Marketing Management*, 6th ed. (New York: Pearson, 2015).

35. "Which Industry Spends Most on Marketing?" Marketing-Interactive.com, March 16, 2017, https://www.marketing-interactive.com/which-industry-spends-most-on-marketing.

36. Russ Winer and Ravi Dhar, *Marketing Management*, fourth ed. (New York: Pearson Prentice Hall, 2010).

37. Venkatesan, Farris, and Wilcox, *Marketing Analytics: Essential Tools for Data-Driven Decisions.*

38. Lenke Harmath, "A Focus on Visualizations: Scatter Plot," Sweetspot.com, May 30, 2014, https://www.sweetspot.com/en/2014/05/30/focus-visualizations-scatter-plot/.

39. "Prescriptive Analytics," Gartner.com, accessed May 7, 2022, https://www.gartner.com/en/information-technology/glossary/prescriptive-analytics.

40. Adam Hayes, "Multiple Linear Regression (MLR)," Investopedia.com, January 2, 2022, https://www.investopedia.com/terms/m/mlr.asp; and Rebecca Bevans, "Multiple Linear Regression: A Quick and Simple Guide," Scribbr.com, October 26, 2020, https://www.scribbr.com/statistics/multiple-linear-regression/.

41. Will Kenton, "A–B Split," Investopedia.com, February 3, 2021, https://www.investopedia.com/terms/a/a-b-split.asp.

42. "Test Market," Common Language Marketing Dictionary, Marketing-Dictionary.org, accessed May 9, 2022, https://marketing-dictionary.org/t/test-market/.

43. Ron Ruggless, "Wendy's to Test Spicy Black Bean Burger in 3 Markets," National Restaurant News, June 24, 2021, https://www.nrn.com/quick-service/wendy-s-test-spicy-black-bean-burger-3-markets.

44. Ali Francis, "Fast Food Took a Gamble on Fake Meat. It's Not Paying Off," BonAppetit.com, August 8, 2022, https://www.bonappetit.com/story/mcdonalds-ends-mcplant-test-us-stores.

45. Philip Kotler, Hermawan Kartajaya, and Iwan Setiawan, *Marketing 5.0: Technology for Humanity* Hoboken, NJ: Wiley, 2021).

46. Sarah Armstrong, Dianne Esber, Jason Heller, and Bjorn Timelin, "Modern Marketing: What It Is, What It Isn't, and How to Do It," McKinsey.com, March 2, 2020, https://www.mckinsey.com/business-functions/marketing-and-sales/our-insights/modern-marketing-what-it-is-what-it-isnt-and-how-to-do-it.

47. SpotBowl.com, accessed May 9, 2022, https://spotbowl.com/.

48. "Budweiser "Fence," Kate Witshire, YouTube.com, February 15, 2021, https://www.youtube.com/watch?v=1rAuu9Yd0uo.

49. Keith A. Quesenberry and Michael K. Coolsen, "What Makes a Super Bowl Ad Super? Five-Act Dramatic Form Impacts Consumer Super Bowl Advertising Ratings," *Journal of Marketing Theory and Practice* 22, no. 4 (2014): 437–54.

50. Quesenberry and Coolsen, "What Makes a Super Bowl Ad Super?"

Index